Roadside Silhouettes

1. MOURNING DOVE
2. HOUSE SPARROW
3. GRACKLE
4. STARLING
5. COWBIRD
6. RED-WINGED BLACKBIRD
7. KINGFISHER
8. BLUE JAY
9. MOCKINGBIRD
10. SONG SPARROW
11. SHRIKE
12. FLICKER
13. BLUEBIRD
14. NIGHTHAWK
15. ROBIN
16. KILLDEER
17. PHEASANT
18. PURPLE MARTIN
19. BARN SWALLOW
20. CLIFF SWALLOW
21. KESTREL
22. CARDINAL
23. MEADOWLARK
24. KINGBIRD
25. HORNED LARK
26. PHOEBE
27. BOBWHITE
28. CROW

A Field Guide to the Birds

of Eastern and Central North America

THE PETERSON FIELD GUIDE SERIES®

A Field Guide to the Birds

A Completely New Guide to All the Birds of Eastern and Central North America

Text and Illustrations by
ROGER TORY PETERSON

Maps by
VIRGINIA MARIE PETERSON

• Fourth Edition •
Completely Revised and Enlarged

Sponsored by the National Audubon Society
and National Wildlife Federation

HOUGHTON MIFFLIN COMPANY
BOSTON   NEW YORK

Conservation Note

Birds undeniably contribute to our pleasure and standard of living. But they also are sensitive indicators of the environment, a sort of "ecological litmus paper," and hence more meaningful than just chickadees and cardinals to brighten the suburban garden, grouse and ducks to fill the sportsman's bag, or rare warblers and shorebirds to be ticked off on the birder's checklist. The observation of birds leads inevitably to environmental awareness.

Help support the cause of wildlife conservation by taking an active part in the work of the National Audubon Society (950 Third Avenue, New York City 10022), the National Wildlife Federation (1412 16th St., N.W., Washington, D.C. 20036), the Defenders of Wildlife (1244 19th Street, N.W., Washington, D.C. 20036), and your local Audubon or Natural History Society. On the international level, don't forget the World Wildlife Fund (Suite 800, 1601 Connecticut Ave., N.W., Washington, D.C. 20009). These and other conservation organizations merit your support.

For information about permission to reproduce selections from this book, write to Permissions, Houghton Mifflin Company, 215 Park Avenue South, New York, New York 10003

PETERSON FIELD GUIDES and PETERSON FIELD GUIDE SERIES are registered trademarks of Houghton Mifflin Company.

For information about this and other Houghton Mifflin trade and reference books and multimedia products, visit The Bookstore at Houghton Mifflin on the World Wide Web at http://www.hmco.com/trade/ .

Library of Congress Cataloging in Publication Data

Peterson, Roger Tory, date.
A field guide to the birds.
(The Peterson field guide series; 1)
"Sponsored by the National Audubon Society and National Wildlife Federation."
Includes index.
1. Birds—North America. I. Title.
QL681.P45   1980   598.297   80-14304
ISBN 0-395-91175-3
ISBN 0-395-91176-1 (pbk.)
ISBN 0-395-91177-X (Flexi-book)

Printed in the United States of America
RVG 34 33 32 31 30 29 28 27 26

to the memory of
CLARENCE E. ALLEN
and
WILLIAM VOGT

Bird Songs and Calls

Not everything useful for identifying birds can be crammed into a pocket-sized *Field Guide*. In the species accounts I have included a brief entry on **Voice,** and I have done this in my own way, trying to give the reader some handle on the songs or calls he hears. Authors of bird books have attempted with varying success to fit songs into syllables, words, and phrases. Musical notations, comparative descriptions, and even ingenious systems of symbols have also been employed. But since the advent of sound recording these older techniques have been eclipsed. A visual spinoff of the tape recording is the sonogram, but most people are not technologically oriented enough to interpret it easily.

Use the second edition of the *Field Guide to Bird Songs,* which is arranged to match this edition of the *Field Guide to Birds*. It comprises two 12-inch LP records or cassettes. This comprehensive collection of sound recordings includes the calls and songs of more than 200 land and water birds — a large percentage of all the species found in eastern and central North America. They were recorded and prepared under the direction of Dr. James Gulledge of the Laboratory of Ornithology, Cornell University. To prepare yourself for your field trips play the records or cassettes; then read the descriptions in the *Field Guide* for useful clues and analysis. In learning bird voices (and some birders do 90 percent of their field work by ear) there is no substitute for the actual sounds.

Bird Nests

Most birders are not too skilled at finding nests. In most cases there would be an appalling gap between the number of species ticked off on their checklists and the number of nests they have discovered. To remedy this Hal Harrison, the premier nest photographer, has prepared *A Field Guide to Birds' Nests in the United States east of the Mississippi River*. This *Field Guide* (No. 21 in the Field Guide Series) will expand your ornithological expertise.

Watching Birds

A valuable tool for learning bird identification is my videocassette *Watching Birds* (available in home and institutional formats), which shows over 200 birds, live and in color, with stereophonic sound. Another useful aid is the *Field Guide to Birds Coloring Book*. Both are published by Houghton Mifflin.

Introduction

In 1934 my first *Field Guide* was published, covering the birds east of the 90th meridian in North America. This book was designed so that live birds could be readily identified at a distance by their "field marks" without resorting to the bird-in-hand characters that the early collectors relied on. During the last half century the binocular and the spotting scope have replaced the shotgun.

The "Peterson System," as it now is called, is based on patternistic drawings with arrows that pinpoint the key field marks. These rather formal schematic illustrations and the direct comparisons between similar species are the core of the system, a practical method that has gained universal acceptance not only on this continent but also in Europe where *Field Guides* now exist in 12 languages. This system, which is, in a sense, a pictorial key based on readily noticed visual impressions rather than on technical features, has been extended to other branches of natural history and there are now more than two dozen titles in the Field Guide Series.

This edition of *A Field Guide to the Birds,* the flagship book of the Peterson Field Guide Series, is more than a revision; it is completely new, with 136 plates, as against 60 in the previous edition. Every illustration is new or redrawn. All species are now shown in color; some are repeated in monochrome, but only when flight patterns are more clearly diagnosed in that way.

There are also 390 three-color maps, a new feature. My wife, Virginia Marie Peterson, and I researched these together and she then carefully carried out their execution. Her expertise had previously been used at the U.S. Coast Guard Research and Development Center where she worked out critical methods for identifying oil spills by means of infrared spectroscopy. She wrote the original *Infrared Field Manual for Oil Spill Identification.*

With this new fourth edition, long overdue, the *Field Guide to the Birds* has come of age. Years ago I had concluded that for comparative purposes the ideal number of species per color plate would be about 4 (rather than 10 to 12 as in the previous editions), but the cost factor prohibited this ideal format when we first broke ground. In fact, there were only 4 plates in color and 26 in black and white in the 1934 edition. In 1939, 4 more black-and-white plates were added. When the book was extensively revised in 1947 and its scope extended to the 100th meridian, all the old plates were retired and replaced by 60 new ones, 36 in color. The success of the *Field Guide* with its well-tested practical system has grown steadily over the years and the economics of distribution as well as technical advances in fine offset printing now make it possible to surmount earlier restraints.

The *Field Guide* user will find one major format change that will be particularly helpful: all species descriptions now face the species illustrations. Over the years many birders have urged me to arrange text and plates in this way, and I am pleased to be able to provide this means of quicker reference in this new edition.

Area of this Field Guide: Roughly this guide covers North America east of the 100th meridian as shown in the map on p. 16. Rather than a restrictive political boundary, an ecological one is more practical. In the U.S. the logical division of the avifauna is in the belt between the 100th meridian (midway across Oklahoma, Kansas, Nebraska, and the Dakotas) and the edge of the Rockies. This is by no means a sharp division, but people living in that ecological "twilight zone" will find that *A Field Guide to Western Birds* covers all species they are likely to encounter. In a general way, eastern birds follow the valleys west while the western forms edge eastward along the more arid uplands. In Canada eastern influences extend much further west, bridging the gap to the Rockies via the conifer forests north of the plains.

The birds resident in the eastern third of Texas are adequately covered in this *Field Guide*. Not so those in the Rio Grande Valley and along the lower and central coasts of Texas, where many western species reach their eastern outposts and a few Mexican species occur. These will be found in *A Field Guide to the Birds of Texas* (No. 13 in the Peterson Series). Texas is the only state with its own *Field Guide*.

The Maps: Instead of detailed range accounts, maps are now employed; they have been conveniently assembled in an appendix. Because most projections are large enough to show state and provincial lines, ranges are defined more critically. Extra information is included in notes on the maps. For quick reference, the map section is marked with a gray corner that serves as a thumb index. Furthermore, our knowledge of bird distribution is becoming ever more exact because of the proliferation of field observers. By grouping the maps we can update them more frequently without affecting the rest of the pagination.

Although some birds (waterfowl, game birds, seabirds) had already been mapped continentally in the *Handbook of North American Birds* (R.S. Palmer) and in other books, Mrs. Peterson and I researched our own maps using state and regional sources, but we found these very uneven. We urge anyone who is planning such a publication to do it right and include maps. The following areas have books with maps: Canada (W.E. Godfrey), Alabama (T.A. Imhof); Florida (A. Sprunt; H.M. Stevenson); Kentucky (R.M. Mengel); Maryland (R.E. Stewart and C. Robbins); Minnesota (J.C. Green and R.B. Janssen); New York (J. Bull); North Dakota (R.E. Stewart); Pennsylvania (W.E.C. Todd; E.L. Poole); South Dakota (South Dakota Ornithologists Union); Texas (H.C. Oberholser and E.B. Kincaid, Jr.); Wisconsin (O.J. Gromme; S. Robbins; in MS); and the Great Plains states (P.A. Johnsgard). The breeding birds of Canada are mapped in *Birds of Canada* (E. Godfrey). Another 15 states and provinces have good books that unfortunately lack maps. Using these we managed to approximate a good many range contours, but often with some uncertainty. Six or 7 states are almost *terra incognita* and our only sources were a few local checklists, not all of them critically useful. We consulted all of the pertinent state and regional books in the annotated selection prepared by S.R. Drennan which is included in the *Special Book Supplement* published by *American Birds;* and equally important, the files of *American Birds* edited by R. Arbib (National Audubon Society, 950 Third Ave., New York, N.Y. 10022).

The Ranges of Birds: A number of species have been added to the avifauna of eastern North America since the previous edition of the *Field Guide* was published in 1947. Notable is the Cattle Egret that spread explosively after it arrived in the U.S. under its own wing-power about 1952. Equally explosive has been the spread of the House Finch, which received its initial assist from cage bird dealers. Some accidental wanderers, such as the Little Gull and Black-headed Gull of the Old World, have become regular visitors and are starting to breed. The Lesser Black-backed Gull may follow a similar pattern. A number of exotic escapes are doing well, especially in Florida (Budgerigar, Canary-winged Parakeet, Red-whiskered Bulbul, Spotted Oriole, etc.).

The ranges of many species have changed markedly during the past 30–40 years. Some are expanding because of decades of protection; others have diminished alarmingly or have dropped out of parts of their range due to environmental changes. The passion for winter feeding has had its effect on the expanding ranges of Cardinals, Tufted Titmice, Evening Grosbeaks, Mourning Doves, and a number of other birds. *Field Guides* may have played no small part in these range expansions—by introducing birds to so many people.

Drawings vs. Photographs: Because of the increasing sophistication of birders I have leaned more toward detailed portraiture in the new illustrations while trying not to lose the patternistic effect developed in the previous editions. A drawing can do much more than a photograph to emphasize the field marks. A photograph is a record of a fleeting instant; a drawing is a composite of the artist's experience. The artist can edit out, show field marks to best advantage, and delete unnecessary clutter. He can choose position and stress basic color and pattern unmodified by transitory light and shade. A photograph is subject to the vagaries of color temperature, make of film, time of day, angle of view, skill of the photographer, and just plain luck. The artist has more options and far more control even though he may at times use photographs for reference. This is not a diatribe against photography; I am an obsessive photographer as well as an artist and fully aware of the differences. Whereas a photograph can have a living immediacy, a good drawing is really more instructive.

Subspecies: These simply represent subdivisions within the geographic range of a species. They are races, usually determined by morphological characteristics such as slight differences in measurements, shades of color, etc. These subtle subdivisions can usually be distinguished with accuracy only with a collecting gun and by comparison of museum series. The distinctions, often vague, are seldom apparent in the field and should not concern the field observer. To illustrate: the House Wrens of the Atlantic Coast (*Troglodytes aedon aedon*) differ very slightly from those of the Appalachians (*T. a. baldwini*) and are given different subspecific names. Only a trained expert comparing series of specimens would detect the differences. Unlike species, subspecies are not reproductively isolated; they are capable of mating with each other where their populations meet or mingle.

Subspecies have a meaning to the student of bird distribution and evolution and are of practical value to conservation and wildlife management practices. Should occasion demand, the professional or the scholar can refer to his copy of the A.O.U. (American Ornithologists Union) Checklist which gives a detailed breakdown of races and ranges. So do not be concerned with subspecies. They were listed extensively in previous editions of this guide but those pages have been put to other uses in this edition. However, a few subspecies are recognized when field distinctions are obvious. The most publicized and controversial example is the Baltimore Oriole, now lumped with Bullock's Oriole under the new name Northern Oriole. Others are Myrtle and Audubon's Warblers (now known as the Yellow-rumped Warbler), Slate-colored and Oregon Juncos (Northern Junco), Ipswich Sparrow (a race of the Savannah Sparrow), etc. These names and a few others have been retained (in quotes) in deference to long established usage.

Acknowledgments: It was William Vogt, the first editor of *Audubon* magazine, who suggested that I put together a *Field Guide* using my methods of teaching field identification. He was the spark plug. I had already written articles on the subject for *Nature* magazine (gulls) and *Field and Stream* (ducks). Vogt and I enjoyed many field trips together during my art school days and when we were on the staff of the National Audubon Society. He was to distinguish himself later as one of the early gurus of the environmental movement.

INTRODUCTION

There was no efficient bird guide in the modern sense in my youth. I used the little checkbook-sized *Reed's Bird Guide:* but it was not until I met the young members of the Bronx County Bird Club — Allan Cruickshank, Richard Herbert, Joseph Hickey, Irving Kassoy, and the Kuerzi brothers — that I really learned my birds. The man to whom we all owed our inspiration and expertise was Ludlow Griscom of the Museum of Comparative Zoology at Cambridge, Massachusetts. He was the court of last resort in matters of field identification and to him I always turned for a final appraisal of difficult species and knotty problems. Throughout the preparation of the early editions of the *Field Guide* he unselfishly gave me the benefit of his long and varied field experience. Charles A. Urner of Elizabeth, New Jersey, whose specialty was the water birds, also graciously criticized the original manuscript. So did Francis H. Allen of Boston, who was my first editor. He contributed many valuable notes and was responsible for a complete perusal and polishing of the original text as well as that of the first and second revisions.

I shall not list again the 100 or more correspondents and others who contributed notes or helped in other ways in previous editions. Their names are in the *Preface* of the Second Revised and Enlarged Edition (1947). However, I would like to acknowledge here the following persons who offered suggestions for this new edition, or helped in other tangible ways: Ira J. Abramson, E. Ahlquist, Forrest Alexander, Horace Alexander, Robert Arbib, Mrs. R.A. Arny, Elisha Atkins, Harold & Rachel Axtell, H.D. Bain, James Baird, Wesley Biggs, Dr. J.D. Black, Don Bleitz, Bradford G. Blodget, Leonard C. Brecher, Paul Brooks, Maurice Broun, Carter Bundy, A. Chamberlain, J. Cohn, C. Collins, Mrs. C.N. Collister, G.D. Constantz, R. Crawford, Davis Crompton, Mrs. Allan D. Cruickshank, Robert H. Curry, Owen Davies, Susan Roney Drennan, Sam Elliot, Owen W. Ellis, John G. Ericson, Richard Ferren, John Farrand, Jr., Mrs. Bradley Fisk, E.R. Ford, N.L. Ford, William Foster, Mrs. Leonard I. French, Peter Gilchrist, F. Gill, Earl Greene, Fred Hall, Samuel A. Harper, Miss O.C. Hazlett, Donald S. Heintzelman, Fred J. Helgren, R.E. Herman, Philip B. Heywood, Joseph J. Hickey, D.H. Hirth, Stuart Houston, J.B. Hubbard, S.H. Hubbard, Sara Hugus, H. Roy Ivor, Joseph R. Jehl, Jr., Herbert W. Kale II, J. Kleiman, John Lane, David Lank, M.A. Linton, Mrs. R. Cutler Low, George H. Lowery, Jr., J. Ludwig, Elizabeth F. MacDonald, J. Steven Makasa, Carl Maslowski, Russell Mason, Ian McLaren, Gordon M. Meade, James K. Merrit, Roy Moore, J. Morlan, B.G. Murray, Jr., Robert J. Newman, Isabel O'Brien, John Ogden, Oscar T. Owre, Henry E. Parmer, Wayne Petersen, Allan R. Phillips, Helen Phillips, Charles Chauncey Pool, Peter Post, J.S. Prendergast, Frank W. Preston, Noble Proctor, J.V. Remsen, Tudor Richards, Sam Robbins, William B. Robertson, Jr., Dudley & Vivian Ross, William C. Rowe, Alvah W. Sanborn, D.B.O. Saville, F.G. Scheider, Fritz

Scheider, Seymour Schiff, Ralph Schreiber, Paul W. Schueler, Charles W. Schulze, Frank Shields, William J. Sladen, Mrs. Charles L. Smith, Doug Smith, J. Murray Speirs, Sally Spofford, Henry M. Stevenson, Robert W. Storer, Mr. & Mrs. S.J. Strickler, Robert Sundell, Wendell Taber, Harrison B. Tordoff, Mary M. Tremaine, Peter Vickery, Robert B. Weeden, F.D. Weinstein, Harold Werner, Mimi Westervelt, Francis M. Weston, S.F. White, David Wingate, P. Woodward, William Shepherd, and Paul Sykes.

For assistance with the range maps Mrs. Peterson and I are especially indebted to Dr. Noble Proctor, Rev. Sam Robbins, Richard Ferren, Wayne Petersen, and Peter Vickery.

The specimen material used in the preparation of the new color plates came almost entirely from the cabinets of the American Museum of Natural History in New York City. I am deeply grateful to the staff and curators of the Department of Ornithology of that institution for their assistance, especially Dr. Dean Amadon, John Bull, Allan O'Connor, Dr. Eugene Eisenmann, Dr. John Farrand, and Dr. Wesley Lanyon.

I owe a special debt of gratitude to Cornelia Eastland, Elaine Giambattista, Kerry Pado, and Barbara C. Peterson for their secretarial labors and office assistance in connection with this book, and particularly to Charles W. Schulze who typed and retyped the final manuscript several times. Those on the staff of Houghton Mifflin Company who wrestled with the involved problems of actual editing, production, and publication of this edition were Morton Baker, Carol Goldenberg, Richard McAdoo, Austin Olney, Stephen Pekich, Richard Tonachel, and especially Lisa Fisher, Peggy Burlet, and James Thompson, who are models of editorial thoroughness.

The quality of the color work is the result of close collaboration with the printer, Case-Hoyt of Rochester, N.Y., under the critical eyes of Anson Hosley, Director of Research and Development, Gary Meicht, Technical Director, Dan Cooney, and Paul Nedderlik. Mrs. Peterson carefully checked all proofs of the maps with Charles Cruickshank, W.C. Pevc, and D.L. Milligan. In addition to the skill of these craftsmen and the production department of Houghton Mifflin, under the direction of Morton Baker, I have drawn on the color expertise of Ian Ballantine and also Robert and Richard Lewin of Mill Pond Press, publishers of my limited edition bird prints.

Space prevents me from listing again the mass of ornithological literature digested in the preparation of the earlier editions of the *Field Guide,* as well as the regional works, checklists, papers, and periodicals that went into the compilation of this one. Assiduously I consulted them all and intentionally ignored none. A list of these sources is on file and available in my library.

Contents

CONTENTS

CONTENTS

THE GEOGRAPHIC AREA
COVERED BY THIS FIELD GUIDE

Eastern and Central North America, roughly east of the 100th meridian on the Great Plains. This includes the Canadian Arctic but not southern Texas. For full coverage of this state, refer to *A Field Guide to the Birds of Texas.*

N.W. TERR.

Hudson Bay

LAB.

NFLD.

MANITOBA

QUEBEC

ONTARIO

N.B.

ME.

N.S.

N.D.

MINN.

VT.

N.Y.

N.H.

MASS.

R.I.

CONN.

S.D.

WISC.

MICH.

L.I.

NEB.

IOWA

ILL.

IND.

OHIO

PENN.

N.J.

DEL.

MD.

Atlantic Ocean

KANS.

MO.

KY.

W.VA.

VA.

OKLA.

ARK.

TENN.

N.C.

S.C.

TEXAS

LA.

MISS.

ALA.

GA.

FLA.

Gulf of Mexico

Systematic Checklist

Keep a "Life List." Check the birds you have seen.

This list covers the eastern half of the continent west to the 100th meridian on the Great Plains. It includes only those species that are described and illustrated in the main body of the *Field Guide.* It excludes those accidentals, introductions, and escapes that are listed or illustrated on pp. 290-304 and some of the escaped parrots on pp. 178-179, but space is left at the end of the checklist for recording any such species that are observed.

For a convenient and complete continental list, the *A.B.A. Checklist,* prepared by the Checklist Committee of the American Birding Association (Box 6599, Colorado Springs, Colorado 80934), is recommended. It lists every species recorded north of the Mexican border, including the accidentals.

In the following list, birds are grouped first under orders (identified by the Latin ending *-formes*), followed by families (*-dae* ending), sometimes subfamilies (*-nae* ending), and then species. Scientific names of genera and species are not given below but will be found in the species accounts throughout the book. The vernacular names given here are the ones finally decided upon by the Checklist Committee of the American Birding Association (A.B.A.). They are essentially the same as those that will be adopted in the next checklist of the American Ornithologists Union (A.O.U.). So that there will be no confusion, names used in previous editions of the *Field Guide* that differ from ones in the current edition are given in parentheses under the headings of the species accounts. All scientific names in the *Field Guide* are the latest official ones decreed by the A.O.U. Checklist Committee (and accepted by the A.B.A.).

ORDER GAVIIFORMES
LOONS: Gaviidae
__COMMON LOON
__YELLOW-BILLED LOON
__ARCTIC LOON
__RED-THROATED LOON

ORDER
PODICIPEDIFORMES
GREBES: Podicipedidae
__RED-NECKED GREBE
__HORNED GREBE
__EARED GREBE
__WESTERN GREBE
__PIED-BILLED GREBE

ORDER
PROCELLARIIFORMES
SHEARWATERS, PETRELS:
Procellariidae
__NORTHERN FULMAR
__CORY'S SHEARWATER
__GREATER SHEARWATER
__SOOTY SHEARWATER
__MANX SHEARWATER
__AUDUBON'S SHEARWATER
__BERMUDA PETREL
__BLACK-CAPPED PETREL
STORM PETRELS: Hydrobatidae
__LEACH'S STORM PETREL
__WILSON'S STORM PETREL

ORDER PELECANIFORMES
TROPICBIRDS: Phaethontidae
__WHITE-T. TROPICBIRD
PELICANS: Pelecanidae
__AM. WHITE PELICAN
__BROWN PELICAN
GANNETS, BOOBIES: Sulidae
__MASKED BOOBY
__BROWN BOOBY
__NORTHERN GANNET
CORMORANTS: Phalacrocoracidae
__GREAT CORMORANT
__DOUBLE-CR. CORMORANT
__OLIVACEOUS CORMORANT
DARTERS: Anhingidae
__AMERICAN ANHINGA
FRIGATEBIRDS: Fregatidae
__MAGNIFICENT FRIGATEBIRD

ORDER CICONIIFORMES
HERONS, BITTERNS: Ardeidae
__GREAT BLUE HERON
___"WURDEMANN'S" H.
___"GREAT WHITE" H.
__GREEN HERON
__LITTLE BLUE HERON
__CATTLE EGRET
__REDDISH EGRET
__GREAT EGRET
__SNOWY EGRET
__LOUISIANA HERON
__B.-CR. NIGHT HERON
__Y.-CR. NIGHT HERON
__LEAST BITTERN
__AMERICAN BITTERN
STORKS: Ciconiidae
__WOOD STORK
IBISES, etc.: Threskiornithidae
__GLOSSY IBIS
__WHITE-FACED IBIS
__WHITE IBIS
__ROSEATE SPOONBILL
FLAMINGOS: Phoenicopteridae
__AMERICAN FLAMINGO

ORDER ANSERIFORMES
WATERFOWL: Anatidae
SWANS: Cygninae
__MUTE SWAN
__WHISTLING SWAN
GEESE: Anserinae
__CANADA GOOSE
__BRANT
__BARNACLE GOOSE
__WHITE-FRONTED GOOSE
__SNOW GOOSE
___"BLUE" GOOSE
__ROSS' GOOSE
WHISTLING DUCKS:
Dendrocygninae
__FULVOUS WHISTLING DUCK

MARSH DUCKS: Anatinae
__MALLARD
__AM. BLACK DUCK
__MOTTLED DUCK
__GADWALL
__COMMON PINTAIL
__GREEN-WINGED TEAL
___"EURASIAN" TEAL
__BLUE-WINGED TEAL
__CINNAMON TEAL
__EURASIAN WIGEON
__AMERICAN WIGEON
__NORTHERN SHOVELER
__WOOD DUCK
DIVING DUCKS: Aythyinae
__REDHEAD
__RING-NECKED DUCK
__CANVASBACK
__GREATER SCAUP
__LESSER SCAUP
__TUFTED DUCK
__COMMON GOLDENEYE
__BARROW'S GOLDENEYE
__BUFFLEHEAD
__OLDSQUAW
__HARLEQUIN DUCK
__COMMON EIDER
__KING EIDER
__WHITE-WINGED SCOTER
__SURF SCOTER
__BLACK SCOTER
STIFFTAILS: Oxyurinae
__RUDDY DUCK
MERGANSERS: Merginae
__HOODED MERGANSER
__COMMON MERGANSER
__RED-BR. MERGANSER

ORDER FALCONIFORMES
AM. VULTURES: Cathartidae
__TURKEY VULTURE
__BLACK VULTURE
HAWKS, etc.: Accipitridae
KITES: Elaninae and Milvinae
__WHITE-TAILED KITE
__SWALLOW-TAILED KITE
__MISSISSIPPI KITE
__SNAIL KITE
ACCIPITERS: Accipitrinae
__NORTHERN GOSHAWK
__SHARP-SHINNED HAWK
__COOPER'S HAWK
BUTEOS, EAGLES: Buteoninae
__RED-TAILED HAWK
___"HARLAN'S" HAWK
___"KRIDER'S" HAWK
__RED-SHOULDERED HAWK
__BROAD-WINGED HAWK
__SWAINSON'S HAWK
__SHORT-TAILED HAWK
__ROUGH-LEGGED HAWK
__FERRUGINOUS HAWK

__GOLDEN EAGLE
__BALD EAGLE
HARRIERS: Circinae
__NORTHERN HARRIER
OSPREYS: Pandionidae
__OSPREY
FALCONS, etc.: Falconidae
CARACARAS: Caracarinae
__CRESTED CARACARA
FALCONS: Falconinae
__GYRFALCON
__PEREGRINE FALCON
__MERLIN
__AMERICAN KESTREL

ORDER GALLIFORMES
GROUSE: Tetraonidae
__SPRUCE GROUSE
__RUFFED GROUSE
__WILLOW PTARMIGAN
__ROCK PTARMIGAN
__GR. PRAIRIE CHICKEN
__L. PRAIRIE CHICKEN
__SHARP-TAILED GROUSE
QUAIL, etc.: Phasianidae
__COMMON BOBWHITE
__SCALED QUAIL
__RING-NECKED PHEASANT
__GRAY PARTRIDGE
TURKEYS: Meleagrididae
__WILD TURKEY

ORDER GRUIFORMES
CRANES: Gruidae
__WHOOPING CRANE
__SANDHILL CRANE
LIMPKINS: Aramidae
__LIMPKIN
RAILS, etc.: Rallidae
__KING RAIL
__CLAPPER RAIL
__VIRGINIA RAIL
__SORA
__YELLOW RAIL
__BLACK RAIL
__CORN CRAKE
__PURPLE GALLINULE
__COMMON GALLINULE
__AMERICAN COOT

ORDER CHARADRIIFORMES
OYSTERCATCHERS:
Haematopodidae
__AMERICAN OYSTERCATCHER
STILTS, AVOCETS:
Recurvirostridae
__BLACK-NECKED STILT
__AMERICAN AVOCET
PLOVERS: Charadriidae
__RINGED PLOVER
__SEMIPALMATED PLOVER

__WILSON'S PLOVER
__KILLDEER
__PIPING PLOVER
__SNOWY PLOVER
__LESSER GOLDEN PLOVER
__BLACK-BELLIED PLOVER
SANDPIPERS, etc.: Scolopacidae
__HUDSONIAN GODWIT
__MARBLED GODWIT
__ESKIMO CURLEW
__WHIMBREL
__LONG-BILLED CURLEW
__UPLAND SANDPIPER
__GREATER YELLOWLEGS
__LESSER YELLOWLEGS
__SOLITARY SANDPIPER
__WILLET
__SPOTTED SANDPIPER
__RUDDY TURNSTONE
__WILSON'S PHALAROPE
__NORTHERN PHALAROPE
__RED PHALAROPE
__AM. WOODCOCK
__COMMON SNIPE
__SHORT-BILLED DOWITCHER
__LONG-BILLED DOWITCHER
__RED KNOT
__SANDERLING
__SEMIPAL. SANDPIPER
__WESTERN SANDPIPER
__LEAST SANDPIPER
__WHITE-R. SANDPIPER
__BAIRD'S SANDPIPER
__PECTORAL SANDPIPER
__PURPLE SANDPIPER
__DUNLIN
__CURLEW SANDPIPER
__STILT SANDPIPER
__BUFF-BR. SANDPIPER
__RUFF
JAEGERS, SKUAS: Stercorariidae
__POMARINE JAEGER
__PARASITIC JAEGER
__LONG-TAILED JAEGER
__GREAT SKUA
__SOUTH POLAR SKUA
GULLS, TERNS: Laridae
GULLS: Larinae
__GLAUCOUS GULL
__ICELAND GULL
__ "KUMLIEN'S" GULL
__GR. BLACK-BACKED GULL
__L. BLACK-BACKED GULL
__HERRING GULL
__THAYER'S GULL
__CALIFORNIA GULL
__RING-BILLED GULL
__BLACK-HEADED GULL
__LAUGHING GULL
__FRANKLIN'S GULL
__BONAPARTE'S GULL
__LITTLE GULL

19

___IVORY GULL
___B.-L. KITTIWAKE
___ROSS' GULL
___SABINE'S GULL
TERNS: Sterninae
___GULL-BILLED TERN
___FORSTER'S TERN
___COMMON TERN
___ARCTIC TERN
___ROSEATE TERN
___SOOTY TERN
___BRIDLED TERN
___LITTLE TERN
___ROYAL TERN
___SANDWICH TERN
___CASPIAN TERN
___BLACK TERN
___BROWN NODDY
___BLACK NODDY
SKIMMERS: Rynchopidae
___BLACK SKIMMER
AUKS (Alcids): Alcidae
___RAZORBILL
___THIN-BILLED MURRE
___THICK-BILLED MURRE
___DOVEKIE
___BLACK GUILLEMOT
___ATLANTIC PUFFIN

ORDER COLUMBIFORMES
PIGEONS, DOVES: Columbidae
___WHITE-CROWNED PIGEON
___ROCK DOVE
___WHITE-WINGED DOVE
___MOURNING DOVE
___RINGED TURTLE DOVE
___COMMON GROUND DOVE
___INCA DOVE

ORDER PSITTACIFORMES
PARROTS: Psittacidae
___MONK PARAKEET
___CANARY-W. PARAKEET
___BUDGERIGAR

ORDER CUCULIFORMES
CUCKOOS, etc.: Cuculidae
___MANGROVE CUCKOO
___YELLOW-BILLED CUCKOO
___BLACK-BILLED CUCKOO
___GREATER ROADRUNNER
___SMOOTH-BILLED ANI
___GROOVE-BILLED ANI

ORDER STRIGIFORMES
BARN OWLS: Tytonidae
___BARN OWL
TYPICAL OWLS: Strigidae
___COMMON SCREECH OWL
___GREAT HORNED OWL
___SNOWY OWL
___HAWK OWL

___BURROWING OWL
___BARRED OWL
___GREAT GRAY OWL
___LONG-EARED OWL
___SHORT-EARED OWL
___BOREAL OWL
___SAW-WHET OWL

ORDER CAPRIMULGIFORMES
GOATSUCKERS: Caprimulgidae
___CHUCK-WILL'S-WIDOW
___WHIP-POOR-WILL
___POOR-WILL
___COMMON NIGHTHAWK
___ANTILLEAN NIGHTHAWK
___LESSER NIGHTHAWK

ORDER APODIFORMES
SWIFTS: Apodidae
___CHIMNEY SWIFT
___VAUX'S SWIFT
HUMMINGBIRDS: Trochilidae
___RUBY-THROATED
   HUMMINGBIRD
___RUFOUS HUMMINGBIRD

ORDER CORACIIFORMES
KINGFISHERS: Alcedinidae
___BELTED KINGFISHER

ORDER PICIFORMES
WOODPECKERS: Picidae
___COMMON FLICKER
   ("YELLOW-SHAFTED")
   ___"RED-SHAFTED" FLICKER
___PILEATED WOODPECKER
___RED-BELLIED WOODPECKER
___RED-HEADED WOODPECKER
___YELLOW-B. SAPSUCKER
___HAIRY WOODPECKER
___DOWNY WOODPECKER
___RED-COCKADED WOODP.
___BL.-B. THREE-TOED WOODP.
___N. THREE-TOED WOODP.
___IVORY-BILLED WOODP.

ORDER PASSERIFORMES
FLYCATCHERS: Tyrannidae
___EASTERN KINGBIRD
___GRAY KINGBIRD
___WESTERN KINGBIRD
___SCISSOR-T. FLYC.
___GR. CRESTED FLYCATCHER
___ASH-THROATED
   FLYCATCHER
___EASTERN PHOEBE
___SAY'S PHOEBE
___YELLOW-B. FLYCATCHER
___ACADIAN FLYCATCHER
___WILLOW FLYCATCHER
___ALDER FLYCATCHER
___LEAST FLYCATCHER

___EASTERN PEWEE
___OLIVE-SIDED FLYC.
___VERMILION FLYCATCHER
LARKS: Alaudidae
___HORNED LARK
SWALLOWS: Hirundinidae
___TREE SWALLOW
___BANK SWALLOW
___ROUGH-WINGED SWALLOW
___BARN SWALLOW
___CLIFF SWALLOW
___PURPLE MARTIN
JAYS, CROWS: Corvidae
___GRAY JAY
___BLUE JAY
___SCRUB JAY
___BLACK-BILLED MAGPIE
___NORTHERN RAVEN
___WHITE-NECKED RAVEN
___AMERICAN CROW
___FISH CROW
TITMICE: Paridae
___BLACK-CAPPED CHICKADEE
___CAROLINA CHICKADEE
___BOREAL CHICKADEE
___TUFTED TITMOUSE
NUTHATCHES: Sittidae
___WHITE-BR. NUTHATCH
___RED-BR. NUTHATCH
___BROWN-H. NUTHATCH
CREEPERS: Certhiidae
___BROWN CREEPER
BULBULS: Pycnonotidae
___RED-WH. BULBUL
WRENS: Troglodytidae
___HOUSE WREN
___WINTER WREN
___BEWICK'S WREN
___CAROLINA WREN
___MARSH WREN
___SEDGE WREN
___ROCK WREN
MIMIC THRUSHES: Mimidae
___N. MOCKINGBIRD
___GRAY CATBIRD
___BROWN THRASHER
THRUSHES: Turdidae
___AMERICAN ROBIN
___VARIED THRUSH
___WOOD THRUSH
___HERMIT THRUSH
___SWAINSON'S THRUSH
___GRAY-CHEEKED THRUSH
___VEERY
___EASTERN BLUEBIRD
___MOUNTAIN BLUEBIRD
___NORTHERN WHEATEAR
___TOWNSEND'S SOLITAIRE
KINGLETS, etc.: Sylviidae
___BLUE-GR. GNATCATCHER
___GOLDEN-CROWNED
KINGLET

___RUBY-CROWNED KINGLET
PIPITS, etc.: Motacillidae
___WATER PIPIT
___SPRAGUE'S PIPIT
WAXWINGS: Bombycillidae
___BOHEMIAN WAXWING
___CEDAR WAXWING
SHRIKES: Laniidae
___NORTHERN SHRIKE
___LOGGERHEAD SHRIKE
STARLINGS: Sturnidae
___EUROPEAN STARLING
VIREOS: Vireonidae
___BLACK-CAPPED VIREO
___WHITE-EYED VIREO
___BELL'S VIREO
___YELLOW-THR. VIREO
___SOLITARY VIREO
___BL.-WHISKERED VIREO
___RED-EYED VIREO
___PHILADELPHIA VIREO
___WARBLING VIREO
WOOD WARBLERS: Parulidae
___BL.-AND-WHITE WARBLER
___PROTHONOTARY WARBLER
___SWAINSON'S WARBLER
___WORM-EATING WARBLER
___GOLDEN-WINGED WARBLER
___BLUE-WINGED WARBLER
___"BREWSTER'S" W. (HYBR.)
___"LAWRENCE'S" W. (HYBR.)
___BACHMAN'S WARBLER
___TENNESSEE WARBLER
___ORANGE-CR. WARBLER
___NASHVILLE WARBLER
___N. PARULA WARBLER
___"SUTTON'S" W. (HYBR.)
___YELLOW WARBLER
___MAGNOLIA WARBLER
___CAPE MAY WARBLER
___BL.-THR. BLUE WARBLER
___YELLOW-RUMPED
WARBLER
___"MYRTLE" WARBLER
___"AUDUBON'S" WARBLER
___BL.-THR. GRAY WARBLER
___BL.-THR. GREEN WARBLER
___CERULEAN WARBLER
___BLACKBURNIAN WARBLER
___YELLOW-THR. WARBLER
___CHESTNUT-S. WARBLER
___BAY-BREASTED WARBLER
___BLACKPOLL WARBLER
___PINE WARBLER
___KIRTLAND'S WARBLER
___PRAIRIE WARBLER
___PALM WARBLER
___OVENBIRD
___N. WATERTHRUSH
___LA. WATERTHRUSH
___KENTUCKY WARBLER
___CONNECTICUT WARBLER

__MOURNING WARBLER
__COMMON YELLOWTHROAT
__YELLOW-BREASTED CHAT
__HOODED WARBLER
__WILSON'S WARBLER
__CANADA WARBLER
__AMERICAN REDSTART
WEAVER FINCHES: Ploceidae
__HOUSE SPARROW
__EUR. TREE SPARROW
BLACKBIRDS, etc.: Icteridae
__BOBOLINK
__EASTERN MEADOWLARK
__WESTERN MEADOWLARK
__YELLOW-H. BLACKBIRD
__RED-WINGED BLACKBIRD
__ORCHARD ORIOLE
__NORTHERN ORIOLE
____"BALTIMORE" ORIOLE
____"BULLOCK'S" ORIOLE
__SPOTTED ORIOLE
__RUSTY BLACKBIRD
__BREWER'S BLACKBIRD
__GREAT-TAILED GRACKLE
__BOAT-TAILED GRACKLE
__COMMON GRACKLE
__BROWN-HEADED COWBIRD
TANAGERS: Thraupidae
__WESTERN TANAGER
__SCARLET TANAGER
__SUMMER TANAGER
__BLUE-GRAY TANAGER
FINCHES, etc.: Fringillidae
__NORTHERN CARDINAL
__ROSE-BREASTED
  GROSBEAK
__BLACK-HEADED GROSBEAK
__BLUE GROSBEAK
__INDIGO BUNTING
__LAZULI BUNTING
__PAINTED BUNTING
__DICKCISSEL
__EVENING GROSBEAK
__PURPLE FINCH
__HOUSE FINCH

__PINE GROSBEAK
__HOARY REDPOLL
__COMMON REDPOLL
__PINE SISKIN
__AMERICAN GOLDFINCH
__RED CROSSBILL
__WHITE-W. CROSSBILL
__RUFOUS-SIDED TOWHEE
__LARK BUNTING
__SAVANNAH SPARROW
____"IPSWICH" SPARROW
__GRASSHOPPER SPARROW
__BAIRD'S SPARROW
__HENSLOW'S SPARROW
__LeCONTE'S SPARROW
__SHARP-TAILED SPARROW
__SEASIDE SPARROW
____"DUSKY" S. SPARROW
____"CAPE SABLE" S.
  SPARROW
__VESPER SPARROW
__LARK SPARROW
__RUFOUS-CROWNED
  SPARROW
__BACHMAN'S SPARROW
__NORTHERN (DARK-EYED)
  JUNCO
____"SLATE-COLORED" JUNCO
____"OREGON" JUNCO
__AMERICAN TREE SPARROW
__CHIPPING SPARROW
__CLAY-COLORED SPARROW
__FIELD SPARROW
__HARRIS' SPARROW
__WHITE-CR. SPARROW
__WHITE-THR. SPARROW
__FOX SPARROW
__LINCOLN'S SPARROW
__SWAMP SPARROW
__SONG SPARROW
__McCOWN'S LONGSPUR
__LAPLAND LONGSPUR
__SMITH'S LONGSPUR
__CHESTNUT-C. LONGSPUR
__SNOW BUNTING

Accidentals, Strays, and Others

_____   _____

_____   _____

_____   _____

_____   _____

_____   _____

_____   _____

_____   _____

How to Identify Birds

Veteran birders will know how to use this book. Beginners, however, should spend some time becoming familiar in a general way with the illustrations. They are not arranged in systematic or phylogenetic order as in most ornithological works but are grouped in 8 main visual categories:

    (1) **Swimmers** — Ducks and ducklike birds
    (2) **Aerialists** — Gulls and gull-like birds
    (3) **Long-legged Waders** — Herons, cranes, etc.
    (4) **Smaller Waders** — Plovers, sandpipers, etc.
    (5) **Fowl-like Birds** — Grouse, quail, etc.
    (6) **Birds of Prey** — Hawks, eagles, owls
    (7) **Nonpasserine Land Birds**
    (8) **Passerine (Perching) Birds**

Within these groupings it will be seen that ducks do not resemble loons; gulls are readily distinguishable from terns. The needlelike bills of warblers immediately differentiate them from the seed-cracking bills of sparrows. Birds that could be confused are grouped together when possible and are arranged in identical profile for direct comparison. The arrows point to outstanding "field marks" which are explained opposite. The text also gives aids such as voice, actions, habitat, etc., not visually portrayable, and under a separate heading discusses species that might be confused. The brief notes on general range are keyed by number to detailed 3-color range maps in the rear of the book (pp. 305–370).

In addition to 129 plates of birds normally found in the area of this *Field Guide* there are 7 color plates depicting 80 accidentals from Europe, the sea, and the tropics, as well as some of the exotic escapes that are sometimes seen.

What Is the Bird's Size?

Acquire the habit of comparing a new bird with some familiar "yardstick" — a House Sparrow, a Robin, a Pigeon, etc., so that you can say to yourself, "smaller than a Robin; a little larger than a House Sparrow." The measurements in this book represent lengths in inches (with centimeters in parentheses) from bill tip to tail tip of specimens on their backs as in museum trays. However, specimen measurements vary widely depending on the preparator, who may have stretched the neck a bit. In most cases the species accounts give minimum and maximum lengths, but in life, not lying in a tray, most birds are closer to the minimum lengths given.

What Is Its Shape?

Is it plump like a Starling (left) or slender like a cuckoo (right)?

What Shape Are Its Wings?

Are they rounded like a Bobwhite's (left) or sharply pointed like a Barn Swallow's (right)?

What Shape Is Its Bill?

Is it small and fine like a warbler's (1); stout and short like a seed-cracking sparrow's (2); dagger-shaped like a tern's (3); or hook-tipped like that of a bird of prey (4)?

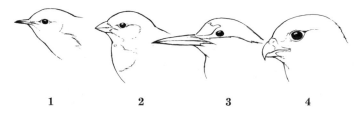

1   2   3   4

What Shape Is Its Tail?

Is it deeply forked like a Barn Swallow's (1); square-tipped like a Cliff Swallow's (2); notched like a Tree Swallow's (3); rounded like a Blue Jay's (4); or pointed like a Mourning Dove's (5)?

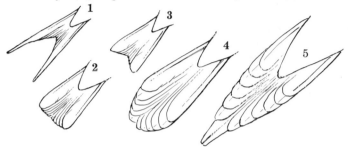

How Does It Behave?

Does it cock its tail like a wren or hold it down like a flycatcher? Does it wag its tail? Does it sit erect on an open perch, dart after an insect, and return as a flycatcher does?

Does It Climb Trees?

If so, does it climb in *spirals* like a Creeper (left), in jerks like a woodpecker (center) using its tail as a brace, or does it go down headfirst like a nuthatch (right)?

How Does It Fly?

Does it undulate (dip up and down) like a Flicker (1)? Does it fly straight and fast like a Dove (2)? Does it hover like a Kingfisher (3)? Does it glide or soar?

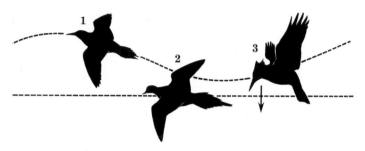

Does It Swim?

Does it sit low in the water like a loon (1) or high like a gallinule (2)? If a duck, does it dive like a deepwater duck (3); or does it dabble and upend like a Mallard (4)?

Does It Wade?

Is it large and long-legged like a heron or small like a sandpiper? If one of the latter, does it probe the mud or pick at things? Does it teeter or bob?

What Are Its Field Marks?

Some birds can be identified by color alone, but most birds are not that easy. The most important aids are what we call field marks, which are, in effect, the "trademarks of nature." Note whether the breast is spotted as in the Wood Thrush (1); streaked as in the Thrasher (2); or plain as in a cuckoo (3).

Tail Patterns

Does the tail have a "flash pattern" — a white tip as in the King-bird (1); white patches in the outer corners as in the Towhee (2); or white sides as in the Junco (3)?

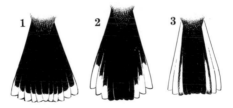

Rump Patches

Does it have a light rump like a Cliff Swallow (1) or Flicker (2)? The Harrier, Myrtle Warbler, and many of the shorebirds also have distinctive rump patches.

Eye-Stripes and Eye-Rings

Does the bird have a stripe above, through, or below the eye, or a combination of these stripes? Does it have a striped crown? A ring around the eye or "spectacles"? A "mustache" stripe? These details are important in many small songbirds.

Wing Bars

Do the wings have light wing bars or not? Their presence or absence is important in recognizing many warblers, vireos, and flycatchers. Wing bars may be single or double, bold or obscure.

Wing Patterns

The basic wing patterns of ducks (shown below), shorebirds, and other water birds are very important. Notice whether the wings have patches (1) or stripes (2); are solidly colored (3) or have contrasting black tips (Snow Goose, etc.).

Caution in Sight Records: Fifty years ago, prior to the *Field Guide* era, most ornithologists would not accept sight records of unusual birds unless they were made along the barrel of a shotgun. Today it is difficult to secure a collecting permit unless one is a professional or a student training to be one. Moreover, rarities may show up in parks, refuges, or on other lands where collecting is out of the question. There is no reason why we should not trust our increasingly educated eyes.

To validate the sight record of a very rare or accidental bird — a state "first," for example — the rule is that at least 2 competent observers should see the bird and document it in detail in their notes. A 35 mm camera equipped with a 400 mm lens is becoming an increasingly useful tool for substantiating such sightings. Rarities are sometimes caught in mist nets by bird banders and can be photographed, hand-held, for the record. For this purpose a 50 mm close-up lens, such as a Micro-Nikkor, is best and may be used with or without a strobe light.

There are some species — or plumages — where even the expert will hedge. And it is the mark of an expert to occasionally put a question mark after certain birds on his list: for example, accipiter, sp.?, or empidonax, sp.?, or "peep," sp.?, or immature Thayer's Gull? Do not be embarrassed if you cannot name *every* bird you see. Allan Phillips argued convincingly in *American Birds* that practically all of the Semipalmated Sandpipers so freely reported in winter on the southern coasts of the U.S. were really Western Sandpipers. It is quite impossible to identify many individuals of these 2 species correctly unless they are collected for critical examination — or unless their distinctive call notes are heard.

A Few Key Sources for the Birder: Every active birder should subscribe to *American Birds* edited by Robert Arbib, National Audubon Society, 950 Third Avenue, New York, N.Y. 10022. Issued bimonthly, it gives detailed reports on migration, breeding, wintering, population trends, and accidental occurrences for every section of North America. Susan Roney Drennan, the Associate Editor, has prepared an annotated selection of the best state and regional books. These are listed in a *Special Book Supplement* published by *American Birds* and need not be listed again here.

Birders who wish to keep up to date should also subscribe to *Birding* edited by James A. Tucker, American Birding Association, Inc., P.O. Box 4335, Austin, Texas 78765. A must.

There are also literally hundreds of journals, newsletters, and checklists published by local Audubon societies and bird clubs. These are listed, along with meetings and field trips, in *A Guide to North American Bird Clubs* by Jon E. Rickert, Sr., an extremely useful source book produced by Avian Publications, Inc., P.O. Box 310, Elizabethtown, Kentucky 42701.

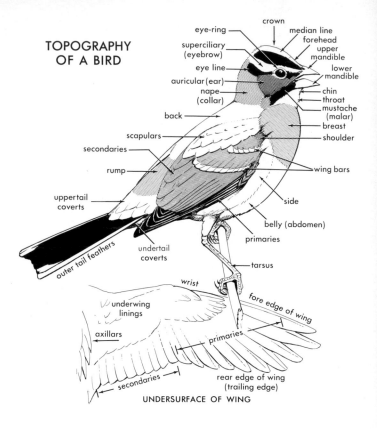

TOPOGRAPHY OF A BIRD

crown
median line
forehead
upper mandible
lower mandible
chin
throat
mustache (malar)
breast
shoulder
eye-ring
superciliary (eyebrow)
eye line
auricular (ear)
nape (collar)
back
scapulars
secondaries
rump
uppertail coverts
outer tail feathers
undertail coverts
wing bars
side
belly (abdomen)
primaries
tarsus

wrist
underwing linings
axillars
fore edge of wing
primaries
rear edge of wing (trailing edge)
secondaries

UNDERSURFACE OF WING

Other Terms Used in this Book

Sex symbols: ♂ means male, ♀ means female. These symbols are used frequently on the plates, sparingly in the text.

Accidental: In the area of this book, recorded fewer than 12 or 15 times; far out of range (see pp. 290–301). On the state level only 1 or 2 records; might not be expected again.

Casual: Very few records, but might be expected again because the normal range of the species is not too distant.

Introduced: Not native; deliberately released.

Exotic: Not native; either released or escaped.

In part: A well-marked subspecies or morph — part of a species.

A Field Guide to the Birds

of Eastern and Central North America

■ LOONS Family Gaviidae.

Large swimming birds with daggerlike bills; may dive from surface or submerge. Thrash along the water on takeoff. Flight slower than most ducks'; outline hunchbacked, with a sagging look; large webbed feet project rudderlike beyond the stubby tail. Sexes alike. See grebes (shorter bodies, thinner necks) and cormorants (thinner necks, longer tails). **Food:** Small fish, crustaceans, other aquatic life. **Range:** N. parts of N. Hemisphere. **No. of species:** World, 4; East, 4.

COMMON LOON *Gavia immer* 28–36″ (70–90 cm) **M 1**

Large, long-bodied, low-swimming; bill stout, daggerlike. *Summer:* Note the *checkered back,* broken white collar. *Winter:* Dark above, whitish below. Note *stout, straight* bill.

Similar species: See (1) other loons; (2) cormorants.

Voice: In summer, falsetto wails, weird yodeling, maniacal quavering laughter; at night, a tremulous *ha-oo-oo.* In flight, a barking *kwuk.* Loons are usually silent in winter.

Range: Alaska, Canada, n. U.S., Greenland, Iceland. In winter, chiefly coasts to n. Mexico, w. Europe. **East:** Map 1. **Habitat:** Wooded lakes, tundra ponds (summer); coastal waters.

YELLOW-BILLED LOON *Gavia adamsii* 33–38″ (83–95 cm)

Similar to Common Loon but bill pale *ivory,* distinctly upturned, straight above, slightly angled below. In winter, a *dark ear patch. Caution:* Bills of many winter Common Loons are pale toward the base but always have a *dark upper ridge.*

Range: Arctic, north of tree limit, from n. U.S.S.R. to nw. Canada. Winters along Pacific Coast of n. Eurasia, se. Alaska, B. Columbia. **East:** Overlaps range of Common Loon north and west of Hudson Bay. Accidental on Atlantic Coast. **Habitat:** Tundra lakes (summer), coastal waters.

RED-THROATED LOON *Gavia stellata* 25″ (63 cm) **M 2**

The sharp thin bill, distinctly *upturned,* is the key mark. *Summer:* Note the gray head, plain back, *rufous* throat patch. *Winter:* Similar to Common Loon but smaller, slimmer; back and head paler, less contrasty; profile more snaky.

Similar species: (1) Common Loon; larger with a more robust, *straight* bill. (2) Arctic Loon has a slender *straight* bill.

Voice: Usually silent. In Arctic, falsetto wails, falling in pitch; a series of ducklike quacks; a repeated *kwuk.*

Range: Arctic, circumpolar. Winters south along coasts to Mediterranean, China, nw. Mexico. **East:** Map 2. **Habitat:** Tundra lakes (summer), bays, estuaries, ocean.

ARCTIC LOON *Gavia arctica* 26″ (65 cm) **M 3**

Smaller than Common Loon with a thin, straight bill. *Summer:* Crown and nape *pale gray.* Checkered back divided into 4 patches. *Winter:* Bill slender, *straight* (not upturned).

Similar species: Winter Red-throat; paler with a tilted bill.

Voice: A deep barking *kwow.* Falsetto wails, rising in pitch.

Range: N. Eurasia, nw. N. America. Winters along coasts to Mediterranean, India, nw. Mexico. **East:** Map 3. **Habitat:** Tundra lakes (summer), ocean.

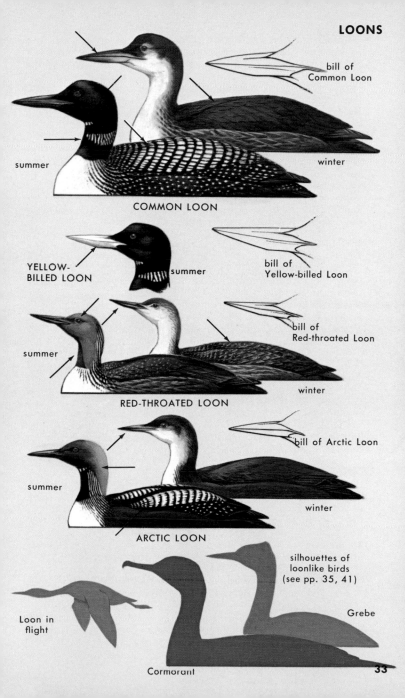

bill of
Common Loon

summer

winter

COMMON LOON

YELLOW-
BILLED LOON

summer

bill of
Yellow-billed Loon

summer

bill of
Red-throated Loon

winter

RED-THROATED LOON

bill of Arctic Loon

summer

winter

ARCTIC LOON

silhouettes of
loonlike birds
(see pp. 35, 41)

Loon in
flight

Grebe

Cormorant

33

■ **GREBES Family Podicipedidae.** Ducklike divers with thin necks, small heads, lobed toes, tail-less appearance; all but Pied-bill have white wing patches, pointed bills. Sexes alike. Most young grebes have striped heads. May dive from surface or submerge. Skitter when taking wing; flight labored (with sagging neck). **Food:** Small fish, crustaceans, tadpoles, insects. **Range:** Cosmopolitan. **No. of species:** World, 20; East, 5 (+1 accidental).

HORNED GREBE *Podiceps auritus* 12–15″ (30–38 cm) **M 4**
   Breeding: Note the combination of *golden ear tufts* and *chestnut neck. Winter:* Contrastingly patterned with dark and white. Note the clean-cut black cap, thin straight bill.
   Similar species: On Great Plains, see Eared Grebe.
   Voice: When nesting, a squeaking trill; harsh *kerra's.*
   Range: N. parts of N. Hemisphere. Winters to s. U.S., s. Eurasia.
   East: Map 4. **Habitat:** Lakes, ponds, coastal waters.

EARED GREBE *Podiceps nigricollis* 12–14″ (30–35 cm) **M 5**
   Breeding: Crested black head, golden ear tufts, *black* neck (Horned Grebe has *chestnut* neck). *Winter:* Similar to Horned Grebe; neck thinner, *gray;* bill slightly tilted; cap ill-defined. Gray cheek sets off white throat, *white ear patch.*
   Voice: On nesting ponds a froglike *poo-eep* or *krreep.*
   Range: Eurasia, Africa, w. N. America. **East:** Map 5. **Habitat:** Prairie lakes, ponds; in winter, salt bays, ocean.

PIED-BILLED GREBE *Podilymbus podiceps* 13″ (33 cm) **M 6**
   Note the thick, ungrebelike "chicken bill," puffy white stern. No white wing patch. *Breeding:* Key marks are the *black throat patch* and a *ring* around the thick whitish bill. *Winter:* Browner; throat patch and bill-ring *absent.*
   Similar species: Other grebes have pointed bills, wing patches.
   Voice: A cuckoolike *kuk-kuk-cow-cow-cow-cow-cowp-cowp,* etc.
   Range: S. Canada to Argentina. Migratory in North. **East:** Map 6.
   Habitat: Ponds, lakes, marshes; in winter, salt bays.

RED-NECKED GREBE *Podiceps grisegena* 18″ (45 cm) **M 7**
   (Holboell's Grebe) The largest eastern grebe. *Breeding:* Long *rufous-red* neck, *light cheek,* black cap. *Winter:* Grayish (incl. neck); *white crescent* on side of face (often absent in immature). In flight, a double white wing patch.
   Voice: A rapid *kik-kik-kik,* etc.; harsh complaining notes.
   Range: Eurasia, n. N. America. Winters to n. Africa, s. U.S. **East:** Map 7. **Habitat:** Lakes, ponds; in winter, salt water.

WESTERN GREBE *Aechmophorus occidentalis* 25″ (63 cm) **M 8**
   A large slate-and-white grebe with a *long swanlike* neck. Bill very thin, *pale yellow.* Downy young gray, without stripes.
   Voice: A shrill rolling *kirik-kirik-kirik-rik-rik-rik* etc.
   Range: W. N. America. Winters to Mexico. **East:** Map 8. **Habitat:** Rushy lakes, sloughs; in winter, bays, ocean.

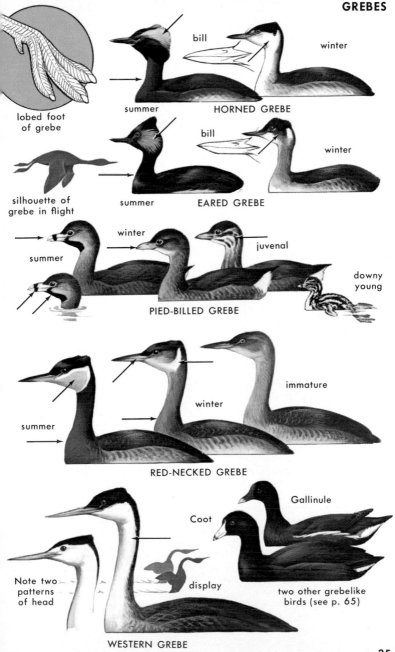

lobed foot of grebe

silhouette of grebe in flight

bill

winter

HORNED GREBE

summer

bill

winter

summer

EARED GREBE

winter

summer

juvenal

downy young

summer

PIED-BILLED GREBE

summer

winter

immature

RED-NECKED GREBE

Gallinule

Coot

Note two patterns of head

display

two other grebelike birds (see p. 65)

WESTERN GREBE

35

■ AUKS, ETC. Family Alcidae.

Auks ("alcids") are black-and-white seabirds that suggest penguins and replace them in the N. Hemisphere. They dive expertly, using their wings underwater, flipperlike, as penguins do, but can also use them to propel themselves through the air in a rapid whir. In flight they are given to much veering, and spread their feet wide as brakes before landing. Swimming, they are ducklike but have short necks and pointed, stubby, or laterally flat bills. Sexes alike. On rocky islands where most species nest in crowded colonies they stand nearly erect, penguinlike. Birds of open sea, they rarely appear on fresh water, descending to the latitudes of northern U.S. in fall or winter. Watch for them from coastal points during nasty weather. **Food:** Fish, crustaceans, mollusks, algae. **Range:** N. Atlantic, N. Pacific, Arctic Ocean. **No. of species:** World, 22; East, 6 (+2 accidental, 1 extinct).

RAZORBILL   *Alca torda*   16–18″ (40–45 cm)   M 9

Size of a small duck. Black above and white below; characterized by a rather heavy head, thick neck, *deep and flat bill* that is crossed midway by a white mark. On the water the *cocked pointed tail* is often characteristic.
Similar species: Immature Razorbill has a smaller bill than the adult, and it lacks the white marks (hence resembling Thick-billed Murre) but the bill is stubby and rounded enough to suggest the bird's parentage.
Voice: A weak whirring whistle; a deep growling *Hey Al.*
Range: N. Atlantic (both sides) breeding from Arctic south to Maine, British Isles. **East:** Map 9. **Habitat:** Sea cliffs (nesting); open ocean.

THICK-BILLED MURRE   *Uria lomvia*   17–19″ (43–48 cm)   M 10

(Brunnich's Murre)   Similar to Thin-billed Murre but a bit larger, blacker; bill thicker, with a *whitish line* along the gape. Note also the sharper peak of the white on the throat. In winter, black of crown extends *below eye;* no dark stripe through white ear coverts; white bill mark less evident.
Voice: Very similar to Thin-billed Murre's.
Range: Cold oceans of N. Hemisphere. **East:** Map 10. **Habitat:** Sea cliffs when nesting; open ocean.

THIN-BILLED MURRE   *Uria aalge*   16–17″ (40–43 cm)   M 11

(Common Murre)   Size of a small duck, with a *slender* pointed bill. *Breeding:* Head, back, and wings dark brown; underparts and line on rear edge of wing white. *"Ringed" phase:* A few birds have a narrow white eye-ring and line behind it. *Winter:* Similar, but throat and cheeks white. A *black mark* extends from the eye onto the white cheek. Murres raft on water, fly in lines. Very gregarious in nesting colonies.
Voice: Hoarse, deep growls, *arrr* or *arra.*
Range: N. parts of N. Pacific, N. Atlantic. **East:** Map 11. **Habitat:** Sea cliffs (breeding); ocean, large salt bays.

ALCIDS (AUKS)

immature

summer

RAZORBILL   winter

winter

THICK-BILLED MURRE

summer

winter

← THIN-BILLED MURRE →

"Bridled" form

summer   summer   THICK-BILLED MURRE

summer

RAZORBILL
summer

1844

GREAT
AUK
extinct

37

DOVEKIE *Alle alle* 7½–9″ (19–23 cm)

The smallest auk, about the size of a Starling; chubby and seemingly neckless. Flying flocks bunch tightly, Starling-like. The contrasting alcid pattern, *black above, white below,* together with the *small size and very stubby bill,* renders it unlike anything else. By far the smallest winter seabird.

Similar species: Young of other alcids are really larger (size is deceptive on the ocean); all have *larger bills.*

Voice: A shrill chatter. Noisy on nesting grounds.

Range: Breeds coastal Greenland, n. Iceland, Spitzbergen, etc. Winters at sea to e. U.S., Mediterranean. **East:** Winters well offshore in N. Atlantic from ice-line south to New Jersey, irregularly to Florida. Accidental inland when "wrecked" by November storms. **Habitat:** Oceanic; offshore to pelagic.

BLACK GUILLEMOT *Cepphus grylle* 12–14″ (30–35 cm)   **M 12**

Note the large *white wing patch. Breeding:* A small *black* ducklike bird with a large *white* shoulder patch, *bright red* feet, and a pointed bill. Inside of mouth *orange-red. Winter:* Pale with white underparts, barred back. Wings black with a white patch as in summer. *Immature:* Darker above than winter adult, with a dingier, mottled wing patch.

Similar species: No other Atlantic alcid has a white wing patch (although others show a narrow line of white on the trailing edge of the wing). In winter the much larger White-winged Scoter (which has a white wing patch) is quite black, whereas the Black Guillemot is usually whitish. The wing patch of the White-winged Scoter is positioned at the rear of the wing.

Voice: A wheezing or hissing *peeeee;* very high-pitched.

Range: N. Atlantic sector of Arctic south to New England, British Isles. **East:** Map 12. **Habitat:** Inshore waters of ocean; breeds in small groups or singly in holes or under rocks of rocky shores, islands. Less pelagic than other auks.

ATLANTIC PUFFIN *Fratercula arctica* 12″ (30 cm)   **M 13**

The *colorful triangular bill* is the most striking feature of the chunky little "Sea Parrot." On the wing, it is a stubby, short-necked, thick-headed bird with a buzzy flight. No white line on wing. *Breeding:* Upper parts black, underparts white, cheeks *pale gray;* triangular bill broadly tipped with *red.* Feet bright orange. *Winter:* Cheeks grayer; bill smaller, yellower; but obviously a Puffin. *Immature:* Bill much smaller, blackish, but both mandibles distinctly curved. The chunky shape and the gray cheeks are unmistakably those of a Puffin.

Similar species: Immature Puffin may be mistaken for young Razorbill. Note the gray cheeks, all-black underwing.

Voice: Usually silent. When nesting a low growling *ow* or *arr.*

Range: N. Atlantic from s. Greenland and Iceland to New England, British Isles. **East:** Map 13. **Habitat:** Coastal and offshore waters, open sea. Colonial; breeds in holes in turf and among the rocks of sea islands.

ALCIDS (AUKS)

winter

summer

DOVEKIE

summer

winter

summer

BLACK GUILLEMOT

winter

summer

summer

immature

ATLANTIC PUFFIN

winter

adults
summer

**BLACK
GUILLEMOT**
summer

DOVEKIE
summer

**ATLANTIC
PUFFIN**

39

■ **CORMORANTS Family Phalacrocoracidae.** Large, blackish water birds; often stand erect on rocks or posts with neck in an S; may strike a "spread-eagle" pose. Adults may have colorful face skin, gular pouch, and eyes (usually green). Bill slender, hook-tipped. Sexes alike. Flocks fly in lines or wedges like geese (but are silent). Swim low like loons, but bill tilted up at an angle. **Food:** Fish, crustaceans. **Range:** Nearly cosmopolitan. **No. of species:** World, 30; East, 3.

DOUBLE-CRESTED CORMORANT   M 14
Phalacrocorax auritus   33″ (83 cm)
See family discussion (above). The one widespread cormorant of e. N. America; found both on coast and inland.
Voice: Silent, except for piglike grunts in nesting colony.
Range: Most of N. America, winters to Belize (B. Honduras). **East:** Map 14. **Habitat:** Coast, islands, bays, lakes, rivers.

GREAT CORMORANT *Phalacrocorax carbo* 37″ (93 cm)   M 15
(European Cormorant) Larger than Double-crest; note the *heavier* bill, *pale yellow* (not orangish) chin pouch, bordered by a *white throatstrap.* In breeding plumage, a *white "pocket"* on flanks. Immature is *whiter below* than most young Double-crests (which typically have a pale breast but a *dark* belly).
Range: N. Atlantic, Eurasia, Africa, Australia, etc. **East:** Map 15.
Habitat: Sea cliffs (nesting); strictly coastal.

OLIVACEOUS CORMORANT *Phalacrocorax olivaceus* 25″ (63 cm)
(Neotropic or Mexican Cormorant) Similar to Double-crest but smaller. Note the duller (less orange) chin pouch and, in summer, the narrow white mask on the face. At very close range note that feathers of back and scapulars are pointed, not rounded. In nuptial dress, white filoplumes on neck.
Range: Gulf of Mexico to Argentina. **East:** Coastal Texas and sw. Louisiana (Cameron Parish); straggler further east in Louisiana.
Habitat: Tidal waters, lakes near coasts.

■ **DARTERS (ANHINGAS) Family Anhingidae.** The family is best characterized under the one U.S. species (below). **Food:** Fish, small aquatic animals. **Range:** N. and S. America, Africa, India, se. Asia, Australia. **No. of species:** World, 4 (or 1); East, 1.

AMERICAN ANHINGA *Anhinga anhinga* 34″ (85 cm)   M 16
(Water Turkey) Similar to a cormorant, but neck *snakier,* bill *pointed,* tail much *longer.* Note the large *silvery* wing patches. *Male* is black-bodied; *female* has a buffy neck and breast; *immature* is brownish. In flight, flaps and glides, neck extended, long tail spread. Often soars high, hawklike. Perches like a cormorant, often with wings half spread. May swim submerged, with only head emergent, appearing snakelike.
Range: Se. U.S. to Argentina. **East:** Map 16. **Habitat:** Cypress swamps, rice fields, rivers, wooded ponds.

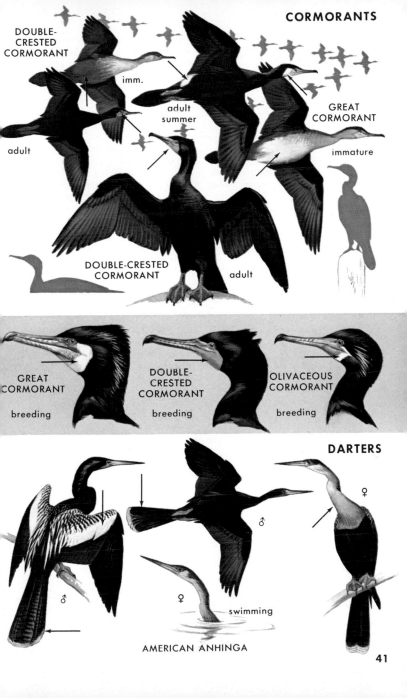

CORMORANTS

DOUBLE-CRESTED CORMORANT

imm.

adult summer

GREAT CORMORANT

immature

adult

DOUBLE-CRESTED CORMORANT

adult

GREAT CORMORANT

breeding

DOUBLE-CRESTED CORMORANT

breeding

OLIVACEOUS CORMORANT

breeding

DARTERS

♂

♂

♀

♂

♀ swimming

AMERICAN ANHINGA

41

■ SWANS, GEESE, DUCKS   Family Anatidae.   Waterfowl;
the subfamilies are discussed separately. **Range:** Cosmopolitan.
No. of species: World, 145; East, 39 (+15 accidental, 1 introduced,
1 extinct).

● SWANS Subfamily Cygninae.   Huge, all-white swimming birds;
larger, longer-necked than geese. Young tinged brown. Sexes alike.
Migrate in lines or V's. Feed by immersing head and neck, or by
"tipping up." **Food:** Aquatic plants, seeds.

MUTE SWAN   *Cygnus olor*   60″ (150 cm)   **M 17**
The ornamental park variety, now well-established in the wild;
spreading. More graceful than Whistling Swan, often swimming
with an S-curve in the neck; wings arched. The *knobbed orange
bill* points downward. Dingy young birds have black at the base of
a pinkish bill. *Wingbeats* make a singing sound.
Range: Eurasia; introduced ne. U.S., elsewhere. **East:** Map 17.
Habitat: Ponds, fresh and salt; coastal lagoons, salt bays.

WHISTLING SWAN   *Olor columbianus*   53″ (133 cm)   **M 18**
Spread 6–7 ft. America's common native swan. Often heard long
before the ribbonlike flock can be spotted. *All-white* wings and
very long necks mark them as swans. Bill *black,* often with a small
yellow basal spot. Young bird dingy with pinkish bill.
Similar species: Trumpeter Swan of Northwest is larger, deep-
voiced. Captives in Minnesota have produced free-flying young.
Voice: A mellow, high-pitched cooing: *woo-ho, woo-woo, woo-ho.*
Range: Breeds from Arctic coast south to Alaska Peninsula and
barren ground of Canada. Winters to seaboards of e. and w. U.S.
East: Map 18. **Habitat:** Tundra (summer), lakes, large rivers, bays,
estuaries, flooded fields.

● GEESE Subfamily Anserinae.   Large waterfowl; heavier-bodied,
longer-necked than ducks; bills thick at base. Noisy in flight; some
fly in line or V formation. Sexes alike. More terrestrial than ducks,
grazing on land (except Brant). Gregarious. **Food:** Grasses, seeds,
aquatic plants; Brant prefers Eelgrass.

SNOW GOOSE   *Chen caerulescens*   25–38″ (63–95 cm)   **M 19**
A *white* goose with *black primaries.* Often rust-stained on head.
Bill and feet pink. Immature pale gray with a dark bill.
Voice: A loud, nasal, resonant *whouk* or *houck* uttered in chorus.
Range: Ne. Siberia, Arctic America. Winters to Japan, n. Mexico,
Gulf Coast. **East:** Map 19. **Habitat:** Tundra (summer), marshes,
grainfields, ponds, bays.

ROSS' GOOSE   *Chen rossii*   23″ (58 cm)
Like a miniature Snow Goose. Bill decidedly stubbier, dark and
warty at base and lacking the black "lips." Hybrids occur.
Range: Nw. Canada; winters California. **East:** Local northwest of
Hudson Bay. A few reach Texas and Louisiana via prairies.

imm.

MUTE SWAN

WHISTLING SWAN

adult

adult

imm.

SWANS, GEESE

adult

MUTE SWAN

imm.

adult   WHISTLING SWAN

ROSS' GOOSE

imm.

adult

SNOW GOOSE
white phase

ROSS'

SNOW GOOSE
intergrade between
gray and white phases   white phase

SNOW

43

SNOW GOOSE (dark phase) **or "BLUE" GOOSE**   **M 19**
Chen caerulescens (in part)   25–30″ (63–75 cm)
  The "Blue" Goose, dark with a *white head,* is now regarded as a
  color morph of the Snow Goose with which it is usually associated.
  Intermediates are frequent (see preceding plate, p. 43).
  Similar species: The immature is dusky, similar to the young
  White-front, but feet and bill *dark;* wings paler, bluish.
  Range: Breeds in e. N. American Arctic, mainly in s. and e. parts of
  Snow Goose range. Migrates through prairies to Gulf of Mexico.
  East: Map 19. **Habitat:** Same as Snow Goose's.

WHITE-FRONTED GOOSE *Anser albifrons* 30″ (75 cm)   **M 20**
  No other goose in our area has *yellow or orange feet.* A *gray* goose
  with a *pink* bill, *white patch on front of face,* and irregular *black
  bars* on belly (variable). The Greenland race has a *yellow* bill.
  Immature: Dusky with a pale bill, yellow or orange feet; lacks
  other marks of adult.
  Voice: High-pitched tootling, *kah-lah-a-luk,* in chorus.
  Range: Arctic; circumpolar; winters to Mexico, Gulf states, n.
  Africa, India. **East:** Map 20. **Habitat:** Marshes, prairies, fields, lakes,
  bays, tundra (summer).

CANADA GOOSE *Branta canadensis* 25–43″ (63–108 cm) **M 21**
  The most widespread goose in N. America. Note the black head
  and neck or "stocking" that contrasts strikingly with the pale
  breast and the *white patch or chinstrap* that runs onto the side of
  the head. Flocks travel in long strings in V formation, announcing
  their approach by musical honking or barking. Considerable variation in size between various races.
  Voice: A deep musical honking or barking *ka-ronk* or *ka-lunk.*
  Range: Alaska, Canada, n. U.S. Winters to Mexico. **East:** Map 21.
  Habitat: Lakes, ponds, bays, marshes, fields.

BRANT *Branta bernicla* 22–26″ (55–65 cm)   **M 22**
  A small black-necked goose near size of Mallard. Has a white stern,
  conspicuous when it upends, and a fleck of white on neck (absent
  in immature). Travels in large irregular flocks.
  Similar species: Canada Goose's breast shows light above water
  (foreparts of Brant are black *to the waterline*). Canada Goose has
  a large white face patch. Brant is more strictly coastal.
  Voice: A throaty *cr-r-r-ruk* or *kurr-onk, krrr-onk.*
  Range: Arctic coasts of n. Eurasia, e. N. America. **East:** Map 22.
  Habitat: Mainly salt bays, estuaries; tundra (summer).

BARNACLE GOOSE *Branta leucopsis* 26″ (65 cm)
  Similar to Brant (white sides, black chest to waterline) but note
  the *white face encircling eye.* Heavily scalloped above.
  Range: Breeds in ne. Greenland, Spitzbergen, nw. Siberia. **East:** A
  casual or accidental visitor to ne. seaboard of N. America. Some
  reports may be referred to aviary escapes.

GEESE

imm.

adult

SNOW GOOSE
gray phase ("Blue" Goose)

adult

imm.

adult **WHITE-FRONTED GOOSE**

adult

Richardson's race

Lesser race

Atlantic race

CANADA GOOSE

BARNACLE GOOSE

BRANT

45

GEESE AND SWANS IN FLIGHT

Many **geese** and **swans** fly in line or wedge formation.

	Text and color plate
CANADA GOOSE *Branta canadensis* Light chest, black neck "stocking," white chinstrap.	**pp. 44, 45**
BRANT *Branta bernicla* Small; black chest, black head and neck.	**pp. 44, 45**
WHITE-FRONTED GOOSE *Anser albifrons* *Adult:* Gray neck, black splotches on belly. *Immature:* Dusky, light bill, light feet.	**pp. 44, 45**
SNOW GOOSE *Chen caerulescens* *Adult:* White with black primaries.	**pp. 42, 43**
SNOW GOOSE (dark phase) **or "BLUE" GOOSE** *Chen caerulescens* (in part) *Adult:* Dark body, white head. *Immature:* Dusky; dark bill, dark feet.	**pp. 44, 45**
WHISTLING SWAN *Olor columbianus* Very long neck; plumage entirely white.	**pp. 42, 43**

GEESE, SWANS

CANADA
GOOSE

below

above

BRANT

adult

immature

WHITE-FRONTED
GOOSE

immature

SNOW
GOOSE

gray phase
("Blue" Goose)

adult

SNOW
GOOSE

white phase

WHISTLING
SWAN

SNOW
GOOSE

gray phase
("Blue" Goose)

adult

47

- **WHISTLING DUCKS Subfamily Dendrocygninae.**

FULVOUS WHISTLING DUCK *Dendrocygna bicolor*
(Fulvous Tree-duck) 18–21″ (45–53 cm)
> Long-legged, gooselike. Note the *tawny* body, dark back, and *pale side stripe*. Flies with neck slightly drooped and feet trailing, showing *black* underwings, *white ring* on rump.
> **Voice:** A squealing slurred whistle, *ka-whee-oo.*
> **Range:** S. U.S. to Cen. America; also S. America, s. Asia, e. Africa.
> **East:** Coastal Texas and Louisiana. Recent invader along s. Atlantic Coast; has nested locally from Florida to North Carolina. Casual (in flocks) north to New England, Maritimes. **Habitat:** Marshes, mostly coastal. Not in trees.

- **MARSH DUCKS Subfamily Anatinae.** Surface-feeders of creeks, ponds, marshes. Feed by dabbling and upending; sometimes feed on land. Take flight directly into air. Most species have an iridescent speculum on rear edge of wing. Sexes unlike; in late summer males molt into drab "eclipse." **Food:** Aquatic plants, seeds, grass, small aquatic animals, insects.

AMERICAN BLACK DUCK   **M 23**
Anas rubripes 21–25″ (53–63 cm)
> The Black Duck in flight is *very dark* with flashing *white wing linings.* Sooty brown with a paler head and metallic violet wing patch; feet may be red or brown. Sexes similar.
> **Voice:** ♂ has a low croak; ♀ quacks like a barnyard Mallard.
> **Range:** Ne. N. America. Winters to Gulf Coast. **East:** Map 23.
> **Habitat:** Marshes, bays, estuaries, ponds, rivers, lakes.

MOTTLED DUCK *Anas fulvigula* 20″ (50 cm)   **M 24**
> A pale brownish or tawny edition of the Black Duck. Note the tan head, *unstreaked buffy throat* and unmarked yellow bill.
> **Range:** Florida to coastal Texas. **East:** Map 24. **Habitat:** Marshes.

GADWALL *Anas strepera* 19–23″ (48–58 cm)   **M 25**
> *Male:* A *gray* duck with a *black rump, white patch* on the rear edge of the wing, and a dull ruddy patch on the forewing. When swimming, the wing patches may be concealed; then note the black stern. Belly white, feet yellow, bill dark. *Female:* Brown, mottled; *white speculum,* yellow feet, yellow on bill.
> **Voice:** ♂ has a low *bek;* a whistling call. ♀ quacks loudly.
> **Range:** Northern N. America, n. Eurasia. Winters to Mexico, Africa, India. **East:** Map 25. **Habitat:** Lakes, ponds, marshes.

MALLARD *Anas platyrhynchos* 20–28″ (50–70 cm) **M 26**
> *Male:* Recognized by the uncrested *glossy-green head* and *white neck-ring.* Grayish with a chestnut chest, white tail; yellowish bill, orange feet, violet-blue speculum. *Female:* Mottled brown; *whitish tail.* Bill patched with orange, feet orange. Flying, shows a white bar *on each side* of the blue speculum.
> **Voice:** ♂, *yeeb;* a low *kwek;* ♀ has a boisterous quacking.
> **Range:** Northern parts of N. Hemisphere. Winters to Mexico, n. Africa, India. **East:** Map 26. **Habitat:** Marshes, wooded swamps, grainfields, ponds, rivers, lakes, bays.

FULVOUS WHISTLING DUCK

sexes similar

MOTTLED DUCK

AMERICAN BLACK DUCK

♂

♀

marsh ducks tip up

GADWALL

♂

♀

marsh ducks spring directly from the water

MALLARD

♂

♀

49

COMMON PINTAIL *Anas acuta* 26–30″ (65–75 cm) **M 27**
Male: A slender, slim-necked, white-breasted duck with a long
needle-pointed tail. A conspicuous *white point* runs from the neck
onto the side of the head. *Female:* Mottled brown; note the rather
pointed tail, slender neck, gray bill. In flight shows *one light
border* on the rear of the brown speculum.
Similar species: See (1) ♀ Mallard; (2) ♀ American Wigeon; (3) ♀
Gadwall. See also (4) Oldsquaw (not a marsh duck).
Voice: ♂ utters a double-toned whistle, *prrip, prrip,* wheezy teal-
like notes. ♀ has a low *quack.*
Range: Northern parts of N. Hemisphere. Winters south to n. S.
America, Africa, India. **East:** Map 27. **Habitat:** Marshes, prairies,
fresh ponds, lakes, salt bays.

AMERICAN WIGEON *Anas americana* 18–23″ (45–58 cm) **M 28**
(Baldpate) In flight, the Wigeon is recognized by the *large white
patch on the forewing.* (The similarly placed blue patches of
Shoveler and Blue-winged Teal may also appear whitish.) On the
water, it rides high, picking at the surface like a Coot. Often grazes
on land. *Male:* Note the *shining white crown.* Brownish; head gray
with a deep green patch. *Female:* Brown with gray head and neck;
belly and forewing whitish.
Similar species: ♀ is easily confused with (1) ♀ Gadwall, and (2) ♀
Pintail, but note the whitish patch on the forewing, bluish bill, and
contrasting gray head. (3) See Eurasian Wigeon.
Voice: ♂, a whistled *whee whee whew.* ♀, *qua-ack.*
Range: Alaska, w. Canada, n. U.S. Winters to Cen. America, W.
Indies. **East:** Map 28. **Habitat:** Marshes, lakes, bays, fields.

EURASIAN WIGEON *Anas penelope* 18–20″ (45–50 cm)
Male: Note the *red-brown* head, buff crown. A *gray* wigeon with a
vinaceous breast. *Female:* Very similar to ♀ American Wigeon but
head tinged with rust (not gray). The surest point when held in the
hand is the dusky (not white) axillars or "wingpits."
Similar species: See (1) American Wigeon; (2) Redhead.
Voice: ♂, a whistle, *whee-oo.* ♀, a *purr;* a *quack.*
Range: Breeds in Eurasia, Iceland. **East:** Rare visitor, chiefly near
coast in fall and winter, interior in spring.

WOOD DUCK *Aix sponsa* 17–20½″ (43–51 cm) **M 29**
Highly colored; often perches in trees. In flight, the white belly
contrasts with the dark breast and wings. Note also the long
square dark tail, short neck, and angle at which the bill points
downward. *Male:* The bizarre face pattern, swept-back crest, and
rainbow iridescence are unique. *Female:* Dull-colored; note the
dark crested head and *white eye patch.*
Voice: ♂, a loud distressed *whoo-eek;* a finchlike *jeee,* with rising
inflection. ♀, *crrek, crrek.*
Range: S. Canada, nw. and e. U.S., Cuba. Winters to Mexico,
Cuba. **East:** Map 29. **Habitat:** Wooded swamps, rivers, ponds.

MARSH DUCKS
(Dabblers)

♀

♂

COMMON PINTAIL

♂   ♀

AMERICAN WIGEON

♂   ♀

EURASIAN WIGEON

♀

♂   ♂ in eclipse
(autumn)

WOOD DUCK

POSTURES OF DUCKS ON LAND

Marsh
Ducks
(dabblers)

Sea and
Bay Ducks
(divers)

Mergansers
(divers)

Ruddy
Duck
(diver)

Whistling
Ducks
(dabblers)

NORTHERN SHOVELER *Anas clypeata* 17–20″ (43–50 cm) **M 30**
Note the *spoon-shaped bill.* A small duck; in flight the long bill
makes the wings seem set well back. Swimming, it sits low, bill
pointed toward the water. *Male:* Much black and white; belly and
sides rufous; pale blue patch on forewing; orange feet. *Female:*
Brown; big bill, blue wing patch, orange feet.
Voice: ♂, a low *took, took, took;* ♀, a light *quack.*
Range: Widespread in N. Hemisphere. Winters to Cen. America,
Africa. **East:** Map 30. **Habitat:** Fresh marshes, ponds, sloughs; in
winter, also salt bays.

BLUE-WINGED TEAL *Anas discors* 15–16″ (38–40 cm) **M 31**
A little half-sized marsh duck. *Male:* Note the *white facial cres-
cent,* and large *chalky blue* patch on the *forewing.* Males hold
eclipse plumage late in the year and may resemble females. *Fe-
male:* Brown, mottled; blue patch on forewing.
Similar species: See (1) Green-winged Teal; (2) Shoveler.
Voice: ♂ utters peeping notes; ♀, a light quack.
Range: Canada to s. U.S. Winters to S. America. **East:** Map 31.
Habitat: Fresh ponds, marshes.

GREEN-WINGED TEAL *Anas crecca* 14″ (35 cm) **M 32**
In flight, teal are recognized by their small size, tight flocks. If they
lack light wing patches they are Green-wings (speculum is *deep
iridescent green*). *Male:* A small compact gray duck with a brown
head (a green head patch shows in sunlight). When swimming note
the *vertical white mark* in front of the wing. *Female:* A diminutive
speckled duck with a green speculum.
Similar species: Blue-winged Teal (♂ and ♀) have light blue wing
patches. In flight, ♂ Blue-wings show dark bellies; Green-wings,
white bellies. ♀ Blue-wings are larger, longer billed.
Voice: ♂, a short whistle; froglike peeping. ♀, a crisp *quack.*
Range: Northern parts of N. America. Winters to Cen. America, W.
Indies. **East:** Map 32. **Habitat:** Marshes, rivers, bays.

GREEN-WINGED TEAL (Eurasian race)
Anas crecca (in part) 13–15½″ (33–39 cm)
Considered conspecific with American Green-winged Teal. *Male:*
Note the longitudinal white stripe on the scapulars. *Female:* In-
distinguishable from ♀ American Green-wing.
Range: Iceland, n. Europe, Asia, Aleutians. **East:** Rare visitor to N.
Atlantic seaboard on ponds along the coast.

CINNAMON TEAL *Anas cyanoptera* 15–17″ (38–43 cm)
Male: A small, *dark chestnut* duck with a large chalky-blue patch
on the fore edge of the wing. In flight resembles Blue-winged Teal.
Female: Very similar to ♀ Blue-wing.
Range: Sw. Canada, w. U.S., Mexico; S. America. **East:** A few east
to prairie states; accidental to Atlantic Coast.

MUSCOVY *Cairina moschata* ♂ 32″ (80 cm); ♀ 25″ (63 cm)
Native of tropical America (Mexico to n. Argentina). A clumsy,
black, gooselike duck with large white wing patches and underwing coverts. *Male:* Has a *bare, knobby, red face. Female:* Duller,
may lack facial knobs. Domestic Muscovy can be white, black, or
patched. Escaped birds often become semiwild.

MARSH DUCKS and MUSCOVY (Dabblers)

♀
♂ NORTHERN SHOVELER

♂ ♀ BLUE-WINGED TEAL

♂ ♀ GREEN-WINGED TEAL
American race

♂ GREEN-WINGED TEAL
Eurasian race

♂ CINNAMON TEAL

ancestral form

domestic variation

MUSCOVY
(A frequent escape from captivity)

- **DIVING DUCKS Subfamily Aythyinae.** Also called "sea ducks" and "bay ducks," but many are found on lakes and rivers and breed in marshes. All dive; surface-feeding ducks rarely do. Legs close to tail; hind toe with a paddlelike flap (lacking in surface feeders). In taking wing they patter while getting underway. Sexes unlike. **Food:** Small aquatic animals and plants. Seagoing species eat mollusks, crustaceans.

WHITE-WINGED SCOTER *Melanitta deglandi* 21″ (53 cm) **M 33**
Scoters are heavy blackish ducks seen coastwide, flying in stringy formation. The White-wing is the largest of the 3 species. On the water the white wing patch is often concealed (wait for the bird to flap or fly). *Male:* Black with a tick of white near the eye; bill orange with a black basal knob. *Female:* Sooty with a white wing patch and 2 light patches on the face (sometimes obscure; more pronounced on young birds).
Similar species: See (1) Surf Scoter and (2) Common Scoter.
Voice: In flight, a low bell-like whistle in a series of 6–8 notes (Kortright). Said to be produced by wings.
Range: Alaska, n. Canada; winters to s. U.S. (both coasts). **East:** Map 33. **Habitat:** Salt bays, ocean; in summer, lakes.

SURF SCOTER *Melanitta perspicillata* 19″ (48 cm) **M 34**
The "Skunk-duck." *Male:* Black, with 1 or 2 *white patches* on the crown and nape. Bill patterned with orange, black, and white. *Female:* Dusky brown; 2 light spots on the side of the head (sometimes obscured; more evident on young birds).
Similar species: ♀ White-wing has similar head pattern, but note the wing patch (which may not show until the bird flaps).
Voice: Usually silent. A low croak; grunting noises.
Range: Alaska, n. Canada. Winters to s. U.S. (both coasts). **East:** Map 34. **Habitat:** Ocean surf, salt bays; in summer, fresh Arctic lakes, tundra.

BLACK SCOTER *Melanitta nigra* 18½″ (46 cm) **M 35**
(American or Common Scoter) *Male:* A sea duck with entirely black plumage. The bright orange-yellow knob on the bill ("butter-nose") is diagnostic. In flight, the underwing shows a 2-toned effect, more pronounced than in the other scoters. *Female:* Sooty; *light cheeks* offer contrast with the *dark cap*.
Similar species: (1) Coot is blackish, but has a white bill, white patch under the tail. Gunners often call scoters "coots." (2) Some young ♂ Surf Scoters may lack head patches and appear all black. Look for a round black spot at the base of the bill. (3) ♀ and immature scoters of other 2 species have light spots on side of head. (4) ♀ Black Scoter may suggest winter Ruddy Duck (p. 60).
Voice: ♂, melodious cooing notes. ♀, growls.
Range: Alaska, ne. Canada, Iceland, n. Eurasia. Winters to s. U.S., Mediterranean. **East:** Map 35. **Habitat:** Seacoast, coastal tundra (summer).

Scoters fly in line or V formation

SEA DUCKS (SCOTERS)
(Divers)

White-winged

Surf

Black

imm.

♂

♀

WHITE-WINGED SCOTER

♂

♀

imm.

SURF SCOTER

inset
LABRADOR DUCK
extinct

1878

♂

♂

♀

BLACK SCOTER

Diving ducks (sea ducks and bay ducks) raft on water, skitter when taking wing.

OLDSQUAW   **M 36**
Clangula hyemalis   ♂ 21″ (53 cm); ♀ 16″ (40 cm)
The only sea duck combining much *white on the body and unpatterned dark wings*. Flies in bunched, irregular flocks. *Male, winter:* Note the needlelike tail, pied pattern, dark cheek. *Female, winter:* Dark wings, white face, dark cheek spot. *Male, summer:* Dark with white flanks and belly. Note the white eye patch. *Female, summer:* Similar, but darker.
Voice: Talkative; a musical *ow-owdle-ow*, or *owl-omelet*.
Range: Arctic, circumpolar. Winters to s. U.S., cen. Europe, cen. Asia. **East:** Map 36. **Habitat:** Ocean, large lakes; in summer, tundra pools and lakes.

HARLEQUIN DUCK   *Histrionicus histrionicus*   18″ (45 cm)   **M 37**
Dark and bizarre. *Male:* A smallish slaty duck with chestnut sides and odd white patches and spots. In flight has stubby shape of Goldeneye, but appears uniformly dark. *Female:* Dusky with 3 round white spots on side of head; no wing patch.
Similar species: (1) ♀ Bufflehead has white wing patch and only 1 face spot. (2) See ♀ scoters (larger with larger bills).
Voice: ♂, a squeak; also *gwa gwa gwa.* ♀, *ek-ek-ek-ek.*
Range: Ne. Asia, Alaska, Canada, w. U.S., Greenland, Iceland. **East:** Map 37. **Habitat:** Turbulent mountain streams (summer); rocky coastal waters (winter).

KING EIDER   *Somateria spectabilis*   21–24″ (53–60 cm)   **M 38**
Male: A stocky sea duck; on the water foreparts appear white, rear parts black, suggesting slightly a Black-backed Gull. Note *orange bill-shield.* Wings with large white patches. *Female:* Stocky; warm brown, heavily barred. Note facial profile (shown). *Immature male:* Dusky, with light breast, dark brown head.
Similar species: (1) ♂ Common Eider has *white* back. (2) ♀ Common Eider has flatter profile, with longer lobe before eye.
Voice: Courting ♂, a low crooning phrase; ♀, grunting croaks.
Range: Arctic regions of N. Hemisphere. **East:** Map 38. **Habitat:** Coasts, ocean.

COMMON EIDER   *Somateria mollissima*   23–27″ (58–68 cm) **M 39**
Oceanic, living about shoals; bulky, thick-necked. Flight sluggish and low, usually in a line. *Male:* The only duck in our area with a *black belly and white back.* Forewing white; head white, with a black crown, greenish nape. *Female:* Large, brown, *closely barred;* long flat profile. *Immature male:* At first grayish brown; later dusky with white collar; may develop chocolate head or breast; white areas come in irregularly.
Similar species: (1) ♂ King Eider has a *black* back; ♀ has a different facial profile, as shown. (2) ♀ scoters are duskier, lack the heavy black barrings of ♀ eiders.
Voice: ♂, a slurred moaning *ow-ooo-urr.* ♀, a grating *kor-r-r.*
Range: Northern parts of N. Hemisphere. **East:** Map 39. **Habitat:** Rocky coasts, shoals; in summer, also islands, tundra.

SEA DUCKS
(Divers)

♂ summer   ♂ winter   OLDSQUAW   ♀ summer

♀ winter

HARLEQUIN DUCK

♂   ♀

♂ imm.   ♀

bill of ♀
King Eider

♂

KING EIDER

♂ imm.   ♀

bill of ♀
Common Eider

♂

COMMON EIDER

King
Eider

Common
Eider

Eiders raft in large flocks

57

CANVASBACK *Aythya valisineria* 20–24″ (50–60 cm) **M 40**
Note the *long sloping profile* (both sexes). Flocks travel in lines or
V formation. *Male:* Very white-looking with a *chestnut-red* head
and neck, black chest, long *blackish* bill. *Female:* Grayish, with a
suggestion of pale rust on head and neck.
Voice: ♂, a low croak; growling notes. ♀, a *quack.*
Range: Alaska, w. Canada, nw. U.S. Winters to Mexico, Atlantic and Gulf coasts. **East:** Map 40. **Habitat:** Fresh marshes
(summer), lakes, salt bays, estuaries.

REDHEAD *Aythya americana* 18–23″ (45–58 cm) **M 41**
Male: Gray with a black chest and *round rufous head;* bill bluish
with a black tip. *Female:* Brownish; note the *suffused light patch*
near the bill. Both sexes have a *gray* wing stripe.
Similar species: (1) ♂ Canvasback is much whiter with a sloping
forehead and black bill. (2) See ♀ Ring-necked Duck.
Voice: ♂, a harsh catlike *meow;* a deep purr. ♀, *squak.*
Range: W. Canada, w. and n.-cen. U.S. Winters to Mexico, W.
Indies. **East:** Map 41. **Habitat:** Fresh marshes (summer), lakes,
saltwater bays, estuaries.

RING-NECKED DUCK *Aythya collaris* 15–18″ (38–45 cm) **M 42**
Male: Like a *black-backed* scaup. Note the *vertical white mark*
before the wing; bill crossed by a white ring. In flight, a broad *gray*
(not white) wing stripe. *Female:* Shaped like ♀ Lesser Scaup but
has an *indistinct* light face patch, dark eye, white eye-ring, and
ring on bill. Wing stripe is *gray.*
Similar species: Tufted Duck, *A. fuligula,* accidental in e. U.S. ♂
has a wispy *crest, white sides, white wing stripe.*
Range: Canada, n. U.S. Winters to Panama. **East:** Map 42. **Habitat:**
Wooded lakes, ponds; in winter, also rivers, bays.

LESSER SCAUP *Aythya affinis* 15–18″ (38–45 cm) **M 43**
Scaups (both species) are our only ducks with a broad white stripe
on the trailing edge of the wing. *Male:* On the water, black at both
ends, white in the middle. Bill *blue;* head glossed with *dull purple.*
Flanks and back finely barred. *Female:* Dark brown, with a
clean-cut white mask near bill.
Similar species: See Greater Scaup.
Voice: A loud *quack* or *scaup;* purring notes. ♂, a low whistle.
Range: Alaska, w. Canada. Winters to n. S. America. **East:** Map 43.
Habitat: Marsh ponds (summer), lakes, bays, estuaries.

GREATER SCAUP *Aythya marila* 16–20″ (40–50 cm) **M 44**
Very similar to Lesser Scaup but male whiter; head rounder, less
domed, glossed mainly with *dull green* rather than *dull purple.*
Black nail on bill larger (seen only at close range). Greater's *wing
stripe is longer,* extending onto primaries.
Range: Alaska, Canada, n. Eurasia. Winters to Mexico, se. U.S.,
Mediterranean, India. **East:** Map 44. **Habitat:** Lakes, rivers, salt
bays, estuaries, tundra ponds (summer).

CANVASBACK

Diving ducks run and patter

REDHEAD

♂

♀

TUFTED DUCK
(accidental)

RING-NECKED DUCK

Lesser

Greater

Greater

Lesser

♂

♀

♂

GREATER SCAUP

♂

LESSER SCAUP

COMMON GOLDENEYE *Bucephala clangula* 20″ (50 cm) **M 45**
Male: Note the large *round white spot* before the eye. A white-looking duck with a black back and puffy green-glossed head (black at a distance). In flight, short-necked; wings whistle or "sing," show large white patches. *Female:* Gray with a white collar and a dark brown head; wings with large square white patches (showing also on the closed wing).
Similar species: See (1) Barrow's Goldeneye; (2) scaups (♂ black chest); (3) ♂ Common Merganser (long-lined, low).
Voice: Courting ♂ has a harsh nasal double note, suggesting *pee-ik* of Nighthawk. ♀, a harsh *quack.*
Range: Northern parts of N. Hemisphere. Winters to Gulf Coast, s. Eurasia. **East:** Map 45. **Habitat:** Forested lakes, rivers; in winter, also salt bays, ocean coasts.

BARROW'S GOLDENEYE *Bucephala islandica* 21″ (53 cm) **M 46**
Male: Note the *white crescent* on the face. Similar to Common Goldeneye, but blacker above; head glossed with *purple* (not green); nape more puffy. *Female:* Very similar to ♀ Goldeneye; bill shorter and deeper, forehead more abrupt. As spring advances the bill may become all *yellow* (often a good field mark).
Voice: Courting ♂, a mewing cry. ♀, a hoarse *quack.*
Range: Alaska, Canada, nw. U.S., sw. Greenland, Iceland. **East:** Map 46. **Habitat:** Wooded lakes, beaver ponds; in winter, coastal waters, a few on inland rivers.

BUFFLEHEAD *Bucephala albeola* 13–15″ (33–38 cm) **M 47**
A small duck. *Male:* Mostly white with a black back; puffy head with a *large bonnetlike white patch.* In flight shows a large white wing patch. *Female:* Dark and compact, with a *white cheek spot,* small bill, white wing patch.
Similar species: (1) See Hooded Merganser (spikelike bill). (2) See also winter Ruddy Duck.
Voice: ♂, a hoarse rolling note; ♀, a harsh *quack.*
Range: Alaska, Canada. Winters to Mexico, Gulf Coast. **East:** Map 47. **Habitat:** Lakes, ponds, rivers; in winter, salt bays.

• **STIFF-TAILED DUCKS** **Subfamily Oxyurinae.** Small, chunky; nearly helpless on land. Spiky tail has 18 or 20 feathers. Sexes unlike. **Food:** Aquatic life, insects, water plants.

RUDDY DUCK *Oxyura jamaicensis* 15–16″ (38–40 cm) **M 48**
Small, chubby; note the *white cheek,* dark cap. Often cocks tail vertically. Flight "buzzy." Cannot walk on land. *Male, summer:* Rusty red with white cheek, black cap, large blue bill. *Male, winter:* Gray with *white cheek,* dull blue or gray bill. *Female:* Similar to winter ♂ but cheek crossed by a dark line.
Similar species: See Masked Duck (*Accidentals,* p. 299).
Voice: Courting ♂, a sputtering *chick-ik-ik-ik-k-k-kwrrrr.*
Range: Canada south locally to n. S. America. **East:** Map 48.
Habitat: Fresh marshes, ponds, lakes; in winter, salt bays.

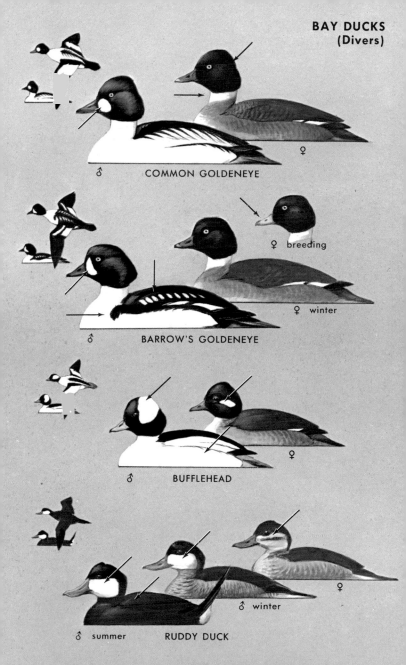

BAY DUCKS
(Divers)

♂ COMMON GOLDENEYE ♀

♀ breeding

♀ winter

♂ BARROW'S GOLDENEYE

♂ BUFFLEHEAD ♀

♂ summer RUDDY DUCK ♂ winter ♀

61

- **MERGANSERS Subfamily Merginae.** Diving fish ducks with spikelike bills, saw-edged mandibles. Most species have crests and are long-lined, slender-bodied. In flight, bill, head, neck, and body on a horizontal axis. Sexes unlike. **Food:** Chiefly small fish.

COMMON MERGANSER   M 49
Mergus merganser   22–27″ (55–68 cm)
> *Male:* Note the long whitish body, black back, green-black head. Bill and feet red; breast tinged delicate peach. *Female:* Gray, with a crested rufous head, clean white chest, large square white wing patch. Bill and feet red. In flight, lines of these slender ducks follow the winding courses of streams. The whiteness of the males and the merganser shape (bill, neck, head, and body held horizontally) identify this species.
> **Similar species:** (1) See ♀ Red-breasted Merganser. (2) ♂ Goldeneye has a white face spot, is stockier, shorter-necked, puffy-headed. (3) ♀ mergansers (rusty-headed) suggest ♂ Canvasback or Redhead, but they have black chests, no crests.
> **Voice:** ♂, low staccato croaks; ♀, a guttural *karrr*.
> **Range:** Northern parts of N. Hemisphere. Winters to Mexico, n. Africa, s. China. **East:** Map 49. **Habitat:** Wooded lakes, ponds, rivers; in winter, open lakes, rivers, rarely coastal bays.

RED-BREASTED MERGANSER   M 50
Mergus serrator   20–26″ (50–65 cm)
> *Male:* Rakish; head black, glossed with green and *conspicuously crested;* breast at waterline dark rusty, separated from head by *wide white* collar; bill and feet red. *Female:* Gray; crested rusty head, large white wing patch, red bill and feet.
> **Similar species:** ♂ Common Merganser is whiter, without collar and breastband effect; lacks crest. In ♀ Common, the white chin and white chest are *sharply defined* (in Red-breast, rufous of head is paler, *blending* into throat and neck).
> **Voice:** Usually silent. A hoarse croak; ♀, *karrr*.
> **Range:** Northern parts of N. Hemisphere. Winters to Mexico, Gulf of Mexico, n. Africa, s. China. **East:** Map 50. **Habitat:** Lakes; in winter, coastal bays, sea.

HOODED MERGANSER   M 51
Lophodytes cucullatus   16–19″ (40–48 cm)
> *Male:* Note the vertical *fan-shaped white crest* that may be raised or lowered. Breast white with 2 black bars on each side. Wing with a white patch; flanks *brown. Female:* Recognized as a merganser by its silhouette and spikelike bill; known as this species by its small size, dusky appearance, *dark head, bill, and chest.* Note the loose *tawny crest.*
> **Similar species:** (1) ♂ Bufflehead; chubbier with *white* sides. See also ♀ Bufflehead. (2) Other ♀ mergansers are larger, *grayer,* with rufous heads, red bills. (3) In flight, white wing patch and silhouette separate ♀ Hooded from ♀ Wood Duck.
> **Voice:** Low grunting or croaking notes.
> **Range:** Se. Alaska, Canada, n. U.S. Winters to n. Mexico, Gulf.
> **East:** Map 51. **Habitat:** Wooded lakes, ponds, rivers.

MERGANSERS
(Divers)

Mergansers fly with bill, head, body, and tail on the same horizontal axis

saw-edged mandibles of merganser

♂

♀

COMMON MERGANSER

♂

♀

RED-BREASTED MERGANSER

♂ crest up

♂ crest down

♀

imm. ♂

HOODED MERGANSER

Common

Red-breasted

Hooded

■ DUCKLIKE SWIMMERS (COOTS, GALLINULES) Family
Rallidae (in part). Coots and gallinules belong to the same family as the rails (see further family discussion on p. 112). Whereas the rails are more henlike and are basically secretive wading birds of the marshes, coots and gallinules are superficially more ducklike except for their smaller heads, forehead shields, and rather henlike bills. They spend most of their time swimming although they may also feed on shores, lawns, golf courses.

AMERICAN COOT *Fulica americana* 13–16″ (33–40 cm) **M 52**
A slaty ducklike bird with a blackish head and neck, *white bill,* and divided white patch under the tail. Its big feet are lobed ("scallops" on toes). Gregarious. Swimming, it pumps its head back and forth (like a gallinule). Dabbles but also dives from the surface. Taking off, it skitters; flight labored; the big feet trail beyond the short tail; a narrow white border shows on the rear of the wing. *Immature:* Paler with a duller bill. Downy young has hairy *orange-red* head and shoulders.
Similar species: Gallinules are smaller, have red bills (with yellow tips). Coots are more ducklike than gallinules and flock more on open water. See Caribbean Coot (p. 298).
Voice: A grating *kuk-kuk-kuk-kuk; kakakakakaka,* etc.; also a measured *ka-ha, ha-ha;* various cackles, croaks.
Range: Canada to Ecuador. **East:** Map 52. **Habitat:** Ponds, lakes, marshes; in winter, also fields, park ponds, salt bays.

COMMON GALLINULE *Gallinula chloropus* 13″ (33 cm) **M 53**
(Florida Gallinule) Note the rather henlike red bill, *red forehead shield,* and white band on the flanks. When walking, flirts white undertail coverts; when swimming, pumps head.
Similar species: (1) American Coot is stockier, shorter-necked; has a gray back, white bill. (2) See Purple Gallinule.
Voice: A croaking *kr-r-ruk,* repeated; a froglike *kup;* also *kek, kek, kek* and loud, complaining, henlike notes.
Range: S. Canada to Argentina; Eurasia, Africa. **East:** Map 53. **Habitat:** Fresh marshes, reedy ponds.

PURPLE GALLINULE *Porphyrula martinica* 13″ (33 cm) **M 54**
Very colorful; swims, wades, and climbs bushes. Size of Common Gallinule but head and underparts *deep violet-purple,* back bronzy green. Shield on forehead *pale blue;* bill red with a yellow tip. Legs *yellow,* conspicuous in flight. *Immature:* Drab; dark above, pale below; *no side stripe;* bill dark.
Similar species: (1) Common Gallinule has a *red* frontal shield, greenish legs, white side stripe; young Common Gallinule also has the whitish side stripe. (2) Young American Coot has a pale bill; black divides the white patch under the tail.
Voice: A henlike cackling *kek, kek, kek,* given when flying; also guttural notes.
Range: Se. U.S. to n. Argentina. Winters mainly south of U.S. **East:** Map 54. **Habitat:** Fresh swamps, marshes, ponds.

Coots skitter on takeoff

lobed foot of Coot

imm.

Coot chick

Gallinule chick

adult

adult

AMERICAN COOT

imm.

adult

COMMON GALLINULE

COMMON GALLINULE

imm.

adult

PURPLE GALLINULE

PURPLE GALLINULE

65

FLIGHT PATTERNS OF MARSH DUCKS

Note: Males are diagnosed below. Females are somewhat similar.

Text and color plate

COMMON PINTAIL (Sprig*) *Anas acuta*　　　**pp. 50, 51**
Overhead: Needle tail, white breast, thin neck.
Topside: Needle tail, neck stripe, one white border on rear edge of wing (speculum).

WOOD DUCK *Aix sponsa*　　　**pp. 50, 51**
Overhead: White belly, dusky wings, long square tail.
Topside: Stocky; long dark tail, white border on dark wing.

AMERICAN WIGEON (Baldpate*) *Anas americana*　**pp. 50, 51**
Overhead: White belly, dark pointed tail.
Topside: Large white shoulder patch.

NORTHERN SHOVELER (Spoonbill*) *Anas clypeata*　**pp. 52, 53**
Overhead: Dark belly, white chest, spoon bill.
Topside: Large bluish shoulder patch, spoon bill.

GADWALL *Anas strepera*　　　**pp. 48, 49**
Overhead: White belly, square white patch on rear edge of wing (speculum).
Topside: White patch on rear edge of wing (speculum).

GREEN-WINGED TEAL *Anas crecca*　　　**pp. 52, 53**
Overhead: Small (teal-sized); light belly, dark head.
Topside: Small, dark-winged; green speculum.

BLUE-WINGED TEAL *Anas discors*　　　**pp. 52, 53**
Overhead: Small (teal-sized); dark belly.
Topside: Small; large bluish shoulder patch.

*The names in parentheses are common duck hunters' names.

Wing of a **marsh duck** showing the iridescent speculum.

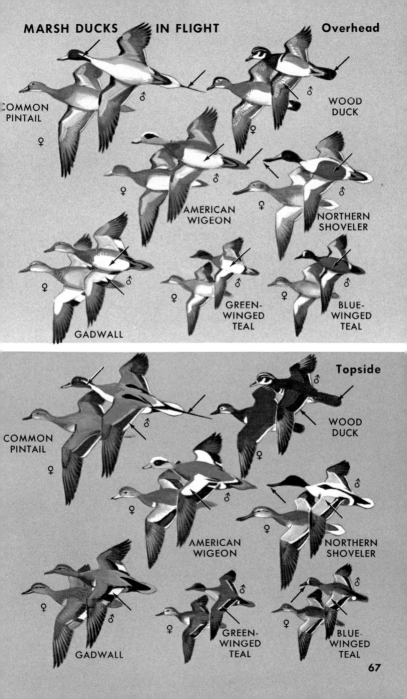

MARSH DUCKS IN FLIGHT   Overhead

COMMON PINTAIL
♀
♂

WOOD DUCK
♂
♀

AMERICAN WIGEON
♀
♂

NORTHERN SHOVELER
♂
♀

GADWALL
♀
♂

GREEN-WINGED TEAL
♀
♂

BLUE-WINGED TEAL
♂
♀

Topside

COMMON PINTAIL
♀
♂

WOOD DUCK
♂
♀

AMERICAN WIGEON
♀
♂

NORTHERN SHOVELER
♂
♀

GADWALL
♀
♂

GREEN-WINGED TEAL
♀
♂

BLUE-WINGED TEAL
♂
♀

67

FLIGHT PATTERNS OF MARSH DUCKS AND MERGANSERS

Note: Males are diagnosed below. Females are somewhat similar. Mergansers have a distinctive flight silhouette with bill, head, neck, body, and tail all on a horizontal axis.

Text and color plate

MALLARD   *Anas platyrhynchos*   pp. 48, 49
  Overhead: Dark chest, light belly, white neck-ring.
  Topside: Dark head, neck-ring, 2 white borders on speculum.

AMERICAN BLACK DUCK   *Anas rubripes*   pp. 48, 49
  Overhead: Dusky body, white wing linings.
  Topside: Dusky body, paler head.

FULVOUS WHISTLING DUCK   *Dendrocygna bicolor*   pp. 48, 49
  Overhead: Tawny, with blackish wing linings.
  Topside: Dark unpatterned wings, white ring on rump.

COMMON MERGANSER*   *Mergus merganser*   pp. 62, 63
  Overhead: Merganser shape; black head, white body, white wing linings.
  Topside: Merganser shape; white chest, large wing patches.

RED-BREASTED MERGANSER*   *Mergus serrator*   pp. 62, 63
  Overhead: Merganser shape; dark chest band.
  Topside: Merganser shape; dark chest, large wing patches.

HOODED MERGANSER*   *Lophodytes cucullatus*   pp. 62, 63
  Overhead: Merganser shape; dusky wing linings.
  Topside: Merganser shape; small wing patches.

*The duck hunter often calls mergansers "sheldrakes" or "sawbills."

DUCKS IN FLIGHT

Overhead

MALLARD

AMERICAN
BLACK DUCK

FULVOUS
WHISTLING
DUCK

♀

♂

COMMON
MERGANSER

♂

♀

♀

RED-BREASTED
MERGANSER

♂

♀

HOODED
MERGANSER

Mergansers fly on a
horizontal axis

Topside

MALLARD

AMERICAN
BLACK DUCK

♂

♀

FULVOUS
WHISTLING
DUCK

♂

♀

♂

RED-BREASTED
MERGANSER

♀

COMMON
MERGANSER

♀

♂

HOODED
MERGANSER

69

FLIGHT PATTERNS OF SEA DUCKS

Note: Only males are diagnosed below.

Text and
color plate

OLDSQUAW   *Clangula hyemalis*   **pp. 56, 57**
  Overhead: Dark unpatterned wings, white belly.
  Topside: Dark unpatterned wings, much white on body.

HARLEQUIN DUCK   *Histrionicus histrionicus*   **pp. 56, 57**
  Overhead: Solid dark below, white head spots, small bill.
  Topside: Stocky, dark with white marks, small bill.

SURF SCOTER*   *Melanitta perspicillata*   **pp. 54, 55**
  Overhead: Black body, white head patches (not readily visible from below).
  Topside: Black body, white head patches.

BLACK SCOTER*   *Melanitta nigra*   **pp. 54, 55**
  Overhead: Black plumage, paler flight feathers.
  Topside: All-black plumage.

WHITE-WINGED SCOTER*   *Melanitta deglandi*   **pp. 54, 55**
  Overhead: Black body, white wing patches.
  Topside: Black body, white wing patches.

COMMON EIDER   *Somateria mollissima*   **pp. 56, 57**
  Topside: White back, white forewing, black belly.

KING EIDER   *Somateria spectabilis*   **pp. 56, 57**
  Topside: Whitish foreparts, black rear parts.

*The three scoters are often called "coots" by duck hunters.

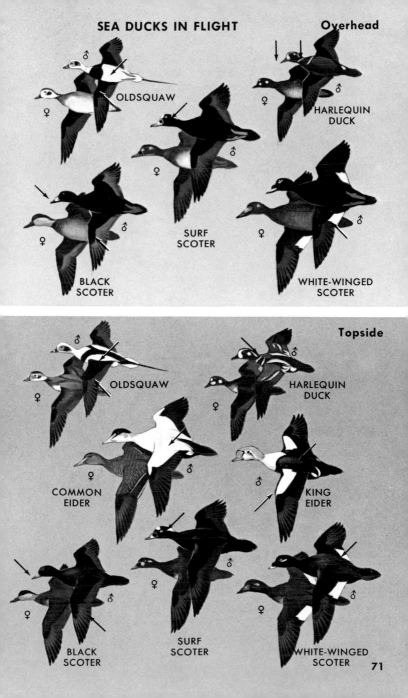

SEA DUCKS IN FLIGHT

Overhead

♂
♀
OLDSQUAW

♂
♀

♀
HARLEQUIN
DUCK

♀
♂
BLACK
SCOTER

SURF
SCOTER

♂
♀
WHITE-WINGED
SCOTER

Topside

♂
♀
OLDSQUAW

♂
♀
HARLEQUIN
DUCK

♀
♂
COMMON
EIDER

♂
♀
KING
EIDER

♀
♂
BLACK
SCOTER

♂
SURF
SCOTER

♂
♀
WHITE-WINGED
SCOTER

71

FLIGHT PATTERNS OF BAY DUCKS

Note: Only males are diagnosed below. The first five all have black chests.

	Text and color plate

CANVASBACK *Aythya valisineria*   **pp. 58, 59**
Overhead: Black chest, long profile.
Topside: White back, long profile.

REDHEAD *Aythya americana*   **pp. 58, 59**
Overhead: Black chest, roundish rufous head.
Topside: Gray back, broad gray wing stripe.

RING-NECKED DUCK *Aythya collaris*   **pp. 58, 59**
Overhead: Not safe to tell from Scaup overhead.
Topside: Black back, broad gray wing stripe.

GREATER SCAUP (Bluebill*) *Aythya marila*   **pp. 58, 59**
Overhead: Black chest, white stripe showing through wing.
Topside: Broad white wing stripe (extending onto primaries).

LESSER SCAUP (Bluebill*) *Aythya affinis*   **pp. 58, 59**
Topside: Wing stripe shorter than that of Greater Scaup.

COMMON GOLDENEYE (Whistler*)   **pp. 60, 61**
Bucephala clangula
Overhead: Blackish wing linings, white wing patches.
Topside: Large white wing-square, short neck, black head.

RUDDY DUCK *Oxyura jamaicensis*   **pp. 60, 61**
Overhead: Stubby; white face, dark chest.
Topside: Small; dark with white cheeks.

BUFFLEHEAD (Butterball*) *Bucephala albeola*   **pp. 60, 61**
Overhead: Like small Goldeneye; note head patch.
Topside: Small; large wing patches, white head patch.

*The names in parentheses are common duck hunters' names.

Marsh and Pond Ducks (Dabblers)	Bay and Sea Ducks (Divers)	Mergansers (Divers)	Ruddy Duck (Diver)	Tree Ducks (Dabblers)

POSTURES OF DUCKS ON LAND

72

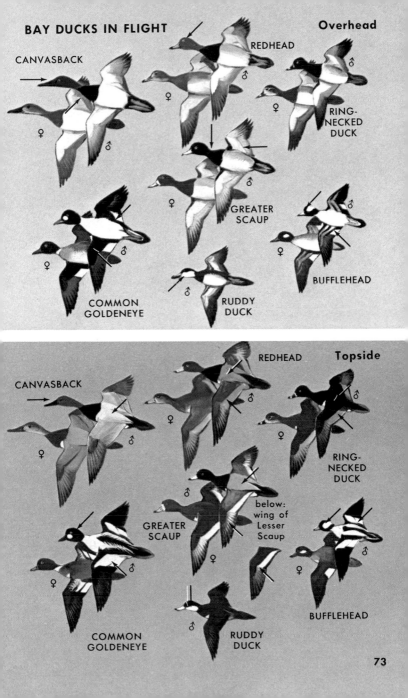

BAY DUCKS IN FLIGHT   **Overhead**

CANVASBACK

REDHEAD ♂

♀ ♀

RING-NECKED DUCK

♂

GREATER SCAUP

♀ ♂

BUFFLEHEAD

♀

♂

COMMON GOLDENEYE

♂

RUDDY DUCK

Topside

CANVASBACK

REDHEAD ♂

♀ ♂

♀

RING-NECKED DUCK

GREATER SCAUP

♂

below: wing of Lesser Scaup

♀

♂

BUFFLEHEAD

COMMON GOLDENEYE

♂

RUDDY DUCK

■ SHEARWATERS, ETC. Family Procellariidae. Gull-like birds
of the *open sea,* with stiff-winged gliding flight low over the waves.
Bills with tubelike external nostrils. Wings narrower than those
of gulls, tail smaller. Sexes alike. On distant nesting grounds noisy
at night; at sea usually silent. **Food:** Fish, squid, crustaceans, ship
refuse. **Range:** Oceans of world. **No. of species:** World, 56; East,
7 (+4 or 5 accidental).

CORY'S SHEARWATER *Puffinus diomedea* 21" (53 cm) **M 55**
Similar to Greater Shearwater, but larger and paler. *Gray* of head
blends into white of throat, whereas Greater has dark-capped look.
Bill of Cory's is *yellow* (Greater's is black). White on rump indis-
tinct or lacking. No smudge on belly.
Range: Breeds in Azores, Canaries, and other islands in e. Atlantic;
also in Mediterranean. Wanders to coastal U.S. in summer. **East:**
Map 55. **Habitat:** Open ocean.

GREATER SHEARWATER *Puffinus gravis* 19" (48 cm) **M 56**
A gull-like seabird, dark above and white below, scaling above the
waves on stiff wings, is likely to be this shearwater or Cory's. This
species has a *dark headcap* separated by a light band across the
nape. Note also the *white rump patch,* usually indistinct or lacking
in Cory's, and the dark smudge on belly.
Range: Breeds mainly on Tristan da Cunha Is. in S. Atlantic.
Wanders at sea north to s. Greenland, Iceland, and back; May–
Oct. **East:** Map 56. **Habitat:** Open ocean, well offshore.

SOOTY SHEARWATER *Puffinus griseus* 17" (43 cm) **M 57**
A gull-like seabird, size of Laughing Gull; looks all dark at a
distance and scales over the waves on narrow rigid wings. Note the
whitish linings on the undersurface of the wings.
Similar species: See dark jaegers (white in primaries), p. 83.
Range: Breeds in New Zealand, s. S. America; ranges in summer to
N. Atlantic, N. Pacific. **East:** Map 57. **Habitat:** Open sea.

MANX SHEARWATER *Puffinus puffinus* 13" (33 cm)
A small *black-and-white* shearwater; half the bulk of Greater
Shearwater; *no white* at base of tail. Dark cap extends below eye.
The gliding, bounding flight is distinctive.
Range: Breeds on sea islands of Europe, w. Mexico, Hawaii. **East:**
Has bred in Newfoundland, Massachusetts. Increasing. Regular at
sea from Newfoundland to Hatteras; casual Florida.

AUDUBON'S SHEARWATER *Puffinus lherminieri* 12" (30 cm)
A very small dark-backed shearwater, similar to the Manx but
with a more rapid or fluttering wing action. Wings *shorter,* tail
longer. Shows *more black* under the tail.
Similar species: See also Little Shearwater (p. 292).
Range: Breeds Bermuda, W. Indies, Cape Verdes, Galapagos, etc.
East: Wanders at sea off Atlantic and Gulf coasts of se. U.S.,
regularly north to Cape Hatteras; rarely to New England.

SHEARWATERS

GREATER
SHEARWATER

CORY'S
HEARWATER

SOOTY
SHEARWATER

MANX
HEARWATER

tubed bill
of shearwater

AUDUBON'S
SHEARWATER

NORTHERN FULMAR *Fulmarus glacialis* 18″ (45 cm) **M 58**
A stiff-winged oceanic glider, stockier than a shearwater; swims buoyantly. Note the bull neck, bulging forehead, *stubby yellow bill,* large dark eye, short tail. Primaries may show a *pale flash.* Legs bluish. *Dark phase:* Smoky gray, wing tips darker; bill yellowish. Intermediates are frequent.
Voice: A hoarse grunting *ag-ag-ag-arrr* or *ek-ek-ek-ek-ek.*
Range: N. oceans of N. Hemisphere. **East:** Map 58. **Habitat:** Open ocean; breeds colonially on open sea cliffs.

BLACK-CAPPED PETREL *Pterodroma hasitata* 16″ (40 cm)
Slightly larger than Audubon's or Manx Shearwater. Note the white forehead, *white collar,* and white rump patch.
Range: Caribbean. Probably regular in Gulf Stream north at least to Cape Hatteras. Accidental inland after storms.

CAHOW (BERMUDA PETREL) *Pterodroma cahow* 15″ (38 cm)
Bermuda only. One of the world's rarest seabirds. Suggests Audubon's or Manx Shearwater but note the *white forehead* and *pale rump patch.* Differs from Black-capped Petrel by grayer rump, absence of white collar.
Range: Known only from certain small islets off the ne. end of Bermuda (a few pairs) where they come and go at night.

■ **STORM PETRELS Family Hydrobatidae.** Little dark birds that flit over the ocean. Like the shearwaters, petrels, etc., they nest on sea islands, returning to burrows at night. Nostrils in fused tube on bill. Sexes alike. **Food:** Plankton, crustaceans, small fish.
Range: Oceans of world (except Arctic). **No. of species:** World, 21; East, 2 (+3 or 4 accidental).

WILSON'S STORM PETREL **M 59**
Oceanites oceanicus 7″ (18 cm)
Smaller than Purple Martin; sooty with a paler wing patch and conspicuous *white rump patch; tail even at end.* Yellow-webbed feet may show beyond tip of tail. Skims like a swallow, pausing to flutter and patter over water. See next species.
Range: Breeds in Antarctic; ranges to N. Hemisphere. **East:** Map 59. **Habitat:** Open ocean. Often follows ships (Leach's Storm Petrel does not). Can be "chummed in" by tossing out ground fish, suet, puffed wheat in fish oil, etc.

LEACH'S STORM PETREL **M 60**
Oceanodroma leucorhoa 8″ (20 cm)
Note the *forked tail.* Otherwise similar to Wilson's Storm Petrel but browner; wings longer, more angled. In flight it bounds about erratically, changing speed and direction (suggesting Nighthawk). The breeding petrel of the North Atlantic (but less often seen at sea). Does not follow ships.
Voice: At night, in flight on breeding grounds, rhythmic falsetto hooting notes. From burrows, long crooning trills.
Range: N. Atlantic, N. Pacific. **East:** Map 60. **Habitat:** Open ocean; nesting colonies in turf on offshore islands.

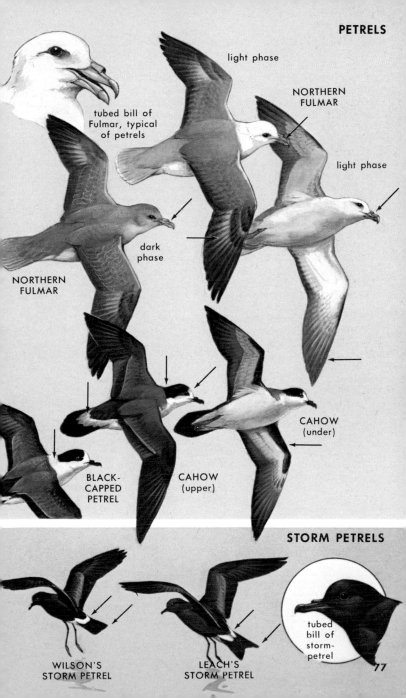

PETRELS

light phase

tubed bill of
Fulmar, typical
of petrels

NORTHERN
FULMAR

light phase

NORTHERN
FULMAR

dark
phase

CAHOW
(under)

BLACK-
CAPPED
PETREL

CAHOW
(upper)

STORM PETRELS

WILSON'S
STORM PETREL

LEACH'S
STORM PETREL

tubed
bill of
storm-
petrel

77

■ **PELICANS Family Pelecanidae.** Huge water birds with long flat bills and great throat pouches (flat when deflated). Neck long, body robust. Sexes alike. Flocks fly in lines, alternating several flaps with a glide. In flight, head is hunched back on shoulders, the long bill resting on breast. Pelicans swim buoyantly. **Food:** Mainly fish, crustaceans. **Range:** N. and S. America, Africa, se. Europe, s. Asia, E. Indies, Australia. **No. of species:** World, 6; East, 2.

WHITE PELICAN *Pelecanus erythrorhynchos* 62″ (155 cm) **M 61**
Huge (wingspread 8–9½ ft.). White with black primaries and a great orange-yellow bill. When breeding the ridge of the bill has a "centerboard." Immature has a dusky bill. Does not plunge from air like Brown Pelican but scoops up fish while swimming. Flocks fly in lines, often circle high on thermals.
Similar species: (1) Swans have no black in wings. (2) Wood Ibis and (3) Whooping Crane fly with necks extended, long legs aft. (4) Snow Goose is much smaller, with a small bill; noisy.
Voice: In colony, a low groan. Young utter whining grunts.
Range: W. and cen. N. America, winters to se. U.S. **East:** Map 61.
Habitat: Lakes, marshes, salt bays, beaches.

BROWN PELICAN *Pelecanus occidentalis* 50″ (125 cm) **M 62**
A ponderous *dark* water bird (spread 6½ ft.); adult with much *white* about head and neck. Immature has a dark head, whitish underparts. Size, shape, and flight (a few flaps and a glide) indicate a pelican; the dark color and habit of *plunging bill-first* proclaim it this species. Lines of pelicans scale close to the water, almost touching it with wing tips.
Voice: Adults silent (rarely a low croak). Nestlings squeal.
Range: Coasts; s. U.S. to n. and w. S. America. **East:** Map 62.
Habitat: Salt bays, beaches, ocean. Perches on posts, boats.

■ **FRIGATEBIRDS Family Fregatidae.** Dark tropical seabirds with extremely long wings (with a greater span in relation to weight than that of any other birds). Bill long, hooked; tail deeply forked. Normally do not swim. **Food:** Fish, jellyfish, squid, young birds. Food snatched from water in flight, scavenged, or taken from other seabirds. **Range:** Pantropical oceans. **No. of species:** World, 5; East, 1 (+1 accidental).

MAGNIFICENT FRIGATEBIRD **M 63**
Fregata magnificens 38–41″ (95–103 cm); spread 7–8 ft.
(Man-o'-war Bird) A large black seabird with extremely long, angled wings and a scissorlike tail (often folded in a point). Soars with extreme ease. Bill long, hooked. *Male:* All black with a red throat pouch (inflated in display). *Female:* White breast, dark head. *Immature:* Head, breast white.
Voice: Voiceless at sea. A gargling whinny during display.
Range: Gulf of Mexico, tropical Atlantic, e. Pacific. **East:** Map 63.
Habitat: Oceanic coasts, islands.

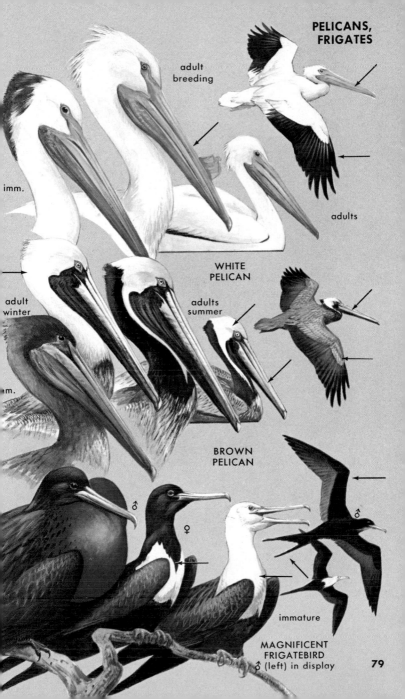

PELICANS, FRIGATES

adult breeding

imm.

adults

WHITE PELICAN

adult winter

m.

adults summer

BROWN PELICAN

♂

♀

immature

♂

MAGNIFICENT FRIGATEBIRD
♂ (left) in display

79

■ **GANNETS, BOOBIES Family Sulidae.** Seabirds with large, tapering bills, pointed tails ("pointed at both ends"). Larger than most gulls; neck longer. Sexes alike. Fish by plunging from air. **Food:** Fish, squid. **Range:** Gannets live in cold seas (N. Atlantic, S. Africa, Australia); boobies, tropical seas. **No. of species:** World, 9; East, 3 (+1 accidental).

NORTHERN GANNET *Morus bassanus* 38″ (95 cm)   **M 64**
A goose-sized white seabird with extensive *black wing ends.* Scales over the ocean and plunges headlong for fish. Much larger than Herring Gull, with a *pointed tail,* longer neck, larger bill (often pointed toward the water). Immature is dusky, but note the "pointed at both ends" shape. Young birds in transition may have a splotched piebald look.
Voice: In colony, a low barking *arrah.*
Range: North Atlantic. **East:** Map 64. **Habitat:** Oceanic; often seen well offshore. Breeds colonially on sea cliffs.

MASKED BOOBY *Sula dactylatra* 27″ (68 cm)
(Blue-faced Booby) A white booby, smaller than Gannet, with a *black* tail and black along *entire rear edge* of wing. *Immature:* Dusky, with a *whitish patch* on upper back and rump.
Range: Tropical oceans. **East:** Occasional off Gulf Coast (on buoys, oil rigs) and s. Florida (regular in Dry Tortugas).

BROWN BOOBY *Sula leucogaster* 28–30″ (70–75 cm)
(White-bellied Booby) Sooty brown with a *white belly* in *clean-cut contrast* to its dark breast. Bill and feet yellowish. *Immature:* Brown above, paler below; feet *yellowish.*
Similar species: Immature Gannet lacks clean-cut breast contrast; feet are *dark* (not yellowish).
Range: Tropical oceans. **East:** Occasional at sea off Gulf Coast and Florida (esp. Dry Tortugas). Accidental to Cape Cod.

■ **TROPICBIRDS Family Phaethontidae.** Although unrelated, tropicbirds resemble large terns with 2 greatly elongated *central* tail feathers and stouter, slightly decurved bills. Ternlike, they dive headfirst. Sexes alike. **Food:** Squid, crustaceans. **Range:** Tropical oceans of world. **No. of species:** World, 3; East, 1 (+1 accidental).

WHITE-TAILED TROPICBIRD *Phaethon lepturus*
(Yellow-billed Tropicbird) 32″ (80 cm), incl. 16″ streamers
Tropicbirds fly pigeonlike on strong quick wings over the sea. Note the *2 extremely long central tail feathers.* Bill yellow to orange-red. Young lack streamers; barred with black above; bill yellow.
Voice: A harsh ternlike scream. Also *tik-et, tik-et.*
Range: Pantropical oceans. **East:** Breeds in Bermuda. Occasionally seen in Gulf Stream off s. Atlantic Coast, Florida Keys. Casual to n. Gulf Coast and Nova Scotia after storms.

80

GANNETS, BOOBIES, TROPICBIRDS

NORTHERN GANNET

adults

1st year

changing

diving

MASKED BOOBY

adults

imm.

BROWN BOOBY

adult

adults

below

imm.

above

imm.

adult

WHITE-TAILED TROPICBIRD

81

■ JAEGERS, SKUAS Family Stercorariidae.

Dark falconlike or hawklike seabirds with slightly hooked beaks; harass gulls and terns, forcing them to disgorge. Light, intermediate, and dark phases. All have a *flash of white* in the primaries. Jaegers have 2 projecting central tail feathers, lacking in immatures, which may be identified (tentatively) by relative size. Skuas lack tail points. Sexes alike. **Food:** In Arctic, lemmings, eggs, young birds. At sea, food taken from other birds or from water. **Range:** Seas of world, breeding in subpolar regions. **No. of species:** World, 5; East, 5.

GREAT SKUA *Catharacta skua* 21–24″ (53–60 cm)
Note the *conspicuous white wing patch.* Near size of Herring Gull but stockier. Dark brown, with rusty underparts and a short, slightly wedge-shaped tail. Flight strong and swift; harasses other seabirds.
Similar species: Dark jaegers may lack tail points. Skuas' wings are wider, less falconlike, wing patches more striking.
Range: Breeds locally in colder parts of e. N. Atlantic, s. S. Atlantic, s. S. Pacific, sub-Antarctic; wanders widely at sea. **East:** Frequent at sea off Maritimes and New England. Skuas of this or next species occur south at least to Cape Hatteras.

SOUTH POLAR SKUA *Catharacta maccormicki* 21″ (53 cm)
Very similar to Great Skua; bill and legs shorter. "Blond" phase is much paler on head and underparts than Great Skua. Dark phase lacks scattered rusty feathers of Great Skua.
Range: Antarctica. Wanders widely into N. Atlantic (as far as Greenland). Summer skuas off our coast may be this one.

PARASITIC JAEGER *Stercorarius parasiticus* 18″ (45 cm) **M 65**
Falconlike; chases gulls, terns. In adult, the sharp tail points project ½–3½ in. Like other jaegers it shows a white wing flash. The jaeger most frequently seen from shore.
Range: Arctic, circumpolar. Winters at sea from latitude of s. U.S. to Tierra del Fuego. **East:** Map 65. **Habitat:** Open ocean, coastal bays, large lakes (rarely); tundra (summer).

POMARINE JAEGER *Stercorarius pomarinus* 22″ (55 cm) **M 66**
Note the *broad and twisted* central tail feathers (projecting 2–7 in.). Larger and heavier than other jaegers, often heavily barred below, with a broad breastband and more white in the primaries. Immature lacks blunt projections, is larger than the other young jaegers, and has a heavier bill.
Range: Arctic; circumpolar. Winters at sea from s. U.S. to S. Hemisphere. **East:** Map 66. **Habitat:** Open sea, coasts (offshore); tundra (summer).

LONG-TAILED JAEGER **M 67**
Stercorarius longicaudus 20–23″ (51–58 cm)
The long tail streamers of adults may project 9–10 in. (usually 3–6). Much whiter below than Parasitic Jaeger; no breastband. The black cap is well separated from the pale gray back. Bill short; legs blue-gray (Parasitic, black).
Range: Arctic, circumpolar. Winters at sea in S. Hemisphere. **East:** Map 67. **Habitat:** Open ocean; tundra (summer).

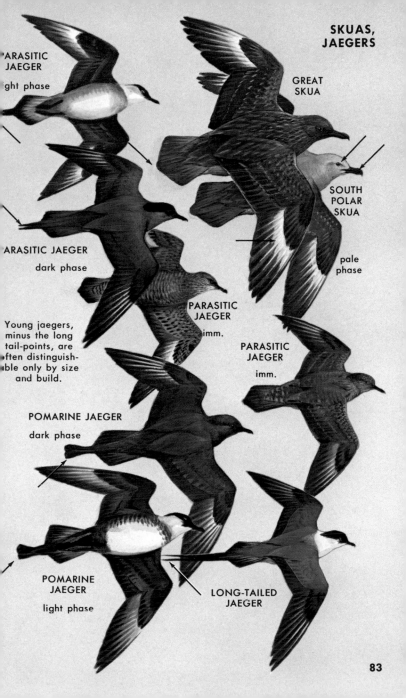

ᴾARASITIC JAEGER

ᴵght phase

ᴾARASITIC JAEGER

dark phase

Young jaegers, minus the long tail-points, are ᴼften distinguishᴬble only by size and build.

POMARINE JAEGER

dark phase

POMARINE JAEGER

light phase

GREAT SKUA

SOUTH POLAR SKUA

pale phase

PARASITIC JAEGER

imm.

PARASITIC JAEGER

imm.

LONG-TAILED JAEGER

■ GULLS (below) **AND TERNS** (p. 94) **Family Laridae.**

- **GULLS Subfamily Larinae.** Long-winged swimming birds with superb flight. More robust, wider-winged, longer-legged than terns. Bills slightly hooked. Tails square or rounded (terns usually have forked tails). They seldom dive (terns hover, plunge headfirst). **Food:** Omnivorous; marine life, plant and animal food, refuse, carrion. **No. of species:** World, 45; East, 17 (+3 accidental).

GLAUCOUS GULL *Larus hyperboreus* 26–32″ (65–80 cm) **M 68**
Note the "frosty" wing tips. A large chalky white gull, size of Greater Black-back. Adults have a pale gray mantle and *unmarked white primaries. Immature:* See pp. 90, 91.
Similar species: Iceland Gull is size of Herring Gull or smaller; bill is smaller than that of Glaucous; head rounder; wing proportionately longer and narrower. Adult has a narrow *red* ring around eye (Glaucous, *yellow*), but this is hard to see.
Range: Arctic; circumpolar. Winters to U.S., Britain, n. China.
East: Map 68. **Habitat:** Mainly coastal; some inland.

ICELAND GULL *Larus glaucoides* 23–26″ (58–65 cm) **M 69**
A pale ghostly gull, near size of Herring Gull. Adult has a pale gray mantle and *whitish or pure white primaries without dark markings. Immature:* See pp. 90, 91. See "Kumlien's" Gull.
Similar species: Glaucous Gull has a more massive bill.
Range: Breeds in Greenland. In winter to e. Canada, e. U.S. **East:** Map 69. **Habitat:** Coastal, less frequent inland.

"KUMLIEN'S" GULL *Larus glaucoides* (in part) **M 69**
This, the race of the Iceland Gull that breeds in eastern Arctic Canada, differs by having *gray or dark markings,* variable in extent, toward the tips of the whitish primaries (not black with white "mirrors" as in the Herring Gull).
Similar species: Thayer's Gull has a darker mantle, dark eyes.
Range: E. Arctic Canada; winters to ne. U.S. **East:** Map 69.

IVORY GULL *Pagophila eburnea* 15–17″ (38–43 cm)
The only *all-white* gull with *black* legs. Pigeon-sized; wings long, flight quite ternlike. Bill black with a yellow tip. *Immature:* See pp. 92, 93.
Similar species: (1) Iceland and (2) Glaucous Gulls are larger with flesh-colored legs.
Voice: Harsh shrill ternlike cries: *keeeer,* etc.
Range: High Arctic; circumpolar. **East:** Breeds locally on Arctic islands of northernmost Canada (NWT). Winters from pack ice south to Gulf of St. Lawrence, casually to New England. Accidental south to New Jersey and on Great Lakes.

ROSS' GULL *Rhodostethia rosea* 12½–14″ (31–35 cm)
A rare gull of the drift ice. *Summer:* Note the *wedge-shaped tail,* rosy underparts, *fine black collar,* blue-gray wing linings. *Winter:* Loses rosy color, black collar. *Immature:* See p. 92.
Range: Breeds mainly in Siberia. **East:** Rare visitor to Arctic Canada; has bred. Accidental Massachusetts, Great Lakes.

"WHITE-WINGED" GULLS
Adults

GLAUCOUS
GULL

ICELAND
GULL

"Kumlien" form   typical form

IVORY
GULL

ROSS'
GULL

winter

breeding

85

HERRING GULL   *Larus argentatus*   23–26″ (58–65 cm)   **M 70**
The common large "seagull." *Adult:* A big gray-mantled gull with *flesh-colored legs.* Wing tips black with white spots; heavy yellow bill with a red spot. *Immature:* See p. 90.
Voice: A loud *hiyak. . .hiyah. . .hyiah-hyak* or *yuk-yuk-yuk-yuk-yuckle-yuckle.* Mewing squeals. Anxiety note, *gah-gah-gah.*
Range: N. parts of N. Hemisphere. **East:** Map 70. **Habitat:** Ocean coasts, bays, beaches, lakes, piers, farmlands, dumps.

THAYER'S GULL   *Larus thayeri*   23–25″ (58–63 cm)   **M 70**
Very similar to Herring Gull, replacing it in Arctic Canada. Adult has (1) *pale to dark brown* (not yellow) eyes, (2) narrow red (not yellow) eye-ring, (3) slate gray (not black) in primaries, (4) slightly darker mantle, (5) *pinker* legs.
Range: Arctic Canada. Winters Pacific Coast. **East:** Map 70.

RING-BILLED GULL   *Larus delawarensis*   19″ (48 cm)   **M 71**
Adult: Similar to Herring Gull but smaller, more buoyant, and dovelike. Note the *black ring* encircling the bill and the *yellowish* or *pale greenish* legs. Shows much more black on *underside* of primaries. *Immature:* See pp. 90, 91.
Similar species: Adult Herring Gull has flesh-colored legs.
Voice: Notes higher pitched than Herring Gull's.
Range: Canada, n. U.S. Winters to Mexico, Cuba. **East:** Map 71.
Habitat: Lakes, bays, coasts, piers, dumps, plowed fields.

CALIFORNIA GULL   *Larus californicus*   20–23″ (50–58 cm)
Adult: Resembles the smaller Ring-billed Gull (both have yellowish green legs), but note the darker mantle, *dark eye,* and *red and black spot* on the lower mandible (not a black ring). Shows more white in wing tips. *Immature:* See pp. 90, 91.
Range: W. N. America; winters from s. B. Columbia to Guatemala.
East: Breeds east to cen. N. Dakota. Accidental east to coast.

BLACK-LEGGED KITTIWAKE   *Rissa tridactyla*   17″ (43 cm)   **M 72**
A small buoyant oceanic gull. In adults the black wing tips are *cut straight across,* as if dipped in ink. Bill small, pale yellow, unmarked. Legs *black. Immature:* See p. 92.
Voice: At nesting colony, a raucous *kaka-week* or *kitti-waak.*
Range: Oceans in northern parts of N. Hemisphere. Winters to coasts of U.S., Mediterranean, Japan. **East:** Map 72.

GREATER BLACK-BACKED GULL   **M 73**
Larus marinus   28–31″ (70–78 cm)
Larger than Herring Gull. *Adult:* Unmistakable; black back and wings, snow-white underparts. *Immature:* See pp. 90, 91.
Similar species: See Lesser Black-backed Gull (casual).
Voice: A harsh deep *kyow* or *owk.*
Range: Mainly coasts of n. N. Atlantic, wintering to mid-Atlantic states, Mediterranean. **East:** Map 73. **Habitat:** Mainly coastal waters, estuaries; a few on large lakes.

LESSER BLACK-BACKED GULL   *Larus fuscus*   23″ (58 cm)
Similar to Greater Black-backed Gull but smaller (size of Herring Gull). Distinguished by *yellow* (not flesh) legs.
Range: N. Europe, wintering to Mediterranean. **East:** In recent years many records from e. Canada to s. Florida.

GULLS
Adults

THAYER'S GULL

HERRING GULL

HERRING GULL

RING-BILLED GULL

CALIFORNIA GULL

BLACK-LEGGED KITTIWAKE

GREATER BLACK-BACKED GULL

LESSER BLACK-BACKED GULL

GREATER BLACK-BACKED GULL

In winter, gulls on this plate may be streaked or clouded with dusky on crown and hind neck.

87

LAUGHING GULL   *Larus atricilla*   16–17″ (40–43 cm)   **M 74**
A small coastal gull. The *dark mantle blends into black wing tips.*
White edge on rear of wing. In summer, head black; in winter,
white with dark smudge. *Immature:* See p. 92.
Voice: A strident laugh, *ha-ha-ha-ha-ha-haah-haah-haah,* etc.
Range: Coast: Nova Scotia to Venezuela, locally in se. California,
w. Mexico. Winters from s. U.S. south. **East:** Map 74. **Habitat:** Salt
marshes, coastal bays, piers, beaches, ocean.

FRANKLIN'S GULL   *Larus pipixcan*   14–15″ (35–38 cm)   **M 74**
Note the *white wing band* separating the black from the gray. In
summer, breast has a rosy bloom, head is black. In fall, head white
with dark cheek and nape. *Immature:* See pp. 92, 93.
Voice: A shrill *kuk-kuk-kuk;* also mewing, laughing cries.
Range: Breeds in w. Canada and nw. and n.-cen. U.S. Winters in
Pacific from Guatemala to Chile. **East:** Map 74. **Habitat:** Prairies,
inland marshes, lakes; in winter, coasts, ocean.

SABINE'S GULL   *Xema sabini*   13–14″ (33–35 cm)   **M 75**
Our only gull with a *well-forked tail.* Note the black outer prima-
ries and *triangular white wing patch.* Bill black with *yellow tip,*
feet black. Slaty hood in summer. *Immature:* See p. 92.
Range: Arctic; circumpolar. Winters in Pacific to Peru; local in
Atlantic. **East:** Map 75. **Habitat:** Tundra (summer); ocean.

BLACK-HEADED GULL   *Larus ridibundus*   14–15″ (35–38 cm)
Similar in pattern to Bonaparte's Gull and associates with it;
slightly larger. Adult in summer has *brown* (not black) head. In
winter loses dark hood. Bill *dark red,* not black. Shows much
blackish on underside of primaries. Immature: See p. 92.
Range: Eurasia, Iceland. **East:** In recent years increasingly frequent along ne. coast of N. America, esp. in Maritimes; less frequent in s. U.S., Great Lakes. Has bred Newfoundland.

BONAPARTE'S GULL   *Larus philadelphia*   13″ (33 cm)   **M 76**
A petite, almost ternlike gull. Note the *long wedge of white* on the
fore edge of the wing. In summer, has a blackish head. Legs red;
bill small, black. In winter, adults have a white head with a *black
earspot. Immature:* See pp. 92, 93.
Voice: A nasal *cheer* or *cherr.* Some notes ternlike.
Range: Alaska, w. and cen. Canada. Winters n. U.S. to Mexico,
Cuba. **East:** Map 76. **Habitat:** Ocean bays, lakes; muskeg (summer).

LITTLE GULL   *Larus minutus*   11″ (28 cm)
The smallest gull. Note the *blackish undersurface* of the *rather
rounded wing* and absence of black above. Head black in summer,
capped in winter. Legs red. In summer, bill dark red, breast pinkish. In winter, bill black. *Immature:* See p. 92.
Range: Eurasia, wintering to Mediterranean. **East:** Rare but regular on Great Lakes and along coast. Has bred in Ontario, Michigan,
Wisconsin. **Habitat:** Lakes, bays; with Bonaparte's.

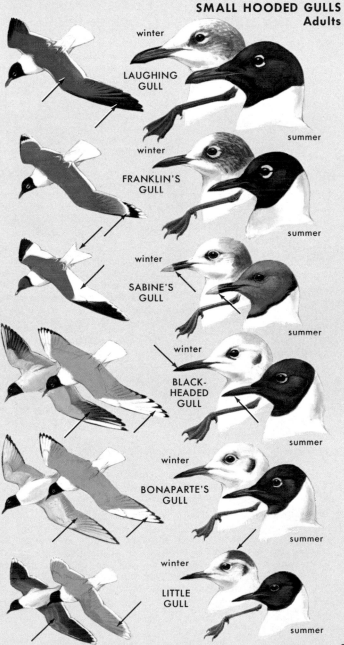

SMALL HOODED GULLS
Adults

winter

LAUGHING GULL

summer

winter

FRANKLIN'S GULL

summer

winter

SABINE'S GULL

summer

winter

BLACK-HEADED GULL

summer

winter

BONAPARTE'S GULL

summer

winter

LITTLE GULL

summer

IMMATURE GULLS (1) LARGER SPECIES

Immature gulls are more difficult to identify than adults. They are usually darkest the first year, lighter the second, and in the larger species may not be fully adult until the third or fourth year. Leg and bill colors of most immatures are not as diagnostic as in adults. Go mainly by pattern and size. The most typical plumages are shown opposite; intermediate stages can be expected. Do not feel you must identify *every* immature gull. Because of variables such as stage of molt, wear, age, individual variation, and even occasional albinism and hybridization, some birds may remain a mystery even to the expert unless the specimen is in hand.

GLAUCOUS GULL *Larus hyperboreus* **Adult pp. 84, 85**
First winter: Recognized by its larger size (size of Greater Black-backed Gull), pale tan coloration, and unmarked *frosty primaries,* a shade lighter than the rest of the wing. Bill *pale flesh* with a dark tip. **Second year:** Very pale or whitish throughout. The pale gray mantle is acquired later, with adulthood.

ICELAND GULL *Larus glaucoides* **Adult pp. 84, 85**
Sequence of plumages similar to Glaucous Gull's but the bird is smaller (size of Herring Gull) with a smaller bill and proportionately longer wings (projecting beyond the tail when at rest). Flight lighter. The bill of the first-year Iceland Gull is almost entirely dark (flesh with dark tip in Glaucous).

HERRING GULL *Larus argentatus* **Adult pp. 86, 87**
First winter: Relatively uniform brown; the common dusky gull. No other young gull is quite as uniformly dark in appearance. **Second and third winter:** Paler. Head and underparts whiter; tail feathers dark-tipped, contrasting with white rump. The gray mantle is acquired with approaching adulthood.

CALIFORNIA GULL *Larus californicus* **Adult pp. 86, 87**
First winter: As *dark* as Herring Gull in its first winter but with a shorter *bicolored bill.*

GREATER BLACK-BACKED GULL *Larus marinus* **Adult p. 86**
Young birds are larger and less brown than first-year Herring Gulls. They are more contrasty, paler on the head, tail, and underparts; the "saddle-back" pattern is suggested. They may resemble the later immature stages of the Herring Gull but the back is darker and the head and bill are larger.

RING-BILLED GULL *Larus delawarensis* **Adult pp. 86, 87**
Immatures may be confused with the second- or third-winter Herring Gull, which has a semblance of a ring near the tip of its longer bill. In the Herring Gull the tail terminates in a *broad* ill-defined band. The subterminal band in the Ring-bill is narrower (a little over 1 in. wide) and usually (but not always) well-defined. The leg color in most instances is not useful, as many young Ring-bills have flesh or flesh-gray legs not unlike those of young Herring Gulls.

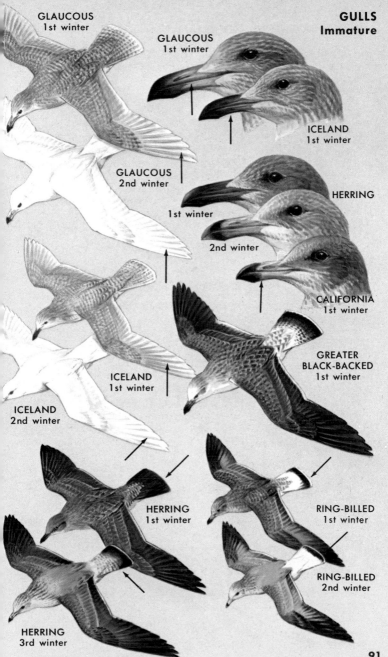

GLAUCOUS
1st winter

GLAUCOUS
1st winter

ICELAND
1st winter

GLAUCOUS
2nd winter

HERRING

1st winter

2nd winter

ICELAND
1st winter

CALIFORNIA
1st winter

GREATER
BLACK-BACKED
1st winter

ICELAND
2nd winter

ICELAND
1st winter

HERRING
1st winter

RING-BILLED
1st winter

HERRING
3rd winter

RING-BILLED
2nd winter

IMMATURE GULLS (2) SMALLER SPECIES

LAUGHING GULL   *Larus atricilla*   **Adult pp. 88, 89**
First year: Very *dark* with a *white rump* and a *white border* on the
trailing edge of the dark wing. **Second winter:** Paler or whiter on
the chest and forehead; not easy to separate from young Franklin's
Gull (see next).

FRANKLIN'S GULL   *Larus pipixcan*   **Adult pp. 88, 89**
The first-winter immature is very similar to the second-winter
Laughing Gull but is smaller-billed and more petite. It perhaps
may best be distinguished by the *darker cheek* and *more distinctly
hooded* effect. Ranges differ — Franklin's inland, Laughing on
coast. First-year Laughing Gull, however, is readily separated from
Franklin's by its brown breast, brown forehead.

BLACK-LEGGED KITTIWAKE   *Rissa tridactyla*   **Adult pp. 86, 87**
Note the *dark bar on the nape,* black outer primaries, and dark
bar across the inner wing. Tail may seem notched.

SABINE'S GULL   *Xema sabini*   **Adult pp. 88, 89**
Dark grayish brown on the back but with the adult's bold *triangular wing pattern.* Note also the *forked* tail. Young Kittiwake is
similar, but has a dark bar on the nape, a diagonal bar across the
wing, and only a slight tail notch.

BONAPARTE'S GULL   *Larus philadelphia*   **Adult pp. 88, 89**
Petite, ternlike. Note the cheek spot, narrow black tail band, and
pattern of black and white in the outer primaries.

BLACK-HEADED GULL   *Larus ridibundus*   **Adult pp. 88, 89**
Similar in pattern to immature Bonaparte's Gull with which it
associates but slightly larger, less ternlike; the longer bill is ochre
at the base, black at tip. Undersurface of wing similar to adult
Black-head's but not as dark.

IVORY GULL   *Pagophila eburnea*   **Adult pp. 84, 85**
A ternlike white gull with irregular gray smudges on the face, a
sprinkling of black spots above, and a narrow black border on the
rear edge of its white wings.

LITTLE GULL   *Larus minutus*   **Adult pp. 88, 89**
Smaller than young Bonaparte's with rounder wings and a *blacker
M pattern* formed by the outer primaries and the dark band across
the wing. Note especially the *dusky cap.*

ROSS' GULL   *Rhodostethia rosea*   **Adult pp. 84, 85**
Similar in pattern to immature Kittiwake but note the *wedge-
shaped,* not square or notched, tail and the blue-gray linings of the
underwing. Lacks the dark nape of immature Kittiwake.

SMALL GULLS
Immature

1st winter

2nd winter

1st winter

LAUGHING

2nd winter

LAUGHING

FRANKLIN'S

1st winter

1st winter

FRANKLIN'S

SABINE'S

BLACK-LEGGED
KITTIWAKE

BONAPARTE'S

BLACK-HEADED

IVORY

LITTLE

ROSS'

93

- **TERNS Subfamily Sterninae.** Graceful water birds, more streamlined than gulls. Bill sharp-pointed, often tilted toward the water. Tail usually forked. Most terns are whitish with black caps; in winter, the black of the forehead is replaced by white. Sexes alike. Terns often hover and plunge headfirst for fish. Normally they do not swim (gulls do). **Food:** Small fish, marine life, large insects. **Range:** Almost worldwide. **No. of species:** World, 42; East, 14 (+2 accidental).

GULL-BILLED TERN *Gelochelidon nilotica* 14″ (35 cm) **M 77**
Note the stout, almost *gull-like black* bill. Stockier and paler than Common Tern; tail much less forked; feet *black*. In winter head is nearly white. Young bird suggests a small gull with a notched tail. Often hawks for insects over land.
Voice: A throaty, rasping *za-za-za;* also *kay-weck, kay-weck.*
Range: Breeds locally, wanders widely in many parts of world.
East: Map 77. **Habitat:** Salt marshes, fields, coastal bays.

SANDWICH TERN *Sterna sandvicensis* 16–18″ (40–45 cm) **M 78**
(Cabot's Tern) Slightly larger than Common Tern. Note the *long black bill* with its *yellow tip* (often obscure in young birds). White forehead acquired during nesting season; feathers on back of crown elongated, forming a crest. Feet black.
Similar species: See Gull-billed Tern (stout black bill).
Voice: A grating *kirr-ick* (higher than Gull-bill's *kay-weck*).
Range: Coasts of se. U.S., British Isles, Europe. Winters to S. America, Africa. **East:** Map 78. **Habitat:** Coastal waters, jetties, beaches. Prefers company of Royal Terns.

ROYAL TERN *Sterna maxima* 18–21″ (45–53 cm) **M 79**
A large tern, slimmer than Caspian, with a large *orange* bill (Caspian's is redder). Tail deeply forked. Although some Royal Terns in spring show a solid cap, they usually have much white on the forehead, the black feathers forming a crest.
Voice: *Keer,* higher than Caspian's note; also *kaak* or *kak.*
Range: Coasts of se. U.S., nw. Mexico, W. Indies, w. Africa. Winters s. U.S. to Argentina; w. Africa. **East:** Map 79. **Habitat:** Coasts, sandy beaches, salt bays.

CASPIAN TERN *Sterna caspia* 19–23″ (48–58 cm) **M 80**
The large size (near that of Herring Gull) and large red bill set the Caspian apart from all other terns except the slimmer Royal. The Caspian ranges inland; the Royal does not. Tail of Caspian is shorter; bill is stouter, *red* rather than orange. Royal has a more *crested* look and usually a *clear white* forehead (in similar plumage, Caspian has clouded, *streaked* forehead). Caspian shows much more black under primaries.
Voice: A hoarse, low *kraa-uh* or *karr;* also repeated *kaks.*
Range: Breeds locally, wanders widely around world. **East:** Map 80.
Habitat: Large lakes, coastal waters, beaches, bays.

LARGE TERNS

Gull-billed

winter

GULL-BILLED TERN

summer

Sandwich

winter

SANDWICH TERN

summer

Royal

most of year

ROYAL TERN

early
summer

Caspian

winter

CASPIAN TERN

summer

95

LITTLE TERN *Sterna albifrons* 9″ (23 cm) **M 81**
(Least Tern) A *very small* pale tern with *yellow* bill and feet, white forehead. Quicker wingbeats than other terns. *Immature:* Dark bill; dark nape; much dark on forewing. In fall, all birds may have dark bills but feet show yellow.
Voice: A sharp repeated *kit;* a harsh squealing *zree-eek* or *zeek;* also a rapid *kitti-kitti-kitti.*
Range: Temperate and tropical oceans. Winters south of U.S. **East:** Map 81. **Habitat:** Sea beaches, bays; large rivers.

ARCTIC TERN *Sterna paradisaea* 14–17″ (35–43 cm) **M 82**
Very similar to Common Tern but *grayer; white cheeks* contrasting with gray throat and breast. The shorter bill is usually *blood-red* to the tip. Legs shorter. Overhead, note the *translucent* effect of the primaries and the *narrow* black border. Adults in fall are more difficult (bill and feet become dark).
Voice: *Kee-yah,* similar to Common Tern's cry; less slurred, higher. A high *keer-keer* is characteristic.
Range: Northern parts of N. Hemisphere; circumpolar. Winters in sub-Antarctic seas. **East:** Map 82. **Habitat:** Open ocean, rocky coasts, islands; tundra lakes (summer).

COMMON TERN *Sterna hirundo* 13–16″ (33–40 cm) **M 83**
A graceful small *black-capped* gull-like bird with a *deeply forked tail. Summer:* White with a pale gray mantle and black cap; bill red-orange with a black tip; feet orange-red. *Immature and winter adult:* Black cap incomplete; bill blackish.
Voice: A drawling *kee-arr* (downward inflection); also *kik-kik-kik;* a quick *kirri-kirri.*
Range: Temperate zone of N. Hemisphere. Winters to S. Hemisphere. **East:** Map 83. **Habitat:** Lakes, ocean, bays, beaches; nests colonially on sandy beaches and small islands.

FORSTER'S TERN *Sterna forsteri* 14–15″ (35–38 cm) **M 84**
A tern with *frosty wing tips.* Very similar to Common Tern, but primaries lighter than rest of wing (darker in Common). Tail grayer; bill more orange. In fall and winter, adult and immature Forster's have a *black mask through eye and ear* (not around nape). Immature lacks dusky forewing of Common Tern.
Voice: A harsh, nasal *za-a-ap* and a nasal *kyarr.*
Range: W. Canada, w. U.S., and cen. Atlantic Coast to Tamaulipas. Winters s. U.S. to Guatemala. **East:** Map 84. **Habitat:** Marshes (fresh, salt), lakes, bays, beaches, ocean. Nests in marshes.

ROSEATE TERN *Sterna dougallii* 14–17″ (35–43 cm) **M 85**
Similar to Common Tern but paler above, with longer tail points. Typically, the *black bill* sets it apart from similar terns, all of which have reddish bills (except in winter). During incubation Roseates may acquire varying amounts of red at the base of the bill; then rely on other points. At rest, the tail extends well beyond the wing tips.
Voice: A rasping *ka-a-ak;* a soft 2-syllabled *chu-ick* or *chivy.*
Range: Breeds locally and wanders widely along coasts of Atlantic, Pacific, and Indian Ocean. **East:** Map 85. **Habitat:** Coastal; salt bays, estuaries, ocean.

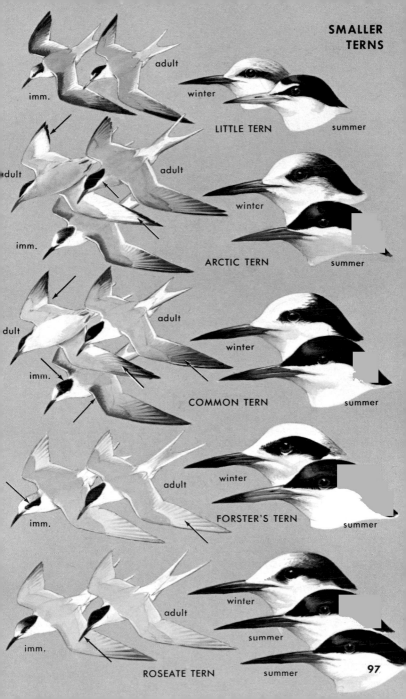

SMALLER TERNS

imm.   adult

winter

LITTLE TERN

summer

dult   adult

imm.

winter

ARCTIC TERN

summer

dult   adult

imm.

winter

COMMON TERN

summer

imm.   adult

winter

FORSTER'S TERN

summer

imm.   adult

winter

summer

ROSEATE TERN

summer

97

BLACK TERN *Chlidonias niger* 9–10″ (23–25 cm) M 86
Our only *black-bodied* tern. *Breeding:* Head and underparts
black; back, wings, and tail dark gray. Mottled molting birds by
midsummer when the black is largely replaced by white. Note the
pied head, smudge on side of breast. Immature similar.
Voice: A sharp *kik, keek,* or *klea.*
Range: Temperate N. America, Eurasia. Winters mainly in S.
America, Africa. **East:** Map 86. **Habitat:** Fresh marshes, lakes; in
migration, coastal waters.

BROWN NODDY *Anous stolidus* 15″ (38 cm)
A sooty *brown tern* with a whitish cap. The *wedge-shaped tail* has
a slight notch. Immature is whitish on forehead only.
Similar species: Black Noddy (*A. tenuirostris*) occurs occasionally
with the Brown Noddies in the Dry Tortugas. It is smaller (12 in.),
blacker, with a whiter cap.
Voice: A ripping *karrrrk* or *arrrrowk.* A harsh *eye-ak.*
Range: Tropical oceans. **East:** Breeds in the Dry Tortugas off Key
West, Florida. Like the Sooty Tern it is sometimes carried north-
ward along the coast by tropical hurricanes.

SOOTY TERN *Sterna fuscata* 15–17″ (38–43 cm)
A cleanly patterned tern that is *black above and white below.*
Cheeks and patch on forehead white; bill and feet black. *Im-
mature:* Dark brown; back spotted with white; tail forked.
Voice: A nasal *wide-a-wake* or *wacky-wack.*
Range: Occurs widely in pantropical oceans. **East:** A large colony in
Dry Tortugas off Florida Keys. Has bred in Louisiana. Often
carried northward along coast by hurricanes.

BRIDLED TERN *Sterna anaethetus* 14″ (35 cm)
A West Indian tern to be looked for after hurricanes. Resembles
Sooty Tern, but back grayer; note the wide *whitish collar* separating the black cap from the back; the white forehead patch extends
behind the eye (in the Sooty, *to* the eye).
Range: Tropical oceans. **East:** Has been carried by tropical storms
along the coast as far north as Massachusetts. Probably regular in
the Gulf Stream north to Cape Hatteras.

■ **SKIMMERS Family Rynchopidae.** Slim, short-legged relatives of gulls and terns. Knifelike red bill; long lower mandible.
Food: Small fish, crustaceans. **Range:** Coasts, large rivers of
warmer parts of world. **No. of species:** World, 3; East, 1.

BLACK SKIMMER *Rynchops niger* 16–20″ (40–50 cm) **M 87**
Note the unequal scissorlike bill. Black above and white below;
more slender than a gull, with extremely long wings. The bright
red bill (tipped with black) is long and flat vertically; the lower
mandible juts a third beyond the upper. Immature brownish,
speckled, smaller-billed. This coastal species skims low, dipping its
knifelike lower mandible in the water.
Voice: Soft, short, barking notes. Also *kaup, kaup.*
Range: Cape Cod to s. S. America. Winters from coast of se. U.S.
south. **East:** Map 87. **Habitat:** Ocean beaches, salt bays, tidewater;
in Florida, also inland lakes.

winter

molting

**DARK TERNS,
SKIMMER**

**BLACK
TERN**

breeding

**BROWN
NODDY**

**BLACK
NODDY**

**SOOTY
TERN**

imm.

adult

**BRIDLED
TERN**

**SOOTY
TERN**

imm.

adult

**BLACK
SKIMMER**

adult

99

■ HERONS, BITTERNS Family Ardeidae.

Medium to large wading birds with long necks, spearlike bills. Stand with neck erect or head on shoulders. In flight, neck folded in an S; legs trail. May have plumes when breeding. Sexes similar. **Food:** Fish, frogs, crawfish, other aquatic life; mice, insects. **Range:** Worldwide except colder regions, some deserts and islands. **No. of species:** World, 59; East, 12 (+1 accidental).

GREAT BLUE HERON   M 88
Ardea herodias   42–52″ (105–130 cm)

A lean gray bird, often miscalled a crane; may stand 4 ft. tall. Its long legs, long neck, daggerlike bill, and, in flight, folded neck indicate a heron. Great size and blue-gray color, white about head (in adults) mark it as this species.
Similar species: See Sandhill Crane (pp. 106, 107).
Voice: Deep harsh croaks: *frahnk, frahnk, frahnk.*
Range: S. Canada to Mexico. Winters to n. S. America. **East:** Map 88. **Habitat:** Marshes, swamps, shores, tideflats.

"WURDEMANN'S" HERON   *Ardea herodias*   (in part)

Florida Keys. Like Great Blue Heron, but its white head *lacks black plumes.* Formerly regarded as a hybrid between Great Blue and "Great White" (p. 103), but presumably an intermediate color morph of the Great Blue–Great White Heron complex.

LITTLE BLUE HERON   *Florida caerulea*   24″ (60 cm)   M 89

A slender, medium-sized heron. *Adult:* Bluish slate with a deep maroon-brown neck; legs dark. *Immature:* All white; legs *dull olive;* bill pale bluish, tipped with black. Birds in transition are boldly pied with white and dark. See pp. 102, 103.
Similar species: Young Snowy Egret may have yellowish stripe up rear of leg. Note the Snowy's all-black bill.
Range: E. U.S. to Peru, Argentina. **East:** Map 89. **Habitat:** Marshes, swamps, rice fields, ponds, shores.

LOUISIANA HERON   *Hydranassa tricolor*   26″ (65 cm)   M 90

Note the contrasting *white belly,* the key field mark of this very slender, dark heron. Rump *white.*
Range: E. U.S. to Brazil. **East:** Map 90. **Habitat:** Marshes, swamps, streams, shores.

REDDISH EGRET   *Dichromanassa rufescens*   29″ (73 cm)   M 91

Note always the *flesh-colored,* black-tipped bill. Two color phases: (1) neutral gray, with rusty head and neck; (2) *white* with *blue* legs (shown on p. 103). Loose-feathered; neck shaggy. When feeding, lurches about, acts drunk.
Similar species: (1) Gray phase resembles adult Little Blue Heron which is darker with bill *pale bluish* at base. (2) White phase suggests Great Egret, but legs bluish (not black).
Range: Gulf states, West Indies, Mexico. **East:** Map 91. **Habitat:** Coastal tidal flats, salt marshes, shores, lagoons.

DARK HERONS

Herons fly with necks pulled in

Herons' necks may stretch or be looped in

immature

adult

GREAT BLUE HERON

adult

"WURDEMANN'S HERON"

adult

LITTLE BLUE HERON
(White immature on next plate)

adult

LOUISIANA HERON

Reddish Egret "dancing"

REDDISH EGRET

dark phase
(white phase on next plate)

GREAT EGRET *Casmerodius albus* 38″ (95 cm) **M 92**
(American Egret) A large, stately, slender white heron with a *yellow bill* (orange when breeding). Legs and feet *black. Straight* plumes on back extend beyond tail when breeding. When feeding, the bird assumes an eager, forward-leaning pose, neck extended, quite unlike the Snowy.
Similar species: Snowy Egret has a *black* bill, *yellow* feet.
Voice: A low hoarse croak. Also, *cuk, cuk, cuk.*
Range: U.S. to s. S. America; warmer parts of Old World. **East:** Map 92. **Habitat:** Marshes, ponds, shores, mud flats.

SNOWY EGRET *Egretta thula* 20–27″ (50–68 cm) **M 93**
Note the *"golden slippers."* A rather small white heron with a *slender black bill,* black legs, *yellow feet. Recurved plumes* on the back during breeding season. A yellow loral spot before the eye (red when breeding). When feeding rushes about, shuffling feet to stir up food.
Similar species: (1) Great Egret (yellow bill); (2) Cattle Egret (yellow bill); (3) young Little Blue Heron (bluish bill).
Voice: A low croak; in colony, a bubbling *wulla-wulla-wulla.*
Range: N. U.S. to Argentina. **East:** Map 93. **Habitat:** Marshes, swamps, ponds, shores, tideflats.

LITTLE BLUE HERON *Florida caerulea*
Immature: *Bluish* bill, dull greenish legs. See p. 100.

CATTLE EGRET *Bubulcus ibis* 20″ (50 cm) **M 94**
Slightly smaller, stockier, thicker-necked than Snowy Egret. When breeding shows *buff* on crown, breast, and back (but appears whitish at a distance); little or no buff at other times. Bill *yellow* (orange-pink when nesting). Legs coral-pink (nesting); yellow, greenish, or dusky (immature).
Similar species: (1) Snowy Egret (*black* bill); (2) immature Little Blue Heron (*bluish* bill); (3) Great Egret (larger).
Range: S. Eurasia, Africa; recent immigrant N. and S. America, Australia. Introduced Hawaii. **East:** Map 94. **Habitat:** Farms, marshes, highway edges (Florida); associates with cattle.

REDDISH EGRET *Dichromanassa rufescens*
White phase: Note the *flesh-pink* bill, bluish legs. See p. 100.

"GREAT WHITE" HERON **M 95**
Ardea herodias (in part) or *A. "occidentalis"* 50″ (125 cm)
Our largest white heron, with the most restricted range. All white with a yellow bill and *yellowish legs,* the latter separating it positively from the smaller Great Egret, which has blackish legs. Formerly believed to be a distinct species (*A. occidentalis*); now regarded as a white morph of the Great Blue Heron (*A. herodias*), p. 100, and much like it in build.
Range: S. Florida, Cuba, coastal Yucatan. **East:** Map 95. **Habitat:** Mangrove keys, salt bays, marl banks, open mud flats.

GREAT EGRET

SNOWY EGRET

changing

immature

LITTLE BLUE HERON
(adult on p. 101)

CATTLE EGRET

immature

breeding

REDDISH EGRET

(dark phase on p. 101)

white phase

"GREAT WHITE" HERON
(regarded as s. Florida color morph of Great Blue Heron)

103

BLACK-CROWNED NIGHT HERON
Nycticorax nycticorax   23–28″ (58–70 cm)

Stocky, thick-billed, short-legged. Usually hunched and inactive; flies to feed at dusk. *Adult:* Note the *blackish back and black cap* in contrast to the pale gray or whitish underparts, gray wings. Eyes red; legs yellowish or yellow-green (pink when breeding). 2 long white head plumes when breeding. *Immature:* Brown, *spotted* and streaked with white and buff.

Similar species: See (1) American Bittern; (2) immature Yellow-crowned Night Heron.

Voice: A flat *quok!* or *quark!* Most often heard at dusk.

Range: S. Canada to Argentina; Eurasia, Africa, Pacific Is. **East:** Map 96. **Habitat:** Marshes, shores; roosts in trees.

YELLOW-CROWNED NIGHT HERON
Nyctanassa violacea   22–28″ (55–70 cm)

A chunky *gray* heron; head black with a *whitish cheek patch and crown. Immature:* Very similar to young Black-crown, but duskier, *more finely speckled.* Bill stouter, legs *longer,* yellower. In flight the entire foot extends beyond the tail.

Voice: *Quark,* higher pitched than note of Black-crown.

Range: E. U.S. to n. and e. S. America. **East:** Map 97. **Habitat:** Cypress swamps, mangroves, bayous, marshes, streams.

GREEN HERON   *Butorides striatus*   16–22″ (40–55 cm)
A small dark heron that in flight looks crowlike (but flies with bowed wingbeats). When alarmed it stretches its neck, elevates a shaggy crest, and jerks its tail. The comparatively *short* legs are *greenish yellow* or *orange* (breeding). Back bluish, neck deep chestnut. Immature has a streaked neck.

Voice: A series of *kuck's;* a loud *skyow* or *skewk.*

Range: Nw. U.S., se. Canada to n. S. America. **East:** Map 98. **Habitat:** Lakes, ponds, marshes, swamps, streamsides.

LEAST BITTERN   *Ixobrychus exilis*   11–14″ (28–35 cm)
Very small, thin, furtive; straddles reeds. Note the large *buff wing patch* (lacking in rails). There is also a very rare dark chestnut color phase ("Cory's" Least Bittern).

Voice: Song, a low, muted *coo-coo-coo* heard in the marsh.

Range: Se. Canada, U.S. to S. America. **East:** Map 99. **Habitat:** Fresh marshes, reedy ponds; not easy to flush.

AMERICAN BITTERN   *Botaurus lentiginosus*   23″ (58 cm)
A stocky brown heron; size of a young night heron but warmer brown. In flight, the outer wing shows *blackish* and the bill is held more horizontal. At rest, often stands rigid, its bill pointing up. A *black stripe* shows on the neck.

Voice: "Pumping," or song, a slow, deep *oong-ka' choonk, oong-ka' choonk, oong-ka' choonk,* etc. Flushing note, *kok-kok-kok.*

Range: Canada to Gulf states; winters to Panama. **East:** Map 100. **Habitat:** Marshes, reedy lakes. Seldom sits in trees.

HERONS,
BITTERNS

adult

BLACK-CROWNED
NIGHT HERON

imm.

adult

YELLOW-CROWNED
NIGHT HERON

imm.

typical

dark
phase
(rare)   LEAST
           BITTERN

imm.

adult

GREEN
HERON

AMERICAN
BITTERN

■ STORKS Family Ciconiidae.
Large, long-legged heronlike birds with long bills (straight, recurved, or decurved); some with naked heads. Sexes alike. Gait a sedate walk. Flight deliberate; neck and legs extended. **Food:** Frogs, crustaceans, lizards, rodents. **Range:** S. U.S., Cen. and S. America, Africa, Eurasia, E. Indies, Australia. **No. of species:** World, 17; East, 1.

WOOD STORK   M 101
Mycteria americana   34–47″ (85–118 cm)

(Wood Ibis) Very large (spread 5½ ft.); white, with a *dark naked head* and *much black* in the wing; black tail. Bill long, *thick, decurved.* Immature has a yellow bill. When feeding, keeps head down and walks. In flight, alternately flaps and glides. Often soars very high on thermals.
Similar species: White Pelican, which also soars on thermals, has a similar wing pattern.
Voice: A hoarse croak; usually silent.
Range: S. U.S. to Argentina. **East:** Map 101. **Habitat:** Cypress swamps (nesting colonies); marshes, ponds, lagoons.

■ CRANES Family Gruidae.
Stately birds, more robust than herons, often with *red facial skin.* Note the *tufted appearance* over the rump. In flight, neck extended; migrates in V's or lines like geese. Large herons are sometimes wrongly referred to as cranes. **Food:** Omnivorous. **Range:** Nearly cosmopolitan except Cen. and S. America and Oceania. **No. of species:** World, 14; East, 2 (+1 accidental).

WHOOPING CRANE   *Grus americana*   50″ (125 cm)

The tallest North American bird and one of the rarest. Spread 7½ ft. A large *white* crane with a *red face.* Primary wing feathers *black.* Young birds are washed with rust color, especially the head.
Similar species: (1) Wood Stork has a dark head, more black in the wing; (2) egrets and (3) swans lack black in the wings. See also (4) White Pelican, p. 78, and (5) Snow Goose, p. 42.
Voice: A shrill buglelike trumpeting *ker-loo! ker-lee-oo!*
Range: Breeds in n. Alberta (Wood Buffalo Park); migrates through Great Plains (via Nebraska) to coastal Texas (Aransas). **Habitat:** Muskeg (summer); prairie pools, marshes.

SANDHILL CRANE   M 102
Grus canadensis   40–48″ (100–120 cm)

Spread 6–7 ft. Note the *bald red crown,* bustlelike rear. A long-legged, long-necked, gray bird, often stained with rust. The immature is quite brown. In flight, the neck is extended and the wings beat with an upward flick.
Similar species: Great Blue Heron (p. 100) is sometimes wrongly called a crane.
Voice: A shrill rolling *garooo-a-a-a;* repeated.
Range: Ne. Siberia, N. America, Cuba. Winters to Mexico. **East:** Map 102. **Habitat:** Prairies, fields, marshes, tundra (summer).

elow, for comparison:
left, White Ibis
right, Wood Stork

adult

WOOD
STORK

imm.

orks, ibises and
cranes fly with
cks outstretched

adult

imm.

WHOOPING
CRANE

adult

imm.

SANDHILL
CRANE

■ **LIMPKINS Family Aramidae.** A monotypic family, characterized under the one species. **Food:** Mostly large freshwater snails;
a few insects, frogs. **Range:** Se. U.S., W. Indies, s. Mexico to Argentina. **No. of species:** World, 1; East, 1.

LIMPKIN *Aramus guarauna* 28″ (70 cm) **M 103**
A large spotted swamp wader, a bit larger than an ibis. Its long legs
and *drooping bill* give it an ibislike aspect but no ibis is brown with
white spots and streaks. Flight cranelike (smart upward flaps).
Similar species: Immature ibises, night herons, Am. Bittern.
Voice: A piercing, repeated wail, *kree-ow, kra-ow,* etc., etc., espe-
cially at night and on cloudy days.
Range: Se. U.S., W. Indies, s. Mexico to Argentina. **East:** Map 103.
Habitat: Fresh swamps, marshes with large snails.

■ **IBISES AND SPOONBILLS Family Threskiornithidae.**
Ibises are long-legged heronlike waders with slender *decurved* bills.
Spoonbills have spatulate bills. Both fly in V's or lines and, unlike
herons, with necks *outstretched*. **Food:** Small crustaceans, small
fish, insects, etc. **Range:** Tropical and warm temperate regions. **No.
of species:** World, 28; East, 4 (+1 introduced).

GLOSSY IBIS *Plegadis falcinellus* 22–25″ (55–63 cm) **M 104**
A medium-sized marsh wader with a long *decurved* bill; *deep
glossy purplish chestnut;* at a distance it appears quite black, like a
large black curlew. Flies in lines with neck extended, flapping and
gliding with quicker wingbeats than herons'.
Voice: A guttural *ka-onk,* repeated; a low *kruk, kruk.*
Range: E. U.S., W. Indies, s. Eurasia, Africa, Australia, etc. **East:**
Map 104. **Habitat:** Marshes, rice fields, swamps.

WHITE-FACED IBIS *Plegadis chihi* 22–25″ (55–63 cm) **M 104**
(White-faced Glossy Ibis) Very similar to Glossy Ibis but in
summer has *reddish legs and lores,* and a narrow *white strip* about
the base of the bill. Many Glossy Ibises show a narrow line of
whitish but in this species the white goes *back of the eye and under
the chin*. This is lost in winter.
Range: W. U.S. to Argentina. **East:** Map 104. S. Louisiana to s.
Texas; occasional in Florida. **Habitat:** Same as Glossy's.

WHITE IBIS *Eudocimus albus* 22–27″ (55–68 cm) **M 105**
Note the *red face,* long *decurved red bill,* and restricted black wing
tips. Immature is dark; note the *white belly, white rump,* curved
red bill. In flight, the neck is outstretched; flocks fly in strings,
flapping and gliding; often soar in circles.
Similar species: (1) Wood Stork is larger, with much more black
(comparison on p. 107). (2) Immature Glossy differs from immature White Ibis by uniformly dark appearance. (3) Immature
could be mistaken for Louisiana Heron except for the bill.
Range: Se. U.S. to n. S. America. **East:** Map 105. **Habitat:** Salt,
brackish, and fresh marshes, rice fields, mangroves.

LIMPKIN,
IBISES

below, for facial
comparison in
breeding season

WHITE-FACED
IBIS

GLOSSY
IBIS

LIMPKIN

GLOSSY
IBIS
adult

GLOSSY
IBIS
imm.

WHITE IBIS
adult

WHITE IBIS
imm.

SCARLET IBIS *Guara rubra* 22–25″ (55–63 cm)
A *bright scarlet* ibis; the same size, structure, and pattern (black wing tips) as the White Ibis.
Range: N. South America. **East:** Accidental in Gulf states. Pinkish birds, sometimes reported, may be zoo escapes (they often lose color in captivity). Young hatched from eggs placed in White Ibis nests in Miami were recently reared to adulthood. Later, some hybrids resulted from this experiment.

ROSEATE SPOONBILL *Ajaia ajaja* 32″ (80 cm)   **M 106**
A *bright pink* wading bird with a long, flat spoonlike bill. Adults are *shell-pink* with a blood-red "drip" on the shoulders, and an orange tail. The head is naked, greenish gray. Immature birds are whitish, acquiring the glow of pink as they mature. When Spoonbills feed, the bill is swept rapidly from side to side. In flight the neck is extended like that of an ibis, and the bird often glides between series of wing strokes.
Voice: About nesting colony, a low grunting croak.
Range: Gulf states to Chile, Argentina. **East:** Map 106. **Habitat:** Coastal marshes, lagoons, mud flats, mangrove keys (nesting).

■ **FLAMINGOS Family Phoenicopteridae.**   Pinkish white to vermilion wading birds with extremely long necks and legs. The thick bill is bent sharply down and lined with numerous lamellae for straining food. **Food:** Small mollusks, crustaceans, blue-green algae, diatoms. **Range:** W. Indies, Yucatan, Galapagos, S. America, Africa, s. Eurasia, India. **No. of species:** World, 6; East, 1.

AMERICAN FLAMINGO *Phoenicopterus ruber* 45″ (113 cm)
An extremely slim rose-pink wading bird as tall as a Great Blue Heron but much more slender. Note the sharply bent bill or broken "Roman nose." Feeds with the bill or head immersed. In flight it shows much black in the wings; its extremely long neck is extended droopily in front and the long legs trail behind, giving the impression that the bird might as easily fly backward as forward. Pale washed-out birds may be escapes from zoos as the color often fades under captive conditions. Immatures are also much paler than normal adults.
Voice: Gooselike calls, gabbling; *ar-honk,* etc.
Range: W. Indies, Yucatan, Galapagos Is. **East:** Occasional on the Florida coast; accidental elsewhere. It is difficult to determine whether vagrants are truly wild or escapes. Hialeah Race Track, Bok Sanctuary, Busch Gardens, etc., may be the sources of strays.
Habitat: Salt flats, saline lagoons.

SCARLET IBIS

adult

ROSEATE SPOONBILL

imm.

adult

AMERICAN FLAMINGO

adult

111

■ RAILS, GALLINULES, AND COOTS Family Rallidae.

Rails are compact, rather hen-shaped marsh birds of secretive habits and mysterious voices; more often heard than seen. Flight brief and reluctant with legs dangling. Gallinules and coots swim; resemble ducks except for smaller heads, forehead shields, and chickenlike bills. They are treated separately on pp. 64, 65 (heads are also shown on p. 115). Sexes in all the Rallidae are alike. **Food:** Aquatic plants, seeds, buds, insects, frogs, crustaceans, mollusks. **Range:** Widespread in nonpolar regions. **No. of species:** World, 132; East, 9 (+5 accidental).

VIRGINIA RAIL *Rallus limicola* 9″ (23 cm)   M 107
A small rusty rail with gray cheeks; black bars on the flanks and a long, slightly decurved reddish bill. The only small rail, near the size of a meadowlark, with a *long slender* bill. Full-grown young in late summer show much black.
Voice: *Wak-wak-wak,* etc., descending; also *kidick, kidick,* etc., and various "kicking" and grunting sounds.
Range: S. Canada to s. S. America. Winters mainly from s. U.S. south. **East:** Map 107. **Habitat:** Mainly fresh and brackish marshes; in winter, also salt marshes.

KING RAIL *Rallus elegans* 15–19″ (38–48 cm)   M 108
A large, rusty rail with a long, slender bill; twice the size of a Virginia Rail, or about that of a small hen. Similar to Clapper Rail but more rusty; prefers fresh marshes.
Similar species: (1) Virginia Rail is half the size and has slaty gray cheeks. (2) See Clapper Rail (grayer).
Voice: A low, grunting *bup-bup, bup-bup-bup,* etc., or *chuck-chuck-chuck* (deeper than Virginia Rail; not descending).
Range: E. U.S., to Cuba, Mexico (rarely). Migrant in North. **East:** Map 108. **Habitat:** Fresh and brackish marshes, rice fields, swamps. In winter, sometimes salt marshes.

CLAPPER RAIL *Rallus longirostris* 14–16″ (35–40 cm)   M 109
The large gray-brown "marsh hen" of the coastal marshes. Note the henlike appearance, strong legs, long, slightly decurved bill, barred flanks, and white patch under the short tail which is usually cocked or flirted. It sometimes swims.
Similar species: King Rail prefers fresh (sometimes brackish) marshes. It averages larger, has blacker stripes on the back and flanks, *rusty brown* on the wings. Its breast is cinnamon, but some Clappers show similar warm tawny tones. The Clapper has *grayer cheeks.* In fact, where they occur in adjacent salt and fresh marshes they occasionally hybridize, leading one to suspect they may be ecological races of the same species.
Voice: A clattering *kek-kek-kek-kek,* etc., or *cha-cha-cha,* etc.
Range: Coasts of e. U.S. and California to n. S. America. **East:** Map 109. **Habitat:** Salt marshes, rarely brackish; locally mangroves.

adult

immature

VIRGINIA RAIL

KING RAIL

chick

CLAPPER RAIL

Limpkin for comparison

SORA *Porzana carolina* 8–9¾″ (20–24 cm) **M 110**
Note the *short yellow* bill. The adult is a small plump gray-brown
rail with a *black patch* on the face and throat. The short cocked
tail reveals white or buff undertail coverts. The immature lacks the
black throat patch, is buffy brown.
Similar species: Immature Sora may be confused with the smaller
and rarer Yellow Rail. See Virginia Rail (slender bill).
Voice: A descending whinny. In spring, a plaintive whistled *ker-
wee?* When a stone is tossed into the marsh, a sharp *keek*.
Range: Canada; w., n.-cen., and ne. U.S. Winters from s. U.S. to
Peru. **East:** Map 110. **Habitat:** Fresh marshes, wet meadows; in
winter, also salt marshes.

CORN CRAKE *Crex crex* 9–10″ (23–25 cm)
An accidental visitor from Europe; about 15 records (not recent).
An upland field rail of the short-billed Sora type, but larger;
yellowish buff with conspicuous *rufous* wings.

BLACK RAIL *Laterallus jamaicensis* 5–6″ (13–15 cm) **M 111**
A tiny blackish rail with a small *black* bill; about the size of a
bobtailed young sparrow. Nape deep chestnut. Very difficult to
flush or glimpse, but may be attracted at night by a tape recording
of its calls.
Similar species: *Caution:* All young rails in downy plumage are
glossy black (but they lack bars on the flanks).
Voice: Male at night, *kiki-doo* or *kiki-krrr* (or *"kitty go"*).
Range: Ne. and cen. U.S. and cen. California south locally to W.
Indies, Chile. **East:** Map 111. **Habitat:** Tidal marshes, salicornia
(coast); grassy marshes, stubble fields (inland).

YELLOW RAIL *Coturnicops noveboracensis* 7″ (18 cm) **M 112**
Note the *white wing patch* (in flight). A small buffy rail, suggesting
a week-old chick. Bill very short, greenish. Back striped and
checkered with buff and black. Mouselike; difficult to flush, but
can be attracted at night by a tape recording.
Similar species: Immature Sora is larger, not as buffy below; lacks
the wing patch. Note the very different back pattern.
Voice: Nocturnal ticking notes, often in long series: *tic-tic, tic-
tic-tic, tic-tic, tic-tic-tic,* etc. (groups of 2 and 3).
Range: Mainly Canada, n. U.S. Winters s. U.S. **East:** Map 112.
Habitat: Grassy fresh marshes, meadows; in winter, also open
grainfields, rarely salt marshes.

AMERICAN COOT *Fulica americana*
White bill. See pp. 64, 65.

COMMON GALLINULE *Gallinula chloropus*
Red frontal shield, red bill. See pp. 64, 65.

PURPLE GALLINULE *Porphyrula martinica*
Pale blue frontal shield, red bill. See pp. 64, 65.

SHORT-BILLED RAILS
(often called "crakes")

SORA

adult

immature

chick

SORA

SORA

BLACK RAIL

CORN CRAKE
(accidental)

YELLOW RAIL

COOT, GALLINULES

AMERICAN COOT

COMMON GALLINULE

PURPLE GALLINULE

(Swimmers related to rails; see p. 65)

115

■ OYSTERCATCHERS Family Haematopodidae.
Large waders with long, laterally flattened, chisel-tipped, red bills. Sexes alike. **Food:** Mollusks, crabs, marine worms. **Range:** Widespread on coasts of world; inland in some areas of Europe and Asia. **No. of species:** World, 6; East, 1.

AMERICAN OYSTERCATCHER   M 113
Haematopus palliatus   17–21″ (43–53 cm)
A very noisy, thick-set, black-headed shorebird with a dark back, white belly, large white wing and tail patches. The outstanding feature is the *large straight red bill,* flattened laterally. Legs pale flesh.
Similar species: See Black Skimmer, pp. 98, 99.
Voice: A piercing *wheep!* or *kleep!*; a loud *pic, pic, pic.*
Range: Shores of Cape Cod south to Chile and Argentina. **East:** Map 113. **Habitat:** Coastal beaches, tidal flats.

■ AVOCETS AND STILTS Family Recurvirostridae.
Slim waders with very long legs and very slender bills (bent upward in avocets). Sexes alike. **Food:** Insects, crustaceans, other aquatic life. **Range:** U.S., Cen. and S. America, Africa, s. Eurasia, Australia, Pacific region. **No. of species:** World, 7; East, 2.

BLACK-NECKED STILT   M 114
Himantopus mexicanus   13–17″ (33–43 cm)
A large, extremely slim wader; black above, white below. Note the *grotesquely long red legs,* needlelike bill. In flight it has black *unpatterned* wings, which contrast with the white rump, tail, and underparts.
Voice: A sharp yipping *kyip, kyip, kyip.*
Range: W. and se. U.S. to Peru. Winters mainly south of U.S. **East:** Map 114. **Habitat:** Grassy marshes, mud flats, pools, shallow lakes (fresh or alkaline).

AMERICAN AVOCET   M 115
Recurvirostra americana   16–20″ (40–50 cm)
A large, slim shorebird with a very slender, *upturned,* somewhat godwitlike bill. This and the striking white-and-black pattern make it unique. In breeding plumage, the head and neck are pinkish tan; in winter this is replaced with pale gray. Avocets feed with a scythelike sweep of the head and bill.
Voice: A sharp *wheek* or *kleet,* excitedly repeated.
Range: Breeds sw. Canada, w. U.S. Winters from s. U.S. to Guatemala. **East:** Map 115. **Habitat:** Beaches, flats, shallow lakes, prairie ponds.

OYSTERCATCHER, STILT, AVOCET

AMERICAN
OYSTERCATCHER

BLACK-NECKED
STILT

summer

winter

AMERICAN AVOCET

117

■ **PLOVERS Family Charadriidae.** Wading birds, more compactly built, thicker-necked than most sandpipers, with shorter, pigeonlike bills and larger eyes. Call notes assist identification. Unlike most sandpipers, plovers run in short starts and stops. Sexes alike. *Note:* The Ruddy Turnstone shown at the bottom, opposite, was until recently assigned to the plover family but is now regarded as more closely allied to the sandpipers, Scolopacidae (see p. 126). **Food:** Small marine life, insects, some vegetable matter. **Range:** Nearly worldwide. **No. of species:** World, 63; East, 8 (+4 accidental).

BLACK-BELLIED PLOVER   M 116
Pluvialis squatarola   10½–13½″ (26–34 cm)

A large plover; in breeding plumage with a *black breast* and pale speckled back. Winter birds and immatures are gray-looking, recognized as plovers by their stocky shape, hunched posture, and short pigeonlike bill. In flight, in any plumage, note the *black axillars* ("wingpits") and the white rump and tail.
Similar species: Lesser Golden Plover is browner and lacks the pattern of white in the wings and tail. Axillars are not black.
Voice: A plaintive slurred whistle, *tlee-oo-eee* or *whee-er-ee* (middle note lower).
Range: Arctic; circumpolar. Winters from coastal U.S. and s. Eurasia to S. Hemisphere. **East:** Map 116. **Habitat:** Mud flats, open marshes, beaches; in summer, tundra.

LESSER GOLDEN PLOVER   *Pluvialis dominica*   M 117
(American Golden Plover)   9½–11″ (24–28 cm)

Size of Killdeer. Breeding adults are dark, spangled with *golden spots* above; underparts black. A *broad white stripe* runs over the eye and down the side of the neck and breast. Young birds and winter adults are brown, darker above than below: they are recognized in flight by their *lack of pattern.*
Similar species: Black-bellied Plover is larger, paler above, with a *white rump and upper tail* and a *white wing stripe.* The *black axillar patch* (in the "wingpit") is diagnostic.
Voice: A whistled *queedle* or *que-e-a* (dropping at end).
Range: Siberia, Arctic America. Winters in S. America, s. Asia, Hawaii to Australia. **East:** Map 117. **Habitat:** Prairies, mud flats, shores; tundra (summer).

RUDDY TURNSTONE   M 118
Arenaria interpres   8–10″ (20–25 cm)

Note the harlequin pattern. A squat, robust, *orange-legged* shorebird. In breeding plumage with russet back and curious face and breast pattern the bird is unique, but in flight is even more striking. Young birds and winter adults are duller but retain enough of the basic pattern to be recognized.
Voice: A staccato *tuk-a-tuk* or *kut-a-kut;* also a single *kewk.*
Range: Arctic, sub-Arctic; circumpolar. Winters coastal U.S., Hawaii, s. Eurasia to S. Hemisphere. **East:** Map 118. **Habitat:** Beaches, mud flats, jetties, rocky shores; tundra (summer).

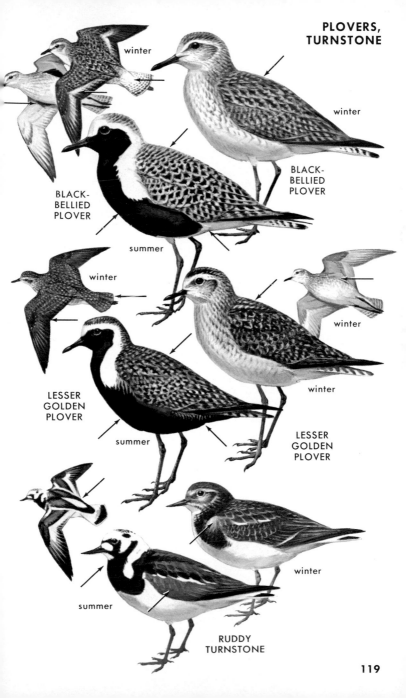

**PLOVERS,
TURNSTONE**

winter

winter

BLACK-
BELLIED
PLOVER

BLACK-
BELLIED
PLOVER

summer

winter

winter

winter

LESSER
GOLDEN
PLOVER

LESSER
GOLDEN
PLOVER

summer

summer

winter

RUDDY
TURNSTONE

119

SEMIPALMATED PLOVER
Charadrius semipalmatus   6½–7½″ (16–19 cm)
A small, plump, brown-backed plover, half the size of a Killdeer, with a *single dark breastband*. Bill deep yellow with black tip, or (in winter) all dark. Legs orange or yellow.
Similar species: Piping Plover is pale, the color of dry sand (Semi-palmated is darker, like wet sand or mud).
Voice: A plaintive upward-slurred *chi-we* or *too-li*.
Range: Arctic America. Winters to S. America. **East:** Map 119.
Habitat: Shores, tideflats.

RINGED PLOVER   *Charadrius hiaticula*   7½″ (19 cm)
Very similar to Semipalmated Plover, replacing it in Greenland, n. Baffinland, Devon and Ellesmere Islands. Migrates to Europe. Distinguished in the hand by the lack of basal webs between the inner and middle toes. The breastband may be a bit wider.

PIPING PLOVER   *Charadrius melodus*   6–7½″ (15–19 cm)   M 120
As pallid as a beach flea or sand crab, the color of dry sand. A complete or incomplete dark ring around neck. Legs yellow; bill yellow with a black tip. In winter, bill and legs dark.
Voice: A plaintive whistle; *peep-lo* (first note higher).
Range: S. Canada to ne. and cen. U.S. **East:** Map 120. **Habitat:** Sand beaches, tidal flats.

SNOWY PLOVER   *Charadrius alexandrinus*   6½″ (16 cm)   M 121
A pale plover of the Gulf Coast. Similar to Piping Plover but with a *slim black bill, blackish legs,* and a *dark ear patch*.
Similar species: Juvenal Piping Plovers and winter birds may have dark legs and bills, but they have *white rumps* and lack the black collars and dark ear patches.
Voice: A musical whistle; *pe-wee-ah* or *o-wee-ah*.
Range: S. U.S., Mid. and S. America, Eurasia, Africa, Australia, etc. **East:** Map 121. **Habitat:** Beaches, sand flats.

WILSON'S PLOVER   *Charadrius wilsonia*   7–8″ (18–20 cm)   M 122
A "ringed" plover, larger than Semipalmated with a wider breast-band and a much longer *heavy black bill*. Legs flesh-gray.
Voice: An emphatic whistled *whit!* or *wheet!*
Range: New Jersey to n. S. America. **East:** Map 122. **Habitat:** Open beaches, tidal flats, sandy islands.

KILLDEER   *Charadrius vociferus*   9–11″ (23–28 cm)   M 123
The common noisy breeding plover of the farm country. Note the 2 black breastbands (chick has 1 band). In flight displays a *golden-tawny rump,* longish tail, white wing stripe.
Voice: Noisy; a loud insistent *kill-deeah,* repeated; a plaintive *dee-ee* (rising); *dee-dee-dee,* etc. Also a low trill.
Range: Canada to cen. Mexico, W. Indies; also coastal Peru. Migrant in North. **East:** Map 123. **Habitat:** Fields, airports, lawns, river banks, shores.

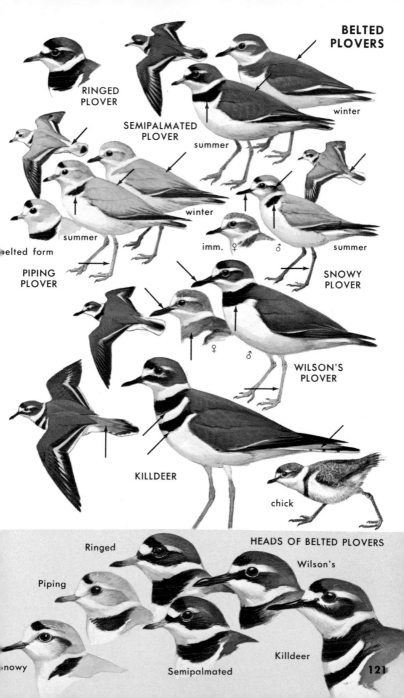

RINGED PLOVER

BELTED PLOVERS

SEMIPALMATED PLOVER

summer

winter

PIPING PLOVER

belted form

summer

winter

imm. ♀   ♂

SNOWY PLOVER

summer

WILSON'S PLOVER

♀   ♂

KILLDEER

chick

HEADS OF BELTED PLOVERS

Ringed

Piping

Wilson's

Snowy

Semipalmated

Killdeer

121

PLOVERS AND TURNSTONE IN FLIGHT

Learn the distinctive flight calls.

Text and color plate

PIPING PLOVER *Charadrius melodus* pp. 120, 121
Pale sand color, black tail spot, *whitish rump.*
Note, a plaintive whistle; *peep-lo* (first note higher).

SNOWY PLOVER *Charadrius alexandrinus* pp. 120, 121
Pale sand color; tail with dark center, white sides; *rump not white.*
Note, a musical whistle; *pe-wee-ah* or *o-wee-ah.*

SEMIPALMATED PLOVER *Charadrius semipalmatus* pp. 120, 121
Mud-brown; dark tail with white borders.
Note, a plaintive upward-slurred *chi-we* or *too-li.*

WILSON'S PLOVER *Charadrius wilsonia* pp. 120, 121
Similar in pattern to Semipalmated; larger; *big bill.*
Different note; an emphatic whistled *whit!* or *wheet!*

KILLDEER *Charadrius vociferus* pp. 120, 121
Tawny-orange rump, longish tail.
Noisy; a loud *kill-deeah* or *killdeer; dee-dee-dee,* etc.

BLACK-BELLIED PLOVER *Pluvialis squatarola* pp. 118, 119
Spring: Black below, *white* undertail coverts. Pattern above as in fall.
Fall: Black axillars ("wingpits"), white in wing and tail.
Note, a plaintive slurred whistle, *whee-er-eee.*

LESSER GOLDEN PLOVER *Pluvialis dominica* pp. 118, 119
Spring: Black below, *black* undertail coverts. Pattern above as in fall.
Fall: Lack of pattern above and below; underwing grayer than Black-belly's; *no black in axillars.*
Note, a harsh whistled *queedle* or *quee.*

RUDDY TURNSTONE *Arenaria interpres* pp. 118, 119
Harlequin pattern.
Note, a low chuckling *ket-a-kek* or *kut-a-kut.*

PLOVERS and TURNSTONE
In flight

PIPING PLOVER

SNOWY PLOVER

SEMIPALMATED PLOVER

WILSON'S PLOVER

KILLDEER

winter

BLACK-BELLIED PLOVER

winter

summer

BLACK-BELLIED PLOVER

winter

LESSER GOLDEN PLOVER

winter

LESSER GOLDEN PLOVER

summer

LESSER GOLDEN PLOVER

summer

RUDDY TURNSTONE

■ SANDPIPERS, PHALAROPES Family Scolopacidae.

Small to medium-sized waders. Bills more slender than those of plovers. Sexes similar, except in phalaropes (swimmers that were formerly regarded as a separate family). **Food:** Insects, crustaceans, mollusks, worms, etc. **Range:** Cosmopolitan. **No. of species:** World, 80; East, 33 (+14 accidental).

AMERICAN WOODCOCK *Philohela minor* 11″ (28 cm) **M 124**
A rotund, almost neckless brown bird with a dead-leaf pattern, broadly barred crown. Near size of Bobwhite, with an extremely long bill, large pop eyes. Usually flushed from a thicket, producing a whistling sound with its short, *rounded* wings.
Voice: At dusk in spring, ♂ utters a nasal *beezp* (suggesting Nighthawk). Aerial "song," a chippering trill (made by wings) as bird ascends, changing to a bubbling warble on descent.
Range: Se. Canada to Gulf states. Winters in se. U.S. **East:** Map 124. **Habitat:** Wet thickets, moist woods, brushy swamps. Nocturnal display high over semi-open fields, pastures.

COMMON SNIPE *Capella gallinago* 11″ (28 cm) **M 125**
Note the *extremely long bill.* A tight-sitting bog wader; brown with *buff stripes on back, striped head.* Flies off in a *zigzag,* showing a *short orange tail* and uttering a rasping *scaip.*
Voice: A rasping *scaip.* Song, a measured *chip-a, chip-a, chip-a,* etc. In aerial display, a winnowing *huhuhuhuhuhuhu.*
Range: N. North America, n. Eurasia. Winters to Brazil, cen. Africa. **East:** Map 125. **Habitat:** Marshes, bogs, wet meadows.

SHORT-BILLED DOWITCHER **M 126**
Limnodromus griseus 10½–12″ (26–30 cm)
A snipelike bird of open *mud flats.* Note the very long bill and the *long white wedge* up the back. In summer, breast rich rusty; by fall, gray. Feeds with a sewing machine motion.
Voice: A staccato *tu-tu-tu;* pitch of Lesser Yellowlegs.
Range: S. Alaska, Canada. Winters s. U.S. to Brazil. **East:** Map 126.
Habitat: Mud flats, tidal marshes, pond edges.

LONG-BILLED DOWITCHER
Limnodromus scolopaceus 11–12½″ (28–31 cm)
Bill lengths of the 2 dowitchers overlap, but birds of this species with very long bills (3″) are easily recognized. In breeding plumage, sides of breast *barred* rather than spotted; underparts *reddish to lower belly.* In fall, best clue is voice.
Voice: A single thin *keek,* occasionally doubled or trebled.
Range: Ne. Siberia to nw. Canada. Winters s. U.S. to Guatemala.
East: Migrant; preferring freshwater margins. Winter range in s. U.S. as in Short-bill (Map 126); arrives later.

RED KNOT *Calidris canutus* 10–11″ (25–28 cm) **M 127**
Stocky, with a rather short bill; much larger than Sanderling. *Spring:* Breast *pale robin-red. Fall:* A dumpy wader with a washed-out gray look; short bill, pale rump, greenish legs. At close range shows *scaly white feather edgings.*
Voice: A low *knut;* also a low mellow *tooit-wit* or *wah-quoit.*
Range: Arctic; circumpolar. Winters to S. Hemisphere. **East:** Map 127. **Habitat:** Tidal flats, shores; tundra (summer).

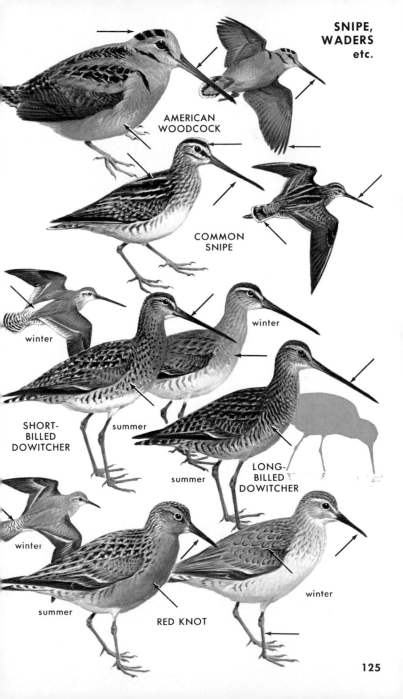

SNIPE,
WADERS
etc.

AMERICAN
WOODCOCK

COMMON
SNIPE

winter

winter

SHORT-
BILLED
DOWITCHER

summer

summer

LONG-
BILLED
DOWITCHER

winter

summer

RED KNOT

winter

HUDSONIAN GODWIT   **M 128**
Limosa haemastica   13–16″ (33–40 cm)
   Note the flight pattern. The rather large size and long straight or
slightly upturned bill mark this wader as a godwit; the black tail,
ringed broadly with white, proclaims it this species. The underwing is *blackish.* In spring, ♂ ruddy-breasted, ♀ duller; in fall,
gray-backed, pale-breasted.
   Voice: *Tawit!* (or *godwit!*); higher pitched than Marbled's.
   Range: Mainly Arctic Canada; winters in S. America. **East:** Map
128. **Habitat:** Beaches, prairie pools; tundra (summer).

MARBLED GODWIT   *Limosa fedoa*   16–20″ (40–50 cm)   **M 129**
   Godwits are large shorebirds with very long, straight or slightly
upturned bills. The rich mottled *buff-brown* color identifies this
species. The linings of the raised wing are *cinnamon.*
   Similar species: Hudsonian Godwit has white on wings and tail.
   Voice: An accented *kerwhit!* (*godwit!*); also *raddica, raddica.*
   Range: N. Great Plains. Winters s. U.S. to n. S. America. **East:**
Map 129. **Habitat:** Prairies, pools, shores; tideflats.

LONG-BILLED CURLEW   **M 130**
Numenius americanus   20–26″ (50–65 cm)
   Note the *very long sickle bill* (4–8½ in.). Much larger than
Whimbrel, more buffy; lacks the bold crown stripes. Overhead,
shows *cinnamon wing linings.* In young birds the bill may be
scarcely longer than that of the Whimbrel.
   Voice: A loud *cur-lee* (rising inflection); a rapid, whistled *kli-li-li-li.*
"Song," a trilled, liquid *curleeeeeeeeuuu.*
   Range: Sw. Canada, w. U.S. Winters s. U.S. to Guatemala. **East:**
Map 130. **Habitat:** High plains, rangeland. In winter, also culti-
vated land, tideflats, beaches, salt marshes.

ESKIMO CURLEW   *Numenius borealis*   12–14″ (30–35 cm)
   Much smaller than Whimbrel. Bill shorter (1¾–2½″), thinner, *only
slightly curved.* More patterned above than Whimbrel, more like
Long-billed Curlew, strong buff interspersed with black. Linings of
raised wing, *cinnamon-buff.* Legs slate-gray. In the hand note the
unbarred primaries.
   Voice: The call has been variously described as *tee-dee-dee,* or a
repeated *tee-dee,* or a note suggestive of Common Tern.
   Range: Nearly extinct. Formerly Arctic America, wintering in s. S.
America. Migrated along East Coast in fall, through Great Plains
in spring. Recent sight records in several states.

WHIMBREL   *Numenius phaeopus*   15–19″ (38–48 cm)   **M 131**
   (Hudsonian Curlew)   A large gray-brown wader with a long
decurved bill. Grayer than Long-billed Curlew; bill shorter (2¾–4
in.), crown *striped.* Whimbrels fly in lines.
   Voice: 5–7 short rapid whistles: *ti-ti-ti-ti-ti-ti.*
   Range: Arctic, circumpolar. Winters to s. S. America. **East:** Map
131. **Habitat:** Shores, mud flats, marshes, prairies; tundra.

LARGE SANDPIPERS

summer

winter

HUDSONIAN GODWIT

winter

♂ summer

MARBLED GODWIT

LONG-BILLED CURLEW

ESKIMO CURLEW

WHIMBREL

127

Catoptrophorus semipalmatus 14–17″ (35–43 cm)

In flight, note the striking black-and-white wing pattern. At rest, when the banded wings cannot be seen, this large wader is nondescript; gray above, somewhat scaled below in summer, unmarked below in fall and winter; legs bluish gray.

Similar species: When standing, stockier than Greater Yellowlegs; differing by its grayer look, heavier bill, dark legs.

Voice: A musical repetitious *pill-will-willet* (in breeding season); a loud *kay-ee* (2nd note lower). Also a rapidly repeated *kip-kip-kip,* etc. In flight, *whee-wee-wee.*

Range: Cen.-s. Canada to Gulf of Mexico, W. Indies. Winters s. U.S. to Brazil. **East:** Map 132. **Habitat:** Marshes, wet meadows, mud flats, beaches.

GREATER YELLOWLEGS *Tringa melanoleuca* 14″ (35 cm) **M 133**

Note the *bright yellow legs* (shared with the next species, but leg joints thicker). A slim gray sandpiper; back checkered with gray, black, and white. Flying, it appears *dark-winged* (no stripe) with a *whitish rump and tail.* Bill long, slightly upturned.

Similar species: See Lesser Yellowlegs.

Voice: A 3-note whistle, *whew-whew-whew,* or *dear! dear! dear!*

Range: Alaska, Canada. Winters U.S. to Tierra del Fuego. **East:** Map 133. **Habitat:** Open marshes, mud flats, streams, ponds; in summer, wooded muskegs, spruce bogs.

LESSER YELLOWLEGS *Tringa flavipes* 10–11″ (25–28 cm) **M 134**

Like Greater Yellowlegs but noticeably smaller. Its shorter slimmer bill is quite straight; that of the Greater often appears slightly uptilted. Readily identified by voice (below).

Similar species: (1) Stilt Sandpiper and (2) Wilson's Phalarope (fall) have similar flight patterns. (3) See also Solitary Sandpiper.

Voice: *Yew* or *yu-yu* (1 or 2 notes); lower, less forceful than clear 3-syllabled *whew-whew-whew* of Greater Yellowlegs.

Range: Alaska, Canada. Winters from s. U.S. to Argentina. **East:** Map 134. **Habitat:** Marshes, mud flats, shores, pond edges; in summer, open boreal woods.

SOLITARY SANDPIPER *Tringa solitaria* 8–9″ (20–23 cm) **M 135**

Note the dark wings and conspicuous *white sides of the tail* (crossed by bold black bars). A dark-backed sandpiper, whitish below, with a *light eye-ring.* Nods like a yellowlegs.

Similar species: (1) Lesser Yellowlegs has yellow (not greenish) legs, white (not dark) rump. (2) Spotted Sandpiper teeters more; has a white wing stripe. Spotted has a shallow wing arc; Solitary, a darting, almost swallowlike wing stroke.

Voice: *Peet!* or *peet-weet-weet!* (higher than Spotted).

Range: Alaska, Canada. Winters Gulf of Mexico to Argentina. **East:** Map 135. **Habitat:** Streamsides, wooded swamps and ponds, fresh marshes.

STILT SANDPIPER *Micropalama himantopus*   See p. 132

Winter: Long yellow-green legs, white rump, light eyebrow.

WILSON'S PHALAROPE *Steganopus tricolor*   See p. 136

Winter: Needle bill, clear white underparts, dull yellow legs.

SANDPIPERS

summer

winter

WILLET

GREATER
YELLOWLEGS

(in flight
on p. 141)

LESSER
YELLOWLEGS

SOLITARY
SAND-
PIPER

STILT
SANDPIPER

winter

WILSON'S
PHALAROPE

winter

129

SANDERLING *Calidris alba* 7–8″ (18–20 cm) **M 136**
Note the bold *white wing stripe.* A plump active sandpiper of the outer beaches, where it chases the retreating waves like a clockwork toy. *Summer plumage:* Bright rusty about the head, back, and breast. *Winter plumage:* The palest sandpiper; snowy white below, pale gray above with *black shoulders.*
Voice: A short *twick* or *quit* is distinctive.
Range: Arctic; circumpolar. Winters from U.S., Britain, China to S. Hemisphere. **East:** Map 136. **Habitat:** Outer beaches, tideflats, lakeshores; stony tundra (summer).

BUFF-BREASTED SANDPIPER *Tryngites subruficollis* 7½″ (19 cm)
No other small shorebird is so *evenly buff below* (to undertail coverts). A tame buffy wader with an erect stance, short bill, light eye-ring, yellowish legs. In flight or in "display" the buff body contrasts with the underwing (white with marbled tip).
Voice: A low, trilled *pr-r-r-reet.* A sharp *tik.*
Range: Local in w. N. American Arctic. Winters in Argentina. **East:** Migrant through Great Plains; a few reach East Coast in fall.
Habitat: Short-grass prairies; tundra ridges (summer).

UPLAND SANDPIPER **M 137**
Bartramia longicauda 11½″ (29 cm)
(Upland Plover) A "pigeon-headed" brown sandpiper; larger than a Killdeer. The short bill, *small head,* shoe-button eye, thin neck, and *long tail* are helpful points. Often perches on fenceposts and poles; holds wings elevated upon alighting.
Voice: A mellow whistled *kip-ip-ip-ip,* often heard at night. Song, weird windy whistles: *whoooleeeeee, wheeloooooooooo.*
Range: Mainly Canada, n. U.S. Winters on pampas of Argentina.
East: Map 137. **Habitat:** Grassy prairies, open meadows, fields.

PECTORAL SANDPIPER **M 138**
Calidris melanotos 8–9″ (20–23 cm)
Note the heavy breast streaks, ending *abruptly,* like a bib. Medium-sized (variable). Neck longer than in smaller "peeps." The dark back is *lined* snipelike with white; wing stripe faint or lacking; crown rusty. Legs and bill dull yellowish green.
Voice: A reedy *krik, krik,* or *trrip-trrip.*
Range: Ne. Siberia, American Arctic. Winters in S. America. **East:** Map 138. **Habitat:** In migration, prairie pools, muddy shores, fresh and tidal marshes; in summer, tundra.

RUFF *Philomachus pugnax* ♂ 12″ (30 cm); ♀ 9″ (23 cm)
Male (Ruff), *summer:* Unique, with erectile *ruffs* and *ear tufts* that may be black, brown, rufous, buff, white, or barred, in various combinations. Legs may be green, yellow, orange, or flesh. Bill also variable (red, yellow, brown, or blackish). *Male, winter:* Rather plain, with a scaly brown back, unstreaked ashy-buff breast. Note the *erect stance* and (in flight) the *oval white spot* on each side of dark tail. *Female* (Reeve): Similar to winter ♂ but smaller.
Voice: Flight note, a low *too-i* or *tu-whit.*
Range: N. Eurasia; winters in s. Eurasia, Africa. Rare visitor to N. America. **East:** Recorded annually, mostly in fall (less often in spring) in ne. U.S. and Maritime Provinces.

SANDPIPERS

summer

winter

SANDERLING

BUFF-
BREASTED
SANDPIPER

UPLAND
SANDPIPER

PECTORAL
SANDPIPER

winter
♂

Breeding dress
of ♂ variable

♂

♂

RUFF

♀ (Reeve)

131

STILT SANDPIPER *Micropalama himantopus* 8″ (20 cm)   **M 139**
In spring, heavily marked below with *transverse bars*. Note the
rusty cheek patch. In fall, yellowlegs-like; gray above, white below;
dark-winged and *white-rumped;* note the *greenish legs* and *white
eyebrow stripe*. Bill long, tapering, with slight droop at tip. Feeds
like Dowitcher (sewing machine motion).
Voice: A single *whu,* like Lesser Yellowlegs; lower, hoarser.
Range: American Arctic. Winters in S. America. **East:** Map 139.
Habitat: Shallow pools, mud flats, marshes; tundra (summer).

CURLEW SANDPIPER *Calidris ferruginea* 7–9″ (18–23 cm)
Note the slim, *downcurved bill, whitish rump. Spring:* Dark russet
on head and underparts. *Fall:* Resembles fall Dunlin but longer-
legged, less streaked on breast; bill *curved slightly throughout*.
Main distinction is the *whitish rump.*
Voice: A liquid *chirrip,* less grating than Dunlin's note.
Range: E. Arctic Asia. Migrant to Africa. **East:** Rare straggler to e.
N. America. **Habitat:** As Dunlin's.

DUNLIN *Calidris alpina* 8–9″ (20–23 cm)   **M 140**
(Red-backed Sandpiper) Slightly larger than Sanderling, with a
slight *downward droop* at the tip of its rather long stout bill.
Summer: Rusty-red back; *black patch across belly. Winter:* Unpatterned gray-brown above with a grayish wash across the breast
(not clean white as in Sanderling). Note the droop-tipped bill.
When feeding, the bird's posture is hunched.
Voice: A nasal, rasping *cheezp* or *treezp.*
Range: Arctic; circumpolar. Winters from coasts of U.S., s. Eurasia
to Mexico, n. Africa, India. **East:** Map 140. **Habitat:** Tidal flats,
beaches, muddy pools; wet tundra (summer).

PURPLE SANDPIPER *Calidris maritima* 8–9″ (20–23 cm) **M 141**
Dumpy, dark sandpipers about rocks, jetties, or breakwaters along
the northern coasts in winter are likely to be this hardy species.
The rather juncolike coloration, slate-gray with a white belly, is a
good clue. At close range note the short yellow legs, yellowish base
of the bill, and the white eye-ring. In summer the bird is much
browner, heavily streaked above and below. See winter Dunlin
(black bill and legs).
Voice: A low *weet-wit* or *twit.*
Range: Arctic; winters along coasts of N. Atlantic (both sides).
East: Map 141. **Habitat:** Wave-washed rocks, jetties.

SPOTTED SANDPIPER *Actitis macularia* 7½″ (19 cm)   **M 142**
The most widespread sandpiper along the shores of small lakes and
streams. Teeters up and down as if a bit too delicately balanced. In
summer, note the *round breast spots*. In fall and winter, no spots;
olive-brown above, with a white line over the eye. A dusky smudge
enclosing a white wedge near the shoulder is a good aid. The flight
is distinctive; the wings beat in a *shallow arc,* giving a stiff, bowed
appearance.
Voice: A clear *peet* or *peet-weet!* or *pee-weet-weet-weet-weet.*
Range: Alaska, Canada to cen. U.S. Winters s. U.S. to n. Argentina. **East:** Map 142. **Habitat:** Pebbly lakeshores, ponds, streamsides; in winter, also seashores.

SANDPIPERS

winter

summer

STILT SANDPIPER

winter

summer

CURLEW SANDPIPER

winter

summer

DUNLIN

winter

summer

PURPLE SANDPIPER

winter

summer

SPOTTED SANDPIPER

LEAST SANDPIPER *Calidris minutilla* 5–6½″ (13–16 cm) **M 143**
Collectively the sparrow-sized sandpipers are called "peeps." Most have similar streaked patterns. The Least may be known by its smaller size, *browner* look, *yellowish or greenish* (not blackish) legs, *slighter bill,* more streaked breast.
Voice: A thin *kree-eet.* More of an *ee* sound than Semipalmated.
Range: Alaska, Canada. Winters s. U.S. to Brazil. **East:** Map 143.
Habitat: Mud flats, grass marshes, rainpools, shores.

SEMIPALMATED SANDPIPER **M 144**
Calidris pusilla 5½–6½″ (14–16 cm)
Coastally, the most numerous "peep" *in migration.* Compared to the Least, it has a relatively shorter, *stouter* bill. It is noticeably larger, grayer above, and usually has *blackish* legs.
Similar species: Often confused with Western Sandpiper.
Voice: Note, *chit* or *cheh* (lacks *ee* sound of Least, Western).
Range: N. American Arctic. Winters mainly in n. S. America. **East:** Map 144. **Habitat:** Beaches, mud flats; tundra (summer).

WESTERN SANDPIPER *Calidris mauri* 6–7″ (15–18 cm) **M 145**
Very similar to Semipalmated Sandpiper; may be a trifle larger. In typical adult females the bill is definitely thicker at the base and longer, drooping slightly at the tip. Summer adults are rustier on the back and crown (a trace of rusty may persist on scapulars in fall, giving a 2-toned effect). Perhaps the palest "peep" in winter. Short-billed winter males are almost impossible to separate from Semipalmateds except by voice. The latter species seldom winters in the U.S., the Western does.
Voice: A thin *jeet* or *cheep;* unlike soft *chit* of Semipalmated.
Range: Breeds Alaska; winters s. U.S. to Peru. **East:** Map 145.
Habitat: Shores, beaches, mud flats.

BAIRD'S SANDPIPER *Calidris bairdii* 7–7½″ (18–19 cm) **M 146**
Larger than Semipalmated or Western, with a more *pointy look* (wings extend ½″ beyond tail tip). Browner; buffier across the breast. Suggests a large Least Sandpiper with black legs. Back of immature has a rather *scaled* look.
Similar species: (1) Buff-breasted Sandpiper is buffy from throat to undertail coverts, and has *yellowish* (not *blackish*) legs. See also (2) summer Sanderling; (3) Pectoral Sandpiper.
Voice: Note, *kreep* or *kree;* a rolling trill.
Range: Ne. Siberia and American Arctic. Winters in w. and s. S. America. **East:** Map 146. **Habitat:** Rainpools, pond margins, mud flats, shores.

WHITE-RUMPED SANDPIPER **M 147**
Calidris fuscicollis 7–8″ (18–20 cm)
Larger than Semipalmated Sandpiper, smaller than Pectoral. The only *small* streaked sandpiper with a completely *white rump,* conspicuous in flight. In spring it is quite rusty; in fall grayer than the other "peeps." At rest, wing tips extend well beyond tail; sides show *streaks below wings,* a good point.
Voice: A mouselike *jeet,* like scraping of 2 flint pebbles.
Range: Arctic N. America. Winters in s. S. America. **East:** Map 147.
Habitat: Prairies, shores, mud flats; tundra (summer).

"PEEP" SANDPIPERS

winter summer
LEAST
SANDPIPER

winter summer
SEMIPALMATED
SANDPIPER

winter summer
WESTERN
SANDPIPER

winter summer
BAIRD'S
SANDPIPER

winter summer
WHITE-
RUMPED
SANDPIPER

Least   Semipalmated   Western
BILLS OF SMALL "PEEPS"   ♀   **135**

- **PHALAROPES.** These sandpiperlike birds with lobed toes are equally at home wading or swimming. They are placed by some taxonomists in a family of their own, Phalaropodidae. When feeding they often spin like tops, rapidly dabbing at the disturbed water for plankton, marine invertebrates, brine shrimp, mosquito larvae, and insects. Females are larger, more colorful than males. 2 of the 3 species are circumpolar, wintering at sea; the other breeds in the N. American plains and winters in S. America.

WILSON'S PHALAROPE *Steganopus tricolor* 9″ (23 cm)   **M 148**
This trim phalarope is dark-winged (no stripe), with a white rump. The breeding female is unique, with a broad black face and neck stripe *blending into cinnamon.* Males are duller, with just a wash of cinnamon on the sides of the neck and a white spot on the hind-neck. *Fall:* Suggests Lesser Yellowlegs (dark wings, white rump); but whiter below, with no breast-streaking; bill *needlelike,* legs greenish or straw-colored (not canary yellow).
Similar species: The other phalaropes show wing stripes.
Voice: A low nasal *wurk;* also *check, check, check.*
Range: Sw. Canada, w. U.S. Winters in s. S. America. **East:** Map 148. **Habitat:** Shallow prairie lakes, fresh marshes, pools, shores, mud flats; in migration, also salt marshes.

NORTHERN PHALAROPE   **M 149**
Lobipes lobatus 7–8″ (18–20 cm)
A Sanderling-like bird at sea is most likely to be a phalarope. This is the commonest of the 2 "sea snipes" and the one most likely to occur inland. Breeding females are gray above, with a patch of *rufous on the neck* and a white throat. Males are browner, but similar in pattern. In winter, both sexes are gray above (strongly streaked) and white below. Note the dark "phalarope patch" through the eye and the needlelike black bill.
Voice: A sharp *kit* or *whit,* similar to note of Sanderling.
Range: Circumboreal. Winters at sea to S. Hemisphere. **East:** Map 149. **Habitat:** Ocean, bays, lakes, ponds; tundra (summer).

RED PHALAROPE   **M 150**
Phalaropus fulicarius 8–9″ (20–23 cm)
The seagoing habits (swimming buoyantly like a tiny gull) distinguish this as a phalarope; in breeding plumage, deep *reddish underparts* and *white face* designate it as this species. Male duller than female. In fall and winter, gray above, white below: suggests Sanderling but with a *dark patch* through the eye.
Similar species: Fall Northern Phalarope is darker, with a strongly striped back, blacker crown. Its wing stripe contrasts more; its bill is more needlelike. The thicker bill of the fall Red Phalarope may be yellowish at the base (but usually not).
Voice: Similar to Northern Phalarope's *whit* or *prip.*
Range: Arctic; circumpolar. Winter range at sea poorly known; from N. Atlantic to S. Hemisphere. **East:** Map 150. **Habitat:** More strictly pelagic than Northern's. In summer, tundra.

PHALAROPES

winter

♀ summer

winter

WILSON'S PHALAROPE

♂ summer

winter

winter

♀ summer

NORTHERN PHALAROPE

♂ summer

winter

RED PHALAROPE

winter

♀ summer

♂ summer

lobed foot of
phalarope

137

LARGE SHOREBIRDS IN FLIGHT

Learn to know their flight calls which are quite diagnostic.

**Text and
color plate**

HUDSONIAN GODWIT *Limosa haemastica*   **pp. 126, 127**
   Upturned bill, white wing stripe, ringed tail.
   Overhead, shows blackish wing linings.
   Flight call, tawit! (or *godwit!*), higher pitched than Marbled's.

WILLET *Catoptrophorus semipalmatus*   **pp. 128, 129**
   Contrasty black, gray, and white wing pattern.
   Overhead, the wing pattern is even more striking.
   Flight call, a whistled *whee-wee-wee.*

MARBLED GODWIT *Limosa fedoa*   **pp. 126, 127**
   Long upturned bill, tawny brown color.
   Overhead, shows cinnamon wing linings.
   Flight call, an accented *kerwhit!* (or *godwit!*).

WHIMBREL *Numenius phaeopus*   **pp. 126, 127**
   Decurved bill, gray-brown color, striped crown.
   Overhead, grayer than next species, lacks cinnamon wing linings.
   Flight call, 5–7 short rapid whistles, *ti-ti-ti-ti-ti-ti.*

LONG-BILLED CURLEW *Numenius americanus*   **pp. 126, 127**
   Very long sicklelike bill; lacks head striping.
   Overhead, shows bright cinnamon wing linings.
   Flight call, a rapid, whistled *kli-li-li-li.*

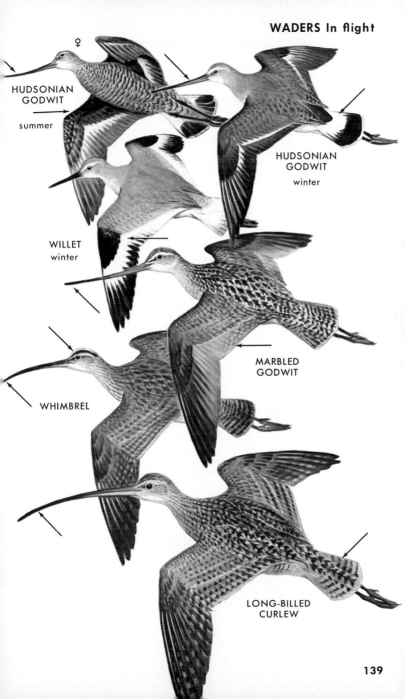

WADERS In flight

HUDSONIAN
GODWIT

summer

♀

HUDSONIAN
GODWIT

winter

WILLET
winter

MARBLED
GODWIT

WHIMBREL

LONG-BILLED
CURLEW

SNIPE, SANDPIPERS, ETC. IN FLIGHT

These and the shorebirds on the next plate are figured in black-and-white to emphasize their basic flight patterns. Most of these have unpatterned wings, lacking a central stripe. All are shown in full color on previous plates. Learn their distinctive flight calls.

Text and color plate

COMMON SNIPE *Capella gallinago*   **pp. 124, 125**
Long bill, pointed wings, tawny orange tail, zigzag flight.
Flight note, when flushed, a rasping *scaip.*

AMERICAN WOODCOCK *Philohela minor*   **pp. 124, 125**
Long bill, rounded wings, chunky shape.
Wings whistle in flight. At night, an aerial flight "song."

SOLITARY SANDPIPER *Tringa solitaria*   **pp. 128, 129**
Dark unpatterned wings, conspicuous bars on white sides of tail.
Flight note, peet! or *peet-weet-weet!* (higher than Spotted's).

LESSER YELLOWLEGS *Tringa flavipes*   **pp. 128, 129**
Similar to Greater Yellowlegs (next), but smaller, with a smaller bill. Distinguish by call, 1 or 2 notes (not 3).
Flight call, yew or *yu-yu,* softer than Greater's call.

GREATER YELLOWLEGS *Tringa melanoleuca*   **pp. 128, 129**
Dark unpatterned wings, whitish rump and tail.
Flight call, a forceful 3-note whistle, *whew-whew-whew!*

WILSON'S PHALAROPE *Steganopus tricolor*   **pp. 128, 136**
Fall: Suggests Lesser Yellowlegs; smaller, whiter, bill needlelike.
Flight note, a low nasal *wurk.*

STILT SANDPIPER *Micropalama himantopus*   **pp. 128, 132**
Suggests Lesser Yellowlegs, but legs greenish.
Flight note, a single *whu,* lower than Lesser Yellowlegs'.

UPLAND SANDPIPER *Bartramia longicauda*   **pp. 130, 131**
Brown; small head, long tail. White line on trailing edge of wing.
Often flies "on tips of wings," like Spotted Sandpiper.
Flight note, a mellow whistled *kip-ip-ip-ip.*

BUFF-BREASTED SANDPIPER *Tryngites subruficollis*   **pp. 130, 131**
Evenly buff below, contrasting with white wing linings.
Flight note, a low trilled *pr-r-r-reet.*

PECTORAL SANDPIPER *Calidris melanotos*   **pp. 130, 131**
Like double-sized Least Sandpiper. Wing stripe faint or lacking.
Flight note, a reedy *krik, krik.*

WADERS In flight

COMMON SNIPE

AMERICAN WOODCOCK

SOLITARY SANDPIPER

GREATER YELLOWLEGS

LESSER YELLOWLEGS

WILSON'S PHALAROPE
winter

STILT SAND-PIPER
winter

UPLAND SANDPIPER

BUFF-BREASTED SANDPIPER

PECTORAL SANDPIPER

SANDPIPERS, PHALAROPES IN FLIGHT

Most of these have a light wing stripe. Learn their calls.

WADERS In flight

SHORT-BILLED DOWITCHER
(Long-billed has similar pattern)

winter

RED KNOT

winter

DUNLIN

PURPLE SANDPIPER

WHITE-RUMPED SANDPIPER

CURLEW SANDPIPER

winter

winter

RUFF

winter

SPOTTED SANDPIPER

SANDERLING

winter

RED PHALAROPE

winter

NORTHERN PHALAROPE

LEAST SANDPIPER

SEMIPALMATED SANDPIPER

BAIRD'S SANDPIPER

143

■ **TURKEYS Family Meleagrididae.** Very large fowl, iridescent, naked-headed; ♂ with tail erected fanwise in display; ♀ smaller. **Food:** Berries, acorns, nuts, seeds, insects. **Range:** E. and s. U.S.
to Mexico, Guatemala. Domesticated throughout much of world.
No. of species: World, 2; East, 1.

WILD TURKEY   M 151
Meleagris gallopavo   ♂ 48″ (120 cm); ♀ 36″ (90 cm)
A streamlined version of the barnyard Turkey, with *rusty* instead
of white tail tips. Head naked; bluish with red wattles, intensified
in male's display. Tail of male erected like a fan in display. Bronzy
iridescent body; barred wings (primaries and secondaries); "beard"
on breast. Female smaller, with a smaller head; less iridescent; is
less likely to have a beard.
Voice: "Gobbling" of ♂ like domestic Turkey's. Alarm, *pit!* or *put-
put!* Flock call, *keow-keow.* Hen clucks to brood.
Range: E. and sw. U.S. to n. Mexico. Introduced elsewhere. **East:**
Map 151. **Habitat:** Woods, mountain forests, wooded swamps.

■ **GROUSE, ETC. Family Tetraonidae.**   Ground-dwelling
chickenlike birds; larger than quail, lacking the long tails of
pheasants. **Food:** Insects, seeds, buds, berries, etc. **Range:** N. America, Europe, Asia. **No. of species:** World, 18; East 7.

RUFFED GROUSE   *Bonasa umbellus*   16–19″ (40–48 cm)   M 152
Note the fan-shaped tail with a broad *black band* near the tip. A
large *red-brown* or *gray-brown* chickenlike bird of brushy woodlands, usually not seen until it flushes with a startling whir. 2 color
morphs occur: "red" birds with rufous tails, and "gray" birds with
gray tails. Red birds are in preponderance in the southern parts of
the range, gray birds northward.
Voice: Drumming of ♂ suggests a distant motor starting up. The
muffled thumping starts slowly, accelerating into a whir:
Bup. . .bup. . .bup. . .bup. .bup.bup.up.r-rrrrrr.
Range: Alaska, Canada, n. U.S. **East:** Map 152. **Habitat:** Ground
and understory of deciduous or mixed woodlands.

■ **PHEASANTS Family Phasianidae** (in part). See p. 148.

RING-NECKED PHEASANT   M 153
Phasianus colchicus   ♂ 30–36″ (75–90 cm); ♀ 21–25″ (53–63 cm)
Note the long, sweeping, pointed tail. A large chickenlike or
gamecock-like bird. Runs swiftly; flight strong (takeoff noisy).
Male, highly colored and iridescent, with scarlet wattles on its face
and a *white neck-ring* (not always present). Female, mottled
brown, with a moderately *long pointed tail.*
Voice: Crowing ♂ has a loud double squawk, *kork-kok,* followed by
a brief whir of wing flapping. When flushed, harsh croaks. Roosting
call, a 2-syllabled *kutuck-kutuck,* etc.
Range: Eurasia. Introduced widely in N. America and elsewhere.
East: Map 153. **Habitat:** Farms, fields, marsh edges, brush.

MISC. FOWL-LIKE BIRDS

display

♂

♂

♀

WILD
TURKEY

♂

♂

RUFFED
GROUSE

gray phase

red phase

♂

♂

display

♂

♀

♂

RING-NECKED PHEASANT

145

SPRUCE GROUSE   M 154
Canachites canadensis   15–17″ (38–43 cm)
Look for this *very tame,* dusky grouse in the dark conifer forests of
the North. Male has a sharply defined *black breast,* white barring
on the sides and a *chestnut band* on the tail tip. A comb of red skin
above the eye is visible at close range. Female, dark rusty brown,
thickly barred; tail short and dark, with a rusty tip.
Range: Alaska, Canada, n. U.S. **East:** Map 154. **Habitat:** Conifer
forests, jack pines, muskeg, blueberry patches, etc.

SHARP-TAILED GROUSE   M 155
Pedioecetes phasianellus   15–20″ (38–50 cm)
Note the *short pointed tail,* which in flight shows *white* at the
sides. A pale speckled brown grouse of the prairie brush. The
displaying male inflates *purplish* neck sacs.
Similar species: (1) Female Pheasant (p. 144) has a *long* pointed
tail. (2) Prairie chickens have *short, rounded, dark* tails. (3)
Ruffed Grouse (p. 144) has a larger *fan-shaped* tail.
Voice: A cackling *cac-cac-cac,* etc. Courting note, a single low *coot*
or *coo-oo,* accompanied by quill-rattling, shuffling.
Range: Alaska, Canada, nw. and n.-cen. U.S. **East:** Map 155. **Habitat:** Prairies, brushy groves, open thickets, forest edges, clearings,
coulees, open burns in coniferous forests, etc.

GREATER PRAIRIE CHICKEN   M 156
Tympanuchus cupido   17–18″ (43–45 cm)
Note the short *rounded dark tail* (black in males, barred in females). A brown henlike bird of the prairies; heavily barred.
Courting males in communal "dance" inflate orange neck sacs and
erect hornlike pinnae (blackish neck feathers).
Similar species: (1) ♀ Pheasant (p. 144) has a long pointed tail.
(2) Sharp-tailed Grouse (often called Prairie Chicken) has a whit-
ish tail. (3) Ruffed Grouse (p. 144) lives in woods, has a large
fan-shaped tail. (4) See Lesser Prairie Chicken.
Voice: "Booming" male in dance makes a hollow *oo-loo-woo,*
suggesting the sound made by blowing across a bottle.
Range: Canadian prairies (where now very rare) to coastal Texas.
East: Map 156. **Habitat:** Tall-grass prairie, now very limited.

LESSER PRAIRIE CHICKEN
Tympanuchus pallidicinctus   16″ (40 cm)
A small, pale prairie chicken; best identified by its range (see
below). The gular sacs of the male are dull purplish red or plum-
colored (not orange as in Greater Prairie Chicken).
Voice: Courtship "booming" not as rolling nor as loud as Greater
Prairie Chicken's. Both have clucking, cackling notes.
Range: Resident locally in se. Colorado, e. New Mexico, and n.
Texas Panhandle, entering our area in extreme w. Kansas and
Oklahoma, just west of the range of the Greater Prairie Chicken as
shown on Map 156. **Habitat:** Sandhill country (sage and bluestem
grass, oak shinnery).

GROUSE

♀

♂

SPRUCE
GROUSE

♂ display

♂
SHARP-
TAILED
GROUSE

♂ display

♂
GREATER
PRAIRIE
CHICKEN

♂ display

♂
LESSER
PRAIRIE CHICKEN

WILLOW PTARMIGAN *Lagopus lagopus* 16″ (40 cm) **M 157**
Ptarmigan are small arctic grouse that change their brown summer plumage to white in winter. The 2 eastern species are similar;
in breeding plumage variable, brown with white wings; in winter,
white with black tails. In summer, the Willow Ptarmigan is usually more deeply chestnut than the Rock.
Similar species: Some races of the Rock Ptarmigan are decidedly
gray, finely barred. The bill is smaller, more slender. In winter,
most Rocks have a *black mark* between the eye and bill. Habitats
differ; the Rock prefers higher, more barren hills.
Voice: Deep raucous calls, *go-out, go-out.* ♂ a staccato crow; *kwow,
kwow, tobacco, tobacco,* etc., or *go-back, go-back.*
Range: Arctic regions; circumpolar. **East:** Map 157. **Habitat:** Tundra, willow scrub, muskeg; in winter, sheltered valleys.

ROCK PTARMIGAN *Lagopus mutus* 13″ (33 cm) **M 158**
See Willow Ptarmigan (above).
Range: Arctic and alpine regions of N. Hemisphere. **East:** Map 158.
Habitat: Above timberline in mountains (to lower levels in winter);
also bleak tundra of northern coasts.

■ QUAILS, PARTRIDGES, ETC. Family Phasianidae.
Quails and partridges are usually smaller than grouse. Pheasants
are chicken-sized with long sweeping tails. Sexes alike or unlike.
Food: Insects, seeds, buds, berries. **Range:** Nearly cosmopolitan.
No. of species: World, 165; East, 2 (+2 introduced successfully;
others have failed).

GRAY PARTRIDGE *Perdix perdix* 12–14″ (30–35 cm) **M 159**
In flight, note the *short rufous tail.* A rotund gray and brown
partridge, larger than Bobwhite; has a dark U-shaped splotch on
the belly, rusty face, chestnut bars on flanks.
Similar species: The Chukar (*Alectoris chukar*), another Old
World partridge, has been introduced successfully in the West,
unsuccessfully in the Northeast. See p. 302.
Voice: A hoarse *kar-wit, kar-wit.* When flushed, a cackle.
Range: Eurasia; introduced in N. America. **East:** Map 159. **Habitat:**
Open farmland, grainfields.

COMMON BOBWHITE **M 160**
Colinus virginianus 8½–10½″ (21–26 cm)
A small, rotund fowl, near the size of a Meadowlark. Ruddy, with
a short, dark tail. The male has a conspicuous white throat and
white brow stripe. In the female these are buff.
Similar species: Ruffed Grouse is larger with a fanlike tail.
Voice: A clearly whistled *Bob-white!* or *Poor, Bob-whoit!* Covey
call, *ka-loi-kee?* answered by *whoil-kee!*
Range: Cen. and e. U.S. to Guatemala, Cuba. **East:** Map 160.
Habitat: Farms, brushy open country, roadsides, wood edges.

SCALED QUAIL *Callipepla squamata* 10–12″ (25–30 cm)
A gray, scaly "cotton-topped" quail of the arid Southwest that just
crosses the 100th meridian into our area in extreme sw. Kansas and
sw. Oklahoma. See inset of head.

PTARMIGANS

♀ summer

winter

♂ summer

WILLOW PTARMIGAN

♀ summer

winter

♂ summer

ROCK PTARMIGAN

QUAIL, etc.

GRAY PARTRIDGE   sexes similar

SCALED QUAIL

COMMON BOBWHITE   ♂   ♀

■HAWKS, EAGLES, ETC. Family Accipitridae. Diurnal
birds of prey, with hooked beaks, hooked claws. The several subfamilies are presented separately. Persecuted and misunderstood,
but important in the ecosystem. **Range:** Almost worldwide. **No. of
species:** World, 208; East, 17 (+5 accidental).

• KITES Subfamilies Elaninae and Milvinae. Graceful birds of
prey of southern distribution. U.S. species (except Snail Kite) are
falcon-shaped with pointed wings. **Food:** Large insects, reptiles,
rodents. Snail Kite specializes in snails.

SWALLOW-TAILED KITE   M 161
Elanoides forficatus   24″ (60 cm)
Shaped like a giant Barn Swallow, this kite flies with swallowlike
grace. Note the black upper parts, clean white head and under-
parts, and the long, mobile, *deeply forked* tail.
Voice: A shrill, keen *ee-ee-ee* or *pee-pee-pee.*
Range: Se. U.S. and tropical America. Leaves U.S. in winter. **East:**
Map 161. **Habitat:** Wooded river swamps.

MISSISSIPPI KITE   *Ictinia mississippiensis*   14″ (35 cm)   M 162
Falcon-shaped, graceful and gray. Body dark above, lighter below;
head *very pale gray;* tail and underwing blackish. No other
falconlike bird has a black unbarred tail. In flight, shows a broad
pale patch on rear of wing (not visible when bird is overhead).
Immature is heavily streaked on underparts; tail shows banding.
Voice: *Phee-phew* (G. M. Sutton); a clear *kee-ee.*
Range: Mainly U.S.; winters Cen. and n. S. America. **East:**
Map 162. **Habitat:** Wooded streams; groves, shelterbelts.

WHITE-TAILED KITE   *Elanus leucurus*   15–17″ (38–43 cm)
This whitish kite is falcon-shaped with long, pointed wings and a
long white tail. Soars and glides like a small gull; *often hovers.*
Adult: Pale gray with white head, underparts, and tail. A *large
black patch* toward the fore edge of the upperwing. *Immature:*
Recognizable, but has a rusty breast, brown back, and a narrow
band near the tip of its pale tail.
Range: California and s. Texas to Chile, Argentina; extending
range. **East:** A rare straggler in se. U.S. (La., Fla., S.C.) **Habitat:**
Open groves, river valleys, marshes.

SNAIL KITE   *Rostrhamus sociabilis*   17–19″ (43–48 cm)   M 162
(Everglade Kite) Suggests Marsh Hawk at any distance, but
without the gliding, tilting flight; flies more floppily, with head
looking down, searching for snails. *Male:* All black except for a
broad white band across the base of its tail; legs *red. Female:*
Heavily streaked on the buffy body; white stripe over eye and
white band across the black tail.
Voice: A cackling *kor-ee-ee-a, kor-ee-ee-a.*
Range: Florida, W. Indies, Mexico, to Argentina **East:** Map 162.
Habitat: Fresh marshes and canals with Pomacea Snails.

Overhead flight patterns on p. 171

KITES

SWALLOW-TAILED KITE

MISSISSIPPI KITE

adult

imm.

adult

imm.

imm.

adult

WHITE-TAILED KITE

adult

imm.

♀

♂

SNAIL KITE

♂

151

- **ACCIPITERS (BIRD HAWKS) Subfamily Accipitrinae.** Long-tailed woodland hawks with short, rounded wings. Typical flight is several quick beats and a glide. Sexes similar; females larger. **Food:** Chiefly birds, some small mammals.

SHARP-SHINNED HAWK   M 163
Accipiter striatus   10–14″ (25–35 cm)
A small, slim-bodied woodland hawk with a slim tail and *short, rounded wings*. Flies with several quick beats and a glide. Adult has a dark back, rusty-barred breast. Folded tail of male is *slightly notched* or *square* (may seem rounded when spread). Immature is browner, streaked on underparts.
Similar species: ♀ Cooper's Hawk is obviously larger with a *well-rounded* tail; but ♂ Cooper's and ♀ Sharp-shin may approach each other so closely in size and tail shape that many cannot be safely identified in the field. See *American Birds,* May 1979.
Voice: Like Cooper's Hawk's, but shriller; a high *kik, kik, kik.*
Range: Tree limit in Canada to Gulf states; winters from n. U.S. south. **East:** Map 163. **Habitat:** Woods, thickets.

COOPER'S HAWK   *Accipiter cooperii*   14–20″ (35–50 cm)   M 164
A short-winged, long-tailed hawk very similar to Sharp-shinned Hawk but larger, ♀ averaging not quite as long as a Crow. The tail of ♀ is *well-rounded,* even when folded; that of ♂ less so.
Voice: About nest, a rapid *kek, kek, kek;* suggests Flicker.
Range: S. Canada to n. Mexico. **East:** Map 164. **Habitat:** Broken woodlands, river groves.

NORTHERN GOSHAWK   M 165
Accipiter gentilis   20–26″ (50–65 cm)
Adult: A large, robust hawk with a longish tail, rounded wings. Crown and cheek blackish, *white stripe over eye.* Underparts pale gray, finely barred; back paler and grayer than in Cooper's or Sharp-shin. *Immature:* Like immature Cooper's; usually larger; note pale stripe over eye and zigzag tailbanding.
Voice: *Kak, kak, kak,* or *kuk, kuk, kuk,* heavier than Cooper's.
Range: Eurasia, n. N. America. **East:** Map 165. **Habitat:** Northern forests; in winter, also deciduous woodlands.

- **HARRIERS Subfamily Circinae.** Slim hawks with slim wings, long tails. Flight low, languid, gliding, with wings in a shallow V. Sexes unlike. They hunt in open country.

NORTHERN HARRIER   M 166
Circus cyaneus   17½–24″ (44–60 cm)
(Marsh Hawk)   Note the *white rump.* A slim hawk. *Males* are pale gray; *females,* streaked brown; *young birds,* rich russet below. Glides and tilts buoyantly low over the ground with wings slightly above horizontal, suggesting Turkey Vulture's dihedral. Wing tips of pale male have a "dipped in ink" look.
Voice: A weak, nasal whistle, *pee, pee, pee.*
Range: Alaska, Canada to s. U.S.; n. Eurasia. Winters to n. S. America, n. Africa. **East:** Map 166. **Habitat:** Marshes, fields, etc.

ACCIPITERS,
HARRIERS

imm.

adult

ACCITERS
(True Hawks)
have small heads,
ort, rounded wings,
and long tails

SHARP-SHINNED
HAWK

COOPER'S
HAWK

imm.

adult

NORTHERN
GOSHAWK

adult

imm.

Northern
Harrier

imm.

♂

NORTHERN
HARRIER
Marsh Hawk

♀

153

- **BUTEOS (BUZZARD HAWKS) Subfamily Buteoninae** (in part). Large thick-set hawks with broad wings and wide rounded tails. Habitually soar high in wide circles. Much variation; sexes similar, females larger. Young birds are usually *streaked* below. Black morphs often occur. **Food:** Rodents, rabbits; sometimes small birds, reptiles, grasshoppers.

RED-TAILED HAWK *Buteo jamaicensis* 19–25″ (48–63 cm) **M 167**
When this large, broad-winged, round-tailed hawk veers in its soaring, the *rufous* of the upperside of the tail can be seen (if adult). From below the tail is pale but may transmit a hint of red. Immature birds have dark gray tails that may or may not show banding. Underparts of typical Red-tails are "zoned" (whitish breast, broad band of streaks across belly). There is much variation westward where one might encounter the pale *kriderii* form, the blackish *harlani,* as well as various melanistic and rusty birds.
Voice: An asthmatic squeal, *keeer-r-r* (slurring downward).
Range: Alaska, Canada, to Panama. **East:** Map 167. **Habitat:** Open country, woodlands, prairie groves, mountains, plains.

"KRIDER'S" RED-TAILED HAWK *Buteo jamaicensis kriderii*
A pale prairie race or form of the Red-tail with a white tail that may be tinged with pale rufous.
Range: Prairie provinces of Canada and northern prairie states. In winter south through the southern plains to Texas, Louisiana.

"HARLAN'S" RED-TAILED HAWK *Buteo jamaicensis harlani*
A variable blackish race of the Red-tail; regarded as a distinct species by some. Tail never solid red but usually dirty white with a *longitudinal* mottling and freckling of black merging into a dark terminal band, giving a *white-rumped look.* Usually a hint of red on tail. Very similar to other melanistic Red-tails.
Range: Breeds in e. Alaska and nw. Canada. Winters southeastward to Texas and the lower Mississippi Valley.

SWAINSON'S HAWK **M 168**
Buteo swainsoni 19–22″ (48–55 cm)
A buteo of the plains; proportioned like Red-tail but wings a bit more pointed. When gliding, wings are slightly above horizontal. Typical adults have a *dark breastband.* Overhead, buffy wing linings contrast with *dark* flight feathers. Tail gray above, often shading to white at base. There are confusing individuals with light breasts and dark melanistic birds, but note the underwing with its dark flight feathers.
Voice: A shrill plaintive whistle, *kreeeeeeer.*
Range: Nw. N. America to n. Mexico; winters to Argentina. **East:** Map 168. **Habitat:** Plains, range, open hills, sparse trees.

FERRUGINOUS HAWK *Buteo regalis* 23–25″ (58–63 cm)
A large buteo of the plains, *rufous above* and whitish below, with a *whitish or pale rufous tail* and a light patch on the upper surface of the wing. Head often quite white. Overhead, typical adults show a *dark V* formed by the rufous thighs.
Range: Sw. Canada, w. U.S. Winters sw. U.S., n. Mexico. **East:** Breeds on plains east to s. Sask., cen. N.D., cen. S.D., Neb., w. Kans., w. Okla. Straggler east to Mississippi River.

BUTEOS

Overhead patterns on pp. 165, 169

imm.

BUTEOS have stocky build, wide tail

adult

RED-TAILED HAWK

"HARLAN'S" RED-TAILED HAWK

"Harlan's" Red-tailed

"KRIDER'S" RED-TAILED HAWK

imm.

dark phase

light phase

SWAINSON'S HAWK

FERRUGINOUS HAWK

ROUGH-LEGGED HAWK M 169
Buteo lagopus 19–24″ (48–60 cm)

This big hawk of open country habitually *hovers* on beating wings. A buteo by shape; larger, with somewhat longer wings and tail than most of the others. Typical birds usually show a *dark or blotched belly* and a *black patch* at the "wrist" of the underwing. Tail *white with a broad black band or bands* toward the tip. The black phase lacks extensive white on the tail, but shows much white on the underwing flight feathers.

Similar species: (1) Northern Harrier (white rump) has slimmer wings, slim tail. See (2) Golden Eagle, (3) Red-tailed Hawk.

Range: Arctic; circumpolar. Winters to s. U.S., cen. Eurasia. **East:** Map 169. **Habitat:** Tundra escarpments, Arctic coasts; in winter, open fields, plains, marshes.

RED-SHOULDERED HAWK M 170
Buteo lineatus 17–24″ (43–60 cm)

Adult: Recognized as a buteo by the ample tail and broad wings; as this species by the heavy dark bands across both sides of the tail. Adults have *rufous shoulders* (not always visible from below) and pale robin-red underparts. In flight, note also a translucent patch or "window" at the base of the primaries. *Immature:* Streaked; can be recognized by proportions, tailbanding and, in flight overhead, by the wing "windows."

Similar species: (1) Adult Broad-winged Hawk has paler wing linings, broader white bands on tail. See immature Broad-wing; also (2) Red-tailed Hawk; (3) Cooper's Hawk (different shape).

Voice: A 2-syllabled scream, *kee-yer* (dropping inflection).

Range: Se. Canada, e. U.S., California, Mexico. **East:** Map 170. **Habitat:** Woodlands, wooded rivers, timbered swamps.

BROAD-WINGED HAWK M 171
Buteo platypterus 14–19″ (35–48 cm)

A small chunky buteo, size of Crow. Note the tailbanding of the adult — the white bands are *about as wide* as the black. Wing linings white. *Immature:* Tail bands more numerous, crowding out the white. Often migrates in soaring flocks.

Similar species: Young Red-shouldered Hawk is similar to immature Broad-wing, but the latter is chunkier, with a stubbier tail, shorter wings; underwing is usually whiter.

Voice: A high-pitched shrill *pweeeeeee* (diminuendo).

Range: S. Canada, e. U.S. to Gulf states. Winters mainly in Cen. and S. America. **East:** Map 171. **Habitat:** Woods, groves.

SHORT-TAILED HAWK *Buteo brachyurus* 17″ (43 cm) M 172

A small black or black-and-white buteo, size of a Crow. 2 morphs: (1) black body and black wing linings, and (2) black above, white below, with white wing linings. No other Florida buteo would be jet-black or clear white below.

Range: Florida, Mexico to Chile, Bolivia, n. Argentina. **East:** Map 172. **Habitat:** Pines, wood edges, cypress swamps, mangroves.

BUTEOS

dark phase

light phase

Overhead patterns
on pp. 165, 169

imm.

ROUGH-LEGGED HAWK

pale
Florida
form

imm.

adult

RED-SHOULDERED HAWK

imm.

adult

adult

imm.

BROAD-WINGED HAWK

light
phase
imm.

dark phase

light
phase

light phase
adult

dark phase

SHORT-TAILED HAWK

- **EAGLES Subfamily Buteoninae** (in part). Eagles are distinguished from buteos, to which they are related, by their much greater size and proportionately longer wings. The powerful bill is nearly as long as the head. **Food:** Golden Eagle eats chiefly rabbits and large rodents; Bald Eagle, chiefly dead or dying fish.

BALD EAGLE   **M 173**
Haliaeetus leucocephalus   30–43″ (75–108 cm)
The national bird of the U.S. The adult, with its *white head* and *white tail,* is "all field mark." Bill yellow, massive. The dark immature has a dusky head and tail, dark bill. It shows considerable whitish in the wing linings and often on the breast (see overhead pattern, p. 167). Spread 7–8 ft.
Similar species: See Golden Eagle.
Voice: A harsh creaking cackle, *kleek-kik-ik-ik-ik,* or a lower *kak-kak-kak.*
Range: Alaska, Canada, to s. U.S. **East:** Map 173. **Habitat:** Coasts, rivers, large lakes; in migration, also mountains.

GOLDEN EAGLE   *Aquila chrysaetos*   30–40″ (75–100 cm)   **M 174**
Majestic, the Golden Eagle glides and soars flat-winged with occasional wingbeats. Its greater size, longer wings (spread about 7 ft.) set it apart from the large buteos. *Adult:* Uniformly dark below, or with a slight lightening at the base of the obscurely banded tail. On the hindneck, a *wash of gold. Immature:* In flight, more readily identified than the adult, showing a *white flash in the wings* at the base of the primaries, and a white tail with a broad dark terminal band.
Similar species: (1) Immature Bald Eagle usually has some white in the wing linings and often on the body. Tail may be mottled with white at base; but is not distinctly banded. (2) Black morph of Rough-legged Hawk is smaller, has more white under wing.
Voice: Seldom heard; a yelping bark, *kya;* whistled notes.
Range: Mainly mt. regions of N. Hemisphere. **East:** Map 174. **Habitat:** Open mts., foothills, plains, open country.

- **OSPREYS Family Pandionidae.** A monotypic family comprising a single large bird of prey that plunges feet-first for fish. Sexes alike. **Range:** Occurs on all continents except Antarctica. **No. of species:** World, 1; East, 1.

OSPREY   *Pandion haliaetus*   21–24½″ (53–61 cm)   **M 175**
Our only raptor that plunges into the water. Large (spread 4½–6 ft.); blackish above, white below. Head largely white, suggesting Bald Eagle, but with a *broad black cheek patch.* Often flies with an angle in the wing, showing a black "wrist" patch below. Hovers on beating wings and plunges feet-first for fish.
Voice: A series of sharp, annoyed whistles, *cheep, cheep,* or *yewk, yewk,* etc. Near nest, a frenzied *cheereek!*
Range: Almost cosmopolitan. **East:** Map 175. **Habitat:** Rivers, lakes, coasts.

EAGLES

Overhead patterns on p. 167

BALD EAGLE
adult

BALD EAGLE
imm.

GOLDEN EAGLE
imm.

GOLDEN EAGLE
adult

OSPREY

hovering

OSPREY

adult

159

■ **AMERICAN VULTURES Family Cathartidae.** Blackish
eaglelike birds often seen soaring high in wide circles. Their naked
heads are relatively smaller than those of hawks and eagles. Often
incorrectly called buzzards. Sexes alike. **Food:** Carrion. **Range:**
S. Canada to Cape Horn. **No. of species:** World, 7; East, 2.

TURKEY VULTURE *Cathartes aura* 26–32″ (65–80 cm) **M 176**
Nearly eagle-sized (spread 6 ft.). When overhead note the great
2-toned blackish wings (flight feathers paler). Soars with wings in a
slight dihedral (a shallow V); rocks and tilts unsteadily. At close
range the small naked *red head* of the adult is evident; young
birds have blackish heads.
Similar species: (1) See Black Vulture. (2) Eagles have larger
heads, shorter tails, and soar in a flat plane.
Range: S. Canada to Cape Horn. Migratory in North. **East:**
Map 176. **Habitat:** Usually seen soaring in the sky or perched on
dead trees, posts, carrion, or on the ground.
BLACK VULTURE *Coragyps atratus* 23–27″ (58–68 cm) **M 177**
This big black scavenger is readily identified by the short square
tail that barely projects from rear edge of the wings and by a
whitish patch toward the wing tip. Legs longer and whiter than
Turkey Vulture's. Note the quick labored flapping — alternating
with short glides. Span under 5 ft.
Similar species: Turkey Vulture has a longer tail; flaps wings less,
soars more. Black Vulture is blacker, tail stubby; wings shorter,
wider. *Caution:* Young Turkey Vulture has black head.
Range: Ohio, Pennsylvania to n. Chile, n. Argentina. **East:**
Map 177. **Habitat:** Similar to Turkey Vulture's; avoids higher mts.
KING VULTURE *Sarcoramphus papa* 32″ (80 cm)
A whitish vulture with black flight feathers, gaudy head and neck.
A rare resident of tropical America. Recorded by John and Wil-
liam Bartram on the St. Johns River in Florida in 1765–66 but this
species has never been seen in the U.S. since.

■ **CARACARAS AND FALCONS Family Falconidae.**

● **CARACARAS Subfamily Caracarinae.** Large, long-legged birds
of prey with naked faces. Sexes alike. **Food:** Our one U.S. species
eats chiefly carrion. **Range:** S. U.S. to Tierra del Fuego, Falklands.
No. of species: World, 10; East, 1.

CRESTED CARACARA **M 178**
Caracara cheriway 20–25″ (50–63 cm)
A large, long-legged, long-necked, dark bird of prey often seen
feeding with vultures; its *black crest* and *red face* are distinctive.
In flight, its underbody presents alternating areas of light and
dark; white chest, black belly, and whitish, dark-tipped tail. Note
the combination of *pale* wing patches and *white chest.* Young birds
are browner, streaked on the breast.
Range: Sw. U.S., Fla. to S. America. Often lumped with *C. plancus*
of S. America. **East:** Map 178. **Habitat:** Prairies, rangeland.

SCAVENGERS

adult

imm.

TURKEY
VULTURE

BLACK
VULTURE

adult

adult

mm.

CRESTED
CARACARA

above, King Vulture
(formerly in Florida)

161

- **FALCONS Subfamily Falconinae.** Falcons suggest kites; streamlined birds of prey with pointed wings, longish tails. **Food:** Birds, rodents, insects. **Range:** Almost cosmopolitan. **No. of species:** World, 52; East, 5 (+1 accidental).

AMERICAN KESTREL *Falco sparverius* 9–12″ (23–30 cm) **M 179**
(Sparrow Hawk) A swallowlike falcon, size of a jay. No other *small* hawk has a *rufous back or tail.* Males have blue-gray wings. Both sexes have a mustached black-and-white face pattern. *Hovers* for prey on rapidly beating wings, Kingfisher-like. Sits fairly erect, with an occasional tail lift.
Similar species: (1) Sharp-shinned Hawk has rounded wings. Sharp-shin and (2) Merlin have gray or brown backs and tails.
Voice: A rapid, high *klee klee klee* or *killy killy killy.*
Range: Most of N. and S. America. **East:** Map 179. **Habitat:** Open country, farmland, cities, wood edges, dead trees, wires.

MERLIN *Falco columbarius* 10–13½″ (25–34 cm) **M 180**
(Pigeon Hawk) A small compact falcon, length of a jay; suggests a miniature Peregrine. *Male:* Blue-gray above, with broad black bands on a gray tail. *Female and young:* Dusky brown with banded tails. Both adults and young are boldly streaked below.
Similar species: (1) Sharp-shinned Hawk has rounded wings. (2) Kestrel has a rufous tail, rufous back.
Range: Northern parts of N. Hemisphere. Winters to n. S. America, n. Africa. **East:** Map 180. **Habitat:** Open conifer woodlands; in migration, also foothills, marshes, open country.

PRAIRIE FALCON *Falco mexicanus* 17″ (43 cm)
Like a sandy Peregrine with *narrower mustaches.* In flight overhead shows *blackish patches* in the wingpits (see p. 171).
Similar species: Peregrine has blacker sideburns, slaty back.
Range: Sw. Canada, w. U.S. to s. Mexico. **East:** Occasional wanderer east of 100th meridian in the prairie states. Accidental east of Mississippi River (escapes from falconers?).

PEREGRINE FALCON *Falco peregrinus* 15–20″ (38–50 cm) **M 181**
(Duck Hawk) Note the heavy black "sideburns." Known as a falcon by its pointed wings, narrow tail, and quick wingbeats, not unlike a pigeon's. Size, near that of Crow, and strong face pattern indicate this species. Adults are slaty-backed, barred and spotted below. Young birds are brown, heavily streaked.
Voice: At eyrie, a repeated *we'chew;* a rapid *kek kek kek kek.*
Range: Nearly worldwide. **East:** Map 181. **Habitat:** Mainly open country (mts. to coast); formerly even cities. Endangered.

GYRFALCON *Falco rusticolus* 20–25″ (50–63 cm) **M 182**
A very large arctic falcon, larger, more robust than Peregrine; slightly broader-tailed. Wingbeats deceptively slower. More uniformly colored than Peregrine. In the Arctic there are black, gray, and white types; these are color morphs, not races.
Similar species: Peregrine is more contrastingly patterned, with a dark hood, broad black sideburns; slimmer; tail more tapered.
Range: Arctic regions; circumpolar. **East:** Map 182. **Habitat:** Arctic barrens, seacoasts, open mountains.

FALCONS

FALCONS have long, pointed wings, long tails

Overhead patterns on p. 171

♀ ♂

AMERICAN KESTREL

♂ Kestrel

♀ ♂

MERLIN

♂ Merlin

Peregrine

PRAIRIE FALCON

imm. adult

PEREGRINE FALCON

gray phase

dark phase

white phase

GYRFALCON

163

BUTEOS AND HARRIERS OVERHEAD

The birds shown opposite are mostly adults.

 **Buteos** or **buzzard hawks** are chunky, with broad wings, broad rounded tails. They soar and wheel high in the open sky.

Text and color plate

RED-TAILED HAWK *Buteo jamaicensis* pp. 154, 155
Light chest, streaked belly.
Tail with little or no banding.

RED-SHOULDERED HAWK *Buteo lineatus* pp. 156, 157
Banded tail (white bands narrow).
Translucent wing "windows" (not infallible).

SWAINSON'S HAWK *Buteo swainsoni* pp. 154, 155
Dark chest, light wing linings, dark flight feathers.

BROAD-WINGED HAWK *Buteo platypterus* pp. 156, 157
Adult: Broadly banded tail (white bands wide);
whitish wing linings.
Immature: Narrowly banded tail; whitish wing linings.

SHORT-TAILED HAWK *Buteo brachyurus* pp. 156, 157
Light phase: Clear white belly and wing linings.
(Only Florida buteo so colored.)

ROUGH-LEGGED HAWK *Buteo lagopus* pp. 156, 157
Light phase: Dark belly, black wrist patch.
Whitish tail with broad dark band or bands.

FERRUGINOUS HAWK *Buteo regalis* pp. 154, 155
White or pale rusty tail; dark V formed by rufous legs.

Harriers are slim, with long rounded wings and long tails. They fly low with a vulturelike dihedral.

NORTHERN HARRIER *Circus cyaneus* pp. 152, 153
(Marsh Hawk)
Male: Slim; pale, with black wing tips.
Female: Harrier shape; brown; streaked and barred.

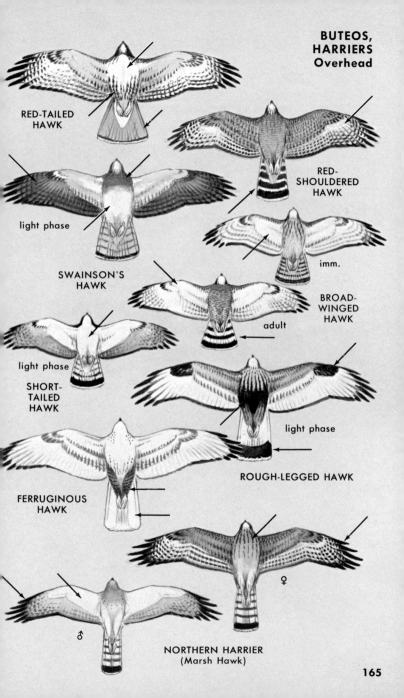

RED-TAILED
HAWK

RED-
SHOULDERED
HAWK

light phase

SWAINSON'S
HAWK

imm.

BROAD-
WINGED
HAWK

adult

SHORT-
TAILED
HAWK

light phase

light phase

ROUGH-LEGGED HAWK

FERRUGINOUS
HAWK

♂

♀

NORTHERN HARRIER
(Marsh Hawk)

EAGLES AND OSPREY OVERHEAD

<table>
<tr><td></td><td align="right">Text and
color plate</td></tr>
<tr><td>**BALD EAGLE**   *Haliaeetus leucocephalus*</td><td align="right">**pp. 158, 159**</td></tr>
</table>

BALD EAGLE   *Haliaeetus leucocephalus*   **pp. 158, 159**
   Adult: White head and tail.
   Immature: Some white in wing linings.

GOLDEN EAGLE   *Aquila chrysaetos*   **pp. 158, 159**
   Adult: Almost uniformly dark; wing linings dark.
   Immature: "Ringed" tail; white patches at base of primaries.

OSPREY   *Pandion haliaetus*   **pp. 158, 159**
   Clear white belly; black wrist patches.

Where the **Bald Eagle, Turkey Vulture,** and **Osprey** all are found, they can be separated at a great distance by their manner of soaring: the Bald Eagle with flat wings; the Turkey Vulture with a dihedral; the Osprey often with a kink or crook in its wings.

BALD EAGLE   adult

BALD EAGLE   immature

GOLDEN EAGLE   adult

GOLDEN EAGLE   immature

OSPREY

BLACKISH BIRDS OF PREY OVERHEAD

Text and
color plate

TURKEY VULTURE   *Cathartes aura*   pp. 160, 161
2-toned wings, small head, longish tail.

BLACK VULTURE   *Coragyps atratus*   pp. 160, 161
Stubby tail, white wing patches.

CRESTED CARACARA   *Caracara cheriway*   pp. 160, 161
Whitish chest, black belly, pale patches on primaries.

SNAIL KITE   *Rostrhamus sociabilis*   pp. 150, 151
(Everglade Kite)
   Immature: Brown, streaked; white tail with black band.
   Adult male: Black body, white tail with black band.

ROUGH-LEGGED HAWK   *Buteo lagopus*   pp. 156, 157
   Dark phase: Dark body, whitish flight feathers; whitish tail
with wide black terminal band.

SWAINSON'S HAWK   *Buteo swainsoni*   pp. 154, 155
   Dark phase: Wings usually dark throughout, including flight
feathers. Tail narrowly banded.

"HARLAN'S" RED-TAILED HAWK   pp. 154, 155
Buteo jamaicensis harlani
   Red-tailed Hawk shape, dark body; pale, mottled tail. Other
melanistic Red-tails may be similar except for tail.

SHORT-TAILED HAWK   *Buteo brachyurus*   pp. 156, 157
   Dark phase: Black body and wing linings, pale banded tail.
The only small *black* buteo in Florida.

DARK BIRDS OF PREY
Overhead

TURKEY
VULTURE

BLACK
VULTURE

CRESTED
CARACARA

SNAIL KITE
imm.

SNAIL KITE
♂

ROUGH-LEGGED
HAWK

dark phase

SWAINSON'S
HAWK

dark phase

"HARLAN'S"
RED-TAILED
HAWK

dark phase

SHORT-TAILED HAWK

169

ACCIPITERS, FALCONS, AND KITES OVERHEAD

Accipiters (bird hawks) have *short rounded wings,* long tails. They fly with several rapid beats and a short glide. Females are larger than males. Immatures (not shown) have streaked breasts.

Text and color plate

COOPER'S HAWK   *Accipiter cooperii*   **pp. 152, 153**
Underparts rusty. Near size of American Crow.
Tail of ♀ *well-rounded,* even when folded; tail of ♂ less so.
NORTHERN GOSHAWK   *Accipiter gentilis*   **pp. 152, 153**
Adult: Larger than American Crow; *pale gray* underbody.
SHARP-SHINNED HAWK   *Accipiter striatus*   **pp. 152, 153**
Small, jay-sized or a bit larger; tail of ♂ *square or notched* when folded; tail of ♀ less so. Fanned tail may seem more rounded.

Falcons have long *pointed* wings, long tails. Their wing strokes are strong and rapid.

GYRFALCON   *Falco rusticolus*   **pp. 162, 163**
Black phase: Blacker below than Peregrine.
Gray phase: More uniformly colored than Peregrine.
White phase (not shown): White as a Snowy Owl.
AMERICAN KESTREL   *Falco sparverius*   **pp. 162, 163**
(Sparrow Hawk)
Small; rufous tail with dark tip or dark bands.
MERLIN   (Pigeon Hawk)   *Falco columbarius*   **pp. 162, 163**
Small; dark; banded gray tail.
PEREGRINE FALCON   *Falco peregrinus*   **pp. 162, 163**
(Duck Hawk)
Falcon-shaped; size near that of Crow; bold face pattern.
PRAIRIE FALCON   *Falco mexicanus*   **pp. 162, 163**
Size of Peregrine; paler; note black patch in wingpit.

Kites (except Snail Kite) are falcon-shaped but, unlike falcons, are buoyant gliders, not power fliers. All are southern.

SWALLOW-TAILED KITE   *Elanoides forficatus*   **pp. 150, 151**
White body and wing linings; deeply forked black tail.
WHITE-TAILED KITE   *Elanus leucurus*   **pp. 150, 151**
Falcon-shaped; white body, whitish tail.
MISSISSIPPI KITE   *Ictinia mississippiensis*   **pp. 150, 151**
Falcon-shaped. *Adult:* Black tail, blackish wings, gray body.
Immature: Streaked breast; banded square-tipped or notched tail.

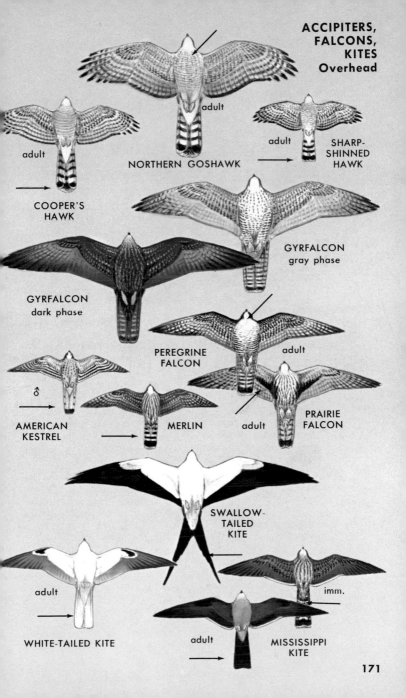

**ACCIPITERS,
FALCONS,
KITES
Overhead**

adult

NORTHERN GOSHAWK

adult

adult

SHARP-
SHINNED
HAWK

COOPER'S
HAWK

GYRFALCON
gray phase

GYRFALCON
dark phase

PEREGRINE
FALCON

adult

adult

PRAIRIE
FALCON

♂

AMERICAN
KESTREL

MERLIN

SWALLOW-
TAILED
KITE

adult

imm.

WHITE-TAILED KITE

adult

MISSISSIPPI
KITE

171

■ OWLS Families Tytonidae (Barn Owls) and Strigidae.

Chiefly nocturnal birds of prey, with large heads, flattened faces forming facial disks, and large forward-facing eyes. Hooked bills, hooked claws, and usually feathered feet (outer toe reversible). Flight noiseless, mothlike. Some species have "horns" or "ears." Sexes similar; ♀ larger. **Food:** Rodents, birds, reptiles, fish, large insects. **Range:** Nearly cosmopolitan. **No. of species:** World, 134; East, 12 (+1 accidental).

SHORT-EARED OWL *Asio flammeus* 13–17″ (33–43 cm) **M 183**

An owl of open country, often abroad by day. Streaked tawny brown color and irregular flopping flight identify it. Large buffy wing patches show in flight and on the underwing, a black carpal ("wrist") patch. *Dark face disks* emphasize yellow eyes.
Similar species: Barn Owl has a white "monkey" face, *dark* eyes.
Voice: An emphatic sneezy bark, *kee-yow!, wow!,* or *waow!*
Range: Nearly worldwide. In N. America breeds from Arctic to cen. U.S. Winters south to Mexico. **East:** Map 183. **Habitat:** Prairies, marshes (fresh and salt), dunes, tundra.

COMMON SCREECH OWL *Otus asio* 7–10″ (18–25 cm) **M 184**

Our only *small* eastern owl with ear tufts. 2 color phases: red-brown and gray. No other eared owl is bright red-brown. Young birds may lack conspicuous ears.
Voice: A mournful whinny, or wail; tremulous, descending in pitch. Sometimes a series on a single pitch.
Range: Se. Alaska, s. Canada to cen. Mexico. **East:** Map 184.
Habitat: Woodlands, farm groves, shade trees.

LONG-EARED OWL *Asio otus* 13–16″ (33–40 cm) **M 185**

A slender, crow-sized owl with long ear tufts. Usually seen "frozen" close to trunk of dense tree. Often roosts in groups. Much smaller than Great Horned Owl. Underparts streaked *lengthwise,* not barred crosswise. Ears closer together, erectile.
Voice: A low moaning *hooooo.* Also a catlike whine.
Range: Canada to sw. and s.-cen. U.S.; Eurasia, n. Africa. **East:** Map 185. **Habitat:** Woodlands, thickets, conifer groves.

GREAT HORNED OWL **M 186**

Bubo virginianus 18–25″ (45–63 cm)

The "Cat Owl." A really *large* owl with ear tufts or "horns." Heavily *barred* beneath; has a conspicuous *white throat bib.* In flight, as large as our largest hawks; looks neckless, large-headed. In Canada, races vary from very dark in the Maritimes to almost as pale as Snowy Owls around Hudson Bay.
Similar species: Long-eared Owl is much smaller (crow-sized in flight), with lengthwise streakings rather than crosswise barring beneath. Ears closer together; lacks white bib.
Voice: A resonant hooting of 3 to 8 hoots. Male usually 4 or 5, in this rhythm: *Hoo, hoo-oo, hoo, hoo.* Female lower in pitch, 6 to 8: *Hoo, hoo-hoo-hoo, hoo-oo, hoo-oo.*
Range: Tree limit to Tierra del Fuego. **East:** Map 186. **Habitat:** Forests, woodlands, thickets, streamsides, open country.

"EARED" OWLS

rufous
phase

SHORT-EARED
OWL

COMMON
SCREECH
OWL

gray
phase

LONG-EARED
OWL

subarctic form

GREAT HORNED OWL

typical form

173

BARRED OWL *Strix varia* 17–24″ (43–60 cm) **M 187**
A large gray-brown, puffy-headed woodland owl. Note the big
moist *brown* eyes and the pattern — barred *across* the chest and
streaked *lengthwise* on the belly. White spots on back.
Similar species: Other owls, except Barn Owl, have yellow eyes.
Voice: The hooting is more emphatic than Great Horned Owl's, not
so deep. May sound like the barking of a dog. Usually consists
of 8 accented hoots, in 2 groups of 4: *hoohoo-hoohoo, hoohoo-
hoohooaw.* The *aw* at the close is characteristic.
Range: Canada (east of Rockies) to Honduras. **East:** Map 187.
Habitat: Woodlands, wooded river bottoms, wooded swamps.

BARN OWL *Tyto alba* 14–20″ (35–50 cm) **M 188**
Our only owl with a *white heart-shaped face.* A long-legged,
knock-kneed, pale, monkey-faced owl. *Dark eyes,* no ear tufts.
Distinguished in flight as an owl by the large head and light
mothlike flight; as this species, by the unstreaked whitish or pale
cinnamon underparts (ghostly at night), and golden-buff or rusty
upper plumage.
Similar species: Short-eared Owl (marshes) is streaked, has darker
face and underparts, shorter legs.
Voice: A shrill rasping hiss or snore: *kschh* or *shiiish.*
Range: Nearly worldwide in tropical and temperate regions; in
New World from s. Canada to Tierra del Fuego. **East:** Map 188.
Habitat: Woodlands, groves, farms, barns, towns, cliffs.

GREAT GRAY OWL *Strix nebulosa* 24–33″ (60–83 cm) **M 189**
The largest North American owl; dusky gray, heavily striped
lengthwise on the underparts. It is round-headed, without ear
tufts; the *strongly lined facial disks* are very large proportionately, dwarfing the yellow eyes. Note the *black chin spot* bordered
by 2 broad white patches like *white mustaches.* The tail is long for
an owl (12″). Often hunts by day. Very tame.
Similar species: Barred Owl is much smaller, browner, with *brown*
(not yellow) eyes, smaller face disks, shorter tail.
Voice: A deep booming *whoo-hoo-hoo.* Also deep single *whoo's.*
Range: Boreal forests of N. Hemisphere; rare. **East:** Map 189.
Habitat: Dense conifer forests, adjacent meadows, bogs.

SNOWY OWL *Nyctea scandiaca* 20–27″ (50–68 cm) **M 190**
A large *white* owl; flecked or barred with dusky. Round head,
yellow eyes. Some birds are much whiter than others. Day-flying.
Perches on dunes, posts, haystacks, etc.
Similar species: (1) Barn Owl is whitish on underparts only; has
dark eyes. (2) Young owls of all species are whitish when in the
downy stage. (3) See Gyrfalcon (white phase).
Voice: Usually silent. Flight note when breeding, a loud repeated
krow-ow; also a repeated *rick.*
Range: Arctic; circumpolar. Has cyclic winter irruptions southward into the U.S. **East:** Map 190. **Habitat:** Prairies, fields, marshes,
beaches, dunes; in summer, arctic tundra.

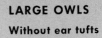

BARRED OWL

BARN OWL

GREAT GRAY OWL

SNOWY OWL

BOREAL OWL *Aegolius funereus* 9–10″ (23–25 cm) **M 191**
(Richardson's Owl) A small, flat-headed, earless owl. Very tame.
Similar to Saw-whet Owl but a bit larger; face disks pale grayish
white *framed with black;* bill pale horn or *yellowish;* forehead
thickly spotted with white. *Juvenal:* Similar to young Saw-whet
Owl but duskier; eyebrows dirty whitish or gray; belly obscurely
blotched, not tawny ochre.
Similar species: (1) Saw-whet Owl is smaller. Adult has a blacker
bill, lacks black facial frames, and has fine white streaks on the
forehead rather than spots. (2) Hawk Owl is larger, grayer, *long-
tailed;* it is *barred below.*
Voice: Like a soft high-pitched bell or dripping of water; an end-
lessly repeated *ting-ting-ting-ting-ting-ting,* etc.
Range: Boreal forests of W. Hemisphere. **East:** Map 191. **Habitat:**
Mixed-wood and conifer forests, muskeg.

SAW-WHET OWL *Aegolius acadicus* 7–8½″ (18–21 cm) **M 192**
A very tame little owl; smaller than Screech Owl, without ear
tufts. Underparts with soft blotchy brown streaks. Young birds in
summer are chocolate-brown, with conspicuous white eyebrows
forming a broad V over the bill. Belly *tawny ochre.*
Similar species: Boreal Owl is somewhat larger, has black facial
frames and a yellowish or pale horn-colored bill.
Voice: Song, a mellow whistled note repeated mechanically in
endless succession, often 100–130 times per minute: *too, too, too,
too, too, too,* etc.
Range: Se. Alaska, Canada, w. and ne. U.S. to cen. Mexico. **East:**
Map 192. **Habitat:** Forests, conifers, groves.

BURROWING OWL **M 193**
Athene cunicularia 9–11″ (23–28 cm)
A small owl of open country, often seen by day standing erect on
the ground or on posts. Note the *long legs* (for an owl). About size
of Screech Owl; barred and spotted, white chin stripe, round head,
stubby tail. Bobs and bows when agitated.
Voice: A rapid, chattering *quick-quick-quick.* At night, a mellow
co-hoo, higher than Mourning Dove's *coo.*
Range: Sw. Canada, w. U.S., Florida to s. Argentina. Migratory in
North. **East:** Map 193. **Habitat:** Open grassland, prairies, farmland,
airfields.

HAWK OWL *Surnia ulula* 14½–17½″ (36–44 cm) **M 194**
A medium-sized, hawklike, day-flying owl (smaller than Crow),
with a *long, rounded tail and completely barred underparts.* Does
not sit as erect as other owls; often perches at the tip of a tree and
jerks its tail like a Kestrel. Shrikelike, it flies low, rising abruptly to
its perch. Note the broad black sideburns framing its pale face.
Voice: A chattering *kikikiki,* more like a falcon than an owl. A
Kestrel-like *illy-illy-illy-illy.* Also a harsh scream.
Range: Boreal forests of N. Hemisphere. **East:** Map 194. **Habitat:**
Conifer forests, birch scrub, tamarack bogs, muskeg.

SMALL OWLS

BOREAL OWL

SAW-WHET OWL juvenal

SAW-WHET OWL adult

BURROWING OWL

HAWK OWL

177

■ **PARROTS, PARAKEETS Family Psittacidae.** Compact, short-necked birds with stout hooked bills. Feet zygodactyl (2 toes fore, 2 aft). Noisy and gaudily colored. **Range:** Most of S. Hemisphere; also tropics and subtropics of N. Hemisphere. **No. of species:** World, 317; East, only one endemic, the **CAROLINA PARAKEET,** *Conuropsis carolinensis,* now extinct (last reported 1920, in Florida). A number of exotic species have been released or have escaped, especially around Miami and New York City. At least two, the Canary-winged Parakeet and the Budgerigar, are breeding and are well established in Florida. Another, the Monk Parakeet, will probably not succeed. At least a score of other species have been observed in a free-flying state.

CANARY-WINGED PARAKEET *Brotogeris versicolorus* 9″ (23 cm) (S. America) White and yellow wing patch. Established in Miami area (hundreds). A few elsewhere, north to N.Y., Mass.

MONK PARAKEET *Myiopsitta monachus* 11½″ (29 cm) (Argentina) Pale gray chest, buff band across belly. Has attempted to nest in a number of states from Mass. to Fla. and west to Okla., but probably will not become established.

BUDGERIGAR *Melopsittacus undulatus* 7″ (18 cm) (Australia) Scalloped back. Usually green; a small minority may be blue, yellow, or white. Thousands are established along the west coast of Florida; lesser numbers on the southeast coast of Florida. Escapes are seen elsewhere north to New England.

1. **YELLOW-HEADED PARROT** *Amazona ochrocephala* 14″ (35 cm) (Tropical America) Occasionally seen.
2. **BLACK-HOODED PARAKEET** *Nandayus nenday* 12″ (30 cm) (S. America) Black head and beak. N.Y., s. Ont. (large flock).
3. **BLOSSOM-HEADED PARAKEET** *Psittacula roseata* 12″ (30 cm) (Himalayas) Rose-colored head, slender tail. Observed N.Y., Vt.
4. **ROSE-RINGED PARAKEET** *Psittacula krameri* 16″ (40 cm) (India) Narrow red-and-black necklace, slender tail. Reported Mass., Conn., N.Y. (flocks), to Fla. (flocks).
5. **MASKED LOVEBIRD** *Agapornis personata* 6″ (15 cm) (E. Africa) Small, stubby; black head, yellow breast; N.Y.
6. **HISPANIOLAN PARAKEET** *Aratinga chloroptera* 12½″ (31 cm) (Hispaniola) Green with red patch under bend of wing; white eye-ring. Reported in Miami with Canary-winged Parakeets.
7. **GREEN PARAKEET** *Aratinga holochlora* 10–12″ (25–30 cm) (Mexico) All green. Fla.
8. **RED-CROWNED PARROT** *Amazona viridigenalis* 12″ (30 cm) (Mexico) Red crown. Frequent in se. Fla. (has nested).
9. **ORANGE-FRONTED PARAKEET** *Aratinga canicularis* 9″ (23 cm) (Mexico) Orange forehead, olive chest, blue in wing. Fla., Pa., N.J., N.Y., etc.
10. **ORANGE-CHINNED PARAKEET** *Brotogeris jugularis* 7″ (18 cm) (Cen. America) Small; orange chin spot, yellow wing linings.
11. **COCKATIEL** *Nymphicus hollandicus* 12–13″ (30–33 cm) (Australia) Gray; crested; white wing patch, orange cheek.

CAROLINA PARAKEET
(Formerly endemic,
now extinct)

PARROTS
(Escapes)

CANARY-
WINGED
PARAKEET

MONK
PARAKEET

BUDGERIGAR
Some individuals
may be blue or yellow

OCCASIONAL ESCAPES

1

2

3

4

5

6

7

8

9

10

11

179

■ **PIGEONS AND DOVES Family Columbidae.** Plump, fast-flying birds with small heads; low cooing voices. Two types: (1) with fanlike tails (Rock Dove) and (2) smaller, brownish, with rounded or pointed tails (Mourning Dove). Sexes similar. **Food:** Seeds, waste grain, fruits, insects. **Range:** Nearly worldwide in tropical and temperate regions. **No. of species:** World, 289; East, 4 (+5 accidental, 3 introduced, 1 extinct).

MOURNING DOVE *Zenaida macroura* 12″ (30 cm) **M 195**
The common wild dove. Brown; smaller and slimmer than Rock Dove. Note the *pointed tail* with large white spots.
Voice: A hollow mournful *coah, cooo, cooo, coo.* At a distance only the 3 *coo's* are audible.
Range: Se. Alaska, s. Canada to Panama. **East:** Map 195. **Habitat:** Farms, towns, open woods, scrub, roadsides, grassland.

GROUND DOVE *Columbina passerina* 6½″ (16 cm) **M 196**
A very small dove, *not much larger than a sparrow.* Note the *stubby black tail* and rounded wings that flash *rufous* in flight. Nods its head as it walks. Feet yellow.
Voice: A soft, monotonously repeated *woo-oo, woo-oo,* etc. May sound monosyllabic, *wooo,* with rising inflection.
Range: Southern U.S. to Costa Rica; n. S. America. **East:** Map 196. **Habitat:** Farms, orchards, wood edges, roadsides.

INCA DOVE *Scardafella inca* 7½″ (19 cm)
A very small, slim dove with a *scaly* appearance; *rufous* in the primaries. Differs from Ground Dove by its *comparatively long* square-ended tail which *flashes white on the sides.*
Range: Sw. U.S. to nw. Costa Rica. **East:** Has bred in Key West, Fla. Casual Louisiana. **Habitat:** Towns, parks, farms.

WHITE-WINGED DOVE *Zenaida asiatica* 11–11½″ (28–29 cm)
Large white patch on the wing. Tail rounded; white corners.
Range: Sw. U.S. to Peru. **East:** Established s. Fla. (imported). A few winter along Gulf; bred La. Accidental n. U.S.

WHITE-CROWNED PIGEON *Columba leucocephala* 13″ (33 cm)
A stocky, obviously wild pigeon, size and build of Rock Dove; *completely dark* except for an immaculate *white crown.*
Voice: A low owllike *wof, wof, wo, co-woo* (Maynard).
Range: W. Indies, s. Florida; locally Caribbean islands, B. Honduras. **East:** Southern tip of Florida and Florida Keys, mainly in summer. **Habitat:** Mangrove keys, wooded islands.

RINGED TURTLE DOVE *Streptopelia risoria* 12″ (30 cm)
Very pale, beige. Note the *narrow black neck-ring.*
Range: Origin unknown; domesticated widely. **East:** Established locally in several Florida cities. **Habitat:** City parks.

ROCK DOVE *Columba livia* 13″ (33 cm)
(Domestic Pigeon) Typical birds are gray with a *whitish rump, 2 black wing bars,* and a broad dark tail band. Domestic stock may have many color variants.
Voice: Familiar to city dwellers; a soft gurgling *co-roo-coo.*
Range: Old World origin; worldwide in domestication. **East:** Sustains self in wild about cities, farms, cliffs, bridges.

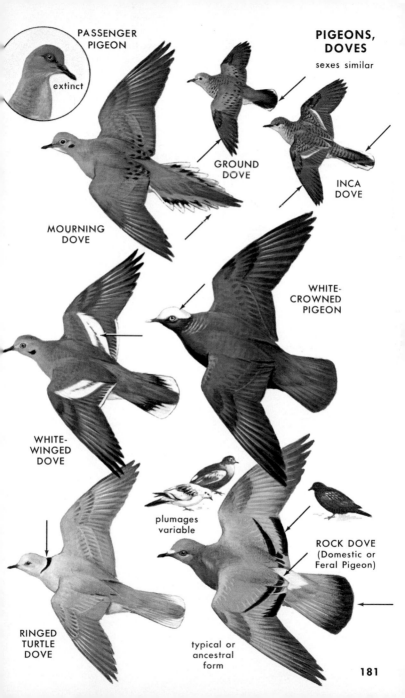

PASSENGER
PIGEON

extinct

**PIGEONS,
DOVES**

sexes similar

GROUND
DOVE

INCA
DOVE

MOURNING
DOVE

WHITE-
CROWNED
PIGEON

WHITE-
WINGED
DOVE

plumages
variable

ROCK DOVE
(Domestic or
Feral Pigeon)

RINGED
TURTLE
DOVE

typical or
ancestral
form

181

■ **CUCKOOS AND ALLIES Family Cuculidae.** Slender, long-tailed birds; feet zygodactyl (2 toes forward, 2 aft). Sexes alike. **Food:** Caterpillars, other insects; Roadrunner eats reptiles; anis eat seeds, fruits. **Range:** Warm and temperate regions of world. **No. of species:** World, 128; East, 6.

YELLOW-BILLED CUCKOO   **M 197**
Coccyzus americanus   11–13″ (28–33 cm)
   Known as a cuckoo by the slim sinuous look, brown back, plain white breast; as this species, by *rufous* in wings, *large white* spots at tips of black tail feathers (most noticeable below), and *yellow* lower mandible on the slightly curved bill.
   Voice: Song, a rapid throaty *ka-ka-ka-ka-ka-ka-ka-ka-ka-ka-ka-ka-kow-kow-kowlp-kowlp-kowlp-kowlp* (retarded toward end).
   Range: S. Canada to Mexico, W. Indies. Winters to Argentina. **East:** Map 197. **Habitat:** Woodlands, thickets, farms, orchards.

BLACK-BILLED CUCKOO   **M 198**
Coccyzus erythropthalmus   11–12″ (28–30 cm)
   Similar to Yellow-billed Cuckoo but bill black; narrow *red* eye-ring (in adult). No rufous in wing; only small tail spots.
   Voice: A fast rhythmic *cucucu, cucucu, cucucu,* etc. The grouped rhythm (3 or 4) is typical. May sing at night.
   Range: S. Canada, cen. and ne. U.S. Winters in n. S. America. **East:** Map 198. **Habitat:** Wood edges, groves, thickets.

MANGROVE CUCKOO   *Coccyzus minor*   12″ (30 cm)   **M 199**
   Similar to Yellow-billed Cuckoo (both live in s. Florida), but belly *creamy buff;* no rufous in wing. Note the *black ear patch.*
   Range: S. Florida, W. Indies, Mexico, to n. Brazil. **East:** Map 199. **Habitat:** In our area, mangroves.

SMOOTH-BILLED ANI   *Crotophaga ani*   12½″ (31 cm)   **M 390**
   A coal-black grackle-sized bird with a *loose-jointed* tail, short wings and huge bill with a *high curved* ridge (giving a puffinlike profile). Flight weak; alternately flaps and sails.
   Voice: A whining whistle. A querulous *que-lick.*
   Range: S. Florida, W. Indies, Caribbean coastal islands to Argentina. **East:** Map 390. **Habitat:** Brushy edges, thickets.

GROOVE-BILLED ANI   *Crotophaga sulcirostris*   13″ (33 cm)
   Very similar to Smooth-billed Ani but with 3 grooves on the upper mandible; *lacks the hump* at the base of the bill.
   Voice: A repeated *whee-o* or *tee-ho,* first note slurring up.
   Range: Gulf of Mexico to Argentina. **East:** Extending range eastward along Gulf; now breeds in coastal Louisiana; casual east to Florida Panhandle. Accidental north to Great Lakes.

GREATER ROADRUNNER   **M 199**
Geococcyx californianus   20–24″ (50–60 cm)
   The cuckoo that runs on the ground (tracks show 2 toes forward, 2 aft). Large, slender, streaked, with a long white-tipped tail, shaggy crest, long legs. White crescent on open wing.
   Voice: 6 to 8 low dovelike *coo's* descending in pitch.
   Range: Sw. U.S. to cen. Mexico. **East:** Map 199. **Habitat:** Dry open country with scattered cover, brush.

CUCKOOS, etc.

sexes similar

YELLOW-BILLED
CUCKOO

adult

BLACK-BILLED
CUCKOO

imm.

MANGROVE
CUCKOO

adult

GROOVE-
BILLED
ANI

SMOOTH-
BILLED
ANI

GREATER ROADRUNNER

183

■ GOATSUCKERS (NIGHTJARS) Family Caprimulgidae.

Nocturnal birds with ample tails, large eyes, tiny bills, large bristled gapes, very short legs. By day they rest horizontally on limbs or on ground, camouflaged by "dead leaf" pattern. Best identified at night by voice. Nighthawks are aberrant goatsuckers, often abroad by day. **Food:** Nocturnal insects. **Range:** Nearly worldwide in temperate and tropical land regions. **No. of species:** World, 67; East, 4 or 5 (+1 accidental).

COMMON NIGHTHAWK *Chordeiles minor* 9½″ (24 cm) **M 200**
A slim-winged gray-brown bird often seen high in the air; flies with easy strokes, "changing gear" to quicker erratic strokes. Note the *broad white bar* across the pointed wings. Male has a white bar across its notched tail and a white throat. An aberrant goatsucker; prefers night, but may be abroad at midday.
Similar species: (1) Antillean Nighthawk (*C. m. gundlachii*), perhaps a distinct species, occurs in Florida Keys. Its voice is a dry 4-syllabled *pity-pit-pit* or *killy-kadick*. (2) Lesser Nighthawk (*C. acutipennis*) of sw. U.S. is casual in La., Fla.; accidental Ont.
Voice: A nasal *peent* or *pee-ik*. In aerial display, the male dives, then zooms up sharply with a sudden deep whir of wings.
Range: Canada to Panama. Winters S. America. **East:** Map 200.
Habitat: Open country to mts.; open pine woods; often seen in air over cities or towns. Sits on ground, posts, rails, roofs.

WHIP-POOR-WILL *Caprimulgus vociferus* 9½″ (24 cm) **M 201**
A voice in the night woods. When flushed by day, the bird flits away on *rounded* wings like a large brown moth. Male shows large white tail patches; in female these are buffish.
Voice: At night, a rolling, tiresomely repeated *whip' poor-weel'*, or *purple-rib*, etc.; accent on first and last syllables.
Range: Cen. and e. Canada to Honduras. Winters from Gulf states to Honduras. **East:** Map 201. **Habitat:** Leafy woodlands.

CHUCK-WILL'S-WIDOW **M 202**
Caprimulgus carolinensis 12″ (30 cm)
Similar to Whip-poor-will; larger, much buffier, with a *brown* (not blackish) throat. Identify by size, brownish look, more restricted white areas in tail of male; also by voice, range.
Voice: Call, *chuck-will'-wid'-ow* (less vigorous than efforts of Whip-poor-will); 4-syllabled, but *chuck* often inaudible.
Range: Se. U.S. Winters south to Colombia. **East:** Map 202. **Habitat:** Pine forests, river woodlands, groves.

POOR-WILL *Phalaenoptilus nuttallii* 7–8″ (18–20 cm) **M 203**
Best known by its night cry in arid hills. It appears smaller than a Nighthawk, has more rounded wings (no white bar), and its short rounded tail has *white corners*.
Voice: At night, a loud repeated *poor-will* or *poor-jill-ip*.
Range: Se. B. Columbia, w. U.S. to cen. Mexico. Winters sw. U.S. south. **East:** Map 203. **Habitat:** Dry hills, open brush.

GOATSUCKERS

wing of
LESSER
NIGHTHAWK
♀

COMMON
NIGHTHAWK

♂

COMMON
NIGHTHAWK ♂

WHIP-POOR-WILL ♂

WHIP-POOR-WILL ♂

POOR-WILL ♂

CHUCK-WILL'S-
WIDOW ♂

CHUCK-WILL'S-
WIDOW ♂

185

■ HUMMINGBIRDS Family Trochilidae.   The smallest birds.
Usually iridescent, with needlelike bills for sipping nectar. Jewel-like throat feathers, or gorgets, adorn adult males of most species. The wing motion is so rapid that the wings appear blurred. Hover when feeding. Pugnacious. **Food:** Nectar of flowers (red flowers are favored); aphids, other small insects, spiders. **Range:** W. Hemisphere; majority in tropics. **No. of species:** World, 319; East, 2 (+6 accidental).

RUBY-THROATED HUMMINGBIRD   M 204
Archilochus colubris   3–3¾″ (8–9 cm)
See family description (above). The male Ruby-throat has a glowing *fiery-red throat,* iridescent green back, forked tail. The female lacks red throat; has a blunt tail with white spots.
Similar species: Ruby-throat is the only eastern species, but Rufous Hummingbird may turn up occasionally along Gulf Coast in late fall and winter. Large sphinx moths (Sphingidae) might be mistaken for hummers, but seldom visit flowers before dusk.
Voice: Male in aerial display swings like a pendulum in a wide arc, each swing accompanied by a hum. Notes, high, squeaky.
Range: S. Canada to Gulf states. Winters Mexico, Cen. America.
East: Map 204. **Habitat:** Flowers, gardens, wood edges.

RUFOUS HUMMINGBIRD   *Selasphorus rufus*   3½″ (9 cm)
Male: No other North American hummingbird has a *rufous back.* Upper parts bright red-brown; throat flaming orange-red. *Female:* Green-backed; dull *rufous on sides and base of tail.*
Range: Breeds in nw. N. America; winters in Mexico; migrates in spring through Pacific states; in fall, through Rockies. **East:** A rare but regular straggler in fall and winter (Nov.–April) eastward along the Gulf Coast from Louisiana to Florida. Casual or accidental elsewhere in e. U.S. **Habitat:** In Louisiana, favors hibiscus and late-blooming salvia.

■ KINGFISHERS Family Alcedinidae.   Solitary birds with
large heads, heronlike bills, small syndactyl feet (2 toes partially joined). American species are fish-eaters, fishing from perches above water, or hovering and plunging headfirst. **Food:** Mainly fish; some species eat insects, lizards. **Range:** Almost worldwide. **No. of species:** World 87; East, 1.

BELTED KINGFISHER   *Megaceryle alcyon*   13″ (33 cm)   M 205
Hovering on rapidly beating wings in readiness for the plunge, or flying with uneven wingbeats (as if changing gear), rattling as it goes, the Kingfisher is easily recognized. Perched, it is big-headed and big-billed, larger than a Robin, blue-gray above, with a ragged bushy crest and a broad gray breastband. The female has an additional rusty breastband.
Voice: A loud dry rattle.
Range: Alaska, Canada to s. U.S. Winters to Panama. **East:** Map 205. **Habitat:** Streams, lakes, bays, coasts; nests in banks.

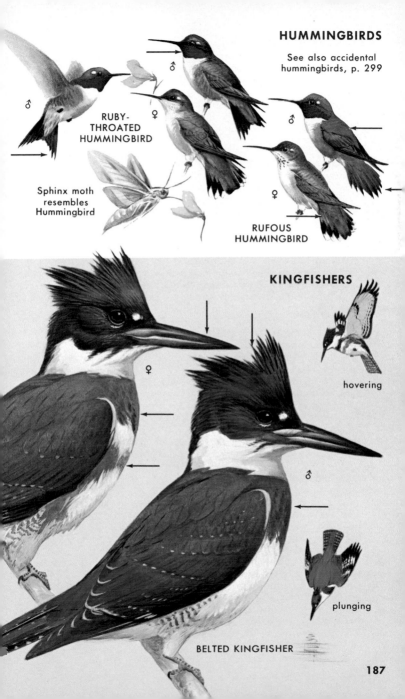

HUMMINGBIRDS

See also accidental hummingbirds, p. 299

♂

RUBY-
THROATED
HUMMINGBIRD

♀

Sphinx moth
resembles
Hummingbird

♂

♀

RUFOUS
HUMMINGBIRD

KINGFISHERS

hovering

♀

♂

plunging

BELTED KINGFISHER

187

■ WOODPECKERS Family Picidae.

Chisel-billed wood-boring birds with strong zygodactyl feet (usually 2 toes front, 2 rear), remarkably long tongues, and stiff spiny tails that act as props when climbing. Flight usually undulating. Most males have some red on the head. **Food:** Tree-boring insects; some species eat ants, flying insects, berries, acorns, sap. **Range:** Mainly wooded parts of world, but absent in Australian region, Madagascar, most oceanic islands. **No. of species** (including allies): World, 210; East, 11 (+2 accidental).

RED-HEADED WOODPECKER   M 206
Melanerpes erythrocephalus   8½–9½″ (21–24 cm)

The only eastern woodpecker with the *entire* head red (others may have a patch of red). Back *solid black,* rump white. Large square white patches are conspicuous on the wing (making the lower back look white when the bird is at rest). Sexes similar. Immature is dusky-headed; large white wing patches identify it.
Voice: A loud *queer* or *queeah,* louder and higher pitched than *churr* of Red-bellied Woodpecker.
Range: East of Rockies from s. Canada to Gulf states. Partial migrant in North. **East:** Map 206. **Habitat:** Groves, farm country, orchards, shade trees in towns, large scattered trees.

PILEATED WOODPECKER   M 207
Dryocopus pileatus   16–19½″ (40–49 cm)

A spectacular black *crow-sized* woodpecker with a flaming-red *crest.* The female has a blackish forehead, lacks the red on the mustache. The great size, sweeping wingbeats, and flashing white underwing areas identify the Pileated in flight. The diggings, large *oval* or *oblong* holes, indicate its presence.
Voice: Call resembles that of Flicker, but louder, irregular: *kik–kik–kikkik—kik-kik,* etc. Also a more ringing, hurried call that may rise or fall slightly in pitch.
Range: Canada to s. U.S. **East:** Map 207. **Habitat:** Conifer, mixed, and hardwood forests; woodlots.

IVORY-BILLED WOODPECKER
Campephilus principalis   20″ (50 cm)

This rarest of North American birds may be known from the Pileated Woodpecker by its larger size, ivory-white bill, large white wing patches *visible at rest,* and different underwing pattern (see opposite). The female has a *black* crest.
Similar species: See Pileated Woodpecker.
Voice: Call unlike that of Pileated, a single loud tooting note constantly uttered as the bird forages about—a sharp nasal *kent* suggesting to some the note of a big nuthatch. Audubon wrote it *pait,* resembling the high false note of a clarinet.
Range: Formerly primeval river-bottom forests of s. U.S. Reports in recent years (needing further verification) from Florida, Louisiana, S. Carolina, and e. Texas (Big Thicket). Very close to extinction, if, indeed, it still exists.

WOODPECKERS

imm.

adult

RED-HEADED WOODPECKER

sexes similar

♂

♀

PILEATED WOODPECKER

under

♀

♂

under

IVORY-BILLED WOODPECKER

near extinction

upper

189

COMMON ("YELLOW-SHAFTED") FLICKER

M 208

Colaptes auratus (in part)   12–14″ (30–35 cm)

Note the conspicuous *white rump,* visible when the bird flies. This and the *brown back* mark it as a Flicker. The flight is deeply undulating. Overhead, it flashes *golden yellow* under the wings and tail. Close up, it displays a black patch across the chest and a red crescent on the nape. The male has a black mustache. Flickers often hop awkwardly on the ground, feeding on ants.

Voice: Song, a loud *wick wick wick wick wick,* etc. Notes, a loud *klee-yer,* and a squeaky *flick-a, flick-a,* etc.

Range: Tree limit in Alaska, Canada south to Gulf states, Cuba. Migrant in n. parts of range. **East:** Map 208. **Habitat:** Open forests, woodlots, groves, farms, towns, semi-open country.

COMMON ("RED-SHAFTED") FLICKER

Colaptes auratus (in part)   12–14″ (30–35 cm)

Similar to "Yellow-shafted" (above), but with the yellow of the wing and tail linings replaced by *salmon-red.* Both sexes lack the red crescent on nape. The male has a *red* (not black) mustache. Where their ranges overlap (western edge of Great Plains), hybrids or intermediates are frequent. These may have orange wing linings or a combination of characters.

Range: Se. Alaska, sw. Canada, w. U.S. to Guatemala. **East:** Migrants, usually hybrids, may occur in western part of our area.

RED-BELLIED WOODPECKER

M 209

Melanerpes carolinus   9–10½″ (23–26 cm)

A *zebra-backed* woodpecker with a *red cap,* white rump. Red covers crown and nape in male, only nape in female. Juvenal is also zebra-backed but has a brown head, devoid of red.

Voice: Note, *kwirr, churr,* or *chaw;* also *chiv, chiv.* Also a muffled Flicker-like series.

Range: S. Great Lakes area and s. New England to Gulf states (Map 209). **Habitat:** Woodlands, groves, orchards, towns.

RED-COCKADED WOODPECKER

M 210

Picoides borealis   8½″ (21 cm)

Zebra-backed, with a *black cap.* The *white cheek* is an obvious field mark. The tiny red cockade of the male is hard to see.

Voice: A rough rasping *sripp* or *zhilp* (suggests flock note of young Starling). Sometimes a higher *tsick.*

Range: Se. U.S. (Map 210). **Habitat:** Open pine woodlands.

YELLOW-BELLIED SAPSUCKER

M 211

Sphyrapicus varius   8–9″ (20–23 cm)

Note the longish white wing patch and red forehead patch. The male has a red throat patch, the female a white throat. The young bird is brown, but note the distinctive white wing patch. Sapsuckers drill orderly rows of small holes in trees for sap.

Voice: A nasal mewing note, or squeal: *cheerrrr,* slurring downward. On nesting grounds, distinctive drumming; several rapid thumps followed by several slow rhythmic ones.

Range: Canada to s. Rocky Mts., s. Appalachians. Winters to Cen. America, W. Indies. **East:** Map 211. **Habitat:** Woodlands, aspen groves; in winter, also orchards, other trees.

Yellow-shafted

Red-shafted

Yellow-shafted

♂

Red-shafted
form

♂

♀

♀

imm.

**COMMON
FLICKER**

Yellow-shafted
form

♂

**RED-BELLIED
WOODPECKER**

♂

imm.

**RED-COCKADED
WOODPECKER**

♂

**YELLOW-BELLIED
SAPSUCKER**

DOWNY WOODPECKER *Picoides pubescens* 6½″ (16 cm) **M 212**
Note the *white* back and the *small* bill. Otherwise this industrious
bird is like a small edition of the Hairy Woodpecker.
Similar species: Hairy Woodpecker is larger, has a large bill.
Voice: A rapid whinny of notes, descending in pitch. Note, a flat
pick, not as sharp as Hairy's *peek!*
Range: Alaska, Canada to s. U.S. **East:** Map 212. **Habitat:** Forests,
woodlots, willows, river groves, orchards, shade trees.

HAIRY WOODPECKER *Picoides villosus* 9½″ (24 cm) **M 213**
Note the *white* back and *large* bill. Other woodpeckers may have
white rumps or white bars on the back, but the Downy and the
Hairy are our only woodpeckers with *white backs.* They are almost identical in pattern, checkered and spotted with black and
white; the *male* with a small red patch on the back of the head, the
female without. The Hairy is like a large Downy; its bill is exag-
gerated compared with the Downy's little bill.
Similar species: The Downy at close range shows spots on the
outer tail feathers. The small bill is the best character.
Voice: A Kingfisher-like rattle, run together more than the call of
the Downy. Note, a sharp *peek!* (Downy says *pick.*)
Range: Alaska, Canada to Panama. **East:** Map 213. **Habitat:** Forests, woodlands, river groves, shade trees.

NORTHERN THREE-TOED WOODPECKER **M 214**
Picoides tridactylus 8–9½″ (20–24 cm)
(American Three-toed Woodpecker) The males of this and the
next species are our only woodpeckers that normally have *yellow*
caps. Both have *barred sides.* The "ladder" back distinguishes this
species. The female lacks the yellow cap and suggests a Downy or
Hairy Woodpecker, but note the *barred sides.*
Similar species: (1) Black-backed Three-toed Woodpecker has a
solid-*black* back. (2) Rarely, an aberrant immature Hairy Wood-
pecker has a yellowish or orange cap, but it lacks the bars on the
flanks and has more white on the face.
Voice: Calls similar to those of next species.
Range: Boreal forests of N. Hemisphere. **East:** Map 214. **Habitat:**
Conifer forests.

BLACK-BACKED THREE-TOED WOODPECKER **M 215**
Picoides arcticus 9–10″ (23–25 cm)
(Arctic Three-toed Woodpecker) Note the combination of *solid-
black back, barred sides.* This and the preceding species (both
have 3 toes) inhabit the cold forests of the North; their presence
can be detected by patches of bark scaled from dead conifers. Their
sides are heavily barred; males have *yellow* caps.
Similar species: Northern Three-toed Woodpecker (*barred* back).
Voice: A short sharp *kik* or *chik.* Also in series.
Range: Boreal forests of n. N. America. **East:** Map 215. **Habitat:**
Boreal forests of firs and spruces.

WOODPECKERS

DOWNY
WOODPECKER

HAIRY
WOODPECKER

southern
form

NORTHERN
THREE-TOED
WOODPECKER

BLACK-BACKED
THREE-TOED
WOODPECKER

193

■ **TYRANT FLYCATCHERS Family Tyrannidae.** Most fly-catchers perch quietly upright on exposed branches and sally forth to snap up insects. Bill flattened, with bristles at base. **Food:** Flying insects. **Range:** New World; majority in tropics. **No. of species:** World, 365; East, 16 (+10 accidental).

SCISSOR-TAILED FLYCATCHER   **M 216**
Muscivora forficata   11–15″ (28–38 cm)
A beautiful bird; pale pearly gray, with an *extremely long scissor-like tail,* usually folded. Sides and wing linings salmon-pink. The young bird with a short tail may suggest Western Kingbird.
Voice: A harsh *keck* or *kew;* a repeated *ka-leep;* also shrill king-birdlike bickerings and stutterings.
Range: Se. Colorado, s. Nebraska south to e. New Mexico, s. Texas. Winters chiefly s. Mexico to Panama. **East:** Map 216. **Habitat:** Semi-open country, ranches, farms, roadsides, wires.

EASTERN KINGBIRD   *Tyrannus tyrannus*   8″ (20 cm)   **M 217**
The *white band* across the tail tip marks the Eastern Kingbird. A concealed red crown mark is rarely seen. Often seems to fly quiveringly on "tips of wings." Harasses crows, hawks.
Voice: A rapid sputter of high bickering notes: *dzee-dzee-dzee,* etc., and *kit-kit-kitter-kitter,* etc. Also a nasal *dzeeb.*
Range: Cen. Canada to Gulf of Mexico. Winters Peru to Bolivia. **East:** Map 217. **Habitat:** Wood edges, river groves, farms, shelterbelts, orchards, roadsides, fencerows, wires.

WESTERN KINGBIRD   *Tyrannus verticalis*   8″ (20 cm)   **M 218**
Size of Eastern Kingbird, but with a *paler* head and back, *yellowish* belly. In this species the black tail has a *narrow white edging* on each side, but no white band across the tip.
Voice: Shrill bickering calls; a sharp *whit* or *whit-ker-whit.*
Range: Sw. Canada, w. U.S., upper Mississippi Valley to n. Mexico. Winters to Costa Rica. **East:** Map 218. **Habitat:** Farms, open country with scattered trees, roadsides, wires.

GRAY KINGBIRD   *Tyrannus dominicensis*   9″ (23 cm)   **M 219**
Resembles Eastern Kingbird, but larger and very much paler. The conspicuously notched tail has *no white band.* The *very large bill* gives a large-headed look. Note the dark ear patch.
Voice: A rolling *pi-teer-rrry* or *pe-cheer-ry.*
Range: S. Florida, W. Indies. Winters W. Indies to n. S. America. **East:** Map 219. **Habitat:** Roadsides, wires, mangroves, edges.

GREAT CRESTED FLYCATCHER   **M 220**
Myiarchus crinitus   8–9″ (20–23 cm)
A kingbird-sized flycatcher with *cinnamon wings and tail,* a gray breast, and a yellow belly. Often erects a bushy crest.
Voice: A loud whistled *wheeep!* Also a rolling *prrrrrreet!*
Range: S. Canada, e. and cen. U.S. Winters e. Mexico to Colombia. **East:** Map 220. **Habitat:** Woodlands, groves.

ASH-THROATED FLYCATCHER   *Myiarchus cinerascens*   8″ (20 cm)
A western stray; suggests a small washed-out Great Crested Flycatcher with a *white throat,* less yellow on belly, less rufous. Casual along Gulf Coast east to Florida; accidental northward. A *Myiarchus* flycatcher in late fall or winter may be this one.

LARGE FLYCATCHERS

sexes similar

EASTERN
KINGBIRD

SCISSOR-TAILED
FLYCATCHER

ASH-
THROATED
FLYCATCHER

WESTERN
KINGBIRD

GREAT
CRESTED
FLYCATCHER

GRAY
KINGBIRD

195

EASTERN PHOEBE *Sayornis phoebe* 6½–7″ (16–18 cm) **M 222**
Note the *tail-bobbing.* A gray-brown sparrow-sized flycatcher
without an eye-ring or strong wing bars (but may have dull ones,
especially young birds). The bill is *all black.*
Similar species: The Pewee and the small *Empidonax* flycatchers
have conspicuous wing bars. Their bills are yellowish or whitish on
the lower mandible. They do not wag their tails.
Voice: Song, a well-enunciated *phoe-be,* or *fi-bree* (2nd note alternately higher or lower). Note, a sharp *chip.*
Range: East of Rockies; cen. Canada to s. U.S. Winters to s. Mexico. **East:** Map 222. **Habitat:** Streamsides, bridges, farms, roadsides,
towns.

EASTERN PEWEE *Contopus virens* 6–6½″ (15–16 cm) **M 221**
(Eastern Wood Pewee) A sparrow-sized flycatcher, about the size
of Eastern Phoebe, but with *2 narrow white wing bars.* Similar to
but slightly larger than *Empidonax* flycatchers, but with *no eye-
ring.* Wings extend a bit farther down the tail.
Similar species: Phoebe lacks white wing bars; bobs its tail.
Voice: A sweet plaintive whistle: *pee-a-wee,* slurring down, then
up. Also *pee-ur,* slurring down.
Range: S. Canada, e. U.S. Winters Costa Rica to Peru. **East:** Map
221. **Habitat:** Woodlands, groves.

LEAST FLYCATCHER *Empidonax minimus* See p. 198
OLIVE-SIDED FLYCATCHER **M 223**
Nuttallornis borealis 7–8″ (18–20 cm)
A rather large, stout, large-headed flycatcher; often perches at the
tip of a dead tree. Note the largish bill and *dark chest patches* with
a narrow strip of white between (suggesting an unbuttoned jack-
et). A *cottony tuft* may poke out from behind wing.
Similar species: Eastern Pewee is smaller, has light wing bars.
Voice: Note, a trebled *pip-pip-pip.* Song, a spirited whistle: *quick-
three-beers,* middle note highest, last sliding.
Range: Alaska, Canada, w. and ne. U.S. Winters Colombia to Peru.
East: Map 223. **Habitat:** Conifer forests, burns, slashings. In migration, usually seen on tips of dead trees.

SAY'S PHOEBE *Sayornis saya* 7–8″ (18–20 cm)
A rather large gray-brown flycatcher with a pale *rusty* belly. The
black tail, rusty belly give it the look of a small Robin.
Voice: A plaintive *pee-ur* or *pee-ee;* also a trilling note.
Range: W. N. America; east to about 100th meridian on Plains
(boundary of our area). Casual or accidental east to Atlantic.

VERMILION FLYCATCHER *Pyrocephalus rubinus* 6″ (15 cm)
Male: Crown (often raised in a bushy crest) and underparts *flaming vermilion;* upper parts and tail dusky to blackish. *Female and
immature:* Underparts whitish, narrowly streaked; belly and
undertail coverts washed with pinkish or yellow.
Similar species: Male Scarlet Tanager has a *scarlet back.*
Voice: A slightly phoebelike *p-p-pit-zee* or *pit-a-zee.*
Range: Sw. U.S. to Argentina. In winter a few wander eastward
along the Gulf Coast from Louisiana to Florida. Casual or accidental northward along the Atlantic seaboard.

FLYCATCHERS

sexes similar except
in Vermilion Flycatcher

EASTERN
PHOEBE

EASTERN
PEWEE

LEAST
FLYCATCHER

Least Flycatcher
is a typical Empidonax.
See others on p. 199

OLIVE-SIDED
FLYCATCHER

SAY'S
PHOEBE

VERMILION
FLYCATCHER
♀

VERMILION
FLYCATCHER
♂

- **THE EMPIDONAX COMPLEX Genus Empidonax.** Five small flycatchers in our area share the characters of *light eye-ring* and *2 whitish wing bars*. When breeding, they are readily separated by voice, habitat, and way of nesting (see *A Field Guide to Birds' Nests* by Hal Harrison). In migration they seldom sing, so we are forced to let most of them go simply as *Empidonax* flycatchers.

ACADIAN FLYCATCHER M 224
Empidonax virescens 5½″ (14 cm)

A greenish *Empidonax* with a yellowish wash on the sides; best separated from others of the genus by habitat, range, and voice. The *only* breeding *Empidonax* in most of the South.

Voice: "Song," a sharp explosive *pit-see!* or *wee-see!* (sharp upward inflection); also a thin *peet.*

Range: E. U.S. (Map 224). Winters Costa Rica to Ecuador. **Habitat:** Deciduous forests, ravines, swampy woods, beech groves.

YELLOW-BELLIED FLYCATCHER M 225
Empidonax flaviventris 5½″ (14 cm)

The decidedly *yellowish* underparts (including throat) separate this northern flycatcher from other small eastern flycatchers.

Similar species: Others of this group may have a tinge of yellow, especially in fall, but none of the rest has a wash of yellow from throat to belly. Eye-ring also yellowish. Some Acadians in fall look very much like Yellow-bellies.

Voice: A simple spiritless *per-wee* or *chu-wee.* Also *killik.*

Range: Canada, ne. U.S. Winters Mexico to Panama. **East:** Map 225. **Habitat:** Woods; in summer, boreal forests, muskegs, bogs.

LEAST FLYCATCHER *Empidonax minimus* 5¼″ (13 cm) M 226
Grayer above and whiter below than the other *Empidonax* flycatchers. Know it by its voice and the open groves it inhabits.

Voice: A sharply snapped dry *che-bek'!* Emphatic.

Range: Canada, east of Rockies; n.-cen. and ne. U.S. Winters Mexico to Panama. **East:** Map 226. **Habitat:** Open woods, aspen groves, orchards, shade trees.

WILLOW FLYCATCHER *Empidonax traillii* 5½″ (14 cm) M 227
The Alder and Willow Flycatchers, formerly lumped as races of *traillii* are now regarded as 2 distinct species. They are almost identical in appearance, a bit larger and browner than the Least Flycatcher. They may be separated from each other only by voice and habitat (below).

Voice: Song, a sneezy *fitz-bew,* quite unlike *fee-bee'-o* of Alder.

Range: Alaska, w. Canada to sw. and e.-cen. U.S. Winters s. Mexico to Argentina. **East:** Map 227. **Habitat:** Somewhat like Alder Flycatcher's (bushes, willow thickets, etc.), but often in drier situations, brushy fields, upland copses, etc.

ALDER FLYCATCHER *Empidonax alnorum* 5½″ (14 cm) M 228
This species and the Willow Flycatcher (formerly lumped) can be separated in the field only by voice and habitat.

Voice: Song, an accented *fee-bee'-o.* Note, *pep* or *wit.*

Range: Canada, ne. U.S. Winters in tropical America. **East:** Map 228. **Habitat:** Willows, alders, brushy swamps, swales.

EMPIDONAX FLYCATCHERS

sexes similar

pit-see!

chu-wee

All 5 Empidonax flycatchers have eye-rings and wing bars. Identify by habitat and voice.

...ciduous woods, ...p. beech trees; ...ooded swamps; ...and cen. U.S.

conifer woods, bogs; Canada, n. edge of U.S.

...ACADIAN

...eener than ...ast, Alder, ...or Willow

che-BEK or chebek

YELLOW-BELLIED

breast washed with yellow

fitz-bew

farms, orchards, groves, open woods; n. U.S. and Canada

LEAST

grayest of the group

fee-bee'-o

...et and dry thickets, ...ushy pastures, old ...orchards, willows; ...n. and cen. U.S.

WILLOW

alder swamps, wet thickets, usually near water; n. U.S., Canada

ALDER

199

■ **LARKS Family Alaudidae.** Most larks are streaked, brown, terrestrial birds. The hindclaw is elongated, almost straight. Songs musical; frequently given high in display flight. Often gregarious. Sexes usually similar. **Food:** Mainly seeds, insects. **Range:** Old World (except for Horned Lark). **No. of species:** World, 75; East, 1.

HORNED LARK *Eremophila alpestris* 7–8″ (18–20 cm) **M 229**
Note the head design. A brown ground bird, larger than a sparrow, with black sideburns, 2 small black *horns* (not always noticeable), and a black breast splotch. *Walks,* does not hop. Overhead, pale with a *black* tail; folds wings after each beat. Female and immature are duller, but with the basic pattern.
Voice: Song, tinkling, irregular, high pitched, often prolonged; from ground or high in air. Note, a clear *tsee-titi.*
Range: Breeds widely in N. Hemisphere (south locally to n. Africa, n. S. America); some migration. **East:** Map 229. **Habitat:** Prairies, open fields, golf courses, airports, shores, tundra.

■ **PIPITS Family Motacillidae.** Streaked brown ground birds with white outer tail feathers, long hindclaws, thin bills. They walk briskly instead of hopping, and bob their tails constantly. **Food:** Insects, seeds. **Range:** Nearly cosmopolitan. **No. of species** (including relatives): World, 48; East, 2.

WATER PIPIT *Anthus spinoletta* 6–7″ (15–18 cm) **M 230**
(American Pipit) A slender, brown, sparrow-sized bird of open country. Bill *slender;* underparts buffy with streaks; the *outer tail feathers are white.* Walks; bobs its tail almost constantly. In flight, dips up and down. Learn the note — most are detected as they fly over.
Similar species: Vesper Sparrow (p. 284) and longspurs (p. 264) have thicker bills, do not bob tails. See also Sprague's Pipit.
Voice: Note, a thin *jeet* or *jee-eet.* In aerial flapping song flight, *chwee chwee chwee chwee chwee chwee chwee.*
Range: Colder parts of N. Hemisphere. Winters to Cen. America, n. Africa, s. Asia. **East:** Map 230. **Habitat:** Tundra, alpine slopes; in migration and winter, plains, bare fields, shores.

SPRAGUE'S PIPIT *Anthus spragueii* 6½″ (16 cm) **M 231**
Note the *pale flesh or yellowish legs.* A buffy sparrowlike bird with a striped back and white outer tail feathers. Suggests a Vesper Sparrow or longspur with a *thin bill.* Back streaked with *buff and black.* More solitary than Water Pipit; when flushed, often towers high in aimless flight, then drops.
Similar species: Water Pipit has a darker (not strongly striped) back, deeper buff breast. Legs brown to black.
Voice: Sings high in the air, a sweet thin jingling series descending in pitch: *ching-a-ring-a-ring-a-ring-a* (Salt, Wilk).
Range: Prairie provinces of Canada, n. prairie states. **East:** Map 231. **Habitat:** Plains, short-grass prairies.

LARKS, PIPITS

sexes similar

immature

prairie race

overhead

northern race

HORNED LARK

topside

overhead

tail-wagging

summer

WATER PIPIT

winter

SPRAGUE'S PIPIT

overhead

towering flight

■ SWALLOWS Family Hirundinidae.

Slim, streamlined form and graceful flight characterize these sparrow-sized birds. Tiny feet, long pointed wings, and short bills with very wide gapes. **Food:** Flying insects; also bayberries (Tree Swallow). **Range:** Cosmopolitan except for polar regions and some islands. **No. of species:** World, 75; East, 5 (+6 accidental).

PURPLE MARTIN   *Progne subis*   7¼–8½″ (18–21 cm)   M 232

The largest North American swallow. The male is uniformly blue-black *above and below;* no other swallow is black-bellied. The female is light-bellied; throat and breast grayish, often with a faint collar above. Glides in circles, alternating quick flaps and glides; often spreads tail.

Similar species: (1) Tree Swallow is much smaller than female Purple Martin; immaculate white, no gray on underparts. (2) Starling in flight (triangular wings) may suggest Purple Martin.
Voice: Throaty and rich *tchew-wew,* etc., or *pew, pew.* Song gurgling, ending in a succession of low rich gutturals.
Range: S. Canada to n. Mexico, Gulf states. Winters in S. America.
East: Map 232. **Habitat:** Towns, farms, open or semi-open country, often near water. Attracted to Martin houses.

CLIFF SWALLOW   M 233
Petrochelidon pyrrhonota   5–6″ (13–15 cm)

Note the *rusty* or *buffy* rump. Overhead, the bird appears square-tailed, with a dark throat patch. Glides in a long ellipse, ending each glide with a steep rollercoaster-like climb.

Similar species: Barn Swallow builds an open nest, *usually* but not always *inside* the barn; when nesting on a barn, Cliff Swallow is colonial, building "mud jugs" outside, under the eaves.
Voice: *Zayrp;* a low *chur.* Alarm note, *keer!* Song, creaking notes and guttural gratings; harsher than Barn Swallow's song.
Range: Alaska, Canada to Mexico. Winters Brazil, Argentina, Chile. **East:** Map 233. **Habitat:** Open to semi-open land, farms, cliffs, river bluffs, lakes. Nests colonially on cliffs, barns.

BARN SWALLOW   *Hirundo rustica*   6–7¾″ (15–19 cm)   M 234

Our only swallow that is truly *swallow-tailed;* also the only one with *white tail spots.* Blue-black above; cinnamon-buff below, with a darker throat. Flight direct, close to the ground; wing tips pulled back at the end of the stroke; not much gliding.

Similar species: Most other North American swallows have notched (not deeply forked) tails. See under Cliff Swallow for comparative manner of nesting.
Voice: A soft *vit* or *kvik-kvik, vit-vit.* Also *szee-szah* or *szee.* Anxiety note around nesting barns, a harsh *ee-tee* or *keet.* Song, a long musical twitter interspersed with gutturals.
Range: Widespread in N. Hemisphere. Winters Costa Rica to Argentina, Africa, s. Asia. **East:** Map 234. **Habitat:** Open or semi-open land; farms, fields, marshes, lakes, wires; usually near habitation.

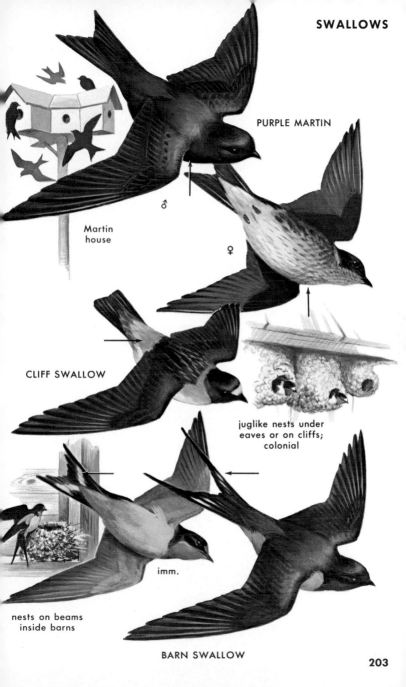

PURPLE MARTIN

♂

Martin
house

♀

CLIFF SWALLOW

juglike nests under
eaves or on cliffs;
colonial

imm.

nests on beams
inside barns

BARN SWALLOW

TREE SWALLOW *Iridoprocne bicolor* 5–6″ (13–15 cm) **M 235**
Steely blue-green-black above, *clear white below.* Immature with
dusky brown back and incomplete breastband may be confused
with Rough-winged Swallow (dingy throat) or Bank Swallow
(complete breastband). Tree Swallow glides in circles, ending each
glide with 3 or 4 quick flaps and a short climb.
Voice: Note, *cheet* or *chi-veet.* A liquid twitter. Song, *weet, trit,
weet,* repeated with variations.
Range: Alaska, Canada to California, cen.-e. U.S. Winters from s.
U.S. to Cen. America. **East:** Map 235. **Habitat:** Open country near
water; marshes, meadows, streams, lakes, wires. Roosts in reeds.
Nests in holes in dead trees, snags, birdhouses.

ROUGH-WINGED SWALLOW **M 236**
Stelgidopteryx ruficollis 5–5¾″ (13–14 cm)
A *brown-backed* swallow, lighter brown than Bank Swallow; *no*
breastband; note the *dusky throat.* Flight unlike Bank Swallow's,
more like Barn Swallow's; wings pulled back at end of stroke.
Voice: A harsh *trrit,* rougher than Bank Swallow's.
Range: S. Canada to Argentina. Winters mostly south of U.S. **East:**
Map 236. **Habitat:** Near streams, lakes, river banks.

BANK SWALLOW *Riparia riparia* 4½–5½″ (11–14 cm) **M 237**
A small *brown-backed* swallow. Note the distinct *dark breast-
band.* Flight irregular, more fluttery than other swallows'.
Similar species: Rough-winged Swallow lacks the breastband, is
usually a solitary nester. (Bank Swallow is colonial.)
Voice: A dry trilled chitter or rattle, *brrt* or *trr-tri-tri.*
Range: Widespread in N. Hemisphere. Winters in S. America,
Africa, s. Asia. **East:** Map 237. **Habitat:** Near water, over fields,
marshes, streams, lakes. Nest colonies in sand banks.

■ **SWIFTS Family Apodidae.** Swallowlike, but structurally
distinct, with flat skull and all 4 toes forward-pointing (hallux
reversible). Flight very rapid, "twinkling," sailing between spurts;
wings often stiffly *bowed.* Sexes similar. **Food:** Flying insects.
Range: Nearly worldwide. **No. of species:** World, 79; East, 2 (+3
accidental).

CHIMNEY SWIFT *Chaetura pelagica* 5–5½″ (12–14 cm) **M 238**
Like a cigar with wings. A blackish swallowlike bird with long,
slightly curved, stiff wings and no apparent tail (unless spread). It
appears to beat its wings not in unison but alternately (actually
this is an illusion); the effect is more batlike, unlike the skimming
of swallows. They seem to fairly twinkle, gliding between spurts,
holding the wings *bowed* in a *crescent.*
Voice: Loud, rapid, ticking or chippering notes.
Range: S. Canada to Gulf of Mexico. Winters in Peru. **East:** Map
238. **Habitat:** Open sky, especially over cities, towns; nests and
roosts in chimneys.

VAUX'S SWIFT *Chaetura vauxi* 4½″ (11 cm)
Like Chimney Swift, but smaller, and paler on underparts.
Range: W. N. America. Very rare, but probably regular in Louisi-
ana from Nov. to March (taken in Baton Rouge).

SWALLOWS,
SWIFTS

sexes similar

TREE
SWALLOW

adult

nests in tree holes
or bird boxes

TREE
SWALLOW

imm.

ank Swallow
colony

BANK SWALLOW

ROUGH-WINGED
SWALLOW

VAUX'S
SWIFT

CHIMNEY
SWIFT

roosting
swifts

SWALLOWS ON A WIRE

Bank

Rough-
winged

Tree

Cliff

Barn

Purple
Martin

■ CROWS, JAYS, ETC. Family Corvidae. Large perching birds with strong longish bills; nostrils covered by forward-pointing bristles. Crows and ravens are very large and black. Jays (p. 208) are often colorful (usually blue). Magpies are black and white with long tails. Sexes alike. Most immatures resemble adults. **Food:** Almost anything edible. **Range:** Cosmopolitan except for s. S. America, some islands, Antarctica. **No. of species:** World, 100; East, 8 (+2 accidental).

FISH CROW *Corvus ossifragus* 16–20″ (40–50 cm)   **M 239**
Listen for this smallish crow near tidewater. Identify it by voice, not size; measurements of the 2 crows broadly overlap.
Similar species: American Crow has a different voice.
Voice: A short nasal *car* or *ca.* Sometimes a 2-syllabled *ca-ha.* (American Crow utters an honest-to-goodness *caw.*) Some calls of young American Crows may sound like those of Fish Crows.
Range: Mostly coastal; s. New England to Florida and e. Texas.
East: Map 239. **Habitat:** Similar to that of American Crow, but more confined to tidewater and lower valleys of large rivers.

AMERICAN CROW   **M 240**
Corvus brachyrhynchos 17–21″ (43–53 cm)
(Common Crow) A large, chunky, ebony bird. Completely black; glossed with purplish in strong sunlight. Bill and feet strong and black. Often gregarious.
Similar species: (1) Northern Raven is larger; has a wedge-shaped tail. (2) Fish Crow is smaller; has a different voice.
Voice: A loud *caw* or *cah* or *kahr;* easily imitated.
Range: Canada to s. U.S., n. Baja California. Partially migratory in the North. **East:** Map 240. **Habitat:** Woodlands, farmland, agricultural fields, river groves, shores.

WHITE-NECKED RAVEN *Corvus cryptoleucus* 19–21″ (48–53 cm)
A small raven of the arid plains, near the size of an American Crow. Flies with the typical flat-winged glide of a raven; has a somewhat wedge-shaped tail. The white feather bases on neck and breast show only when the feathers are ruffled.
Voice: A hoarse *kraak,* flatter and higher than Northern Raven's.
Range: Sw. U.S. to cen. Mexico. **East:** Barely crosses 100th meridian into our area in Oklahoma, Kansas.

NORTHERN RAVEN *Corvus corax* 22–27″ (55–68 cm)   **M 241**
Note the *wedge-shaped tail.* Much larger than American Crow and inclined to be more solitary. Hawklike, it alternates flapping and sailing, gliding on flat wings (Crow's in a slight upward dihedral). When perched, not too distant, note the "goiter" look (shaggy throat feathers) and heavier "Roman nose" bill.
Similar species: American Crow is smaller, has different voice.
Voice: A croaking *cr-r-ruck* or *prruk;* a metallic *tok.*
Range: Widespread in N. America, Eurasia, Africa. **East:** Map 241.
Habitat: Boreal and mt. forests, coastal cliffs, tundra.

CROWS,
RAVENS

Fish Crow

FISH
CROW

American
Crow

WHITE-NECKED
RAVEN

AMERICAN
CROW

Northern
Raven

NORTHERN
RAVEN

207

BLUE JAY *Cyanocitta cristata* 11–12½″ (28–31 cm) **M 242**
A showy, noisy, *blue* bird with a *crest;* larger than a Robin. Bold white spots in wings and tail; whitish or dull gray underparts; black necklace.
Similar species: (1) The dissimilar Bluebird (p. 220) is much smaller (not much larger than a House Sparrow), lacks a crest, and has a ruddy breast. (2) See Belted Kingfisher (p. 186). (3) Scrub Jay of Florida lacks the crest and the white spotting on the wings and tail.
Voice: A harsh slurring *jeeah* or *jay;* a musical *queedle, queedle;* also many other notes. Mimics the calls of Red-shouldered and Red-tailed Hawks.
Range: S. Canada, east of Rockies to Gulf states. **East:** Map 242.
Habitat: Oak and pine woods, suburban gardens, groves, towns.

SCRUB JAY *Aphelocoma coerulescens* 11–12″ (28–30 cm) **M 243**
(Florida Jay) Look for this crestless jay in Florida in stretches of oak scrub. The wings and tail are solid blue (no white markings); the back is brownish tan.
Similar species: The Florida race of the Blue Jay is often present in the same localities, but it has a *crest* and bold white spotting on the wings and tail.
Voice: A rough rasping *kwesh . . . kwesh.* Also a low rasping *zhreek* or *zhrink.*
Range: W. U.S. to s. Mexico. Also cen. Florida. **East:** Map 243.
Habitat: In Florida, mainly scrub, low oaks.

GRAY JAY *Perisoreus canadensis* 11–13″ (28–33 cm) **M 244**
(Canada Jay) A large, fluffy, gray bird of the cool northern woods; larger than a Robin, with a *black* patch or partial cap across the back of the head and a *white forehead* (or crown); suggests a huge overgrown chickadee. Juvenal birds (first summer) are *dark sooty,* almost blackish; the only distinguishing mark is a whitish whisker.
Voice: A soft *whee-ah;* also many other notes, some harsh.
Range: Boreal forests of N. America. **East:** Map 244. **Habitat:** Spruce and fir forests.

BLACK-BILLED MAGPIE **M 245**
Pica pica 17½–22″ (44–55 cm); tail 9½–12″ (24–30 cm)
(American Magpie) A large, slender, black-and-white bird with a long wedge-tipped tail. In flight, the iridescent greenish black tail streams behind; large white patches flash in the wings.
Voice: A harsh rapid *queg queg queg queg.* Also a querulous nasal *maag?* or *aag-aag?*
Range: Eurasia, w. N. America. In winter, a few wander east, rarely to the Great Lakes and casually or accidentally to the northeastern seaboard states. **East:** Map 245. **Habitat:** Rangeland, brushy country, conifers, streamsides.

JAYS,
MAGPIES

sexes alike

BLUE JAY

SCRUB JAY

GRAY JAY
(Canada Jay)

adult

GRAY JAY
juvenal

BLACK-BILLED
MAGPIE

209

■ TITMICE Family Paridae.

Small, plump, small-billed birds; acrobatic when feeding. Often roam in little bands. Sexes usually alike. **Food:** Insects, seeds, acorn masts, berries; at feeders, suet, sunflower seeds. **Range:** Widespread in N. America, Eurasia, Africa. **No. of species:** World, 64; East, 4.

BLACK-CAPPED CHICKADEE   M 246
Parus atricapillus   4¾–5¾″ (12–14 cm)

This small tame acrobat is distinctively patterned with a combination of *black cap and bib, white cheeks.* Sides buffy.
Similar species: See Carolina Chickadee.
Voice: A clearly enunciated *chick-a-dee-dee-dee,* or *dee-dee-dee.* Song, a clear whistle, *fee-bee-ee* or *fee-bee,* first note higher.
Range: Alaska, Canada, northern half of U.S. **East:** Map 246.
Habitat: Mixed and deciduous woods; willow thickets, groves, shade trees. Visits feeders, where it eats suet, sunflower seeds.

CAROLINA CHICKADEE *Parus carolinensis* 4½″ (11 cm) M 247

Nearly identical with the Black-capped Chickadee, but distinctly smaller and lacking the conspicuous white area in the wing created by the white feather edges. The voice is notably different.
Similar species: Replaced by the Black-cap northward. In summer the two are best distinguished by locality and voice. The amount of white in the Black-cap's wing is usually a good distinction, but may not always be reliable because of season, wear, angle of light, etc. Hybrids or intergrades are known.
Voice: The "chickadee" call of this species is higher pitched and more rapid than that of the Black-cap. The 2-noted whistle is replaced by a 4-syllabled *fee-bee, fee-bay.*
Range: Resident from southern edge of range of Black-cap in N.J., Ohio, Mo., Okla. south to Fla., Gulf Coast (Map 247). In borderline areas, check local or state publications for details. Black-cap penetrates range of Carolina in some winters.

BOREAL CHICKADEE *Parus hudsonicus* 5–5½″ (13–14 cm) M 248

Note the *dull brown* cap, rich brown flanks. The small size, black bib, whitish cheeks, and tiny bill mark it as a chickadee, but the general color is *brown* rather than gray.
Voice: Notes, slower, more drawling than the lively *chick-a-dee-dee-dee* of Black-cap; instead, a wheezy *chick-che-day-day.*
Range: Boreal forests of Alaska, Canada, n. New England. **East:** Map 248. **Habitat:** Conifer forests.

TUFTED TITMOUSE *Parus bicolor* 6″ (15 cm)   M 249

A small, gray, mouse-colored bird with a *tufted crest.* Its flanks are rusty. See the waxwings (p. 224).
Voice: A clear whistled chant: *peter, peter, peter,* or *here, here, here, here.* Notes similar to those of chickadees, but more drawling, nasal, wheezy, and complaining.
Range: Southern tip of Ontario south through e. U.S. to Gulf states (Map 249). **Habitat:** Woodlands, shade trees, groves; feeders.

TITMICE

sexes alike

BLACK-
CAPPED
CHICKADEE

CAROLINA
CHICKADEE

BOREAL
CHICKADEE

immature

adult

TUFTED
TITMOUSE

■ **NUTHATCHES Family Sittidae.** Small stout tree-climbers with strong woodpeckerlike bills, strong feet. Stubby square-cut tails not braced like woodpeckers' in climbing. Habitually go down trees *headfirst.* Sexes similar. **Food:** Bark insects, seeds, nuts; attracted by suet, sunflower seeds. **Range:** Most of N. Hemisphere. **No. of species:** World, 31; East, 3.

WHITE-BREASTED NUTHATCH   M 250
Sitta carolinensis   5–6″ (13–15 cm)
Nuthatches climb down trees *headfirst.* This, the most familiar species, is known by its black cap and beady black eye on a white face. The undertail coverts are chestnut.
Voice: Song, a rapid series of low, nasal, whistled notes on one pitch: *whi, whi, whi, whi, whi, whi,* or *who, who, who,* etc. Note, a nasal *yank;* also a nasal *tootoo.*
Range: S. Canada to s. Mexico. **East:** Map 250. **Habitat:** Forests, woodlots, groves, river woods, shade trees; visits feeders.

RED-BREASTED NUTHATCH   M 251
Sitta canadensis   4½″ (11 cm)
A small nuthatch with a *broad black line* through the eye and a white line above it. The underparts are washed with rusty.
Voice: Call higher, more nasal than that of White-breast; *ank* or *enk,* sounding like a baby nuthatch or a tiny tin horn.
Range: Se. Alaska, Canada, w. U.S., ne. U.S. Winters irregularly to s. U.S. **East:** Map 251. **Habitat:** Conifer forests; in winter, also other trees; may visit feeders.

BROWN-HEADED NUTHATCH   *Sitta pusilla*   4½″ (11 cm)   M 252
A dwarf nuthatch of the southern pinelands. Smaller than the White-breast, with a *brown cap coming down to the eye* and a pale or whitish spot on the nape. Travels in groups.
Voice: Unnuthatchlike, a high rapid *kit-kit-kit;* also a squeaky piping *ki-day* or *ki-dee-dee,* constantly repeated, sometimes becoming an excited twitter or chatter.
Range: Se. U.S. (Map 252). **Habitat:** Open pine woods.

■ **CREEPERS Family Certhiidae.** Small, slim, stiff-tailed birds with slender, slightly curved bills used to probe the bark of trees. **Food:** Bark insects. **Range:** Cooler parts of N. Hemisphere. **No. of species:** World, 6; East, 1.

BROWN CREEPER   *Certhia familiaris*   5″ (13 cm)   M 253
A very small, slim, camouflaged tree-climber. Brown above, white below, with a *slender decurved bill,* and a stiff tail, braced when climbing. Ascends trees spirally from the base.
Voice: Note, a single high thin *seee,* similar to quick trebled note (*see-see-see*) of Golden-crowned Kinglet. Song, a thin sibilant *see-ti-wee-tu-wee* or *see-see-see-sisi-see.*
Range: Eurasia, s. Alaska, Canada to Nicaragua. **East:** Map 253. **Habitat:** Woodlands, groves, shade trees.

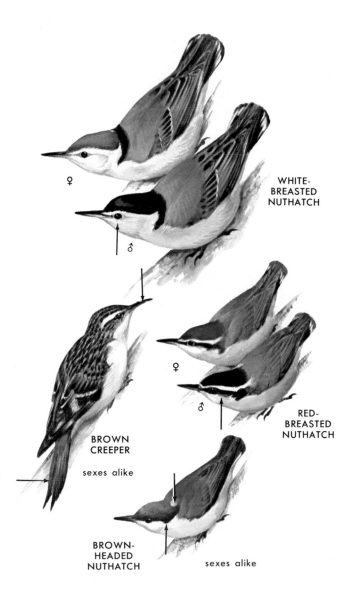

♀

**WHITE-
BREASTED
NUTHATCH**

♂

♀

♂

**RED-
BREASTED
NUTHATCH**

**BROWN
CREEPER**

sexes alike

**BROWN-
HEADED
NUTHATCH**

sexes alike

■ **WRENS Family Troglodytidae.** Small energetic brown birds; stumpy, with slender, slightly decurved bills; tails often cocked. **Food:** Insects, spiders. **Range:** N., Cen., and S. America; only 1 (Winter Wren) in Eurasia. **No. of species:** World, 63; East, 7.

HOUSE WREN *Troglodytes aedon* 4½–5″ (11–13 cm) **M 254**
A small energetic gray-brown wren distinguished from the others by a light eye-ring and lack of facial striping.
Voice: A stuttering gurgling song, rising in a musical burst, then falling at the end.
Range: S. Canada to Argentina (incl. *T. brunneicollis, T. musculus*). Migratory in North. **East:** Map 254. **Habitat:** Open woods, thickets, towns, gardens; often nests in bird boxes.

WINTER WREN *Troglodytes troglodytes* 4″ (10 cm) **M 255**
A very small, round, dark wren known from the House Wren by a *much stubbier tail,* a light line over the eye, and a *dark heavily barred belly.* Often bobs head. Mouselike, stays near the ground.
Voice: Song, a rapid succession of high tinkling warbles and trills, prolonged, often ending on a *very high* light trill. Note, a hard 2-syllabled *kip-kip* (suggests Song Sparrow's *chip*).
Range: Northern parts of N. Hemisphere. **East:** Map 255. **Habitat:** Woodland underbrush; conifer forests (summer).

BEWICK'S WREN *Thryomanes bewickii* 5¼″ (13 cm) **M 256**
Note the long tail with *white corners. White stripe over eye.*
Voice: Song suggests Song Sparrow's, but thinner, starting on 2 or 3 high notes, dropping lower, ending on a thin trill.
Range: S. Canada to Mexico. **East:** Map 256. **Habitat:** Thickets, underbrush, gardens. Often nests in bird boxes.

CAROLINA WREN **M 257**
Thryothorus ludovicianus 5¾″ (14 cm)
A large wren, size of a small sparrow. *Warm reddish brown* above, buff below. Has a conspicuous *white eyebrow stripe.*
Voice: A clear 3-syllabled chant. Variable; *tea-kettle, tea-kettle, tea-kettle, tea,* or *chirpity, chirpity, chirpity, chirp.* Sometimes 2-syllabled.
Range: Resident e. U.S., e. Mexico. **East:** Map 257. **Habitat:** Tangles, brushy undergrowth, suburban gardens, towns.

MARSH WREN *Cistothorus palustris* 5″ (13 cm) **M 258**
(Long-billed Marsh Wren) The conspicuous *white stripes on the back* and the white eyebrow stripe identify this marsh dweller.
Voice: Song, reedy, gurgling, ending in a guttural rattle: *cut-cut-turrrrrrrrr-ur;* often heard at night. Note, a low *tsuck.*
Range: S. Canada to nw. Mexico. Winters to cen. Mexico. **East:** Map 258. **Habitat:** Marshes (cattail, bulrush, brackish).

SEDGE WREN *Cistothorus platensis* 4–4½″ (10–11 cm) **M 259**
(Short-billed Marsh Wren) Differs from Marsh Wren by *buffy* undertail coverts, *streaked* crown. Both have streaked backs.
Voice: Song, a dry staccato chattering: *chap chap chap chap chap chap chap chapper-rrrr.* Call note, *chap.*
Range: S. Canada locally to S. America. **East:** Map 259. **Habitat:** Grassy marshes, sedgy meadows; scarce, local.

ROCK WREN *Salpinctes obsoletus* See p. 216

HOUSE WREN

WINTER WREN

BEWICK'S WREN

CAROLINA WREN

MARSH WREN

SEDGE WREN

ROCK WREN

ROCK WREN *Salpinctes obsoletus* 5½–6½″ (14–16 cm)
(Shown on p. 215.) Western. A gray wren with a *finely streaked breast,* rusty rump, and *buffy tail corners.*
Voice: Song, a harsh chant. A loud dry trill; also *ti-keer.*
Range: Sw. Canada, w. U.S. to Costa Rica. Breeds east to edge of our area in central parts of Dakotas, Neb., Kans., Okla. Accidental east of Miss. River. **Habitat:** Rocky slopes, canyons.

■ **GNATCATCHERS AND KINGLETS** Family Sylviidae.
Tiny active birds with small slender bills. Gnatcatchers have long mobile tails; kinglets short tails, bright crowns. **Food:** Insects, larvae. **Range:** Most large forested areas of world. **No. of species:** World, 332 (including Old World warblers); East, 3.

RUBY-CROWNED KINGLET *Regulus calendula* 4″ (10 cm) **M 261**
A tiny stub-tailed birdlet; olive-gray above, with strong wing bars; male with a *scarlet crown patch* (usually concealed; erect when excited). A conspicuous *broken white eye-ring* gives a big-eyed look. Any kinglet without a crown patch and eye-stripe is this species. Both kinglets flick wings.
Voice: A husky *ji-dit.* Song, quite loud; 3 or 4 high notes, several low notes, and a chant, *tee tee tee, tew tew tew tew, ti-dadee, ti-dadee, ti-dadee.* Variable.
Range: Canada, Alaska, w. U.S. Winters to Gulf, Cen. America. **East:** Map 261. **Habitat:** Conifers; in winter, other woodlands.

GOLDEN-CROWNED KINGLET **M 260**
Regulus satrapa 3½″ (9 cm)
Note the bright crown patch (*yellow* in the female, *orange* in the male) *bordered by black,* and the *whitish eyebrow stripe.* Kinglets are tiny olive-gray birds, smaller than most warblers. An upward flick of the strongly barred wings is characteristic.
Voice: Call note, a high wiry *see-see-see.* Song, a series of high thin notes ascending, then dropping into a little chatter.
Range: S. Alaska, cen. Canada, south in western mts. to Guatemala. In East, to w. N. Carolina; winters to Gulf states. **East:** Map 260. **Habitat:** Conifers; in winter, also other trees.

BLUE-GRAY GNATCATCHER **M 262**
Polioptila caerulea 4½″ (11 cm)
Suggests a miniature Mockingbird. A tiny slender mite, smaller than a chickadee; blue-gray above and whitish below, with a narrow *white eye-ring* and a *long black-and-white tail,* which is often cocked like a wren's tail and flipped about.
Voice: Note, a thin peevish *zpee* or *chee.* Song, a thin, squeaky, wheezy series of notes, easily overlooked.
Range: S. Utah, s. Ontario to Guatemala. Winters to Honduras. **East:** Map 262. **Habitat:** Open woods, oaks, pines, thickets.

■ **BULBULS Family Pycnonotidae.** Birds of Old World tropics; 119 species, 1 of which has been introduced in Florida.

RED-WHISKERED BULBUL *Pycnonotus jocosus* 7″ (18 cm)
Note the *black crest, red cheek patch,* and red undertail coverts. Se. Asia. Established locally in s. Miami, Florida.

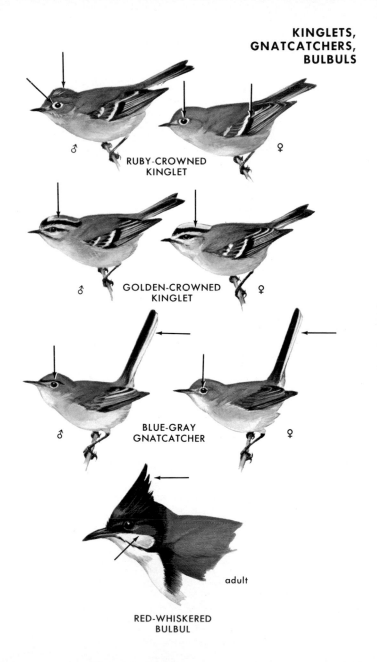

RUBY-CROWNED
KINGLET

♂ ♀

GOLDEN-CROWNED
KINGLET

♂ ♀

BLUE-GRAY
GNATCATCHER

♂ ♀

adult

RED-WHISKERED
BULBUL

■ MOCKINGBIRDS AND THRASHERS Family Mimidae.

Often called "mimic thrushes." Excellent songsters; some mimic other birds. Strong-legged; usually longer-tailed than true thrushes, bill usually more decurved. **Food:** Insects, fruits. **Range:** New World; Canada to Argentina. **No. of species:** World, 30; East, 3 (+3 accidental).

BROWN THRASHER *Toxostoma rufum* 11½″ (29 cm) **M 263**
Slimmer than Robin; *bright rufous* above, *heavily striped* below. Note also wing bars, rather curved bill, long tail, yellow eye.
Similar species: Brown thrushes lack wing bars, are spotted (not striped), and have brown (not yellow) eyes, shorter tails.
Voice: Song, a succession of deliberate notes and phrases resembling Catbird's song, but more musical and each phrase usually *in pairs*. Note, a harsh *chack!*
Range: S. Canada to Gulf states; east of Rockies. **East:** Map 263.
Habitat: Thickets, brush, shrubbery, thorn scrub.

GRAY CATBIRD *Dumetella carolinensis* 9″ (23 cm) **M 264**
Slate-gray; slim. Note the *black cap*. The *chestnut* undertail coverts may not be noticeable. Flips tail jauntily.
Voice: *Catlike mewing,* distinctive. Also a grating *tcheck-tcheck*. Song, disjointed notes and phrases; not repeated as in songs of Mockingbird and Thrasher.
Range: S. Canada, e. and cen. U.S. to Gulf states. Winters mainly s. U.S. to Panama, W. Indies. **East:** Map 264. **Habitat:** Undergrowth, brush, thorn scrub, suburban gardens.

NORTHERN MOCKINGBIRD **M 265**
Mimus polyglottos 9–11″ (23–28 cm)
Gray; slimmer, longer-tailed than Robin. Note the *large white patches* on the wings and tail, conspicuous in flight.
Similar species: Shrikes have black facial masks. See p. 224.
Voice: Song, a varied, prolonged succession of notes and phrases, each repeated a half-dozen times or more before changing. (Thrasher usually repeats once, Catbird does not repeat.) Often heard at night. Many Mockingbirds are excellent mimics of other species. Note, a loud *tchack;* also *chair*.
Range: S. Canada to s. Mexico, W. Indies. Hawaii (introduced).
East: Map 265. **Habitat:** Towns, farms, roadsides, thickets.

■ THRUSHES Family Turdidae. See p. 220.

TOWNSEND'S SOLITAIRE *Myadestes townsendi* 8″ (20 cm)
A slim gray bird with a *white eye-ring, white tail sides,* and *buffy wing patches*. The pattern in the wing and tail give it a not too remote resemblance to a Mockingbird, but note the eye-ring, darker breast, and especially the buff wing patches.
Range: Alaska, nw. Canada to California, n. Mexico. **East:** A very rare or casual winter visitor eastward through the Great Lakes region to the Maritime Provinces and New England.

sexes alike

BROWN THRASHER

GRAY CATBIRD

NORTHERN
MOCKINGBIRD

flight
pattern

wing
flashing

Shrike for
comparison

TOWNSEND'S
SOLITAIRE
(a thrush)

■ THRUSHES Family Turdidae. Large-eyed, slender-billed, usually strong-legged songbirds. The eastern species that bear the name "thrush" are brown-backed with *spotted* breasts. Robins, bluebirds, etc., suggest their relationship through their spot-breasted young. Often fine singers. **Food:** Insects, worms, snails, berries, fruits. **Range:** Nearly worldwide. **No. of species:** World, 304; East, 10 (+2 accidental).

EASTERN BLUEBIRD *Sialia sialis* 7″ (18 cm) **M 266**
A bit larger than a sparrow; a *blue* bird with a *rusty red* breast; appears round-shouldered when perched. Female duller than male; young bird is speckle-breasted, grayish, devoid of red, but always with some telltale blue in wings and tail.
Voice: Note, a musical *chur-wi* or *tru-ly.* Song, 3 or 4 soft gurgling notes.
Range: East of Rockies; s. Canada to Gulf states, also se. Arizona to Nicaragua. Migrant in North. **East:** Map 266. **Habitat:** Open country with scattered trees; farms, roadsides.

MOUNTAIN BLUEBIRD *Sialia currucoides* 7″ (18 cm)
Male: Turquoise-blue, paler below; belly whitish. *Female:* Dull brownish with a touch of blue on rump, tail, and wings.
Range: Alaska, w. Canada to sw. U.S. **East:** Rare wanderer east of 100th meridian on Great Plains. Accidental s. Ont., e. U.S.

AMERICAN ROBIN **M 267**
Turdus migratorius 9–11″ (23–28 cm)
A very familiar bird, often seen walking with an erect stance on lawns. Recognized by its dark gray back and brick-red breast. Head and tail of male are blackish; female's grayer. Young bird has a speckled breast, but the rusty wash identifies it.
Voice: Song, a clear caroling; short phrases, rising and falling, often prolonged. Notes, *tyeep* and *tut-tut-tut.*
Range: Alaska, Canada to s. Mexico. Winters mainly south of Canada. **East:** Map 267. **Habitat:** Cities, towns, farmland, lawns, shade trees, forests; in winter, berry-bearing trees.

VARIED THRUSH *Ixoreus naevius* 9–10″ (23–25 cm)
A casual winter straggler from the Northwest. Similar to Robin; distinguished by *orangish eye-stripe* and *wing bars,* and wide black (male) or gray (female) *band* across the rusty breast.
Range: Alaska, w. Canada, nw. U.S. **East:** Casual; many recent winter records at feeders from maritime Canada to se. U.S.

NORTHERN WHEATEAR *Oenanthe oenanthe* 6″ (15 cm) **M 268**
A dapper sparrow-sized ground bird of arctic barrens. Restless, flitting from rock to rock, fanning its tail, and bobbing. Note the conspicuous white rump and sides of tail. Black of tail forms a broad inverted T. Breeding male has a blue-gray back, black wings, black ear patch, buff underparts. Autumn male is buffier with a brownish back. Female resembles autumn male.
Voice: Note, a hard *chak-chak* or *chack-weet, weet-chack.*
Range: Eurasia, Alaska, nw. and ne. Canada, Greenland. Migrates to Africa, India. Casual autumn stray to e. U.S. **East:** Map 268. **Habitat:** In summer, rocky tundra, barren slopes.

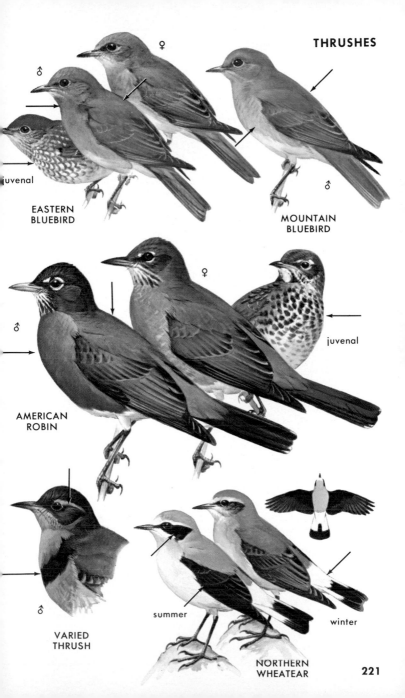

THRUSHES

♂ ♀

juvenal

EASTERN
BLUEBIRD

MOUNTAIN
BLUEBIRD

♂

♀

juvenal

AMERICAN
ROBIN

♂

VARIED
THRUSH

summer

winter

NORTHERN
WHEATEAR

221

GRAY-CHEEKED THRUSH   M 269
Catharus minimus   7–8″ (18–20 cm)

A dull gray-brown thrush, distinguished from Swainson's Thrush by its *grayish* cheeks and less conspicuous eye-ring.
Voice: Song, thin and nasal; suggests Veery's, but often rising abruptly at close (Veery's goes down): *whee-wheeoo-titi-whee.* Note, *vee-a* or *quee-a,* higher and more nasal than Veery's note.
Range: Ne. Siberia, Alaska, Canada, ne. U.S. Winters in W. Indies and n. S. America. **East:** Map 269. **Habitat:** Boreal forests, tundra scrub; in migration, other woodlands.

SWAINSON'S THRUSH   *Catharus ustulatus*   7″ (18 cm)   M 270
(Olive-backed Thrush) A spotted thrush that is uniformly gray-brown above without warm tones is one of 2 species. If it has a *buffy eye-ring* and buff cheeks and upper breast, it is Swainson's Thrush. (Gray-cheek lacks the eye-ring.)
Voice: Song, breezy flutelike phrases; each phrase sliding *upward.* Note, *whit.* Migrants at night, a short *heep.*
Range: Alaska, Canada, w. and ne. U.S. Winters Mexico to Peru.
East: Map 270. **Habitat:** Spruce forests; in migration, other woods.

HERMIT THRUSH   *Catharus guttatus*   7″ (18 cm)   M 271
A spotted brown thrush with a *reddish* tail. When perched it has a habit of cocking its tail and dropping it slowly.
Similar species: (1) Fox Sparrow (reddish tail) has a conical bill, is more streaked. (2) See the other brown thrushes.
Voice: Note, a low *chuck;* also a scolding *tuk-tuk-tuk* and a harsh *pay.* Song, clear, ethereal, flutelike; 3 or 4 phrases at *different pitches,* each with a *long introductory note.*
Range: Alaska, Canada, w. and ne. U.S. Winters U.S. to Guatemala. **East:** Map 271. **Habitat:** Conifer or mixed woods, forest floors; in winter, woods, thickets, parks.

VEERY   *Catharus fuscescens*   6½–7½″ (16–19 cm)   M 272
Note the *uniform warm brown or tawny* cast above. No strong eye-ring (may have a dull whitish ring). Of all our brown thrushes, the least spotted; the spots are often indistinct.
Voice: Song, liquid, breezy, ethereal; wheeling downward: *vee-ur, vee-ur, veer, veer.* Note, a low *phew* or *view.*
Range: S. Canada, n. and cen. U.S. Winters Cen. and n. S. America.
East: Map 272. **Habitat:** Damp deciduous woods.

WOOD THRUSH   *Hylocichla mustelina*   8″ (20 cm)   M 273
Rusty-headed. Smaller than Robin; plumper than the other brown thrushes; distinguished by the deepening redness about the head and the larger, more numerous *round* spots.
Voice: Song, flutelike; phrases rounder than those of other thrushes. Listen for a flutelike *ee-o-lay.* Occasional guttural notes are distinctive. Call, a rapid *pip-pip-pip-pip.*
Range: Se. Canada, e. U.S. (Map 273). Winters to Panama. **Habitat:** Mainly deciduous woodlands.

BROWN THRUSHES

sexes alike

GRAY-CHEEKED THRUSH

SWAINSON'S THRUSH

HERMIT THRUSH

VEERY

WOOD THRUSH

juv.

- **SHRIKES Family Laniidae.** Songbirds with hook-tipped bills and hawklike behavior. Perch watchfully on tree tips, wires. Prey is impaled on thorns, barbed wire. **Food:** Insects, lizards, mice, small birds. **Range:** Widespread in Old World; 2 in N. America. **No. of species:** World, 74; East, 2.

NORTHERN SHRIKE *Lanius excubitor* 9–10″ (23–25 cm) **M 274**
Very similar to Loggerhead Shrike, but note the *faintly barred* breast and *pale base* of lower mandible. Bill longer, more strongly hooked. Young bird brown with *fine bars* on breast.
Similar species: Adult Loggerhead Shrike has a solid-black bill. Black mask meets over base of bill. Juvenal Loggerhead may have faint barring, but is grayer than young Northern.
Voice: Song, a disjointed thrasherlike succession of harsh notes and musical notes. Note, *shek-shek;* a grating *jaaeg.*
Range: Alaska, Canada, Eurasia, n. Africa. Winters to cen. U.S. **East:** Map 274. **Habitat:** Semi-open country with lookout posts.

LOGGERHEAD SHRIKE *Lanius ludovicianus* 9″ (23 cm) **M 275**
A big-headed, slim-tailed, gray, black, and white bird with a *black mask;* a bit smaller than a Robin. Shrikes sit quietly on wires or bush tops; taking off, they fly low with flickering flight, showing white patches; swoop upward to perch.
Similar species: (1) Mockingbird (p. 218) has a longer tail, larger wing patches, and lacks the mask. Flight less flickering (a rowing motion). (2) See Northern Shrike (above).
Voice: Song, harsh deliberate notes and phrases, repeated Mockingbird-like 3–20 times; *queedle, queedle,* over and over, or *tsurp-see, tsurp-see.* Note, *shack, shack.*
Range: S. Canada to s. Mexico. **East:** Map 275. **Habitat:** Semi-open country with lookout posts, wires, trees, scrub.

- **WAXWINGS Family Bombycillidae.** Sleek; crested. Red waxy tips on secondaries. Gregarious. **Food:** Berries, insects. **Range:** N. Hemisphere. **No. of species:** World, 3; East, 2.

BOHEMIAN WAXWING *Bombycilla garrulus* 8″ (20 cm) **M 276**
Similar to Cedar Waxwing; larger, grayer (no yellow on belly); wings with strong white or *white and yellow* markings. Note the *deep rusty* undertail coverts (white in Cedar Waxwing).
Voice: *Zreee,* rougher than note of Cedar Waxwing.
Range: N. Eurasia, nw. N. America. Winters to s. Eurasia, ne. and sw. U.S. **East:** Map 276. **Habitat:** Boreal forests, muskeg; in winter, widespread in search of berries.

CEDAR WAXWING *Bombycilla cedrorum* 7″ (18 cm) **M 277**
Note the *yellow band* at the tail tip. A sleek, crested, brown bird, larger than a House Sparrow. Adults have *waxy red tips* on secondaries. Juvenal is grayer, softly streaked below. Gregarious; fly in compact flocks. Often indulge in fly-catching.
Voice: A high thin lisp or *zeee;* sometimes slightly trilled.
Range: Se. Alaska, Canada, to s.-cen. U.S. Winters s. Canada to Panama. **East:** Map 277. **Habitat:** Open woodlands, fruiting trees, orchards; in winter, widespread, irregular.

SHRIKES

imm.   sexes similar

NORTHERN
SHRIKE

LOGGERHEAD
SHRIKE

WAXWINGS

juvenal

♂

♂

BOHEMIAN
WAXWING

CEDAR
WAXWING

■ VIREOS Family Vireonidae. Small olive- or gray-backed birds, much like wood warblers, but usually less active. Bills with a more curved ridge and a slight hook. May be divided into those with wing bars (and eye-rings) and those without (these have eye-stripes). Those with wing bars and eye-rings may be confused with *Empidonax* flycatchers (p. 198), but do not have the erect posture. **Food:** Mostly insects. **Range:** Canada to Argentina. **No. of species:** World, 41; East, 9 (+2 accidental).

RED-EYED VIREO *Vireo olivaceus* 6″ (15 cm) **M 278**
Note the *gray cap* contrasting with the olive back, and the strong *black-bordered white eyebrow stripe*. The red iris is not obvious at any distance. The iris is brown in immature birds in fall.
Similar species: Warbling Vireo is paler, more uniform above; no black borders on eyebrow stripe. Song very different.
Voice: Song, short abrupt phrases of Robin-like character, separated by deliberate pauses, repeated as often as 40 times per minute; monotonous. Note, a nasal whining *chway.*
Range: Canada to Gulf states. Winters in Amazon basin. **East:** Map 278. **Habitat:** Woodlands, shade trees, groves.

BLACK-WHISKERED VIREO **M 279**
Vireo altiloquus 5″ (13 cm)
Note the narrow *black whisker* on each side of the throat. Otherwise very similar to Red-eyed Vireo. Song similar.
Range: Breeds W. Indies and s. Florida. Winters to n. S. America. **East:** Map 279. **Habitat:** Mangroves; low woods.

WARBLING VIREO *Vireo gilvus* 5″ (13 cm) **M 280**
Three common vireos lack wing bars. In this one, note the whitish breast, and lack of black borders on the eyebrow stripe.
Similar species: (1) Philadelphia Vireo is yellowish below. (2) Red-eyed Vireo has black borders on the eyebrow stripe.
Voice: Song, a languid warble, unlike the broken phrases of other vireos; suggests Purple Finch's song, but less spirited, with a burry undertone. Note, a wheezy querulous *twee.*
Range: Canada to s. U.S., n. and w. Mexico. Winters Mexico and Guatemala. **East:** Map 280. **Habitat:** Deciduous and mixed woods, aspen groves, poplars, shade trees.

PHILADELPHIA VIREO *Vireo philadelphicus* 4¾″ (12 cm) **M 281**
This warblerlike vireo combines unbarred wings and strongly *yellow-tinged* underparts (especially across the breast).
Similar species: (1) Warbling Vireo usually lacks yellow (but may have a tinge on the sides). Note the *dark loral spot* (between the eye and bill) in the Philadelphia. (2) Fall Tennessee Warbler (p. 250) has clear white undertail coverts. (3) See also fall female and immature Black-throated Blue Warbler (p. 250).
Voice: Song similar to Red-eyed Vireo's; higher, slower.
Range: S. Canada, ne. edge of U.S. Winters in Cen. America. **East:** Map 281. **Habitat:** Second growth; poplars, willows, alders.

VIREOS
Without wing bars

sexes similar

imm.

RED-EYED
VIREO

BLACK-WHISKERED
VIREO

WARBLING
VIREO

showing
variation

PHILADELPHIA
VIREO

YELLOW-THROATED VIREO *Vireo flavifrons* 5″ (13 cm) **M 282**
Note the *bright yellow* throat, *yellow* "spectacles," and white wing bars. Our only vireo with *bright* yellow.
Similar species: (1) Yellow-breasted Chat lacks wing bars. (2) Pine Warbler has dusky streaks on sides, white tail spots.
Voice: Song, similar to Red-eyed Vireo's, but more musical, lower pitched; has a burry quality and longer pauses between phrases. One phrase sounds like *ee-yay* or *three-eight*.
Range: E. U.S., se. Canada. Winters in tropical America. **East:** Map 282. **Habitat:** Deciduous woodlands, shade trees.

WHITE-EYED VIREO *Vireo griseus* 5″ (13 cm) **M 283**
Note the combination of *yellow* "spectacles," *whitish* throat. Additional points are 2 wing bars, yellowish sides, *white eyes*.
Similar species: See (1) Solitary Vireo (*white* "spectacles"); (2) Yellow-throated Vireo (*yellow* throat); (3) *Empidonax* flycatchers (p. 198).
Voice: Song, unvireolike, a sharply enunciated *chick'-a-per-weeoo-chick'*. Variable: note the *chick'* at beginning or end.
Range: E. U.S. Winters s. U.S. to Nicaragua. **East:** Map 283. **Habitat:** Wood edges, brush, brambles, undergrowth.

BELL'S VIREO *Vireo bellii* 4½–5″ (11–13 cm) **M 284**
Small, grayish; nondescript. 1 or 2 light wing bars, pale yellowish-washed sides. Distinguished from Warbling Vireo by the wing bar(s) and whitish eye-ring.
Similar species: Young White-eyed Vireo has dark eyes.
Voice: Sings as if through clenched teeth; husky, unmusical phrases at short intervals: *cheedle cheedle chee? cheedle cheedle chew!* First phrase ends with a rising inflection; second phrase has a downward inflection.
Range: Cen. and sw. U.S., n. Mexico. Winters Mexico to Nicaragua. **East:** Map 284. **Habitat:** Willows, streamsides.

SOLITARY VIREO *Vireo solitarius* 5–6″ (13–15 cm) **M 285**
Note the *white* "spectacles," *blue-gray* head, olive back, and *snow-white* throat. 2 white wing bars. Earliest spring vireo.
Voice: Song, whistled phrases with short pauses. Similar to Red-eyed Vireo's song, but more deliberate, higher, sweeter.
Range: Canada to El Salvador. Winters s. U.S. to Nicaragua, Cuba. **East:** Map 285. **Habitat:** Mixed conifer-deciduous woods.

BLACK-CAPPED VIREO *Vireo atricapilla* 4½″ (11 cm)
A small sprightly vireo with the top and sides of head *glossy black* in male, slaty gray in female. Conspicuous "spectacles" formed by eye-ring and loral patch; 2 wing bars; eyes *red*.
Similar species: Female may be mistaken for Solitary Vireo, but eyes red.
Voice: Song, hurried, harsh; phrases remarkable for variety, and restless, almost angry quality. Alarm note, a harsh *chit-ah*.
Range: Breeds sw. Kansas, cen. Oklahoma, w. and cen. Texas (Edwards Plateau) to Coahuila, Mexico. Winters in w. Mexico **Habitat:** Oak scrub, brushy hillsides, canyons.

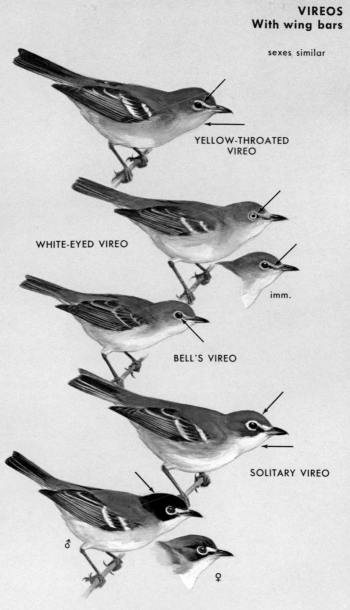

YELLOW-THROATED
VIREO

WHITE-EYED VIREO

imm.

BELL'S VIREO

SOLITARY VIREO

♂

♀

BLACK-CAPPED VIREO

■ WOOD WARBLERS Family Parulidae.

Brightly colored active birdlets, usually smaller than sparrows with thin needle-pointed bills. The majority have some yellow. Identification in autumn is often difficult (see pp. 248–250). **Food:** Mainly insects. **Range:** Alaska and Canada to n. Argentina. **No. of species:** World, 114; East, 40 (+7 accidental).

NORTHERN PARULA WARBLER   M 287

Parula americana   4½″ (11 cm)

A bluish warbler with a yellow throat and breast and 2 conspicuous white wing bars. A suffused greenish patch on the back is a clinching point. In the male the most useful mark is a *dark band* across the breast (indistinct or lacking in the female).

Voice: Song, a buzzy trill or rattle that climbs the scale and trips over at the top: *zeeeeeeeee-up.* Also a series of buzzy notes terminating in the trill *zh-zh-zh-zheeeeee.*

Range: Se. Canada, e. U.S. (Map 287). Winters Florida, Mexico to W. Indies, Nicaragua. **Habitat:** Breeds mainly in humid woods where either *Usnea* or Spanish Moss hangs from the trees (but also in some woods where neither is found).

"SUTTON'S" WARBLER   *Dendroica dominica × Parula americana*

Known from only 2 specimens taken in e. W. Virginia; several sight records. Regarded as a hybrid between Yellow-throated and Parula Warblers. Looks like Yellow-throated, but lacks side stripes; has greenish back of Parula. Song like Parula's, but doubled by repetition: *zeeeeeeeee-up zeeeeeeeee-up.*

YELLOW-THROATED WARBLER   M 288

Dendroica dominica   5–5½″ (13–14 cm)

A gray-backed warbler with a yellow bib. White eyebrow stripe, 2 white wing bars, black stripes on sides. Sexes similar. Creeps about branches of trees.

Voice: Song, a series of clear slurred notes dropping slightly in pitch: *tee-ew, tew, tew, tew, tew, tew wi* (last note rising).

Range: E. and cen. U.S. (Map 288). Winters s. U.S. to Costa Rica. **Habitat:** Open woodlands, groves, especially Live Oaks, pines.

BLACK-THROATED GREEN WARBLER   M 289

Dendroica virens   4½–5″ (11–13 cm)

Male: Note the bright *yellow face,* framed by the black throat and olive-green crown. *Female:* Recognized by the yellow face; much less black on throat. *Immature, fall:* See p. 248.

Voice: A lisping dreamy *zoo zee zoo zoo zee* or *zee zee zee zee zoo zee,* the *zee* notes on same pitch, the *zoo* notes lower.

Range: Canada, ne. U.S. and south in Appalachians. Winters s. Texas to Colombia. **East:** Map 289. **Habitat:** Mainly conifers.

PROTHONOTARY WARBLER   M 286

Protonotaria citrea   5½″ (14 cm)

A golden bird of wooded swamps. Entire head and breast deep yellow, almost orange. Wings blue-gray; no bars. Female duller.

Similar species: See (1) Yellow Warbler, (2) Blue-winged Warbler.

Voice: Song, *zweet zweet zweet zweet zweet zweet,* on one pitch.

Range: Great Lakes area to Gulf states (Map 286). Winters se Mexico to Colombia, Venezuela. **Habitat:** Wooded swamps.

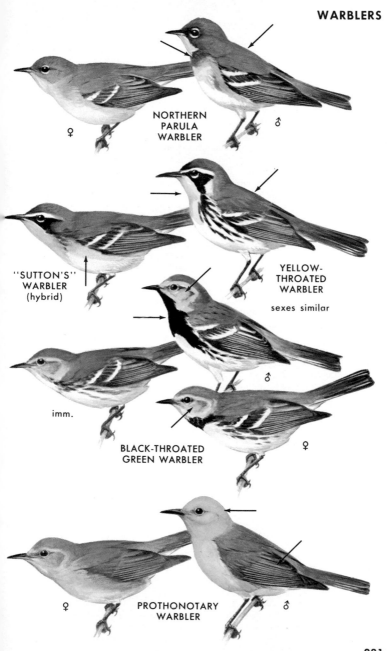

WARBLERS

NORTHERN
PARULA
WARBLER

♀   ♂

"SUTTON'S"
WARBLER
(hybrid)

YELLOW-
THROATED
WARBLER

sexes similar

imm.

BLACK-THROATED
GREEN WARBLER

♂

♀

PROTHONOTARY
WARBLER

♀   ♂

BLACK-AND-WHITE WARBLER M 290
Mniotilta varia   4½–5½″ (11–14 cm)
> *Striped lengthwise* with *black and white;* creeps along the trunks and branches of trees. Has a *striped crown,* white stripes on the back. Female has whiter underparts.
> **Voice:** Song, a thin *weesee weesee weesee weesee weesee weesee;* suggests one of Redstart's songs, but higher pitched and longer. A second, more rambling song drops in pitch midway.
> **Range:** Canada to Gulf states. Winters s. U.S. to n. S. America.
> **East:** Map 290. **Habitat:** Woods; trunks, limbs of trees.

BLACKPOLL WARBLER   *Dendroica striata*   5″ (13 cm)   M 291
> *Male, spring:* A striped gray warbler with a *black cap* and *white cheeks. Female, spring:* Less heavily streaked, lacking black cap; greenish gray above, white below, streaked. *Autumn:* Olive above, greenish yellow below, faintly streaked; 2 wing bars, white under-tail coverts, usually *pale yellowish* legs; see p. 248.
> **Similar species:** (1) Black-and-white Warbler has white stripe through crown. (2) See fall Bay-breasted Warbler (p. 248).
> **Voice:** Song, a thin deliberate, mechanical *zi-zi-zi-zi-zi-zi-zi-zi-zi* on one pitch, becoming stronger, then diminishing.
> **Range:** Alaska, Canada, ne. U.S. Winters in tropical S. America.
> **East:** Map 291. **Habitat:** Conifers; in migration, other trees.

BLACK-THROATED GRAY WARBLER
Dendroica nigrescens   4½–5″ (11–13 cm)
> *Male:* Gray, with black throat, cheek, and crown patches separated by white. *Female: Slaty* crown and cheek, light throat.
> **Range:** W. N. America. **East:** Casual stray east to Atlantic states. Very rare, but perhaps regular in winter in s. La., s. Fla.

BLACK-THROATED BLUE WARBLER M 292
Dendroica caerulescens   5–5½″ (13–14 cm)
> *Male:* Clean-cut; upper parts *blue-gray,* throat and sides *black,* belly white. *Female:* Brown-backed with a light line over the eye and a small *white wing spot* (not always visible). Immature and fall female may lack the white "pocket handkerchief," but note the *dark cheek.* See also p. 250.
> **Voice:** Song, husky, lazy *zur, zur, zur, zreee,* or *beer, beer, beer, bee* (ending higher). May be shortened to 2 or 3 notes.
> **Range:** E. N. America (Map 292). Winters mainly W. Indies. **Habitat:** Undergrowth of deciduous and mixed woodlands.

CERULEAN WARBLER   *Dendroica cerulea*   4½″ (11 cm)   M 293
> *Male: Blue* above, white below. Overhead, note the *narrow black ring* across the chest. *Female:* Blue-gray and olive-green above, whitish below; 2 white wing bars and white eyebrow stripe.
> **Similar species:** Female suggests (1) Tennessee Warbler (p. 240), latter has no wing bars; also (2) fall Blackpoll (p. 248), but greener above, whitish below, with a more conspicuous eyebrow.
> **Voice:** Song suggests Parula's; rapid buzzy notes on same pitch, followed by a longer note on a higher pitch: *zray zray zray zreeeee.* Also has the quality of Black-throated Blue's.
> **Range:** E. U.S. (Map 293). Winters Colombia to n. Bolivia. **Habitat:** Deciduous forests, especially in river valleys.

WARBLERS
**Black-striped,
gray, or bluish**

BLACK-AND-
WHITE WARBLER

♀

♂

BLACKPOLL
WARBLER

winter

summer

♂

♀

BLACK-THROATED
GRAY WARBLER
(accidental)

♂

♀

imm.

BLACK-THROATED
BLUE WARBLER

♀

♂

CERULEAN
WARBLER

♀

♂

MAGNOLIA WARBLER *Dendroica magnolia* 4¾″ (12 cm) **M 294**
The "Black and Yellow" Warbler. Upper parts blackish, with large white patches on the wings and tail; underparts yellow, with heavy black stripes. In any plumage, note the black tail crossed midway by a *broad white band* (from below, the tail looks white with a broad black band at the tip). *Immature:* See p. 248.
Voice: Song suggests Yellow Warbler's but shorter; *weeta weeta weetsee* (last note rising), or *weeta weeta wit-chew*.
Range: Canada, ne. U.S. Winters Mexico, W. Indies to Panama.
East: Map 294. **Habitat:** Low conifers; in migration, other trees.

YELLOW-RUMPED WARBLER   **M 295**
Dendroica coronata 5–6″ (13–15 cm)
("Myrtle" Warbler) Recognized by the bright *yellow rump* and the note (a loud *check*). *Male, spring:* Blue-gray above; heavy black breast patch (like an inverted U); yellow patch on crown and before each wing. *Female, spring:* Brownish; basic pattern similar. *Winter:* Brownish above, whitish below, streaked; *yellow rump.* The western form, "Audubon's" Warbler, accidental in e. U.S., has a *yellow or yellowish* throat.
Voice: Song, a loose Junco-like trill, but rising in pitch or dropping toward the end. Call note, a loud *check*.
Range: Alaska, Canada, ne. U.S. Winters to Panama. **East:** Map 295. **Habitat:** Conifer and mixed forests. In migration and winter, varied; woods, thickets, brush, bayberry scrub.

KIRTLAND'S WARBLER *Dendroica kirtlandii* 6″ (15 cm) **M 296**
Bluish gray above, streaked with black; yellow below, with black spots or streaks *confined to the sides.* Male has a blackish mask. Female is grayer, lacks mask. In autumn, browner. Persistently *jerks tail;* no other gray-backed warbler does this.
Voice: Song, loud and low-pitched for a *Dendroica,* resembles Northern Waterthrush's song; at times suggests House Wren's. Typical song starts with 3 or 4 low staccato notes, continues with rapid ringing notes on a higher pitch, and ends abruptly.
Range: N.-cen. Michigan, nesting in loose colonies in an area about 100 miles long, 60 miles wide (Map 296). Winters Bahamas. **Habitat:** Groves of young Jack Pines 5–18 ft. high with ground cover of blueberries, Bearberry, or Sweetfern.

CANADA WARBLER   **M 297**
Wilsonia canadensis 5–5¾″ (13–14 cm)
The "necklaced" warbler. *Male:* Solid gray above, bright yellow below; with a *necklace of short black stripes. Female and immature* similar, but necklace fainter or lacking. All have yellow "spectacles." In any plumage, gray color above, combined with lack of white in wings and tail, is conclusive.
Voice: Song, a staccato burst, irregularly arranged. *Chip, chupety swee-ditchety* (Gunn). Note, *tchip.*
Range: Canada, ne. U.S.; south in e. mts. Winters n. S. America.
East: Map 297. **Habitat:** Forest undergrowth, shady thickets.

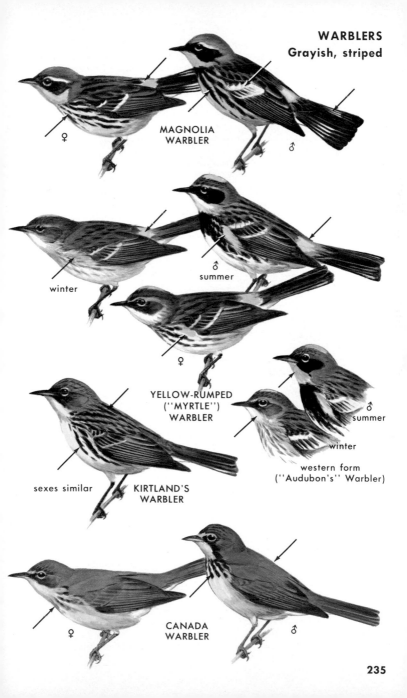

WARBLERS
Grayish, striped

♀

MAGNOLIA
WARBLER

♂

winter

♂
summer

♀

YELLOW-RUMPED
("MYRTLE")
WARBLER

♂
summer

winter

western form
("Audubon's" Warbler)

sexes similar   KIRTLAND'S
WARBLER

♀   CANADA
WARBLER   ♂

235

CAPE MAY WARBLER *Dendroica tigrina* 5″ (13 cm) **M 298**
Male, breeding: Note the *chestnut* cheeks. Yellow below, striped with black; rump yellow, crown black. *Female and autumn:* Lack chestnut cheeks; duller; breast often whitish, streaked. Note the dull *patch of yellow behind the ear.* See also p. 248.
Voice: Song, a very high thin *seet seet seet seet.* Easily confused with song of Bay-breast.
Range: Canada, ne. edge of U.S. Winters in Caribbean area. **East:** Map 298. **Habitat:** Spruces; in migration, other trees.

CHESTNUT-SIDED WARBLER **M 299**
Dendroica pensylvanica 4½–5½″ (11–14 cm)
Adult, spring: Readily identified by the combination of *yellow crown, chestnut sides. Autumn:* Lemon-greenish above, white below. Narrow white eye-ring, 2 pale yellow wing bars. Adults retain some chestnut. *Immature:* See p. 248.
Voice: Song, similar to Yellow Warbler's; *see see see see Miss Beech'er* or *please please pleased to meet'cha,* penultimate note accented, last note dropping. Also a more rambling song.
Range: S. Canada, ne. U.S.; south in mts. Winters in Cen. America. **East:** Map 299. **Habitat:** Slashings, bushy pastures.

BAY-BREASTED WARBLER **M 300**
Dendroica castanea 5–6″ (13–15 cm)
Male, spring: Dark-looking with *chestnut throat, upper breast,* and sides. Note the *large spot* of *pale buff* on the neck. *Female, spring:* Paler, more washed out. *Autumn:* Olive-green above; 2 white wing bars, dull buff-white below. May have trace of bay on sides. *Buff* undertail coverts, dark legs. See p. 248.
Similar species: See fall Blackpoll Warbler (p. 248).
Voice: A high sibilant *tees teesi teesi;* resembles song of Black-and-white; thinner, shorter, more on one pitch.
Range: Canada, ne. edge of U.S. Winters Panama to Venezuela. **East:** Map 300. **Habitat:** Woodlands; conifers (summer).

BLACKBURNIAN WARBLER *Dendroica fusca* 5″ (13 cm) **M 301**
The "fire throat." *Male, spring:* Black and white, with *flaming orange* on head, throat. *Female:* Paler; some orange on throat. *Autumn:* Paler; note yellow head stripes, pale back stripes.
Voice: Song, *zip zip zip titi tseeeeee,* ending on a very high up-slurred note (inaudible to some ears). Also a 2-parted *teetsa teetsa teetsa teetsa zizizizizi,* more like Nashville's song.
Range: Canada, ne. U.S.; south in mts. **East:** Map 301. Winters Costa Rica to Peru. **Habitat:** Woodlands; conifers (summer).

AMERICAN REDSTART *Setophaga ruticilla* 5″ (13 cm) **M 302**
Butterflylike, actively flitting, with drooping wings and spread tail. *Male:* Black; *bright orange patches* on wings and tail. *Female:* Olive-brown; *yellow flash-patches* on wings and tail. *Immature male:* Like female, but tinged with orange.
Voice: Songs (often alternated), *zee zee zee zee zwee* (last note higher), *tsee tsee tsee tsee tsee-o* (last syllable dropping), and *teetsa teetsa teetsa teetsa teet* (notes paired).
Range: Canada, e. U.S. Winters Mexico, W. Indies to Brazil, n. Peru. **East:** Map 302. **Habitat:** Deciduous woods, saplings.

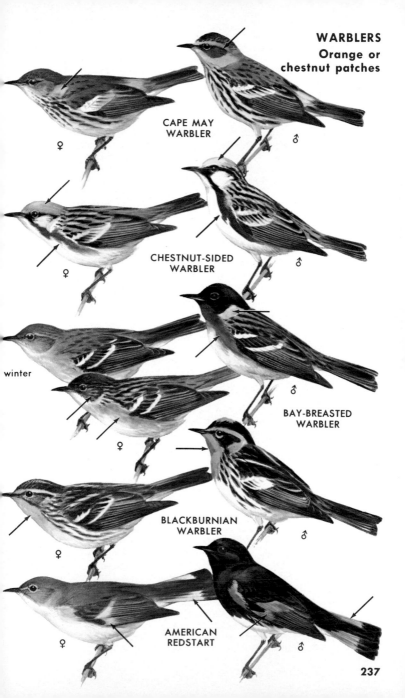

WARBLERS
Orange or
chestnut patches

CAPE MAY
WARBLER

♀

♂

CHESTNUT-SIDED
WARBLER

♀

♂

winter

♀

♂

BAY-BREASTED
WARBLER

BLACKBURNIAN
WARBLER

♀

♂

AMERICAN
REDSTART

♀

♂

237

PINE WARBLER *Dendroica pinus* 5–5½″ (13–14 cm) **M 303**
No other bright yellow–breasted warbler lacking other conspicuous field marks has *white wing bars*. Breast dimly streaked, back
unstreaked; white spots in tail corners. ♀ duller than ♂. Immature
and autumn ♀ obscure; see fall warblers, p. 248.
Voice: Song, a trill on one pitch like Chipping Sparrow's song, but
looser, more musical, slower.
Range: E. N. America, W. Indies. Winters in s. part of range. **East:**
Map 303. **Habitat:** Chiefly open pine woods, pine barrens.

PRAIRIE WARBLER *Dendroica discolor* 5″ (13 cm) **M 304**
This warbler *bobs its tail* (so does Palm Warbler); underparts
yellow; black stripes *confined to sides. 2 black face marks,* 1
through the eye, 1 below. At close range, chestnut marks may be
seen on back of ♂ (reduced in ♀). *Immature:* See p. 248.
Voice: Song, a thin *zee zee zee zee zee zee zee zee;* up scale.
Range: E. N. America (Map 304). Winters Florida to Nicaragua.
Habitat: Brushy slashings, bushy pastures, low pines.

PALM WARBLER **M 305**
Dendroica palmarum 4½–5½″ (11–14 cm)
Note the constant *bobbing* of the tail. Brown above; yellowish or
whitish below, narrowly streaked; *yellow* undertail coverts, white
spots in the tail corners. In spring a *chestnut cap* (obscure in fall,
winter; see p. 248). Sexes similar.
Voice: Song, weak repetitious notes, *zhe-zhe-zhe-zhe-zhe-zhe.*
Range: Canada, ne. edge of U.S. Winters in s. U.S., Caribbean area.
East: Map 305. **Habitat:** Wooded borders of muskeg (summer). In
migration, low trees, bushes, ground. Ground-loving.

"BREWSTER'S" WARBLER
Vermivora chrysoptera × *pinus* or *V. "leucobronchialis"*
Golden-winged and Blue-winged Warblers commonly hybridize
where their ranges overlap, producing 2 distinct types, "Lawrence's" and "Brewster's" (the more frequent hybrid). Typical
"Brewster's" is like Blue-wing with whitish underparts. Some have
white wing bars, others yellow; some are tinged with yellow below.
The black eye mark and the white or largely white (not solid-
yellow) underparts are diagnostic. May sing like either parent.

BLUE-WINGED WARBLER **M 306**
Vermivora pinus 4½–5″ (11–13 cm)
Face and underparts yellow; wings with *2 white bars*. Note the
narrow *black mark through the eye*. Sexes similar.
Voice: Song, a buzzy *beeee-bzzz* (as if inhaled and exhaled).
Range: E. U.S. (Map 306). Winters Mexico to Panama. **Habitat:**
Woodland openings, undergrowth, bushy edges, slashings.

YELLOW WARBLER *Dendroica petechia* 5″ (13 cm) **M 307**
No other warbler is so extensively yellow. Even the *tail spots are
yellow* (white in many other species). Male has *rusty breast
streaks* (in female, faint or lacking). *Fall:* See p. 248.
Voice: Song, a cheerful bright *tsee-tsee-tsee-tsee-titi-wee* or *weet
weet weet weet tsee tsee,* given rapidly. Variable.
Range: Alaska, Canada to cen. Peru. Winters Mexico to Peru. **East:**
Map 307. **Habitat:** Bushes, swamp edges, streams, gardens.

WARBLERS

Olive or yellow with streaks or wing bars

imm.

PINE
WARBLER

♂

♀

PRAIRIE
WARBLER

♂

♂
western race

PALM
WARBLER

winter

♂
yellowish race

hybrid
(Blue-wing X
Golden-wing)

♂

"BREWSTER'S"
WARBLER

♂

BLUE-WINGED
WARBLER

♀

YELLOW
WARBLER

♂

SWAINSON'S WARBLER   M 308
Limnothlypis swainsonii   5″ (13 cm)
A skulker, seldom seen. Olive-brown above, and plain buffy white below, with a *brown crown* and *light eyebrow stripe*. Sexes alike.
Voice: Song suggests Louisiana Waterthrush's, but shorter (5 notes: 2 slurred notes, 2 lower notes, and 1 higher note).
Range: Se. U.S. (Map 308). Winters in W. Indies, Yucatan Peninsula. **Habitat:** Swamps, bogs, stream bottoms, woodland brush; locally in rhododendron-hemlock tangles in cen. Appalachians.

WORM-EATING WARBLER   M 309
Helmitheros vermivorus   5–5½″ (13–14 cm)
A modest forager of leaf-strewn wooded slopes. Heard more often than seen. Dull olive, with *black stripes* on a buffy head. Breast rich buff. Sexes alike.
Voice: Song, a thin dry buzz; resembles trill or rattle of Chipping Sparrow, but thinner, more rapid, and insectlike.
Range: E. U.S. (west to Kansas, ne. Texas); Map 309. Winters W. Indies, Cen. America. **Habitat:** Dry wooded hills, undergrowth, ravines.

TENNESSEE WARBLER   M 310
Vermivora peregrina   4¾″ (12 cm)
Quite plain. *Male, spring:* Note the white eyebrow stripe and gray head contrasting with the greenish back. *Female, spring:* Similar; head less gray, underparts slightly yellowish. *Autumn:* Greenish; note the *unstreaked* yellowish breast, strong yellowish eyebrow stripe, and trace of a wing bar. See also p. 250.
Similar species: (1) See autumn Orange-crowned Warbler (p. 250). (2) See also vireos without wing bars (p. 226).
Voice: Song, staccato, 2- or 3-parted: *ticka ticka ticka ticka, swit swit, chew-chew-chew-chew-chew* (Gunn). Suggests Nashville Warbler's song, but louder, more tirelessly repeated.
Range: Canada, ne. edge of U.S. Winters Mexico to Venezuela. **East:** Map 310. **Habitat:** Deciduous and mixed forests; in migration, groves, brush.

ORANGE-CROWNED WARBLER   M 311
Vermivora celata   4½–5½″ (11–14 cm)
A dingy warbler without wing bars or other distinctive marks; olive-green above, greenish yellow below. Note faint breast streaks, lack of wing bars. "Orange" of crown seldom visible. Many birds in fall and winter are decidedly gray (see p. 250).
Similar species: See (1) autumn Tennessee Warbler (above; p. 250); (2) Philadelphia Vireo (p. 226).
Voice: Song, a colorless trill, becoming weaker toward the end. Often changes pitch, rising then dropping.
Range: Alaska, Canada, w. U.S. Winters to Guatemala. **East:** Map 311. **Habitat:** Brushy clearings, aspens, undergrowth.

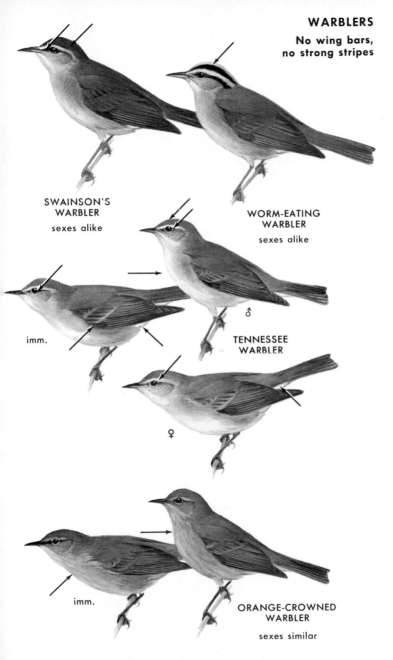

WARBLERS

**No wing bars,
no strong stripes**

SWAINSON'S
WARBLER

sexes alike

WORM-EATING
WARBLER

sexes alike

imm.

TENNESSEE
WARBLER

♂

♀

imm.

ORANGE-CROWNED
WARBLER

sexes similar

WILSON'S WARBLER *Wilsonia pusilla* 4¾″ (12 cm) **M 312**
Male: A yellow warbler with a *round black cap. Female* may, and
immature does not, show trace of a cap. They are small, golden-
looking, with a yellow stripe above a beady eye. See p. 250.
Similar species: (1) Female Hooded has white spots in tail; (2) Yellow Warbler, yellow spots. Wilson's has gray unspotted tail.
Voice: Song, a thin rapid little chatter dropping in pitch at the
end: *chi chi chi chi chi chet chet.*
Range: Alaska, Canada, w. and ne. U.S. Winters Mexico to Panama. **East:** Map 312. **Habitat:** Thickets along wooded streams,
moist tangles, low shrubs, willows, alders.

HOODED WARBLER *Wilsonia citrina* 5½″ (14 cm) **M 313**
The black hood or cowl of the *male* completely encircles the yellow
face and forehead. *Female* and *young* lack this hood, although the
yellow face may be sharply outlined in some females. Aside from
white tail spots, they lack distinctive marks.
Similar species: Female Wilson's is smaller, lacks tail spots.
Voice: Note, a metallic *chink.* Song, a loud whistled *weeta wee-
tee-o.* Also other arrangements; the slurred *tee-o* is a clue.
Range: E. and cen. U.S. Winters in Cen. America. **East:** Map 313.
Habitat: Woodland undergrowth, laurels, wooded swamps.

BACHMAN'S WARBLER *Vermivora bachmanii* 4¼″ (11 cm)
The rarest North American songbird. *Male:* Face and underparts
yellow; *throat patch* and *crown patch black* (suggests a small
Hooded with an incomplete hood). *Female:* Lacks black throat;
forehead yellow; crown and cheek grayish; eye-ring yellow.
Similar species: (1) "Lawrence's" has wing bars, black ear patch.
(2) ♂ Hooded has complete hood. (3) ♀ Hooded and (4) ♀ Wilson's
are similar to ♀ Bachman's. ♀ Bachman's has gray crown and
cheek, yellow eye-ring; lacks tail spots of Hooded.
Voice: Song, a rapid series of flat mechanical buzzes rendered on
one pitch: *bzz-bzz-bzz-bzz-bzz-bzz-bzz-bzz.*
Range: Se. U.S.; very local. Winters in Cuba. Has bred in se.
Missouri, ne. Arkansas, w. Kentucky, n. Alabama, S. Carolina,
Virginia(?). Migrates through Gulf states and Florida.

"LAWRENCE'S" WARBLER
Vermivora chrysoptera × pinus or *V. "lawrencei"*
The recessive hybrid of the Blue-wing–Golden-wing combination.
Yellow below like Blue-wing, but with the black head pattern of
Golden-wing. Note the black ear patch.
Similar species: See Bachman's Warbler (very rare).
Voice: Like either Golden-wing's or Blue-wing's.

GOLDEN-WINGED WARBLER **M 314**
Vermivora chrysoptera 5–5½″ (13–14 cm)
Gray above and white below. The only warbler with the combina-
tion of *yellow wing patch* and *black throat* (in ♀, gray, not black).
Note also the yellow forehead, black ear patch.
Voice: Song, a buzzy note followed by 3 on a lower pitch: *bee-
bz-bz-bz.* (Blue-wing sings a lazier *bee-bzzz.*)
Range: E. U.S. (Map 314). Winters Guatemala to Colombia. **Habi-
tat:** Open woodlands, brushy clearings, undergrowth.

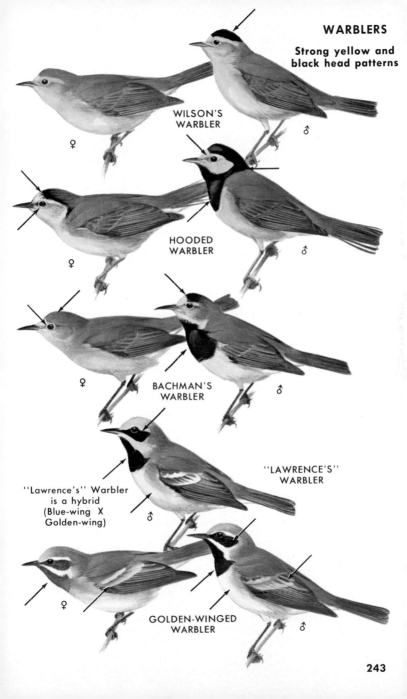

WARBLERS

Strong yellow and black head patterns

WILSON'S
WARBLER

♀

♂

HOODED
WARBLER

♀

♂

BACHMAN'S
WARBLER

♀

♂

''Lawrence's'' Warbler
is a hybrid
(Blue-wing X
Golden-wing)

''LAWRENCE'S''
WARBLER

♂

♀

GOLDEN-WINGED
WARBLER

♂

243

NASHVILLE WARBLER M 315
Vermivora ruficapilla 4¾" (12 cm)
Note the *white eye-ring* in combination with the *yellow* throat.
Head gray, contrasting with the olive-green back. No wing bars.
Males may show a dull chestnut crown patch.
Similar species: Connecticut Warbler also has a white eye-ring and
lacks wing bars, but its throat is *grayish.*
Voice: Song, 2-parted: *seebit, seebit, seebit, seebit, titititititi* (ends
like Chipping Sparrow's song).
Range: S. Canada, w. and n. U.S. Winters s. Texas to Guatemala.
East: Map 315. **Habitat:** Cool open mixed woods with undergrowth,
forest edges, bogs.

CONNECTICUT WARBLER M 316
Oporornis agilis 5¼-6" (13–15 cm)
Similar to Mourning Warbler (gray hood, yellow-and-olive body),
but note the *white eye-ring.* Fall female and young are duller, lack
the gray hood, but have a suggestion of one (a brownish stain
across upper breast). The eye-ring is always present.
Similar species: (1) Breeding Mourning Warbler lacks eye-ring (in
fall, often has a broken one). Male has a black throat. The yellow
undertail coverts reach the middle of the tail (nearly to end in
Connecticut). (2) Nashville Warbler also has an eye-ring, but is
much smaller, more active; has a *yellow throat.*
Voice: A repetitious *chip-chup-ee, chip-chup-ee, chip-chup-ee,
chip,* or *sugar-tweet, sugar-tweet, sugar-tweet* (W. Gunn).
Range: Cen.-s. Canada, cen.-n. U.S. Winters n. S. America. **East:**
Map 316. **Habitat:** Poplar bluffs, muskeg, mixed woods near water;
in migration, undergrowth.

MOURNING WARBLER M 317
Oporornis philadelphia 5–5¾" (13–14 cm)
Olive above, yellow below, with a *gray hood* encircling the head
and neck; male with irregular *black bib. Immature:* See p. 250.
Similar species: See Connecticut Warbler; both are skulkers.
Voice: Song, *chirry, chirry, chorry, chorry* (*chorry* lower). Consid-
erable variation.
Range: Canada and ne. U.S. Winters Cen. and S. America. **East:**
Map 317. **Habitat:** Clearings, thickets, slashings.

KENTUCKY WARBLER *Oporornis formosus* 5½" (14 cm) M 318
Note the broad black sideburns extending down from the eyes, and
also the yellow "spectacles." Sexes similar. Learn the song; 10
Kentuckies are heard for every 1 seen.
Similar species: (1) Yellowthroat (p. 246) lacks "spectacles";
(2) Canada Warbler (p. 234) has a dark necklace.
Voice: Song, a rapid rolling chant, *tory-tory-tory-tory* or *churry-
churry-churry-churry,* suggestive of Carolina Wren's, but less mu-
sical (2-syllabled rather than 3-syllabled).
Range: E. U.S. (west to Texas); Map 318. Winters Mexico to n. S.
America. **Habitat:** Woodland undergrowth.

NASHVILLE
WARBLER

♀   ♂

♀

♂

CONNECTICUT
WARBLER

imm.

♀

♂

imm.

MOURNING
WARBLER

♂

Yellowthroat
for comparison
(see p. 247)

KENTUCKY
WARBLER

sexes similar

245

COMMON YELLOWTHROAT   M 319
Geothlypis trichas   4½–5½" (11–14 cm)

A wrenlike warbler. *Male* with a black mask, or "domino"; throat yellow. *Female* and *immature* are olive-brown with a rich yellow throat, buffy-yellow breast; no black mask. Distinguished from similar warblers by *whitish belly,* brownish sides, and habitat.

Voice: A bright rapid chant, *witchity-witchity-witchity-witch;* sometimes *witchy-witchy-witchy-witch.* Note, a husky *tchep.*

Range: Canada to s. Mexico. Winters s. U.S. to W. Indies, Panama. **East:** Map 319. **Habitat:** Swamps, marshes, wet thickets.

YELLOW-BREASTED CHAT   *Icteria virens*   7" (18 cm)   M 320

Note the *white* "spectacles," bright *yellow* throat and breast. No wing bars. Sexes similar. Size (large for a warbler), bill, longish tail, actions, and habitat suggest a mimic thrush.

Voice: Song, clear repeated whistles, alternating with harsh notes and soft crowlike *caw's.* Suggests Mockingbird, but repertoire more limited; much longer pauses between phrases. Single notes, such as *whoit* or *kook,* are distinctive.

Range: S. Canada to cen. Mexico, Gulf Coast. Winters Cen. America. **East:** Map 320. **Habitat:** Brushy tangles, briars, thickets.

NORTHERN WATERTHRUSH   M 321
Seiurus noveboracensis   6" (15 cm)

Often *walks* along the water's edge and teeters in the manner of a Spotted Sandpiper. Brown-backed, with a *creamy, pale yellow, or buff* eyebrow stripe; *underparts striped,* often yellowish.

Voice: Note, a sharp *chip.* Song, a vigorous, rapid *twit twit twit sweet sweet sweet chew chew chew* (*chew's* drop in pitch).

Range: Alaska, Canada, n. edge of U.S. Winters mainly in American tropics. **East:** Map 321. **Habitat:** Swampy or wet woods, streamsides, lakeshores; in migration, also thickets.

LOUISIANA WATERTHRUSH *Seiurus motacilla* 6" (15 cm) M 322

Similar to Northern Waterthrush, but usually *whitish* below; bill slightly larger. Eyebrow stripe *pure white.*

Similar species: Some Northern Waterthrushes in fall (particularly western race, *notabilis*) have whitish eyebrow stripes. Northern has small spots on throat, which Louisiana lacks (usually).

Voice: Song, musical and ringing; 3 clear slurred whistles, followed by a jumble of twittering notes dropping in pitch.

Range: E. U.S. Winters Mexico, W. Indies to n. S. America. **East:** Map 322. **Habitat:** Brooks, ravines, wooded swamps.

OVENBIRD   *Seiurus aurocapillus*   6" (15 cm)   M 323

A sparrow-sized warbler; usually seen walking on pale *pinkish* legs on floor of woods. Suggests a small thrush; olive-brown above, but striped rather than spotted below. *Orangish patch on crown* visible at close range. Heard more often than seen.

Voice: Song, an emphatic *teach'er, TEACH'ER, TEACH'ER,* repeated rapidly in crescendo. In some areas, monosyllabic, with little change of emphasis, *TEACH, TEACH, TEACH,* etc.

Range: S. Canada, U.S. east of Rockies. Winters from se. U.S. to n. S. America. **East:** Map 323. **Habitat:** Near ground in leafy deciduous woods; in migration, thickets.

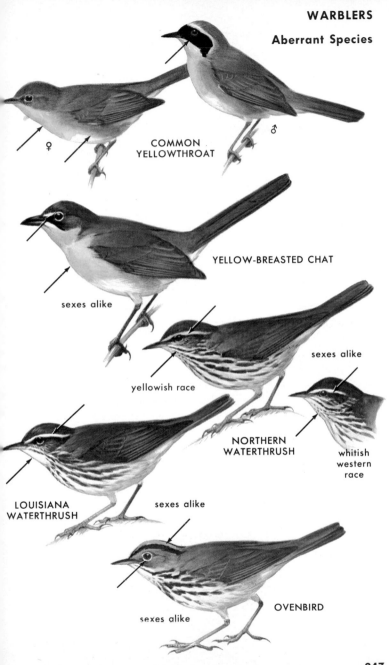

COMMON
YELLOWTHROAT

♀

♂

YELLOW-BREASTED CHAT

sexes alike

yellowish race

sexes alike

NORTHERN
WATERTHRUSH

whitish
western
race

LOUISIANA
WATERTHRUSH

sexes alike

sexes alike

OVENBIRD

sexes alike

CONFUSING FALL WARBLERS

Most of these have streaks or wing bars.

Text

RUBY-CROWNED KINGLET *Regulus calendula* **p. 216**
(Not a warbler.) Broken eye-ring, broad dark wing bar.

CHESTNUT-SIDED WARBLER *Dendroica pensylvanica* **p. 236**
Immature: Yellow-green above, whitish below; eye-ring.

BAY-BREASTED WARBLER *Dendroica castanea* **p. 236**
Note dark legs, buff undertail coverts. Fall adult may retain a
wash of bay on flanks. See Blackpoll Warbler.

BLACKPOLL WARBLER *Dendroica striata* **p. 232**
Very similar to fall Bay-breast, but slimmer. It has (1) a greenish
tinge below and is streaked (Bay-breast is buffier, streaks indistinct
or lacking); (2) white (not buff) undertail coverts; (3) pale yellowish legs (Bay-breast has dark legs, but so may some Blackpolls).

PINE WARBLER *Dendroica pinus* **p. 238**
Separate from the preceding 2 by the unstreaked back. Note white
undertail coverts (in Bay-breast, buff), black legs (in Blackpoll,
pale). Some immatures are very gray or brown.

NORTHERN PARULA WARBLER *Parula americana* **p. 230**
Immature: Combination of bluish and yellow; wing bars.

MAGNOLIA WARBLER *Dendroica magnolia* **p. 234**
Immature: White band at midtail.

PRAIRIE WARBLER *Dendroica discolor* **p. 238**
Immature: Jaw stripe, side stripes. Bobs tail.

YELLOW WARBLER *Dendroica petechia* **p. 238**
Yellow tail spots. Some females and immatures are so dusky that
they may resemble Orange-crowns (pp. 240, 250).

BLACKBURNIAN WARBLER *Dendroica fusca* **p. 236**
Immature: Yellow throat, dark cheek; pale back stripes.

BLACK-THROATED GREEN WARBLER *Dendroica virens* **p. 230**
Immature: Dusky streaks frame yellow cheek.

PALM WARBLER *Dendroica palmarum* **p. 238**
Brownish back, yellowish undertail coverts. Bobs tail.

YELLOW-RUMPED WARBLER *Dendroica coronata* **p. 234**
Immature: Bright yellow rump.

CAPE MAY WARBLER *Dendroica tigrina* **p. 236**
Streaked breast, yellowish rump. Note the pale neck spot (sometimes obscure in young birds).

CONFUSING FALL WARBLERS etc.

RUBY-CROWNED KINGLET ♀
not a warbler

CHESTNUT-SIDED imm.

PINE adult

PINE imm.

BAY-BREASTED imm.

BLACKPOLL

NORTHERN PARULA imm.

MAGNOLIA imm.

PRAIRIE imm.

YELLOW imm.

BLACKBURNIAN imm.

BLACK-THROATED GREEN imm.

PALM

YELLOW-RUMPED imm.

CAPE MAY imm.

CONFUSING FALL WARBLERS

Most of these lack streaks or wing bars.

ORANGE-CROWNED WARBLER *Vermivora celata*   p. 240
Dingy breast, yellow undertail coverts. Fall immature is greenish
drab throughout, barely paler below; it is often quite gray.

TENNESSEE WARBLER *Vermivora peregrina*   p. 240
Trace of a wing bar; white undertail coverts. Very similar to
Orange-crown (above), but note: (1) white undertail coverts; (2)
more conspicuous eyebrow stripe; (3) greener look; (4) paler underparts, with no hint of streaks; (5) trace of a light wing bar.

PHILADELPHIA VIREO *Vireo philadelphicus*   p. 226
(Not a warbler.) "Vireo" song and actions (see p. 226).

HOODED WARBLER *Wilsonia citrina*   p. 242
Immature: Yellow eyebrow stripe, bold white tail spots.

WILSON'S WARBLER *Wilsonia pusilla*   p. 242
Immature: Like a small Hooded; no white in the tail.

BLACK-THROATED BLUE WARBLER   p. 232
Dendroica caerulescens
Dark-cheeked look, white wing spot. Some young birds and females lack this white or light "pocket handkerchief" and may
suggest Philadelphia Vireo or Tennessee Warbler (above), but note
the *dark cheek.*

CONNECTICUT WARBLER *Oporornis agilis*   p. 244
Immature: Suggestion of a hood; complete eye-ring.

MOURNING WARBLER *Oporornis philadelphia*   p. 244
Immature and fall female: Suggestion of a hood; broken eye-ring.
Brighter yellow below than Connecticut.

NASHVILLE WARBLER *Vermivora ruficapilla*   p. 244
Yellow throat, white eye-ring.

COMMON YELLOWTHROAT *Geothlypis trichas*   p. 246
Female: Yellow throat, brownish sides, white belly.

PROTHONOTARY WARBLER *Protonotaria citrea*   p. 230
Female: Dull golden head, gray wings.

CANADA WARBLER *Wilsonia canadensis*   p. 234
Immature: Yellow "spectacles," trace of necklace.

CONFUSING
FALL WARBLERS
etc.

imm.

ORANGE-CROWNED

TENNESSEE

PHILADELPHIA
VIREO
not a warbler

HOODED

WILSON'S

♀

imm.

♀

BLACK-THROATED
BLUE

CONNECTICUT

imm.

MOURNING

imm.

NASHVILLE

♀

COMMON
YELLOWTHROAT

♀

PROTHONOTARY

imm.

CANADA

251

■ BLACKBIRDS, ORIOLES, ETC. Family Icteridae. A varied
group possessing conical, sharp-pointed bills and rather flat pro-
files. Some are black and iridescent, others are highly colored.
Sexes usually unlike. **Food:** Insects, small fruits, seeds, waste grain,
small aquatic life. **Range:** New World; most species in tropics. **No.
of species:** World, 88; East, 14 (+4 accidental).

RED-WINGED BLACKBIRD   M 324
Agelaius phoeniceus   7–9½″ (18–24 cm)
(Red-wing) *Male:* Black, with red *epaulets,* most conspicuous in
spring display. Often the scarlet is concealed; only the yellowish
margin is then visible. *Immature male:* Sooty brown, mottled, but
with red shoulders. *Female and young:* Brownish; identified by the
sharp-pointed bill, "blackbird" appearance, and *well-defined dark
stripings* below. Very gregarious, traveling and roosting in large
flocks.
Voice: Notes, a loud *check* and a high slurred *tee-err.* Song, a liquid
gurgling *konk-la-ree* or *o-ka-lay.*
Range: Canada to W. Indies, Costa Rica. **East:** Map 324. **Habitat:**
Breeds in marshes, brushy swamps, hayfields; forages also in culti-
vated land, along edges of water, etc.

YELLOW-HEADED BLACKBIRD   M 325
Xanthocephalus xanthocephalus   8–11″ (20–28 cm)
Male: A Robin-sized marsh blackbird with an *orange-yellow* head
and breast; shows a *white wing patch* in flight. *Female:* Smaller
and browner; most of the yellow is confined to the throat and
chest; lower breast streaked with white. Gregarious.
Voice: Song, low hoarse rasping notes produced with much effort;
sounds like rusty hinges. Note, a low *kruck* or *kack.*
Range: S. Canada, w. U.S., upper Mississippi Valley to nw. Mexico.
Winters sw. U.S., Mexico. **East:** Map 325. **Habitat:** Fresh marshes.
Forages in fields, open country.

BROWN-HEADED COWBIRD   *Molothrus ater*   7″ (18 cm)   M 326
(Common Cowbird) A rather small blackbird with a short sparrowlike bill. *Male:* Black, with a *brown head. Female:* All gray; note
the short finchlike bill. *Juvenal:* Paler than female, buffy gray,
with soft breast streaks; often seen being fed by smaller birds.
Young males in late summer molt, may be bizarrely patterned
with tan and black. When with other blackbirds, Cowbirds are
smaller and feed on ground with tails lifted high.
Similar species: Gray female Cowbird can be told from (1) female
Rusty and (2) female Brewer's Blackbirds by stubby bill, smaller
size. (3) Young Starling has longer bill, shorter tail.
Voice: Flight call, *weee-titi* (high whistle, 2 lower notes). Song,
bubbly and creaky *glug-glug-gleeee.* Note, *chuck.*
Range: S. Canada to n. Mexico. Migrant in North. **East:** Map 326.
Habitat: Farms, fields, barnyards, roadsides, wood edges, river
groves.

ICTERIDS
(BLACKBIRDS, etc.)

epaulets
concealed

imm. ♂

♀

epaulets
in display

♂

♂

RED-WINGED BLACKBIRD

♀

YELLOW-HEADED
BLACKBIRD

♂

BROWN-HEADED
COWBIRD

juvenal

imm. ♂ molting

253

RUSTY BLACKBIRD *Euphagus carolinus* 9″ (23 cm) **M 327**
  Rusty only in the fall; usually suggests a short-tailed Grackle.
  Male, spring: A Robin-sized blackbird with a pale yellow eye.
  Female, spring: Slate-colored, with *light eyes. Winter adult and
  young:* Washed with rusty; *barred* below.
  Voice: Note, a loud *chack.* "Song," a split creak like a rusty hinge:
  kush-a-lee alternating with *ksh-lay.*
  Range: Alaska, Canada, ne. edge of U.S. Winters to se. U.S. **East:**
  Map 327. **Habitat:** River groves, wooded swamps; muskeg.

BREWER'S BLACKBIRD **M 328**
Euphagus cyanocephalus 9″ (23 cm)
  A western blackbird. *Male:* All black, with a whitish eye; in good
  light *purplish* reflections on head and greenish reflections on body.
  Female: Brownish gray, with a *dark* eye.
  Similar species: Male Rusty Blackbird has dull *greenish* head
  reflections (hard to see); bill longer. Female Rusty has a *light* eye.
  Brewer's does not acquire extensive rusty look in winter.
  Voice: Song, a harsh wheezy, creaking *quee-ee* or *ksh-eee.*
  Range: Sw. Canada, w. and n.-cen. U.S. Winters to s. Mexico. **East:**
  Map 328. **Habitat:** Fields, prairies, farms, parks.

COMMON GRACKLE **M 329**
Quiscalus quiscula 11–13½″ (28–34 cm)
  A large iridescent blackbird larger than a Robin, with a long
  wedge-shaped or keel-shaped tail. Flight more level than that of
  other blackbirds. Male with iridescent purple on head, deep bronze
  or dull purple on back. The "Bronze" Grackle (New England and
  west of Appalachians) and "Purple" Grackle (seaboard south of
  New England) were formerly regarded as separate species.
  Voice: Note, *chuck* or *chack.* "Song," a split rasping note.
  Range: Canada, U.S., east of Rockies. **East:** Map 329. **Habitat:**
  Croplands, towns, groves, streamsides.

BOAT-TAILED GRACKLE **M 330**
Quiscalus major ♂ 16½″ (41 cm); ♀ 13″ (33 cm)
  A very large iridescent blackbird; much larger than Common
  Grackle, with a longer, more ample tail. Female much smaller than
  male; much browner than female Common Grackle; pale breast.
  Similar species: Louisiana westward, see Great-tailed Grackle.
  Voice: A harsh *check check check;* harsh whistles and clucks.
  Range: Atlantic and Gulf coasts from New Jersey to cen. Texas.
  East: Map 330. **Habitat:** Resident near salt water along coasts;
  marshes. Also inland in Florida.

GREAT-TAILED GRACKLE **M 330**
Quiscalus mexicanus ♂ 18″ (45 cm); ♀ 14″ (35 cm)
  Very similar to Boat-tailed Grackle, but somewhat longer-tailed.
  Both sexes have *yellow* eyes. (Male Boat-tails of the Atlantic Coast
  also have yellow eyes; those of the Gulf region have brown eyes,
  but some males may have dull yellowish eyes.)
  Voice: More varied than Boat-tail's; loud *clock's;* a rising whistle.
  Range: Sw. U.S. to Peru. **East:** Map 330. **Habitat:** Whereas the
  Boat-tail is restricted to coastal marshes (except in Florida), the
  Great-tail resorts also to inland areas, parks, towns, etc.

ICTERIDS (BLACKBIRDS, etc.)

♂ summer

♀

♂ winter

RUSTY BLACKBIRD

BREWER'S BLACKBIRD

♀

♂ winter

♂ summer

♂

purple race

bronze race

♀

COMMON GRACKLE

♀

♂

GREAT-TAILED GRACKLE

♂
Atlantic Coast

♂
Gulf states

BOAT-TAILED GRACKLE

255

BOBOLINK *Dolichonyx oryzivorus* 6–8″ (15–20 cm) **M 331**
Male, spring: Our only songbird that is *solid-black below and largely white above,* suggesting a dress suit on backward. *Female and autumn male:* A bit larger than a House Sparrow; rich buff, with dark stripings on the crown and back.
Similar species: (1) Lark Bunting (white confined to wings); (2) female Red-winged Blackbird (heavily striped below).
Voice: Song, in hovering flight and quivering descent, ecstatic and bubbling, starting with low reedy notes and rollicking upward. Flight note, a clear *pink,* heard in migration overhead.
Range: S. Canada, n. U.S. Winters in s. S. America. **East:** Map 331.
Habitat: Hayfields, meadows. In migration, marshes.

EASTERN MEADOWLARK *Sturnella magna* 9″ (23 cm) **M 332**
In grassy country, a chunky brown bird flushes, showing a conspicuous patch of *white* on each side of its short wide tail. Several rapid wingbeats alternate with short glides. Should it perch on a post, the glass reveals a bright yellow breast crossed by a *black V.* Walking, it flicks its tail open and shut.
Voice: Song, 2 clear slurred whistles, musical and pulled out: *tee-yah, tee-yair* (last note skewy and descending). Note, a rasping or buzzy *dzrrt;* also a guttural chatter.
Range: Se. Canada, e. U.S., Cuba; sw. U.S. to Brazil. Partial migrant. **East:** Map 332. **Habitat:** Fields, meadows, prairies.

WESTERN MEADOWLARK *Sturnella neglecta* 9″ (23 cm) **M 333**
Nearly identical with Eastern Meadowlark, but paler above; yellow of throat touches cheek. Readily recognizable by song.
Voice: Song variable; 7–10 notes, flutelike, gurgling and double-noted; unlike clear whistles of Eastern Meadowlark. The note, *chupp,* is lower than the rasping *dzrrt* of Eastern.
Range: Sw. Canada through w. U.S. to cen. Mexico. **East:** Map 333.
Habitat: Fields, meadows, prairies.

■ **STARLINGS Family Sturnidae.** A varied family; some blackbirdlike. Usually short-tailed, sharp-billed. Gregarious. **Food:** Insects, seeds, berries. **Range:** Widespread in Old World. **No. of species:** World, 103; East, 1 (introduced).

EUROPEAN STARLING **M 334**
Sturnus vulgaris 7½–8½″ (19–21 cm)
A gregarious, garrulous, short-tailed "blackbird" with a meadowlark shape. In flight, looks triangular; flies swiftly and directly, not rising and falling like most blackbirds. In spring iridescent; bill *yellow.* In winter *heavily speckled;* bill dark, changing to yellow in spring. Young Starling is dusky, a bit like female Cowbird, but tail shorter, bill longer.
Voice: A harsh *tseeeer;* a whistled *whooee.* Also clear whistles, clicks, bill-rattles, chuckles; sometimes mimics other birds.
Range: Eurasia, n. Africa. Partially migratory. Introduced in N. America and elsewhere. **East:** Map 334. **Habitat:** Cities, parks, farms, open groves, fields, open country.

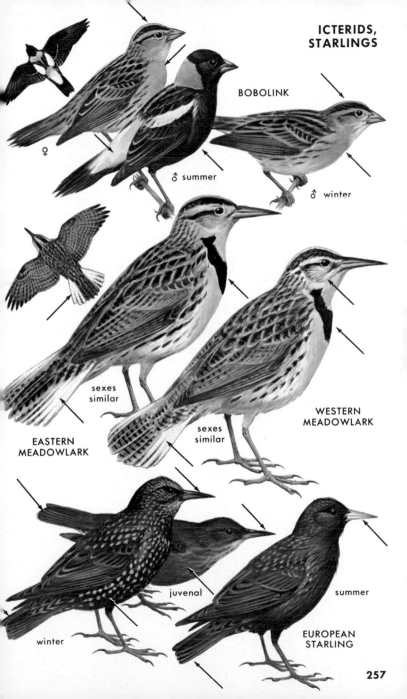

ICTERIDS,
STARLINGS

BOBOLINK

♀

♂ summer

♂ winter

EASTERN
MEADOWLARK

sexes
similar

sexes
similar

WESTERN
MEADOWLARK

winter

juvenal

summer

EUROPEAN
STARLING

- **ORIOLES.** Smaller, slimmer than the Robin; a brightly colored genus (*Icterus*) of the family Icteridae (blackbirds, etc.).

ORCHARD ORIOLE *Icterus spurius* 6–7″ (15–18 cm) **M 335**
Male: An all-dark oriole. Rump and underparts deep chestnut; rest of bird black. *Immature male:* Dull greenish above, yellowish below, with a *black bib. Female and young:* Olive-green above, yellowish below; 2 white wing bars.
Similar species: (1) Female and young "Baltimore" Orioles are not as greenish. Some female "Baltimores" have black throats (as do immature male Orchards), but are more orange. (2) Female Scarlet and (3) female Summer Tanagers lack wing bars (p. 260).
Voice: A fast-moving outburst interspersed with piping whistles, guttural notes. Suggests the Purple Finch's song. A strident slurred *wheeer!* at or near the end is distinctive.
Range: Se. Canada, e. and cen. U.S. to cen. Mexico. Winters in Cen. and n. S. America. **East:** Map 335. **Habitat:** Wood edges, orchards, shade trees.

"BALTIMORE" ORIOLE or NORTHERN ORIOLE (in part) **M 336**
Icterus galbula (in part) 7–8″ (18–20 cm)
Male: Flame-orange and black, with a solid-black head. *Female and young:* Olive-brown above, burnt orange-yellow below; 2 white wing bars. Some females may have traces of black on the head, suggesting the hood of the male.
Similar species: (1) See "Bullock's" Oriole (western). (2) ♀ Orchard Oriole is greener than ♀ "Baltimore." (3) See ♀ tanagers.
Voice: Song, rich, piping whistled notes. Note, a low, whistled *hew-li.* Young (when begging), a plaintive *tee-deedee.*
Range: Canada, e. and cen. U.S. Winters in American tropics. **East:** Map 336. **Habitat:** Open woods, elms, shade trees.

"BULLOCK'S" ORIOLE or NORTHERN ORIOLE (in part) **M 337**
Icterus galbula (in part) 7–8½″ (18–21 cm)
Western. *Male:* Distinguished from male "Baltimore" Oriole by its *orange cheeks, large white wing patches,* different tail pattern. *Female:* Differs from female "Baltimore" by grayer back, *whiter belly. Immature male:* Similar to female, but throat black. Hybridizes with "Baltimore" Oriole.
Voice: A series of accented double notes and 1 or 2 piping notes. Note, a sharp *skip;* also a chatter.
Range: Breeds sw. Canada, w. U.S., n. Mexico. Winters Cen. America. **East:** Map 337. Breeds east to Great Plains (S. Dakota, cen. Nebraska, w. Kansas, w. Oklahoma), where it intergrades or hybridizes with the "Baltimore" Oriole. The two are now regarded as conspecific. Stragglers occur in winter along the eastern seaboard; many records, especially at feeders.

SPOTTED ORIOLE *Icterus pectoralis* 8″ (20 cm) **M 338**
Florida only. Note the *orange crown,* black bib, and *black spots on the sides of the breast.* Much white in the wing. No other oriole in our area has an orange crown.
Range: Sw. Mexico to nw. Costa Rica. Recently established (by introduction or escape) in se. Florida. **East:** Map 338.

ORIOLES

♂
ORCHARD
ORIOLE

imm. ♂

♀

"BALTIMORE"
ORIOLE
(Northern Oriole, in part)

♂

imm. ♂

♀

"BULLOCK'S"
ORIOLE
(Northern Oriole, in part)

♂

♀

♀ similar
but duller

♂

SPOTTED
ORIOLE
(Florida only)

■ TANAGERS Family Thraupidae. Male tanagers are brightly colored; females of our species are greenish above, yellow below, suggesting large thick-billed warblers or vireos. Females may be confused with female orioles, but have darker cheeks and lack wing bars. The rather stout bills are *notched*. **Food:** Insects, fruits. **Range:** New World, most species in tropics. **No. of species:** World, 191; East, 3 (+1 accidental, 1 introduced).

SUMMER TANAGER *Piranga rubra* 7–7¾" (18–19 cm) **M 339**
Male: Rose-red all over, with a yellowish bill; no crest. *Female:* Olive above, deep yellow below. Young males acquiring adult plumage may be patched with red and green.
Similar species: (1) Male Cardinal has a crest, black face. (2) Male Scarlet Tanager has black wings and tail; female has darker wings. (3) Female orioles have wing bars.
Voice: Note, a staccato *pi-tuk* or *pik-i-tuk-i-tuk*. Song, Robin-like phrases, less nasal and resonant than Scarlet Tanager's.
Range: Cen. and s. U.S. to n. Mexico. Winters Mexico to Brazil. **East:** Map 339. **Habitat:** Woods, groves (especially oaks).

SCARLET TANAGER *Piranga olivacea* 7" (18 cm) **M 340**
Male: Flaming scarlet, with jet-black wings and tail. *Female, immature,* and *winter male:* Dull greenish above, yellowish below, with dark brownish or blackish wings.
Similar species: (1) Male Summer Tanager and (2) male Cardinal (crested) are all-red, lack black in wings and tail. (3) Female Summer Tanager is deeper yellow, wings are not as dusky.
Voice: Note, *chip-burr.* Song, 4 or 5 short phrases, Robin-like but hoarse (suggesting a Robin with a sore throat).
Range: Se. Canada, e. U.S. Winters Colombia to w. Amazonia. **East:** Map 340. **Habitat:** Forests and shade trees (esp. oaks).

WESTERN TANAGER *Piranga ludoviciana* 7" (18 cm)
The only U.S. tanager with strong *wing bars. Male:* Yellow, with black back, wings, and tail; 2 wing bars; and a *red face.* Red disappears in autumn and winter. *Female:* Yellowish below, dull olive above, with white and yellow wing bars.
Similar species: Female resembles female orioles (p. 258), but tail and sides of face darker, bill less sharply pointed. *Caution:* A very few young Scarlet Tanagers in fall may have 2 yellowish wing bars, but these birds do not have the "saddle-backed" look of the immature or fall Western Tanager, whose grayish olive back contrasts with its paler head and rump.
Range: W. N. America. Winters Cen. America. **East:** Casual, but there are numerous records from s. Canada to Louisiana and Florida, where it is rare but probably regular in winter.

BLUE-GRAY TANAGER *Thraupis episcopus* 6" (15 cm)
Bluish, with pale shoulders and darker wings and tail. Sexes alike. This native of Cen. and n. S. America has been introduced in Miami, Florida. Its continued survival is uncertain.

TANAGERS

SUMMER
TANAGER

♀

♂
all seasons

n. changing
to adult

SCARLET
TANAGER

♀

♂
summer

♂ changing

♂ winter

♂ orange
variant

WESTERN
TANAGER

♂
summer

♀

♂
winter

BLUE-GRAY
TANAGER
sexes similar

261

■ **WEAVER FINCHES Family Ploceidae.** A varied Old World group, of which the introduced House Sparrow (not related to our native sparrows) is the best known. **Food:** Mainly insects, seeds. **Range:** Widespread in Old World. **No. of species:** World, 263 (sparrow-weavers, 35); East, 2 (introduced).

HOUSE SPARROW *Passer domesticus* 6″ (15 cm) **M 341**
Familiar to everyone. Sooty city birds often bear a poor resemblance to clean country males with the black throat, white cheeks, chestnut nape. Females and young lack the black throat; have a plain dingy breast and a dull eye-stripe.
Range: Eurasia, n. Africa. Introduced N. and S. America, S. Africa, Australia, etc. **East:** Map 341. **Habitat:** Cities, farms.

EURASIAN TREE SPARROW **M 342**
Passer montanus 5½″ (14 cm)
Both sexes resemble male House Sparrow, but the black throat patch is smaller. Note the *black earspot.* Crown *brown.*
Voice: Higher pitched than House Sparrow's. A metallic *chik* or *chup,* a repeated *chit-tchup.* In flight, a hard *tek, tek.*
Range: Eurasia. Introduced; local resident about St. Louis, Missouri, and in nearby Illinois (Map 342). **Habitat:** Farmland.

■ **GROSBEAKS, FINCHES, SPARROWS, BUNTINGS Family Fringillidae.** These birds have seed-cracking bills of 3 main types: (1) very large and thick (grosbeaks); (2) rather canarylike (finches, sparrows, buntings); (3) cross-tipped (crossbills). **Food:** Seeds, insects, small fruits. **Range:** Worldwide. **No. of species:** World, 245; East, 50 (+10 accidental).

DICKCISSEL *Spiza americana* 6–7″ (15–18 cm) **M 343**
A grassland bird, near size of House Sparrow. *Male:* Suggests a small meadowlark, with a black bib on a yellow chest. (In fall the bib is obscure or lacking.) *Female:* Very much like ♀ House Sparrow; paler, with a much lighter stripe over the eye, a touch of yellow on the breast, and a bluish bill. The chestnut shoulder is also an aid. Often travels in large flocks.
Voice: Song, a staccato *Dick-ciss-ciss-ciss* or *chup-chup-klip-klip-klip.* A short buzzing call often heard in migration.
Range: S. Ontario and interior of U.S. between Rockies and Appalachians. Winters mainly from Mexico to n. S. America. **East:** Map 343. **Habitat:** Alfalfa and other fields, meadows, prairies. May rarely winter in e. U.S. (at feeding trays with sparrows).

LARK BUNTING *Calamospiza melanocorys* 7″ (18 cm) **M 344**
A prairie bird. *Male, spring: Black,* with a *large white wing patch. Female, young, and winter male:* Brown, streaked; usually some in the flock show *whitish wing patches.* Gregarious.
Similar species: (1) Male Bobolink has white patches, but not on wings. (2) Brown female suggests female Purple Finch.
Voice: Song, Cardinal-like slurs, unmusical chatlike *chug's;* piping whistles and trills; each note repeated 3–11 times.
Range: Prairies of s. Canada to n. Texas. Winters sw. U.S. to cen. Mexico. **East:** Map 344. **Habitat:** Plains, prairies.

FINCHES and FINCHLIKE BIRDS

HOUSE
SPARROW

♂

♀

EURASIAN
TREE
SPARROW

sexes
similar

DICKCISSEL

♂

♀

fall

Bobolink
for comparison
(see p. 256)

♂

summer

winter ♂
similar to ♀

♀

LARK BUNTING

263

LAPLAND LONGSPUR *Calcarius lapponicus* 6½″ (16 cm) **M 345**
Lapland Longspurs, like Horned Larks and the pipits, are birds of open country; in flight, they appear to have shorter tails. *Male, winter:* Sparse black streaks on the sides, a rusty nape, and a smudge across the breast help identify it. *Male, summer: Black face outlined with white;* rusty collar. *Female, winter:* More nondescript; note the tail pattern (opposite). *Female, summer:* Resembles winter male.
Similar species: Other longspurs have more white in the tail (see opposite). Pipits and Horned Lark have thin bills.
Voice: A musical *teew;* also a rattle and a whistle, *ticky-tick-tew.* Song (in display flight), vigorous, musical.
Range: Arctic; circumpolar. Winters s. Canada to s. U.S. **East:** Map 345. **Habitat:** Tundra; in winter, fields, prairies.

CHESTNUT-COLLARED LONGSPUR **M 346**
Calcarius ornatus 5½–6½″ (14–16 cm)
Male, summer: Solid *black* below except on the throat; nape *chestnut. Female and winter:* Sparrowlike; the best field mark is the tail pattern (a dark triangle on a white tail).
Voice: Song, short, feeble, but musical; suggestive of Western Meadowlark's. Note, a finchlike *ji-jiv.*
Range: S. Canadian prairies; n. prairie states. Winters sw. U.S., n. Mexico. **East:** Map 346. **Habitat:** Plains, prairies.

McCOWN'S LONGSPUR *Calcarius mccownii* 6″ (15 cm) **M 347**
Male, spring: Crown and patch on breast black; tail largely white. Hindneck *gray* (brown or chestnut in other longspurs). *Female and winter male:* Sparrowlike; note the tail pattern (the black is like an inverted T on white).
Similar species: (1) Male Chestnut-collared Longspur in summer has a chestnut collar, black belly. (2) Horned Lark (similar breast splotch) has a thin bill, black face patch.
Voice: Song (in display flight), clear sweet warbles, suggesting Lark Bunting's (Niedrach). Note, a dry rattle.
Range: Prairies of s.-cen. Canada, n.-cen. U.S. Winters sw. U.S. to n. Mexico. **East:** Map 347. **Habitat:** Plains, prairies.

SMITH'S LONGSPUR *Calcarius pictus* 6″ (15 cm) **M 348**
A *buffy* longspur; warm buff on entire underparts. Tail edged with white as in Vesper Sparrow (no dark band at tip). *Male, summer: Deep buff;* ear patch with a *white spot,* strikingly outlined by a *black triangle. Female and winter:* Nondescript; breast lightly streaked; some males may show a white shoulder.
Similar species: See (1) Vesper Sparrow, (2) Sprague's Pipit, and (3) other longspurs (study tail diagrams opposite).
Voice: Rattling or clicking notes in flight (suggesting the winding of a cheap watch). Song, sweet and warblerlike, terminating in a *we'chew* like the Chestnut-sided Warbler's.
Range: N. Alaska to Hudson Bay. Winters s.-cen. U.S. **East:** Map 348. **Habitat:** Prairies, fields, airports; tundra (summer).

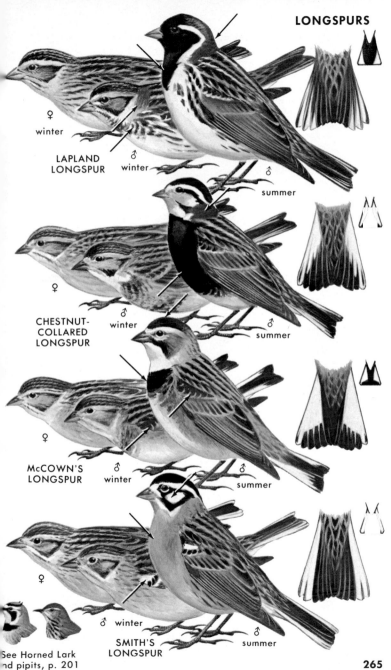

LONGSPURS

♀
winter

LAPLAND
LONGSPUR

♂
winter

♂
summer

♀

CHESTNUT-
COLLARED
LONGSPUR

♂
winter

♂
summer

♀

McCOWN'S
LONGSPUR

♂
winter

♂
summer

♀

♂
winter

SMITH'S
LONGSPUR

♂
summer

See Horned Lark
and pipits, p. 201

"SLATE-COLORED" JUNCO or NORTHERN JUNCO (in part) M 349
Junco hyemalis (in part) 5½–6¾″ (14–17 cm)

This slate-gray, hooded, sparrow-shaped bird is characterized by white outer tail feathers that flash conspicuously as it flies away. The bill and belly are whitish. Males may have blackish hoods; females and immatures are duller. The juvenal bird in summer is finely streaked on the breast, hence its white outer tail feathers might even suggest a Vesper Sparrow.

Similar species: The "Oregon" Junco (below) is now regarded as conspecific. It is a casual stray in the East. Another race, the "White-winged" Junco (*J. h. aikeni*) of the Black Hills, South Dakota, known by its strong white wing bars, has been reported in the East but needs specimen verification.

Voice: Song, a loose trill, suggestive of Chipping Sparrow's song, but more musical; note, a light *smack;* tickering notes.

Range: Cool forests of Alaska, Canada; south in e. mts. to n. Georgia. Winters to Gulf states, n. Mexico. **East:** Map 349. **Habitat:** Conifer and mixed woods. In winter, open woods, undergrowth, roadsides, brush; it also patronizes feeders.

"OREGON" JUNCO or NORTHERN JUNCO (in part)
Junco hyemalis (in part) or *J. "oreganus"* 5½–6¾″ (14–17 cm)

Male: Resembles "Slate-colored" Junco, but back *red-brown,* contrasting sharply with the black hood; sides *buffy* or *rusty. Female:* Head grayer; rusty of the back not so sharply defined, but the "pink" or tawny sides are well separated from the gray hood. Intergrades between *"oreganus"* and typical *hyemalis* are frequent, especially on the Great Plains. Just call them Northern Juncos, now the proper name for the species (A.B.A. Checklist).

Voice: Very similar to that of "Slate-colored" Junco.

Range: Se. Alaska, sw. Canada, nw. U.S., Pacific states. Winters to n. Mexico. **East:** A rare straggler, but occasional birds turn up nearly every winter at feeding trays as far east as the Atlantic seaboard.

SNOW BUNTING   M 350
Plectrophenax nivalis 6–7¼″ (15–18 cm)

No other songbird shows so much white. In winter some individuals may look quite brown, but when they fly their flashing *white wing patches* identify them. Overhead, Snow Buntings look almost entirely white, whereas Water Pipits and Horned Larks are black-tailed. They often swirl over snowy fields in large flocks. In summer dress in the Arctic the male has a black back, contrasting with its white head and underparts.

Voice: Note, a sharp whistled *teer* or *tew;* also a rough purring *brrt.* Song, a musical *ti-ti-chu-ree,* repeated.

Range: Arctic, circumpolar. In winter to cen. Eurasia, cen. U.S. **East:** Map 350. **Habitat:** Tundra (summer); prairies, fields, dunes, shores.

"SNOWBIRDS"

"SLATE-COLORED" JUNCO
(Northern Junco,
in part)

juv.

♂

♀

"OREGON" JUNCO
(Northern Junco,
in part)

♂

♀

♀ winter

♂ winter

♂ summer

SNOW
BUNTING

NORTHERN CARDINAL
Cardinalis cardinalis   7½–9″ (19–23 cm)

Male: An all-red bird with a pointed crest, and a black patch at the base of its heavy triangular red bill. *Female:* Buff-brown, with some red on the wings and tail. The crest, dark face, and heavy red bill are distinctive. *Immature:* Similar to the female, but with a blackish bill.

Similar species: The male Summer Tanager, the other all-red bird of the southern and central states, has no crest.

Voice: Song, clear slurred whistles, lowering in pitch. Several variations: *what-cheer cheer cheer,* etc.; *whoit whoit whoit* or *birdy birdy birdy,* etc. Note, a short thin *chip.*

Range: S. Ontario to Gulf states; sw. U.S., Mexico to Belize (B. Honduras). **East:** Map 351. **Habitat:** Woodland edges, thickets, suburban gardens, towns.

RED CROSSBILL
Loxia curvirostra   5¼–6½″ (13–16 cm)

Note the *crossed mandibles.* Near size of a House Sparrow; with a heavy head, short tail. The sound made when it cracks open the cones of evergreen trees often betrays its presence. It acts like a small parrot as it dangles while feeding. *Male: Dull red,* brighter on the rump; wings and tail blackish. The young male is more orange. *Female:* Dull olive-gray; yellowish on the rump and underparts. *Immature:* Striped above and below, suggesting a large Pine Siskin.

Similar species: White-winged Crossbill has white wing bars in all plumages.

Voice: Note, a hard *jip-jip* or *jip-jip-jip.* Song, finchlike warbled passages, *jip-jip-jip-jeeaa-jeeaa,* or warbled passages, trills, and chips.

Range: Conifer forests of N. Hemisphere. In N. America, south in mts. to Nicaragua; in East, locally to s. Appalachians. Erratic movements in winter. **East:** Map 352. **Habitat:** Conifers (spruces, firs, hemlocks, etc.).

WHITE-WINGED CROSSBILL
Loxia leucoptera   6–6¾″ (15–17 cm)

Note the wing bars, crossed mandibles. *Male: Dull rose-pink,* with black wings crossed by *2 broad white wing bars;* tail black. *Female:* Olive-gray, with a yellowish rump similar to female Red Crossbill's, but with *2 broad white wing bars.* The wing bars are often quite evident in flight and help to pick out this species from mixed flocks of crossbills.

Similar species: See (1) Pine Grosbeak (p. 270) and (2) Red Crossbill (above).

Voice: Notes, a liquid *peet* and a dry *chif-chif.* Song, a succession of loud trills on different pitches.

Range: Boreal forests of N. Hemisphere. **East:** Map 353. **Habitat:** Spruce and fir forests, hemlocks.

RED FINCHES

♂

♀

juv.

NORTHERN
CARDINAL

♂

♀

imm.

RED
CROSSBILL

♂

♀

WHITE-WINGED
CROSSBILL

269

COMMON REDPOLL   *Carduelis flammea*   5″ (13 cm)   **M 354**
Note the *bright red cap* on the forehead. A little, streaked, gray-brown finch with a *black chin* and dark streaks on the flanks. The male is pink-breasted. In size, shape, and actions, resembles an American Goldfinch or a Pine Siskin.
Similar species: (1) Male House Finch and (2) male Purple Finch are larger, redder, and have red rumps; lack the black chin.
Voice: In flight, a rattling *chet-chet-chet-chet.* Song, a trill, followed by the rattling *chet-chet-chet-chet.*
Range: Circumboreal. Winters irregularly to n. and cen. U.S. **East:** Map 354. **Habitat:** Birches, tundra scrub. In winter, weeds, brush.

HOARY REDPOLL   *Carduelis hornemanni*   5″ (13 cm)   **M 355**
Among Redpolls look for a "frostier" bird with an *unstreaked whitish rump.* In males, rump may be pink-tinged; bill more conical than Common Redpoll's; undertail coverts unstreaked.
Range: Arctic; circumpolar. Winters irregularly to n. U.S. **East:** Map 355. **Habitat:** Similar to Common Redpoll's.

HOUSE FINCH   **M 356**
Carpodacus mexicanus   5–5¾″ (13–14 cm)
This recent addition to our eastern avifauna is often mistaken for the Purple Finch, with which it may associate at the feeding tray. It is smaller; male brighter red. Note the dark *stripes* on the sides and belly. The striped brown female is distinguished from the female Purple Finch by its smaller bill and bland face pattern (no heavy mustache or dark cheek patch).
Voice: Song, bright, but loose and disjointed; frequently ends in a harsh nasal *wheer* or *che-urr.* Notes, finchlike; some suggest House Sparrow's, but more musical.
Range: W. U.S. to s. Mexico. Introduced in ne. U.S. about 1940; spreading. **East:** Map 356. **Habitat:** Cities, suburbs, farms.

PURPLE FINCH   **M 357**
Carpodacus purpureus   5½–6″ (14–15 cm)
Like a sparrow dipped in raspberry juice. *Male:* Dull rose-red, brightest on head and rump. *Female and immature:* Heavily striped, brown, sparrowlike. Note the *broad dark jaw stripe,* dark ear patch, broad light stripe behind eye, and largish bill.
Similar species: See House Finch (above).
Voice: Song, a fast lively warble; note, a dull metallic *tick.*
Range: Canada, Pacific states, ne. U.S. Winters to s. U.S. **East:** Map 357. **Habitat:** Woods, groves; in winter, also suburbs.

PINE GROSBEAK   *Pinicola enucleator*   8–10″ (20–25 cm)   **M 358**
Near size of Robin; a large tame winter finch with a longish tail. In flight, undulates deeply. *Male, adult:* Dull rose-red, dark wings with 2 white bars. *Male, immature:* Similar to female, but touch of reddish on head and rump. *Female:* Gray, with 2 white wing bars; head and rump tinged dull yellow.
Voice: Call, a whistled *tee-tew-tew,* suggesting that of Greater Yellowlegs, but finchlike; also a musical *chee-vli.*
Range: Boreal forests of N. Hemisphere, wintering irruptively southward. **East:** Map 358. **Habitat:** Conifer forests; in winter, also mixed woods, fruiting trees.

RED FINCHES
etc.

♀

orange
variant
♂

♂

♀

HOUSE
FINCH

COMMON
REDPOLL

♂

HOARY
REDPOLL

♂

♀

PURPLE
FINCH

♂

imm. ♂

♂

♀

PINE GROSBEAK

271

EVENING GROSBEAK M 359
Hesperiphona vespertina 8″ (20 cm)
A chunky short-tailed finch, the size of a Starling, with a very large, conical, whitish or pale greenish bill. The undulating flight indicates a finch; its stocky shape and *large white wing patches* identify it as this species. *Male:* Dull yellow, with a dark head, yellow eyebrow stripe, and black-and-white wings; suggests an overgrown American Goldfinch. *Female:* Silvery gray, with just enough yellow, black, and white to be recognizable. Gregarious.
Voice: A ringing finchlike *chirp, cleer,* or *clee-ip* (suggesting a glorified House Sparrow's). Song, a short uneven warble.
Range: Spruce belt of Canada, w. and ne. U.S., Mexico. Winters to se. U.S., Mexico. **East:** Map 359. **Habitat:** Conifer forests; in winter, Box Elders and other maples; also fruiting shrubs, feeding trays.

AMERICAN GOLDFINCH *Carduelis tristis* 5″ (13 cm) **M 360**
A small finch with deeply undulating flight. *Male, summer: Yellow,* with *black wings,* tail, and forehead patch. *Female, summer:* Dull yellow-olive, darker above, with blackish wings and conspicuous wing bars; distinguished from other small olive-yellow birds by its short conical bill. *Winter, both sexes:* Much like summer female, but grayer.
Similar species: Yellow Warbler (p. 238) is yellowish all over, including the wings and tail.
Voice: Song, sustained, clear, light, canarylike. In flight, each dip often punctuated by *ti-dee'-di-di* or *per-chik-o-ree.*
Range: S. Canada to s. U.S., n. Baja California. **East:** Map 360.
Habitat: Patches of thistles and weeds, dandelions on lawns, roadsides, open woods, edges; in winter, also feeders.

PINE SISKIN *Carduelis pinus* 4½–5″ (11–13 cm) **M 361**
A small, dark, *heavily* streaked finch with a deeply notched tail, sharply pointed bill. A *touch of yellow* in wings and at base of tail is not always evident. In size and actions, resembles Goldfinch. Most Siskins are detected by voice, flying over.
Similar species: (1) Winter Goldfinch lacks streaks. (2) Female House Finch has stubbier bill, less notch in tail. (3) Redpoll has red forehead. All lack yellow in wings and tail.
Voice: Call, a loud *clee-ip* or *chlee-ip;* also a light *tit-i-tit;* a buzzy *shreeeee.* Song suggests Goldfinch's; coarser, wheezy.
Range: S. Canada to s. U.S. Winters to n. Mexico. **East:** Map 361.
Habitat: Conifers, mixed woods, alders, weedy areas.

EUROPEAN GOLDFINCH *Carduelis carduelis* 5½″ (14 cm)
Slightly larger than American Goldfinch; tawny, with a *red face patch* and *broad yellow band* across wing. Sexes similar.
Similar species: See Western Tanager (p. 260).
Voice: Song, liquid, canarylike; more twittering than song of American Goldfinch. Note, *swit-wit-wit.*
Range: Eurasia. Introduced Bermuda. A colony established on Long Island is now extirpated. Escapes are still reported.

272

YELLOW
FINCHES
etc.

♂

♀

EVENING
GROSBEAK

♂ winter

♂ summer

♀

AMERICAN
GOLDFINCH

♂

♀

PINE SISKIN

sexes similar

EUROPEAN GOLDFINCH

273

BLUE GROSBEAK *Guiraca caerulea* 6–7½" (15–19 cm) **M 362**
Male: Deep *dull blue,* with a thick bill and *2 broad tan wing bars.*
Often flips its tail. Immature male is a mixture of brown and blue.
Female: About the size of a Cowbird; warm brown, lighter below,
with 2 *buff wing bars;* rump tinged with blue.
Similar species: Indigo Bunting is smaller, lacks wing bars.
Voice: Song, a rapid warble; short phrases rising and falling; sug-
gests the song of Purple Finch, House Finch, or Orchard Oriole, but
slower and more guttural. Note, a sharp *chink.*
Range: Cen. U.S. to Costa Rica. Winters Mexico to Panama. **East:**
Map 362. **Habitat:** Brushy places, roadsides, streamside thickets.

INDIGO BUNTING *Passerina cyanea* 5½" (14 cm) **M 363**
Male: A small finch; rich deep blue *all over.* In autumn the male
becomes more like the brown female, but there is usually some
blue in the wings and tail. *Female:* Plain brown; breast paler, with
indistinct streaks; a small brown finch devoid of obvious stripes,
wing bars, or other marks.
Similar species: Blue Grosbeak (larger) has tan wing bars.
Voice: Song, lively, high, and strident, with well-measured phrases
at different pitches; notes usually paired: *sweet-sweet, chew-chew,*
etc. Note, a sharp thin *spit.*
Range: Se. Canada, e. U.S. (west to Black Hills, Great Plains).
East: Map 363. **Habitat:** Brushy pastures, bushy wood edges.

LAZULI BUNTING *Passerina amoena* 5–5½" (13–14 cm)
Male: A small turquoise-blue finch, patterned somewhat like a
Bluebird (blue upper parts, pale cinnamon across breast and sides),
but with *2 white wing bars. Female:* Rather nondescript; a small
finch with an unstreaked brown back, a trace of blue in wings and
tail, 2 pale wing bars (stronger than in female Indigo Bunting).
Hybrids are very frequent where the ranges of Indigo and Lazuli
Buntings overlap.
Similar species: Female Indigo Bunting has less pronounced wing
bars and may show faint streaks on breast.
Voice: Song, similar to Indigo Bunting's; faster.
Range: Sw. Canada, w. U.S. Winters in Mexico. **East:** Breeds east
to western edge of our area (cen. North Dakota, w. Nebraska, cen.
Oklahoma). **Habitat:** Open brush, streamside shrubs.

PAINTED BUNTING *Passerina ciris* 5¼" (13 cm) **M 364**
The most gaudily colored North American songbird. *Male:* A little
finch the size of a Chipping Sparrow, with a patchwork of *blue-
violet* on head, *green* on back, red on rump and underparts. *Fe-
male:* Very plain; greenish above, paling to lemon-green below; *no
other small finch is all green.*
Voice: Song, a bright pleasant warble; resembles song of Warbling
Vireo, but more "wiry." Note, a sharp *chip.*
Range: S. U.S., ne. Mexico. Winters to Panama. **East:** Map 364.
Habitat: Woodland edges, roadsides, brush, towns, gardens.

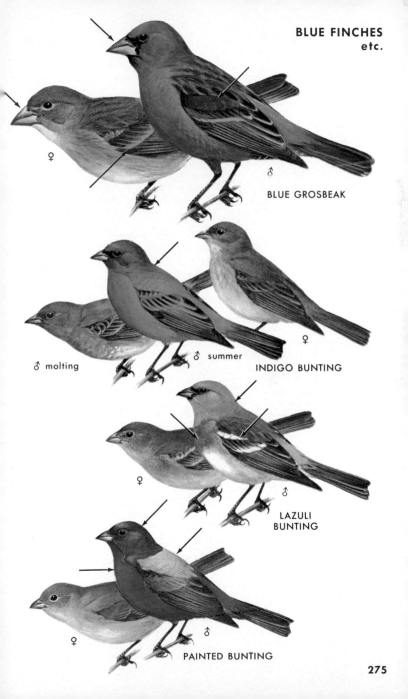

BLUE FINCHES
etc.

♀

BLUE GROSBEAK

♂

♂ molting

♂ summer

♀

INDIGO BUNTING

♀

♂

LAZULI
BUNTING

♀

♂

PAINTED BUNTING

275

ROSE-BREASTED GROSBEAK
Pheucticus ludovicianus   7–8½″ (18–21 cm)

Male: Black and white, with a large triangle of rose-red on the breast and a thick pale bill. In flight a pattern of white flashes across the black upper plumage. *Female:* Streaked, like a large sparrow or female Purple Finch (p. 270); recognized by the large "grosbeak" bill, broad white wing bars, striped crown, and broad white eyebrow stripe. Wing linings yellow.

Similar species: See Black-headed Grosbeak (next).

Voice: Song, rising and falling passages; resembles Robin's song, but mellower, given with more feeling (as if a Robin has taken voice lessons). Note, a metallic *kick* or *eek.*

Range: S. Canada, e. and cen. U.S. Winters W. Indies, Mexico to nw. S. America. **East:** Map 365. **Habitat:** Deciduous woods, orchards, groves, thickets.

BLACK-HEADED GROSBEAK
Pheucticus melanocephalus   6½–7¾″ (16–19 cm)

Male: Size and shape of Rose-breasted Grosbeak, but breast, collar, and rump *dull orange-brown.* The black head, boldly marked black-and-white wings, and pale bill are similar to those of the Rose-breasted Grosbeak. *Female:* Like female Rose-breast, but breast strongly washed with ochre-brown; streaks much finer or nearly absent across chest.

Range: Sw. Canada, w. U.S. to s. Mexico. Winters in Mexico. **East:** Breeds east to about the 100th meridian in the central parts of North and South Dakota and Nebraska. Sometimes hybridizes with Rose-breast where their ranges overlap. Strays occasionally to Atlantic states, where it has wintered at feeding trays.

GREEN-TAILED TOWHEE   *Pipilo chlorurus*   6½″ (16 cm)
This slender western finch may be known by its *rufous cap,* conspicuous *white throat,* white mustache, gray chest, and plain *olive-green back.* It has strayed casually to at least 20 eastern states and provinces from e. Canada to the Gulf states. (Usually recorded in winter at feeders.)

RUFOUS-SIDED TOWHEE
Pipilo erythrophthalmus   7–8½″ (18–21 cm)

Readily recognized by the *rufous sides.* Smaller and more slender than Robin; rummages noisily among dead leaves. *Male:* Head and upper parts black; sides robin-red, belly white. Flashes large white patches in the tail corners. Eye usually red (but white in birds of s. Atlantic Coast and Florida). *Female:* Similar, but brown where male is black. *Juvenal, summer:* Streaked below like a large sparrow, but with the diagnostic Towhee wing and tail pattern.

Similar subspecies: The western race, known as the "Spotted" Towhee, is accidental in the East. It may be known by the additional white wing bars and numerous white spots on the back.

Voice: Song, *drink-your-teeeee,* last syllable higher, wavering. Call, a loud *chewink!* The southern white-eyed race gives a more slurred *shrink* or *zree;* song, *cheet cheet cheeeeee.*

Range: S. Canada to Florida, Guatemala. Migrant in North. **East:** Map 366. **Habitat:** Open woods, undergrowth, brushy edges.

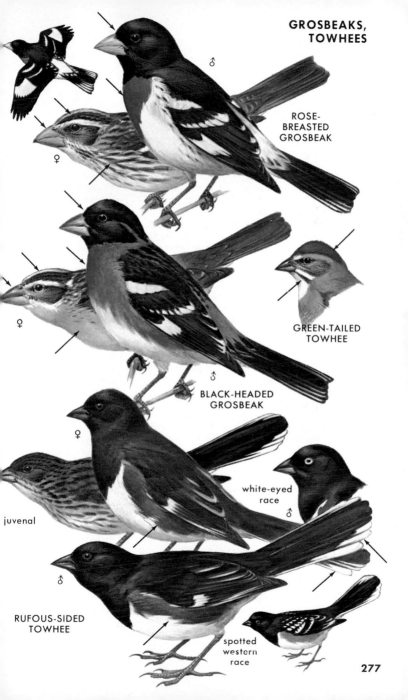

GROSBEAKS, TOWHEES

ROSE-BREASTED GROSBEAK

♂

♀

GREEN-TAILED TOWHEE

BLACK-HEADED GROSBEAK

♀

♂

white-eyed race ♂

juvenal

♂

RUFOUS-SIDED TOWHEE

spotted western race

WHITE-THROATED SPARROW M 367
Zonotrichia albicollis 6½–7″ (16–18 cm)
A gray-breasted sparrow with a *white throat patch* and a *yellow spot* between the eye and bill. Bill blackish. Polymorphic; adults with *black and white head stripes* mate with birds having *brown and tan head stripes. Winter:* Duller; head stripes varying shades of black, brown, tan, and whitish.
Similar species: See White-crowned Sparrow (pinkish bill).
Voice: Song, several clear pensive whistles, easily imitated; 1 or 2 clear notes, followed by 3 quavering notes on a different pitch. Note, a slurred *tseet;* also a hard *chink.*
Range: Canada, ne. U.S. Winters to s. U.S., ne. Mexico (rarely). **East:** Map 367. **Habitat:** Thickets, brush, undergrowth of conifer and mixed woodlands. Patronizes feeders.

WHITE-CROWNED SPARROW M 368
Zonotrichia leucophrys 6½–7½″ (16–19 cm)
Adult: A clear grayish breast and a puffy crown *striped with black and white* make this one of the handsomest sparrows. Bill *pink. Immature:* Browner, with head stripes of dark red-brown and light buff; *bill bright pinkish.* The race *Z. l. gambelii* ("Gambel's" White-crown), which migrates through the Great Plains, can be separated from the nominate race by the white eye-stripe, which extends *from the bill* instead of from the eye.
Similar species: White-throated Sparrow is browner, has a well-defined white throat, yellow spot before the eye, *black* bill.
Voice: Song, 1 or more clear plaintive whistles (suggesting White-throat's), followed by husky trilled whistles. Variable.
Range: Across Canada to Alaska; south through w. U.S. Winters w. and s. U.S., Mexico, Cuba. **East:** Map 368. **Habitat:** Brush, edges, tangles, roadsides; in summer, boreal scrub.

HARRIS' SPARROW *Zonotrichia querula* 7½″ (19 cm) M 369
A large sparrow, the size of a Fox Sparrow. In breeding plumage, has a *black crown, face, and bib encircling a pink bill.* In winter adults, the black crown is veiled with gray. Young in the first winter are *white on the throat,* less black on the crown, buffy brown on the rest of the head, and blotched and streaked on the breast. In the second winter the chin is black.
Voice: Song has the quavering quality of White-throat's song; clear whistles on the same pitch, or 1 or 2 at one pitch, the rest slightly higher or lower; the general effect is *minor.* Alarm note, *weenk* or *wink* (G. Sutton).
Range: N.-cen. Canada. Winters s.-cen. U.S. **East:** Map 369. **Habitat:** Stunted boreal forests; in winter, brush, open woods.

GOLDEN-CROWNED SPARROW
Zonotrichia atricapilla 6–7″ (15–18 cm)
Similar to White-crowned Sparrow, but central crown dull yellow, bordered widely with black. Some winter birds may look like large female House Sparrows, but are longer-tailed, darker; usually with a dull yellow suffusion on the forecrown.
Range: Nw. N. America, wintering through Pacific states. Casual or accidental in winter east to N.S., L.I., Mass.

SPARROWS

WHITE-THROATED SPARROW

tan-striped form

summer
similar in winter

white-striped form

summer
duller in winter

WHITE-CROWNED SPARROW

imm.

adult

imm.

adult

GOLDEN-CROWNED SPARROW

adult summer

HARRIS' SPARROW

imm. winter

CHIPPING SPARROW *Spizella passerina* 5¼″ (13 cm)   **M 370**
Breeding: A small gray-breasted sparrow with a bright *rufous cap,* a *black line* through the eye, and a *white line* over it. *Winter:* Browner, not so gray-breasted; cap and eyebrow line duller. *Immature:* Browner; light crown stripe, gray rump.
Voice: Song, a chipping rattle on one pitch. Note, a dry *chip.*
Range: Canada to Nicaragua. Winters s. U.S. south. **East:** Map 370.
Habitat: Open woods, conifers, orchards, farms, towns.

FIELD SPARROW *Spizella pusilla* 5″ (13 cm)   **M 371**
Note the *pink bill* of this rusty-capped sparrow. It has rather rusty upper parts and a clear breast; less noticeable facial striping than the other rusty-capped sparrows. A narrow light *eye-ring* may give it a big-eyed expression. Juvenal has a finely streaked breast. Note the eye-ring.
Voice: Song, opening on deliberate, sweet, slurring notes, speeding into a trill (which ascends, descends, or stays on the same pitch). Note, *tsee;* has a querulous quality.
Range: Se. Canada, U.S. (east of Rockies). Winters to ne. Mexico.
East: Map 371. **Habitat:** Bushy pastures, brush, scrub.

SWAMP SPARROW   **M 372**
Melospiza georgiana 5–5¾″ (13–14 cm)
A rather stout, dark, rusty sparrow with a dull gray breast, outlined *white throat, reddish cap. Immature* is dimly streaked and has little or no reddish on its striped crown.
Similar species: (1) Chipping Sparrow is less robust and shows a white or buffy stripe over the eye. (2) Field and (3) Tree Sparrows have prominent wing bars. (4) Immature is sometimes misidentified as Lincoln's Sparrow (p. 284).
Voice: Song, a loose trill, similar to Chipping Sparrow's, but slower, sweeter, and stronger (sometimes on 2 pitches simultaneously). Note, a hard *chink,* similar to White-throat's.
Range: Canada (east of Rockies), ne. U.S. Winters to Gulf states.
East: Map 372. **Habitat:** Fresh marshes with tussocks, bushes, or cattails; sedgy swamps.

AMERICAN TREE SPARROW   **M 373**
Spizella arborea 6–6½″ (15–16 cm)
To identify the "Winter Chippy," note the single *dark spot* or "stickpin" on the breast, and the solid *red-brown cap.* Bill dark above, yellow below; 2 white wing bars.
Voice: Song, sweet, variable; opening on 1 or 2 high clear notes. Note, *tseet;* feeding note, a musical *teelwit.*
Range: Alaska, n. Canada. Winters s. Canada to cen. U.S. **East:** Map 373. **Habitat:** Arctic scrub, willow thickets; in winter, brushy roadsides, weedy edges, marshes; patronizes feeders.

RUFOUS-CROWNED SPARROW
Aimophila ruficeps 5–6″ (13–15 cm)
Note the *black whiskers* bordering the throat. A dark sparrow with a plain dusky breast, rufous cap; different habitat.
Voice: Song, stuttering, gurgling. Note, nasal *dear, dear, dear.*
Range: Sw. U.S. **East:** Breeds east locally to e. Oklahoma, w. Arkansas. **Habitat:** Dry, open, brushy slopes.

RUSTY-CAPPED SPARROWS

sexes similar

winter

summer

CHIPPING SPARROW

juv.

for comparison with winter Chipping Sparrow, above

FIELD SPARROW

juv.

CLAY-COLORED SPARROW (See p. 283)

SWAMP SPARROW

imm.

RUFOUS-CROWNED SPARROW

AMERICAN TREE SPARROW

LARK SPARROW   **M 374**
Chondestes grammacus   5½–6½″ (14–16 cm)
Note the *black tail with much white in the corners* (as in Towhee, not as in Vesper Sparrow); also the *single central breast spot* and quaillike head pattern with chestnut ear patch, striped crown. Young are finely streaked, lack the central spot.
Similar species: See Vesper Sparrow (p. 284).
Voice: A broken song; clear notes and trills with pauses between; characterized by buzzing and churring passages.
Range: S. Canada south (west of Appalachians) to n. Mexico. Winters s. U.S. to El Salvador. **East:** Map 374. **Habitat:** Open country with bushes, trees; pastures, farms, roadsides.

CLAY-COLORED SPARROW   *Spizella pallida*   5¼″ (13 cm) **M 375**
A small pale sparrow of midcontinent; plain-breasted, Chipping Sparrow–like, but buffier. Note the *light crown stripe and sharply outlined ear patch.* In fall, more obscure (see below).
Similar species: Chipping and Clay-colored Sparrows both have brown ear patches in fall and winter. Clay-color has sharper head markings and a buffier breast, contrasting with its gray collar or nape. Rump *brown* in Clay-color, *gray* in Chipping.
Voice: Unbirdlike; 3 or 4 low flat buzzes: *bzzz, bzzz, bzzz.*
Range: W. and cen. Canada, n.-cen. U.S. In winter, to Mexico. **East:** Map 375. **Habitat:** Scrub, brushy prairies, Jack Pines.

GRASSHOPPER SPARROW   **M 376**
Ammodramus savannarum   4½–5¼″ (11–13 cm)
A little sparrow of open fields with a short sharp tail, flat head, yellow shoulder. Crown with a pale median stripe; back striped with chestnut and black. Differs from other sparrows of meadows in having a relatively unstriped buffy breast. Flight feeble.
Similar species: Juvenal (late summer) with streaked breast resembles adult Henslow's Sparrow, but wing not so reddish.
Voice: Two songs: (1) 2 faint introductory notes and a thin dry buzz, *pi-tup zeeeeeeeeeeeee;* (2) a thin buzzy tumble of notes.
Range: S. Canada to s. U.S., W. Indies; also s. Mexico to Ecuador. **East:** Map 376. **Habitat:** Grassland, hayfields, prairies.

BACHMAN'S SPARROW   **M 377**
Aimophila aestivalis   5¾″ (14 cm)
In dry open woods of the South, this shy sparrow flushes reluctantly, then drops back into the brush, where it plays hide-and-seek. A glimpse shows it to be striped with reddish brown above and washed with dingy buff across its plain breast.
Similar species: (1) Field Sparrow is smaller, with a smaller *pink* bill. (2) Grasshopper Sparrow lives in meadows, has a light crown stripe, and a tail half as long. (3) Young summer Bachman's has eye-ring and streaked buffy breast; suggests Lincoln's Sparrow, which would not be in the South in summer.
Voice: Song, variable; usually a clear liquid whistle, followed by a loose trill or warble on a different pitch, for example, *seeeee, slip slip slip slip slip* (vaguely suggests Hermit Thrush's).
Range: Se. U.S. (Map 377). **Habitat:** Open pine or oak woods, palmetto scrub, bushy pastures.

SPARROWS
(Mostly clear-breasted)

sexes similar

juvenal

adult

LARK SPARROW

summer

winter

CHIPPING SPARROW

winter

See summer adult on p. 281

CLAY-COLORED SPARROW

GRASSHOPPER SPARROW

See juvenal on p. 287

adult

BACHMAN'S SPARROW

HENSLOW'S SPARROW

juvenal

See adult on p. 287

FOX SPARROW *Passerella iliaca* 6¾–7½″ (17–19 cm)   **M 378**
Larger than the House Sparrow, with a *rufous tail,* conspicuous in
flight. The rusty combined with gray about the neck gives the bird
its foxy look. Breast very heavily streaked with rusty. Action
Towhee-like; rustles among dry leaves.
Similar species: Hermit Thrush (p. 222) has a reddish tail, but
lacks streaks on back, is thin-billed, spotted not striped.
Voice: Song, brilliant and musical; a varied arrangement of short
clear notes and sliding whistles.
Range: Alaska, Canada; w. mts. to cen.-w. U.S. Winters to s. U.S.
East: Map 378. **Habitat:** Wooded undergrowth, brush.

SONG SPARROW *Melospiza melodia* 5–6½″ (13–16 cm) **M 379**
Note the heavy breast streaks confluent into a *large central spot.*
The bird pumps its tail as it flies. Young birds are more finely
streaked, often without the central spot.
Similar species: (1) Savannah Sparrow (p. 286) is more of a field
bird; it often shows yellowish over the eye, has a shorter *notched*
tail, pinker legs. (2) See Lincoln's Sparrow (below).
Voice: Song, a variable series of notes, some musical, some buzzy;
usually starts with 3 or 4 bright repetitious notes, *sweet sweet
sweet,* etc. Call note, a low nasal *tchep.*
Range: Alaska, Canada to cen. Mexico. **East:** Map 379. **Habitat:**
Thickets, brush, marshes, roadsides, gardens.

VESPER SPARROW *Pooecetes gramineus* 6″ (15 cm)   **M 380**
Note the *white outer tail feathers,* conspicuous when the bird flies.
Otherwise suggests a grayish Song Sparrow, but has a *whitish
eye-ring.* Less evident is *chestnut* at bend of wing.
Similar species: Other field birds with white tail sides: (1) meadow-
larks, p. 256, (2) pipits, p. 200, (3) longspurs, p. 264, (4) Junco, p.
266, (5) Lark Sparrow, p. 282.
Voice: Song, throatier than that of Song Sparrow; usually begins
with 2 clear minor notes, followed by 2 higher ones.
Range: Canada to cen. U. S. Winters to Mexico, Gulf. **East:** Map
380. **Habitat:** Meadows, fields, prairies, roadsides.

LINCOLN'S SPARROW *Melospiza lincolnii* 5½″ (14 cm)   **M 381**
A skulker, "afraid of its shadow." Similar to Song Sparrow, but
trimmer, side of face grayer, breast streaks *much finer* and often
not aggregated into a central spot. Note the band of *creamy buff*
across the breast and the narrow eye-ring.
Similar species: Immature Swamp Sparrow is sometimes misidentified as Lincoln's Sparrow; it has a duller breast, with blurry
streaks. Lincoln's is grayer, with a more contrastingly striped
crown (rusty on light gray).
Voice: Song, sweet and gurgling; suggests both House Wren's and
Purple Finch's; starts with low passages, rises abruptly, drops.
Range: Alaska, Canada, w. and ne. U.S. Winters s. U.S. to Guatemala. **East:** Map 381. **Habitat:** Willow and alder thickets, muskeg,
brushy bogs. In winter, thickets, weeds, bushes.

FOX
SPARROW

SONG
SPARROW

VESPER
SPARROW

SWAMP
SPARROW
(See p. 280)

LINCOLN'S
SPARROW

imm.

Purple
Finch
♀

House
Finch
♀

Females for comparison with sparrows
(males shown on p. 271)

SAVANNAH SPARROW
Passerculus sandwichensis 4½–5¾″ (11–14 cm)

This streaked open-country sparrow suggests a Song Sparrow, but usually has a *yellowish* eyebrow stripe, whitish crown stripe, short notched tail, pinker legs. It may lack the yellowish over the eye. The tail notch is an aid when flushing sparrows.
Similar species: Song Sparrow's tail is longer, *rounded*.
Voice: Song, a dreamy lisping *tsit-tsit-tsit, tseeee-tsaaay* (last note lower). Note, a light *tsip*.
Range: Alaska, Canada to Guatemala. Winters to Cen. America, W. Indies. **East:** Map 382. **Habitat:** Open fields, meadows, salt marshes, prairies, dunes, shores.

"IPSWICH" SPARROW or SAVANNAH SPARROW (in part) M 383
Passerculus sandwichensis (in part) 6–6¼″ (15–16 cm)

A large, pale, sandy gray race of the Savannah Sparrow of restricted range. In spring it has a pale yellow eyebrow stripe.
Similar species: It may suggest Vesper Sparrow, but has a white stripe through the crown and lacks white outer tail feathers.
Voice: Similar to nominate Savannah Sparrow's.
Range: Breeds on Sable Island, Nova Scotia. Winters along the coast south to Georgia. **East:** Map 383. **Habitat:** Dunes, beach grass, and edges of salt marshes adjacent to outer beaches.

BAIRD'S SPARROW *Ammodramus bairdii* 5¼″ (13 cm) M 384

An elusive prairie sparrow. The light breast is crossed by a *narrow band* of fine black streaks. Head yellow-brown, streaked with black. The key mark is a broad *ochre* median crown stripe.
Similar species: Savannah Sparrow has more extensive streaking below; stripe in midcrown is narrower (whitish, not ochre).
Voice: Song begins with 2 or 3 high musical *zip's,* and ends with a trill on a lower pitch; more musical than Savannah's song.
Range: N. Great Plains. Winters sw. U.S., n. Mexico. **East:** Map 384. **Habitat:** Native long-grass prairies; local.

HENSLOW'S SPARROW
Ammodramus henslowii 4¾–5¼″ (12–13 cm)

A secretive sparrow of the fields, easily overlooked were it not for its odd song. Short-tailed and flat-headed, with a big pale bill; finely striped across the breast. The striped olive-colored head in conjunction with reddish wings identifies it. Flies low and jerkily with a twisting motion of the tail.
Similar species: See Grasshopper Sparrow (p. 282). Young Henslow's Sparrow (summer) is practically without breast streaks, thus resembles adult Grasshopper. Conversely, young Grasshopper has breast streaks, but lacks the adult Henslow's olive and russet tones.
Voice: Song, a poor vocal effort; a hiccupping *tsi-lick*. May sing on quiet nights.
Range: Cen. and ne. U.S. (Map 385). **Habitat:** Weedy fields.

STREAK-BREASTED GRASS SPARROWS

sexes similar

SAVANNAH SPARROW

typical

SAVANNAH SPARROW

dark northern form

"IPSWICH" SPARROW
(Savannah Sparrow, in part)

BAIRD'S SPARROW

adult

HENSLOW'S SPARROW

(juv. on p. 283)

GRASSHOPPER SPARROW

(adult on p. 283)

juvenal

SHARP-TAILED SPARROW

Ammospiza caudacuta 5–6″ (13–15 cm)

A marsh sparrow. Note the deep *ochre-yellow of the face,* which completely surrounds the gray ear patch. Coastal Sharp-tails have streaked breasts; those of inland prairies are buffier, almost devoid of streaks. Northern coastal birds (Maine north) have grayer backs and blurrier streaks than those to the south.

Similar species: (1) Juvenal Seaside Sparrow in late summer is much like Sharp-tail. (2) In prairies, see LeConte's Sparrow. (3) Savannah Sparrow (p. 286) has a notched tail.

Voice: Song, a gasping buzz, *tuptup-sheeeeeeeee.*

Range: Canadian prairies; Atlantic Coast. Winters coastally. **East:** Map 386. **Habitat:** Marshes, muskeg; coastal marshes.

LeCONTE'S SPARROW

Ammospiza leconteii 4½–5¼″ (11–13 cm)

A sharp-tailed sparrow of weedy prairie marshes. Note the *bright buff-ochre* eyebrow stripe and breast (with streaks *confined to the sides*). Other points are the *pinkish brown nape,* white stripe through the crown, strong stripes on back.

Similar species: (1) Sharp-tailed Sparrow has a solid crown. (2) Grasshopper Sparrow (p. 282) lacks streaks on the sides.

Voice: Song, 2 extremely thin, grasshopperlike hisses.

Range: S.-cen. Canada to n. prairie states. Migrant to Gulf. **East:** Map 387. **Habitat:** Tall grass, weedy hayfields, marshes.

SEASIDE SPARROW *Ammospiza maritima* 6″ (15 cm)

Very dingy looking. A dark, olive-gray, sharp-tailed sparrow of salt marshes, with a short *yellow piece before the eye,* and a whitish streak along the jaw. Shares marshes with Sharp-tails.

Similar species: "Dusky" Seaside and "Cape Sable" Seaside Sparrows (below) are now considered races of this species.

Voice: Song, *cutcut zhe′-eeeeeeee;* very similar to Sharp-tailed Sparrow's song, but usually with a stronger accent (*zhe′*) in the middle. Note, *chack* (like a little Red-winged Blackbird's).

Range: Coastal marshes from s. New England to Florida and along Gulf Coast to Texas (Map 388). **Habitat:** Salt marshes.

"DUSKY" SEASIDE SPARROW

Ammospiza maritima (in part) or *A. "nigrescens"* 6″ (15 cm)

The darkest Seaside Sparrow; *upper parts blackish;* underparts heavily streaked with black. Any Seaside Sparrow on St. Johns River near Titusville, Florida, is this species.

Range: Very local. Marshes on St. Johns River near Titusville, Florida. Formerly also on nearby Merritt Island. Endangered.

"CAPE SABLE" SEASIDE SPARROW

Ammospiza maritima (in part) or *A. "mirabilis"* 6″ (15 cm)

The *only Seaside Sparrow* in southern Florida; greener above and whiter below than any other race of *maritima.* Very local.

Range: Coastal prairies near Cape Sable, Florida (Map 389).

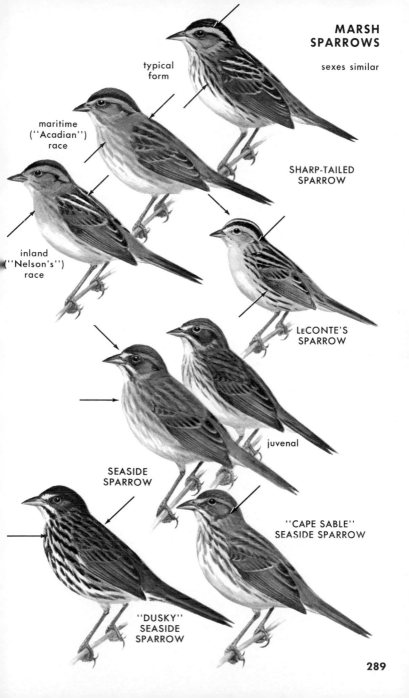

MARSH SPARROWS

sexes similar

typical form

maritime ("Acadian") race

inland ("Nelson's") race

SHARP-TAILED SPARROW

LeCONTE'S SPARROW

juvenal

SEASIDE SPARROW

"CAPE SABLE" SEASIDE SPARROW

"DUSKY" SEASIDE SPARROW

289

ACCIDENTAL SEABIRDS

1. BLACK-BROWED ALBATROSS
Diomedea melanophris 32–34″ (80–85 cm)
Wingspan 7½ ft. Suggests a huge Greater Black-backed Gull, but with a short *blackish tail* and a very large yellow bill with a hooked tip. A *dark eye streak* gives it a frowning look. In stiff-winged gliding flight the underwing is white, broadly outlined with black. (Cold oceans of S. Hemisphere.) Vagrant, far offshore in N. Atlantic; recorded north to Nova Scotia.

2. YELLOW-NOSED ALBATROSS
Diomedea chlororhynchos 29–34″ (73–85 cm)
Wingspan 7–7½ ft. Similar to Black-browed Albatross, but the bill is *black,* with a *yellow ridge* on the upper mandible. In flight the underwing is whiter, with narrower black edgings. (Cold oceans of S. Hemisphere.) Casual vagrant well offshore in N. Atlantic north to Nova Scotia.

3. RED-FOOTED BOOBY *Sula sula* 26–30″ (65–75 cm)
Adults have *bright red feet*. Bill pale blue. *White phase:* Gannetlike; white, with much black in the wing as in Masked Booby, but tail *white*. *Brown phase:* Brown back and wings, paler head; white tail and belly. (Tropical oceans.) Reported La., Fla. (at least a dozen recent sight records, mainly off Dry Tortugas).

4. LESSER FRIGATEBIRD *Fregata ariel* 31″ (78 cm)
Smaller than Magnificent Frigatebird; male distinctive, with a *round white patch on each flank* beneath the wing. Female has a chestnut (not gray) collar on hindneck. (Tropical oceans.) Photographed Maine (1960).

5. RED-BILLED TROPICBIRD
Phaethon aethereus 24–40″ (60–100 cm)
Differs from White-tailed Tropicbird (p. 80) in having a closely *barred back, bright red* (not orange or yellow) bill. (Tropical oceans.) Accidental Fla., L.I., R.I., Nfld. Banks.

6. BAND-TAILED GULL *Larus belcheri*
(Simeon Gull) 20″ (50 cm)
A black-backed gull with a clean-cut *black band* across the tail. Bill broadly tipped with *red;* feet yellow. Winter plumage: *Head blackish.* (S. America.) Collier Co., Fla. (3 years).

7. MEW GULL *Larus canus* 16–18″ (40–45 cm)
Smaller than Ring-billed Gull, with a small, short, *unmarked,* greenish yellow bill; darker back. Legs *greenish*. Immature looks like a "pint-sized" young Herring Gull with a small ploverlike bill. (N. Eurasia, nw. N. America.) Reported from a dozen states and provinces coastally from Nfld. to Fla.

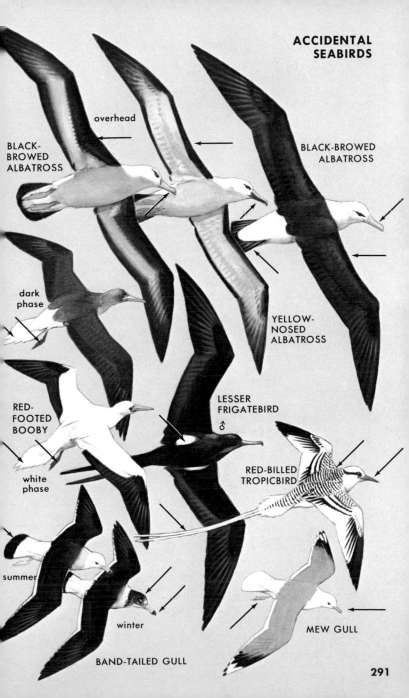

ACCIDENTAL SEABIRDS

overhead

BLACK-
BROWED
ALBATROSS

BLACK-BROWED
ALBATROSS

dark
phase

YELLOW-
NOSED
ALBATROSS

RED-
FOOTED
BOOBY

LESSER
FRIGATEBIRD
♂

white
phase

RED-BILLED
TROPICBIRD

summer

MEW GULL

winter

BAND-TAILED GULL

ACCIDENTAL SEABIRDS

1. **BAND-RUMPED STORM PETREL** *Oceanodroma castro*
(Harcourt's Storm Petrel) 7–8″ (18–20 cm)
> Very similar to Leach's Storm Petrel, but with shorter wings, less bounding flight; tail more squarish. White of rump broad, forming a *straight band* (not divided as in Leach's) and extending onto flanks and undertail coverts. (E. Atlantic, Pacific.) Fla., N.C., Mo., Ind., D.C., Del., Pa., Ont., Que.

2. **BRITISH STORM PETREL** *Hydrobates pelagicus* 6″ (15 cm)
> Smaller than Wilson's Storm Petrel. Shorter legs; feet (lacking yellow webs) do not extend beyond square tail. *Whitish patch* on underwing. (E. N. Atlantic.) Sable I., N.S.

3. **WHITE-FACED STORM PETREL** *Pelagodroma marina* 8″ (20 cm)
> A storm petrel with white head and underparts, dark crown and eye patch. (Se. Atlantic, sw. Pacific, Indian Ocean.) Several sightings far offshore, N.C. to Mass.

4. **LITTLE SHEARWATER** *Puffinus assimilis* 10½–12″ (26–30 cm)
> Smaller than Audubon's (p. 74); shorter tail. Bluish legs contrast with white undertail coverts (Audubon's has flesh-colored legs, blackish undertail coverts). Manx (p. 74) is larger; wings longer; black on face extends below eye level. (E. Atl., oceans of S. Hemisphere.) S.C., N.C., Maine, N.S.

5. **SOUTH TRINIDAD PETREL**
Pterodroma arminjoniana 16″ (40 cm)
> Dark, intermediate, and pale morphs. The 2 N. American specimens are dark; differ from Sooty Shearwater by absence of silvery wing linings. Light area under primaries suggests a jaeger. Feet, legs black. (S. Atl., Indian Ocean.) N.Y., off N.C.

6. **SCALED PETREL** *Pterodroma inexpectata*
(Mottled Petrel) 14″ (35 cm)
> Identified by white chest, dark belly, and black stripe on fore edge of the white underwing. (N.Z., Pacific.) N.Y. (1880).

7. **CAPE PETREL** *Daption capense*
(Cape Pigeon or Pintado Petrel) 14″ (35 cm)
> Size of Bonaparte's Gull; unmistakable pattern, *large white wing patches*. (Cold oceans of S. Hemisphere.) Maine (1873).

Note: There are also a record of a possible **KERMADEC PETREL,** *Pterodroma neglecta,* photographed at Hawk Mt., Pa., and an old record presumably of **WHITE-BELLIED STORM PETREL,** *Fregetta grallaria* (originally recorded as *Fregetta tropica*), off St. Marks, Fla. (specimens lost).

8. **WHITE-WINGED BLACK TERN**
Chlidonias leucopterus 9″ (23 cm)
> In summer, underwing linings *black,* upperwing mostly *white.* In winter, paler than Black Tern; lacks dark shoulder spot. (Eurasia.) Wisc., N.B., Mass., Del., Ga.

9. **LARGE-BILLED TERN** *Phaetusa simplex* 14½″ (36 cm)
> *Very stout yellow bill.* Wing suggests Sabine's Gull (*blackish primaries,* white secondaries). Tail short, gray, nearly square. (S. America.) Reported Ill., Ohio.

ACCIDENTAL SEABIRDS

BRITISH
STORM PETREL

BAND-RUMPED
STORM PETREL

WHITE-FACED
STORM PETREL

LITTLE SHEARWATER

CAPE PETREL

SCALED PETREL

SOUTH TRINIDAD PETREL

WHITE-WINGED BLACK TERN

LARGE-BILLED TERN

293

ACCIDENTALS FROM EURASIA
Shorebirds, etc.

North America and Europe share many species of waders. A number of others have found their way across the Atlantic, east or west, casually or accidentally. Some records are supported by specimens or photographs, others are not. Two Eurasians, Ruff and Curlew Sandpiper, are of rare but regular occurrence, reported every year in eastern North America. For field marks of most of the species below, see *A Field Guide to the Birds of Britain and Europe* (No. 8 in the Peterson Field Guide Series).

1. **GREATER GOLDEN PLOVER** *Pluvialis apricaria* Of regular occurrence in s. Greenland. Recorded Nfld.

2. **NORTHERN LAPWING** *Vanellus vanellus* Baffin I., Lab., Que., N.B., N.S., Maine, R.I., L.I., N.C., S.C., Fla.

3. **MONGOLIAN PLOVER** *Charadrius mongolus* La. Size and bill (heavy) same as in Wilson's Plover. Has rufous breastband, black mask in summer but not in winter.

4. **EUROPEAN WOODCOCK** *Scolopax rusticola* Que., Nfld., Ohio, Pa., N.J., Va., Ala. (all records old).

5. **GREAT SNIPE** *Gallinago media* N.J., Va.

6. **EUROPEAN JACKSNIPE** *Limnocryptes minimus* Lab.

7. **GREENSHANK** *Tringa nebularia* Sight record N.Y.

8. **REDSHANK** *Tringa totanus* Sight records N.S., R.I.

9. **SPOTTED REDSHANK** *Tringa erythropus* Ont., Nfld., Conn., R.I., Pa.

10. **BLACK-TAILED GODWIT** *Limosa limosa* Nfld., Maine., N.J.

11. **BAR-TAILED GODWIT** *Limosa lapponica* Nfld., Miquelon I., L.I., N.J., N.C., Fla.

12. **EURASIAN CURLEW** *Numenius arquata* Nfld., N.S., Mass., L.I. Has white rump.

13. **WHIMBREL** (European race) *Numenius phaeopus* (in part) N.S., Mass., L.I., N.J. Has white rump.

14. **LITTLE EGRET** *Egretta garzetta* (not shown) Nfld. In breeding plumage, differs from Snowy Egret in having 2 very long, slender head plumes.

15. **COMMON CRANE** *Grus grus* (not shown) Photographed Platte R., cen. Neb.

16. **CORN CRAKE** *Crex crex* See p. 115.

winter

1 winter

2

3 summer

4

5

6

7

8

9 summer winter

10

11 winter winter

12

13

295

ACCIDENTALS FROM EURASIA

Field marks of the Eurasian strays listed below can be found in *A Field Guide to the Birds of Britain and Europe* (No. 8 in the series). Some have been substantiated by specimens or photographs; others are convincing sight records. Some sightings of European waterfowl are suspect and could be aviary or zoo escapes. The three passerines shown opposite could have been wind-drifted from Scandinavia to North America during migration and are most likely bona fide stragglers, but the following species (not shown) are more questionable: Chaffinch (N.Y., Pa., La.), Hawfinch (Mass.), Eurasian Siskin (Wisc., w. N.Y.), European Greenfinch (N.B., N.Y.), Linnet (Ont., N.Y.), European Bullfinch (N.Y.), European Robin (N.Y.), Great Tit (Que., N.B., at feeders), and Blue Tit (Ont., at feeders). These may or may not have been escapes. An assist by ship is always possible.

1. **FIELDFARE** *Turdus pilaris* Breeds sw. Greenland. Recorded Nfld., Cape Breton I., Que., Ont., Conn., N.Y., Del.
2. **BRAMBLING** *Fringilla montifringilla* Pa., N.J. (2).
3. **REDWING** *Turdus iliacus* L.I.
4. **GARGANEY** *Anas querquedula* Man., P.E.I., N.B., Mass., N.Y., Del., Tenn., N.C., Ala.
5. **BAIKAL TEAL** *Anas formosa* Ohio, Pa., N.C. (escapes?).
6. **TUFTED DUCK** *Aythya fuligula* Ont., Ill., Ind., Mass., Conn., N.Y., L.I., N.J. Increasingly frequent.
7. **RED-CRESTED POCHARD** *Netta rufina* N.Y.(?); origin of specimen questionable.
8. **SMEW** *Mergus albellus* Ont., Que., R.I.
9. **SHELDUCK** *Tadorna tadorna* Mass., Del.
10. **RUDDY SHELDUCK** *Tadorna ferruginea* Que., Vt., Mass., R.I., N.J., Ky.
11. **GRAYLAG GOOSE** *Anser anser* Mass.
12. **BEAN GOOSE** *Anser fabalis* Ont.
13. **PINK-FOOTED GOOSE** *Anser brachyrhynchus* Mass., L.I.
14. **LESSER WHITE-FRONTED GOOSE** *Anser erythropus* Pa., N.J., Md., Del.
15. **BARNACLE GOOSE** *Branta leucopsis* Lab., Que., N.B., Ont., Vt., Mass., Conn., N.Y., Pa., Md., Okla., N.C., Ala.
16. **RED-BREASTED GOOSE** *Branta ruficollis* Mass., N.Y., Pa. (escapes?).
17. **WHOOPER SWAN** *Olor cygnus* Formerly bred sw. Greenland. Accidental Maine (1903).
18. **EUROPEAN COOT** *Fulica atra* (not shown) Nfld. Lacks white undertail coverts of American Coot.
19. **WHITE-TAILED EAGLE** *Haliaeetus albicilla* (not shown) Mass., Conn.
20. **EUROPEAN SPARROWHAWK** *Accipiter nisus* (not shown) Cape May, N.J. (photograph unconfirmed).
21. **EURASIAN KESTREL** *Falco tinnunculus* (not shown) Mass., N.J.

ACCIDENTALS FROM THE TROPICS

West Indian vagrants are usually spotted in Florida. For their field marks see Bond's *Birds of the West Indies* (abbreviated W.I. below). Strays from Mexico are described in *A Field Guide to Mexican Birds* (No. 20 in the Peterson Field Guide Series—Mex.) or in *A Field Guide to the Birds of Texas* (No. 13 in the series—Tex.). Details of Florida accidentals are being documented elsewhere by Wesley Biggs. Some records are hypothetical.

1. **NORTH AMERICAN JACANA** *Jacana spinosa* (Tex.) Fla.

2. **PAINT-BILLED CRAKE** *Porzana erythrops* (Peru, Galapagos) Va. Smaller than Sora; slaty, with bright coral-red legs and base of bill.

3. **SPOTTED RAIL** *Pardirallus maculatus* (Mex.) Pa.

4. **MASKED DUCK** *Oxyura dominica* (Tex.) S. Fla. (more than 20 records; has probably nested Loxahatchee); also recorded La., Ala., Ga., Md., Mass., Wisc., Vt.

5. **BLACK-BELLIED WHISTLING DUCK** *Dendrocygna autumnalis* (Tex.) La., Ill., Fla. (has bred); escapes?

6. **WHITE-CHEEKED PINTAIL** (Bahama Pintail) *Anas bahamensis* (W.I.) Fla. (several), Va., Ill., Wisc.

7. **LEAST GREBE** *Podiceps dominicus* (Tex.) La., Fla.

8. **CARIBBEAN COOT** *Fulica caribea* (W.I.) S. Fla. (many recent sightings; may breed). Distinguished from American Coot by its broader frontal shield, which is *entirely white* (or tinged with yellow).

9. **ZENAIDA DOVE** *Zenaida aurita* (W.I. or Mex.) Formerly bred Fla. Keys; now accidental s. Fla.

10. **KEY WEST QUAIL DOVE** *Geotrygon chrysia* (W.I.) Key West (before 1900); recently recorded s. Fla.

11. **RUDDY QUAIL DOVE** *Geotrygon montana* (W.I. or Mex.) Dry Tortugas and Fla. Keys.

12. **SCALY-NAPED PIGEON** *Columba squamosa* (W.I.) Key West, Ga.

13. **BLUE-HEADED QUAIL DOVE** *Starnoenas cyanocephala* (not shown; see W.I.) Uncertain. Audubon's sighting at Key West questionable, as is a specimen from Miami (possibly a zoo escape).

14. **LESSER BLACK HAWK** *Buteogallus anthracinus* (not shown; see Tex. or Mex.) Minn., Fla. (at least 4 different birds sighted in Miami area).

1

imm.

adult

2

3

♀

♂

4

5

6

winter

summer   7

5

8

9   10   11   12

ACCIDENTALS FROM THE TROPICS

1. **CAVE SWALLOW** *Petrochelidon fulva* (Mex. or Tex.) Sable I., N.S. (several); Fla. Keys, Dry Tortugas (perhaps regular).
2. **BAHAMA SWALLOW** *Callichelidon cyaneoviridis* (W.I.) Fla. Keys (many records; may have bred).
3. **ANTILLEAN PALM SWIFT** *Tachornis phoenicobia* (W.I.) Key West.
4. **CUBAN EMERALD** *Chlorostilbon ricordii* (W.I.) Fla.; several sightings East Coast and Fla. Keys.
5. **BAHAMA WOODSTAR** *Calliphlox evelynae* (W.I.) S. Fla.
6. **BAHAMA MOCKINGBIRD** *Mimus gundlachii* (W.I.) Fla. Keys, Dry Tortugas. Streaks on flanks; no white wing patches.
7. **FORK-TAILED FLYCATCHER** *Muscivora tyrannus* (Mex.) Fla., Miss., S.C., N.J., Pa., Wisc., N.Y., Mass., N.H., Maine, Ont., N.B., N.S.
8. **KISKADEE** *Pitangus sulphuratus* (Tex.) La., Fla., N.J.
9. **RED-LEGGED THRUSH** *Turdus plumbeus* (W.I.) Miami.
10. **BLACK-COWLED ORIOLE** *Icterus dominicensis* (W.I.) Sight record Seal I., N.S.
11. **TAWNY-SHOULDERED BLACKBIRD** *Agelaius humeralis* (W.I.) Fla. Keys (3 records).
12. **STRIPE-HEADED TANAGER** *Spindalis zena* (W.I.) S. Fla. (at least 20 records).
13. **YELLOW-GREEN VIREO** *Vireo flavoviridis* (Mex.) Fla., Que.
14. **BANANAQUIT** *Coereba flaveola* (W.I.) S. Fla. (20+ records).
15. **CUBAN (MELODIOUS) GRASSQUIT** *Tiaris canora* (W.I.) Miami, Fla. Keys (several sight records).
16. **BLACK-FACED GRASSQUIT** *Tiaris bicolor* (W.I.) S. Fla. (several records).
17. **CUBAN BULLFINCH** *Melopyrrha nigra* (W.I.) Miami.
18. **GREATER ANTILLEAN BULLFINCH** *Loxigilla violacea* (W.I.) S. Fla.
19. **GRAY-RUMPED SWIFT** *Chaetura cinereiventris* (not shown; see W.I.) May be conspecific with No. 3. Dry Tortugas.
20. **CUBAN MARTIN** *Progne cryptoleuca* (not shown; see W.I.) May be a race of Purple Martin. S. Fla., Fla. Keys.
21. **GRAY-BREASTED MARTIN** *Progne chalybea* (not shown; see Mex.) Fla. Keys.
22. **SOUTHERN MARTIN** *Progne modesta* (not shown) Key West.
23. **TROPICAL KINGBIRD** *Tyrannus melancholicus* (not shown; see Tex.) La., Fla. (several), Mass., Maine, N.S.
24. **LOGGERHEAD KINGBIRD** *Tyrannus caudifasciatus* (not shown; see W.I.) S. Fla.
25. **STOLID FLYCATCHER** *Myiarchus stolidus* (not shown) Ala.
26. **VARIEGATED FLYCATCHER** *Empidonomus varius* (not shown) Maine.
27. **THICK-BILLED VIREO** *Vireo crassirostris* (not shown; see W.I.) Se. Fla. (3 possible sight records).
28. **BAHAMA YELLOWTHROAT** *Geothlypis rostrata* (not shown; see W.I.) Fla.

301

EXOTICS
Introduced Birds and Escapes

Most of the successfully introduced birds (Mute Swan, Ring-necked Pheasant, Gray Partridge, Rock Dove, European Starling, House Sparrow, Eurasian Tree Sparrow), well-established escapes (Ringed Turtle Dove, Budgerigar, Red-whiskered Bulbul, Spotted Oriole, House Finch), and successful invaders (Cattle Egret and others) are described and illustrated earlier in this book. So are the various parrots that might be encountered (p. 178). A number of other species, mostly game birds, have been introduced unsuccessfully by fish and game departments. In addition, many zoo and aviary escapes have been reported—everything from hornbills to ostriches and penguins! The possibilities are endless. A few of the most frequently reported exotics are shown opposite.

1. **EUROPEAN GOLDFINCH** *Carduelis carduelis* Formerly established L.I. See also p. 272.
2. **JAVA SPARROW** *Padda oryzivora* Established locally Miami, Fla.; breeding.
3. **RED-CRESTED CARDINAL** (Brazilian Cardinal) *Paroaria coronata* Has bred Fla., Pa., Conn.
4. **COMMON WAXBILL** *Estrilda astrild*
5. **SPOTTED MUNIA** (Ricebird) *Lonchura punctulata*
6. **CHESTNUT MUNIA** *Lonchura malacca*
7. **HILL MYNAH** *Gracula religiosa* Fla. (Homestead to Palm Beach).
8. **TROUPIAL** *Icterus icterus*
9. **CHINESE GOOSE** (Swan Goose) *Anser cygnoides*
10. **BAR-HEADED GOOSE** *Anser indicus*
11. **EGYPTIAN GOOSE** *Alopochen aegyptiacus*
12. **BLACK-NECKED SWAN** *Cygnus melanocoryphus*
13. **BLACK SWAN** *Cygnus atratus*
14. **SPOTBILL DUCK** *Anas poecilorhyncha*
15. **MANDARIN DUCK** *Aix galericulata*
16. **MUSCOVY** *Cairina moschata* See also p. 52.
17. **CHUKAR** *Alectoris chukar* Eastern introductions have had only limited success.
18. **GOLDEN PHEASANT** *Chrysolophus pictus*
19. **COTURNIX** (Migratory Quail) *Coturnix coturnix* Great numbers have been liberated without lasting success.
20. **PLAIN CHACHALACA** *Ortalis vetula* Successfully established Sapelo and Blackbeard Is., Ga.
21. **BLACK FRANCOLIN** *Francolinus francolinus* Successfully established locally s. La., Fla.
22. **SOUTHERN LAPWING** *Vanellus chilensis*
23. **GRAY-NECKED WOOD RAIL** *Aramides cajanea* Near Miami and Vero Beach, Fla. (released?).

ACCIDENTALS FROM THE WEST

Vagrants from western North America, reported fewer than a dozen times *east of the Mississippi River,* are listed below. They are described and illustrated in *A Field Guide to Western Birds.*

STELLER'S EIDER Que., Maine, Mass.
ZONE-TAILED HAWK N.C.
GRAY HAWK Ill.
HARRIS' HAWK La., Fla., Iowa, Mo., Ohio, N.Y.
MOUNTAIN PLOVER Minn., Mich., Mo., Mass., Va., Ala., Fla.
WANDERING TATTLER Ont.
BLACK TURNSTONE Wisc.
SURFBIRD W. Fla. (3 records).
RUFOUS-NECKED STINT Ont., Maine, Conn.
SHARP-TAILED SANDPIPER Ont., Ill., Iowa, Mass., Conn., L.I., Md., Fla.
WESTERN GULL Ill.
ANCIENT MURRELET Man., Ont., Que., Neb., Minn., Wisc., Ill., Ohio.
TUFTED PUFFIN Maine (Audubon's record).
BAND-TAILED PIGEON Ont., N.H., Ohio, Tenn., Ala., Fla.
FLAMMULATED SCREECH OWL La., Fla.
LESSER NIGHTHAWK S. La., Fla., Ont. See p. 184.
BLACK SWIFT Ill.
WHITE-THROATED SWIFT Mich., Ark.
BLACK-CHINNED HUMMINGBIRD La. (regular?), nw. Fla., Ill.
BROAD-TAILED HUMMINGBIRD La., Ark., nw. Fla.
ALLEN'S HUMMINGBIRD La., Miss.
BUFF-BELLIED HUMMINGBIRD S. La. (New Orleans).
GOLDEN-FRONTED WOODPECKER Fla., Mich.
LEWIS' WOODPECKER Man., Ont., Minn., Ill., Mich., Mo., R.I.
CASSIN'S KINGBIRD La., Va., Wisc., Mass., Ont.
BLACK PHOEBE Fla. (several).

WIED'S CRESTED FLYCATCHER La., Fla. (several).
WESTERN PEWEE Minn. (nested), Ont., Mass., Md., Miss.
VIOLET-GREEN SWALLOW Man., Mo., Ill., Fla.
STELLER'S JAY Se. Que., Ill.
CLARK'S NUTCRACKER Man., nw. Ont., Minn., Wisc., Ill., Mich., Mo., Ark.
NORTH AMERICAN DIPPER Ne. Minn.
CURVE-BILLED THRASHER Man., Minn., Wisc., La., Fla.
SAGE THRASHER Ont., Wisc., Ill., L.I., N.C., La., Fla.
WHITE WAGTAIL N. Que.
PHAINOPEPLA Ont., Mass., R.I.
VIRGINIA'S WARBLER Ill., Ont., N.J.
LUCY'S WARBLER La., Mass.
TOWNSEND'S WARBLER Minn., Wisc., Ohio, Pa., N.Y., N.J., Mass., N.S.
GOLDEN-CHEEKED WARBLER Fla.
HERMIT WARBLER Minn., N.Y., Conn., La.
MacGILLIVRAY'S WARBLER Ont., Ind., Mass., Conn., La.
PAINTED REDSTART La., Ark., Ohio, N.Y., Mass., Ont.
SCOTT'S ORIOLE La., Minn., Man., Ont.
BRONZED COWBIRD S. La., w. Fla.
GRAY-CROWNED ROSY FINCH Ont., Minn., Mo., Maine.
CASSIN'S SPARROW Ont., N.S., N.J. Breeds east to 100th meridian in Okla.
BLACK-THROATED SPARROW Wisc., Ill., N.J., Va., La., Fla.
GRAY-HEADED JUNCO Minn., Ill., Ohio.
BREWER'S SPARROW Minn., Mass.

GOLDEN-CROWNED SPARROW Occasional in East. See p. 278.

Range Maps

BY VIRGINIA MARIE PETERSON

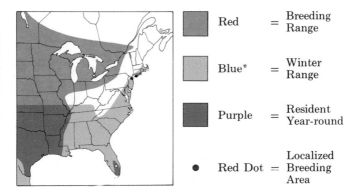

Red	=	Breeding Range
Blue*	=	Winter Range
Purple	=	Resident Year-round
● Red Dot	=	Localized Breeding Area

The maps on the following pages are approximate, giving the general outlines of the range of each species. Within these broad outlines may be many gaps — areas that are ecologically unsuitable for the species. A Marsh Wren must have a marsh, a Meadowlark a meadow, a Ruffed Grouse a woodland or a forest. Certain species may be extremely local or sporadic for reasons that are not clear. Some birds are extending their ranges, a few explosively. Others are declining or even disappearing from large areas where they were formerly found. Some of these increases and declines, as well as extralimital occurrences, are noted. The maps are based on data culled from the many state and regional publications and modified by the observations of a myriad of birders as reported in *American Birds, Birding,* and other journals.

Winter ranges are not as definite as breeding ranges. A species may exist at a very low density near the northern limits of its winter range, surviving through December in mild seasons but often succumbing to the bitter conditions of January and February.

The maps are specific only for the area covered by this *Field Guide.* The Mallard, for example, is found over a large part of the globe. Its world range is briefly stated in the main text. The map shows only its range in eastern North America. The maps are not in phylogenetic sequence (see Systematic List on p. 17) but are arranged in the order in which the species accounts appear in this book.

*Note: In the case of several visiting seabirds from the Southern Hemisphere, blue is used to denote *their* winter range (*during our summer*).

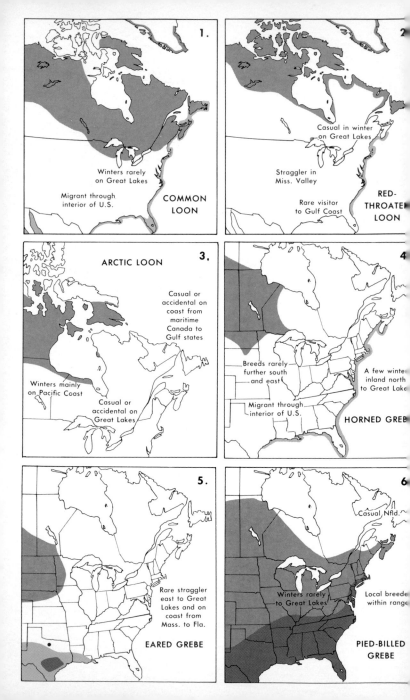

1. **COMMON LOON**
Winters rarely on Great Lakes
Migrant through interior of U.S.

2. **RED-THROATED LOON**
Casual in winter on Great Lakes
Straggler in Miss. Valley
Rare visitor to Gulf Coast

3. **ARCTIC LOON**
Casual or accidental on coast from maritime Canada to Gulf states
Winters mainly on Pacific Coast
Casual or accidental on Great Lakes

4. **HORNED GREBE**
Breeds rarely further south and east
A few winter inland north to Great Lakes
Migrant through interior of U.S.

5. **EARED GREBE**
Rare straggler east to Great Lakes and on coast from Mass. to Fla.

6. **PIED-BILLED GREBE**
Casual, Nfld.
Winters rarely to Great Lakes
Local breeder within range

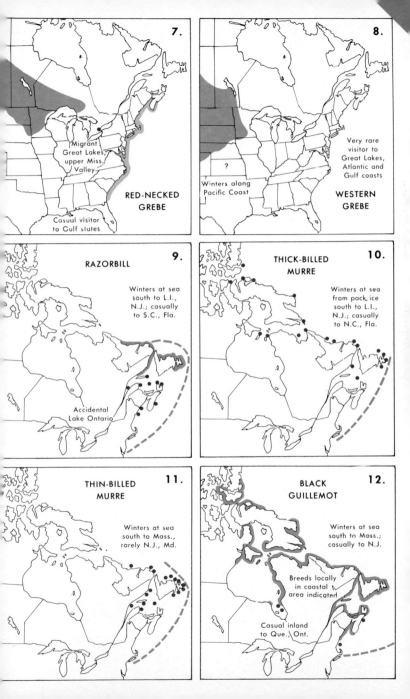

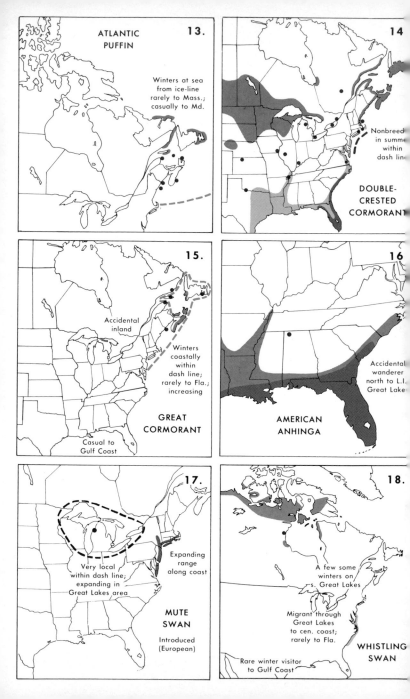

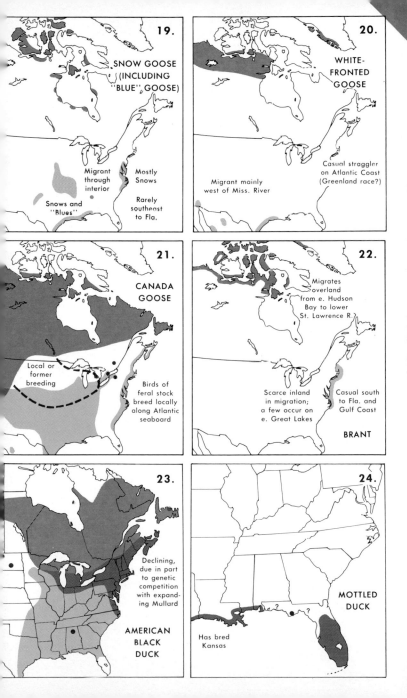

19. SNOW GOOSE (INCLUDING "BLUE" GOOSE)

Migrant through interior

Mostly Snows

Rarely southeast to Fla.

Snows and "Blues"

20. WHITE-FRONTED GOOSE

Casual straggler on Atlantic Coast (Greenland race?)

Migrant mainly west of Miss. River

21. CANADA GOOSE

Local or former breeding

Birds of feral stock breed locally along Atlantic seaboard

22. BRANT

Migrates overland from e. Hudson Bay to lower St. Lawrence R.

Scarce inland in migration; a few occur on e. Great Lakes

Casual south to Fla. and Gulf Coast

23. AMERICAN BLACK DUCK

Declining, due in part to genetic competition with expanding Mullard

24. MOTTLED DUCK

Has bred Kansas

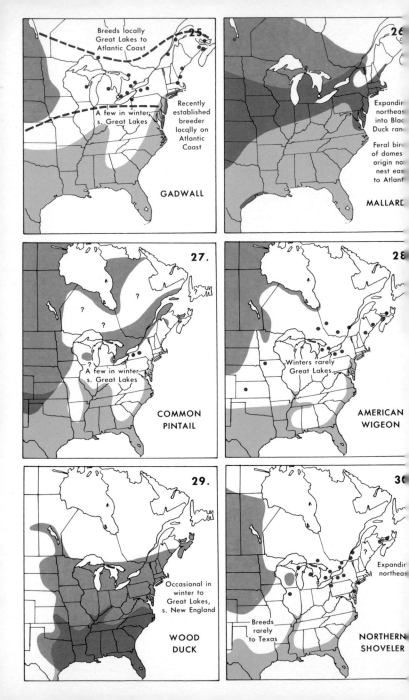

25. Breeds locally Great Lakes to Atlantic Coast

A few in winter, s. Great Lakes

Recently established breeder locally on Atlantic Coast

GADWALL

26. Expandin northeas into Blac Duck ran

Feral bir of domes origin no nest eas to Atlan

MALLARD

27. A few in winter, s. Great Lakes

COMMON PINTAIL

28. Winters rarely Great Lakes

AMERICAN WIGEON

29. Occasional in winter to Great Lakes, s. New England

WOOD DUCK

30. Expandir northeas

Breeds rarely to Texas

NORTHERN SHOVELER

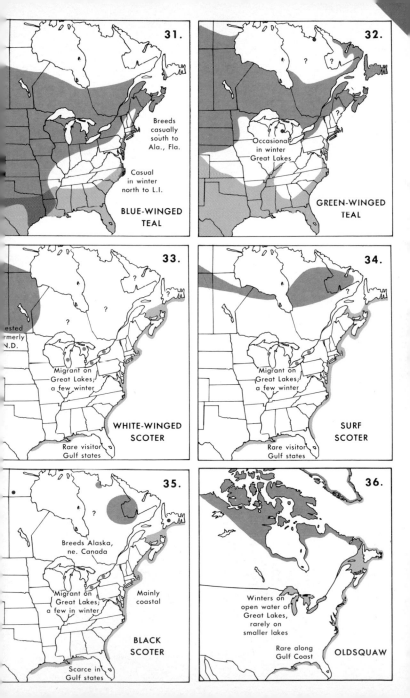

31. Breeds casually south to Ala., Fla.

Casual in winter north to L.I.

BLUE-WINGED TEAL

32. Occasional in winter Great Lakes

GREEN-WINGED TEAL

33. ested rmerly N.D.

Migrant on Great Lakes; a few winter

Rare visitor Gulf states

WHITE-WINGED SCOTER

34. Migrant on Great Lakes; a few winter

Rare visitor Gulf states

SURF SCOTER

35. Breeds Alaska, ne. Canada

Migrant on Great Lakes; a few in winter

Mainly coastal

Scarce in Gulf states

BLACK SCOTER

36. Winters on open water of Great Lakes, rarely on smaller lakes

Rare along Gulf Coast

OLDSQUAW

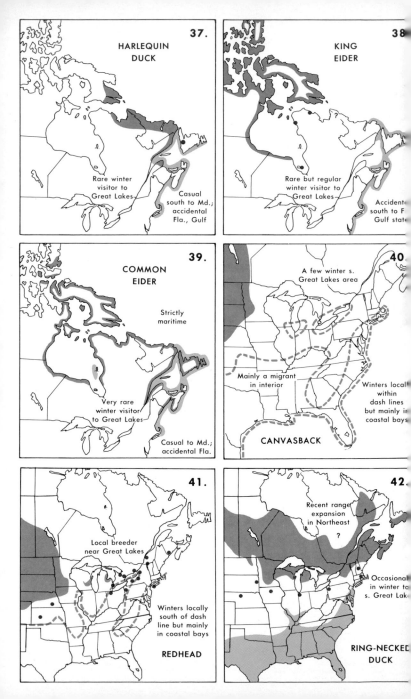

37.
HARLEQUIN DUCK

Rare winter visitor to Great Lakes

Casual south to Md.; accidental Fla., Gulf

38.
KING EIDER

Rare but regular winter visitor to Great Lakes

Accidental south to F Gulf state

39.
COMMON EIDER

Strictly maritime

Very rare winter visitor to Great Lakes

Casual to Md.; accidental Fla.

40.
A few winter s. Great Lakes area

Mainly a migrant in interior

Winters local within dash lines but mainly i coastal bays

CANVASBACK

41.
Local breeder near Great Lakes

Winters locally south of dash line but mainly in coastal bays

REDHEAD

42.
Recent range expansion in Northeast

?

Occasional in winter to s. Great Lak

RING-NECKED DUCK

43.

Mainly migrant on Great Lakes A few winter

Commonest winter Scaup in s. U.S.

LESSER SCAUP

44.

Occasional Miss. Valley in winter

The common winter Scaup of n. U.S.

GREATER SCAUP

45.

Winters locally from Great Lakes, St. Lawrence, south within dash lines

COMMON GOLDENEYE

46.

BARROW'S GOLDENEYE

Breeds mainly w. N. America and Iceland

Rare winter visitor to Great Lakes

Casual on coast south to Md.

47.

BUFFLEHEAD

48.

Rare transient maritime Canada

A few winter north to s. Great Lakes

RUDDY DUCK

Has bred Texas, La., Fla.

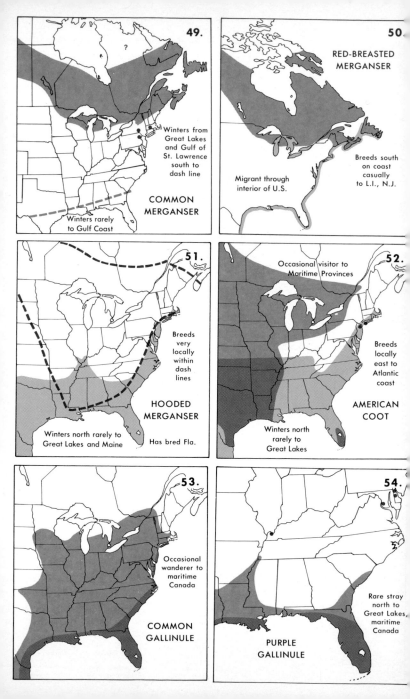

49.

Winters from Great Lakes and Gulf of St. Lawrence south to dash line

Winters rarely to Gulf Coast

COMMON MERGANSER

50.

RED-BREASTED MERGANSER

Migrant through interior of U.S.

Breeds south on coast casually to L.I., N.J.

51.

Breeds very locally within dash lines

Winters north rarely to Great Lakes and Maine

Has bred Fla.

HOODED MERGANSER

52.

Occasional visitor to Maritime Provinces

Breeds locally east to Atlantic coast

Winters north rarely to Great Lakes

AMERICAN COOT

53.

Occasional wanderer to maritime Canada

COMMON GALLINULE

54.

Rare stray north to Great Lakes, maritime Canada

PURPLE GALLINULE

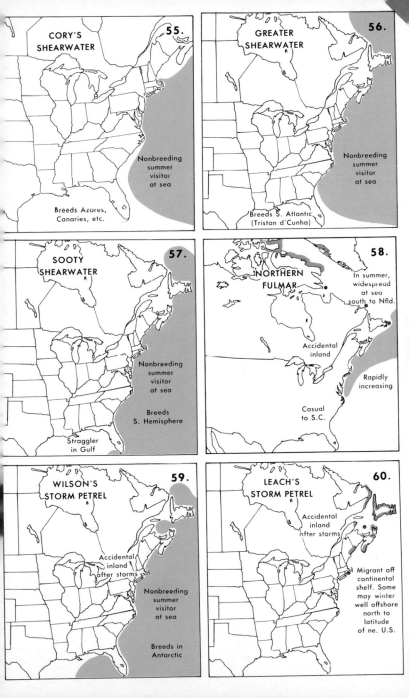

55. CORY'S SHEARWATER
Nonbreeding summer visitor at sea
Breeds Azores, Canaries, etc.

56. GREATER SHEARWATER
Nonbreeding summer visitor at sea
Breeds S. Atlantic (Tristan d'Cunha)

57. SOOTY SHEARWATER
Nonbreeding summer visitor at sea
Breeds S. Hemisphere
Straggler in Gulf

58. NORTHERN FULMAR
In summer, widespread at sea south to Nfld.
Accidental inland
Rapidly increasing
Casual to S.C.

59. WILSON'S STORM PETREL
Accidental inland after storms
Nonbreeding summer visitor at sea
Breeds in Antarctic

60. LEACH'S STORM PETREL
Accidental inland after storms
Migrant off continental shelf. Some may winter well offshore north to latitude of ne. U.S.

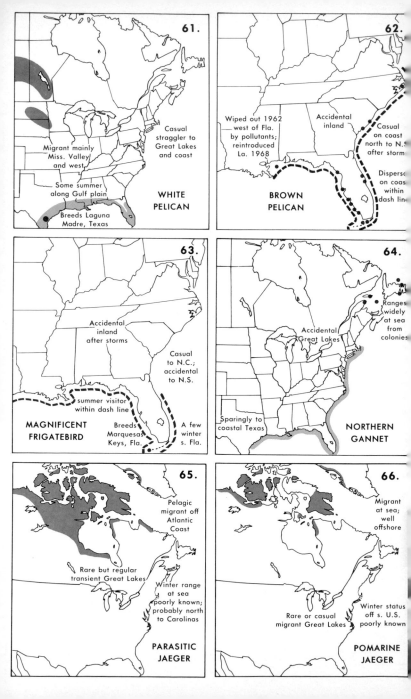

61.

Casual straggler to Great Lakes and coast

Migrant mainly Miss. Valley and west

Some summer along Gulf plain

Breeds Laguna Madre, Texas

WHITE PELICAN

62.

Wiped out 1962 west of Fla. by pollutants; reintroduced La. 1968

Accidental inland

Casual on coast north to N.S. after storm

Dispersed on coast within dash line

BROWN PELICAN

63.

Accidental inland after storms

Casual to N.C.; accidental to N.S.

summer visitor within dash line

Breeds Marquesas Keys, Fla.

A few winter s. Fla.

MAGNIFICENT FRIGATEBIRD

64.

Ranges widely at sea from colonies

Accidental Great Lakes

Sparingly to coastal Texas

NORTHERN GANNET

65.

Pelagic migrant off Atlantic Coast

Rare but regular transient Great Lakes

Winter range at sea poorly known; probably north to Carolinas

PARASITIC JAEGER

66.

Migrant at sea; well offshore

Rare or casual migrant Great Lakes

Winter status off s. U.S. poorly known

POMARINE JAEGER

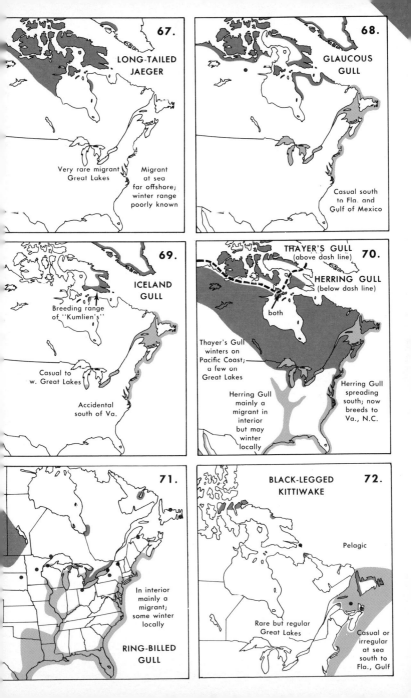

67. LONG-TAILED JAEGER

Very rare migrant Great Lakes

Migrant at sea far offshore; winter range poorly known

68. GLAUCOUS GULL

Casual south to Fla. and Gulf of Mexico

69. ICELAND GULL

Breeding range of "Kumlien's"

Casual to w. Great Lakes

Accidental south of Va.

70. THAYER'S GULL (above dash line)

HERRING GULL (below dash line)

both

Thayer's Gull winters on Pacific Coast; a few on Great Lakes

Herring Gull mainly a migrant in interior but may winter locally

Herring Gull spreading south; now breeds to Va., N.C.

71. In interior mainly a migrant; some winter locally

RING-BILLED GULL

72. BLACK-LEGGED KITTIWAKE

Pelagic

Rare but regular Great Lakes

Casual or irregular at sea south to Fla., Gulf

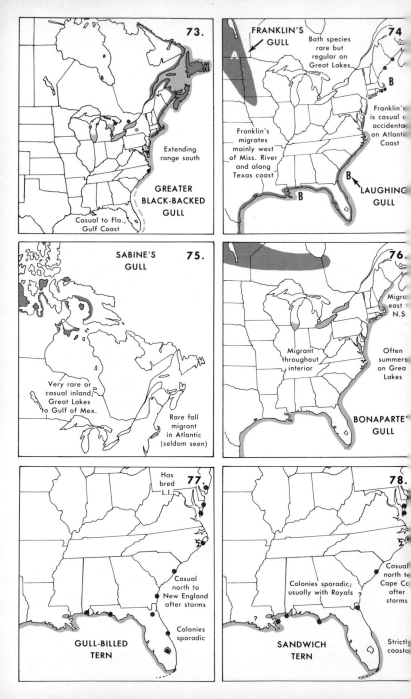

73.

Extending range south

GREATER BLACK-BACKED GULL

Casual to Fla., Gulf Coast

74.

FRANKLIN'S GULL

A

Both species rare but regular on Great Lakes

B

Franklin's is casual or accidental on Atlantic Coast

Franklin's migrates mainly west of Miss. River and along Texas coast

B

B

→ **LAUGHING GULL**

SABINE'S GULL **75.**

Very rare or casual inland; Great Lakes to Gulf of Mex.

Rare fall migrant in Atlantic (seldom seen)

76.

Migrates east to N.S.

Migrant throughout interior

Often summers on Great Lakes

BONAPARTE'S GULL

77.

Has bred L.I.

Casual north to New England after storms

Colonies sporadic

GULL-BILLED TERN

78.

Casual north to Cape Cod after storms

Colonies sporadic; usually with Royals ?

Strictly coastal

SANDWICH TERN

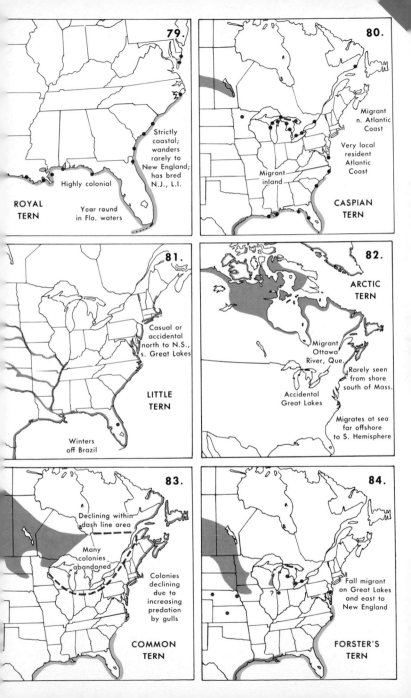

79.
Strictly coastal; wanders rarely to New England; has bred N.J., L.I.
Highly colonial
Year round in Fla. waters
ROYAL TERN

80.
Migrant n. Atlantic Coast
Very local resident Atlantic Coast
Migrant inland
CASPIAN TERN

81.
Casual or accidental north to N.S., s. Great Lakes
LITTLE TERN
Winters off Brazil

82.
ARCTIC TERN
Migrant Ottawa River, Que.
Rarely seen from shore south of Mass.
Accidental Great Lakes
Migrates at sea far offshore to S. Hemisphere

83.
Declining within dash line area
Many colonies abandoned
Colonies declining due to increasing predation by gulls
COMMON TERN

84.
Fall migrant on Great Lakes and east to New England
?
FORSTER'S TERN

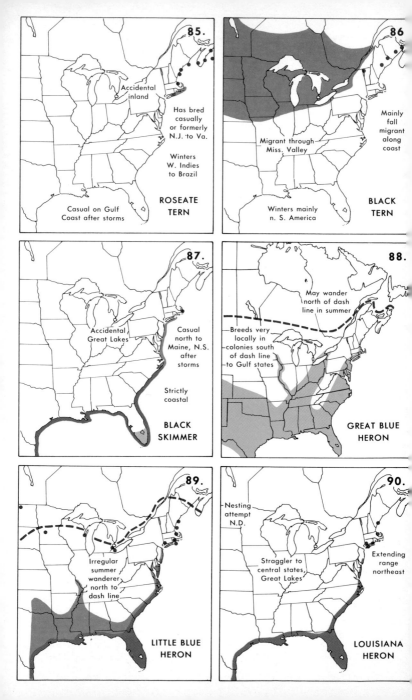

85. ROSEATE TERN

Accidental inland

Has bred casually or formerly N.J. to Va.

Winters W. Indies to Brazil

Casual on Gulf Coast after storms

86. BLACK TERN

Migrant through Miss. Valley

Mainly fall migrant along coast

Winters mainly n. S. America

87. BLACK SKIMMER

Accidental Great Lakes

Casual north to Maine, N.S. after storms

Strictly coastal

88. GREAT BLUE HERON

May wander north of dash line in summer

Breeds very locally in colonies south of dash line to Gulf states

89. LITTLE BLUE HERON

Irregular summer wanderer north to dash line

90. LOUISIANA HERON

Nesting attempt N.D.

Straggler to central states, Great Lakes

Extending range northeast

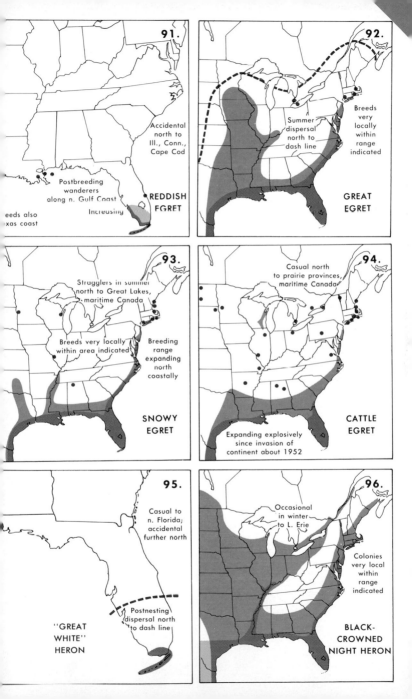

91.

Accidental north to Ill., Conn., Cape Cod

Postbreeding wanderers along n. Gulf Coast

REDDISH EGRET

Increasing

eeds also xas coast

92.

Summer dispersal north to dash line

Breeds very locally within range indicated

GREAT EGRET

93.

Stragglers in summer north to Great Lakes, maritime Canada

Breeds very locally within area indicated

Breeding range expanding north coastally

SNOWY EGRET

94.

Casual north to prairie provinces, maritime Canada

Expanding explosively since invasion of continent about 1952

CATTLE EGRET

95.

Casual to n. Florida; accidental further north

Postnesting dispersal north to dash line

"GREAT WHITE" HERON

96.

Occasional in winter to L. Erie

Colonies very local within range indicated

BLACK-CROWNED NIGHT HERON

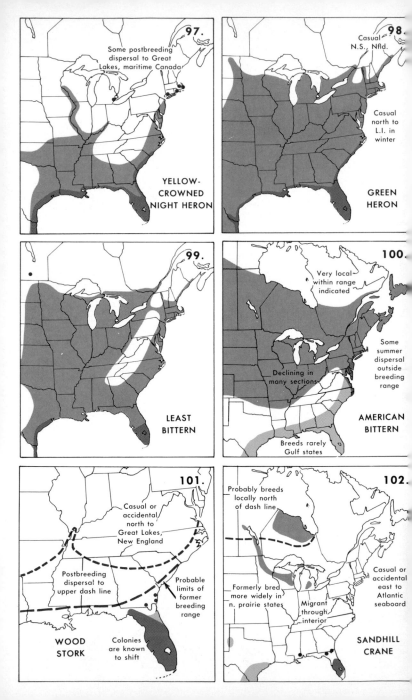

97.
Some postbreeding dispersal to Great Lakes, maritime Canada

YELLOW-CROWNED NIGHT HERON

98.
Casual N.S., Nfld.

Casual north to L.I. in winter

GREEN HERON

99.

LEAST BITTERN

100.
Very local within range indicated

Some summer dispersal outside breeding range

Declining in many sections

Breeds rarely Gulf states

AMERICAN BITTERN

101.
Casual or accidental north to Great Lakes, New England

Postbreeding dispersal to upper dash line

Probable limits of former breeding range

Colonies are known to shift

WOOD STORK

102.
Probably breeds locally north of dash line

Casual or accidental east to Atlantic seaboard

Formerly bred more widely in n. prairie states

Migrant through interior

SANDHILL CRANE

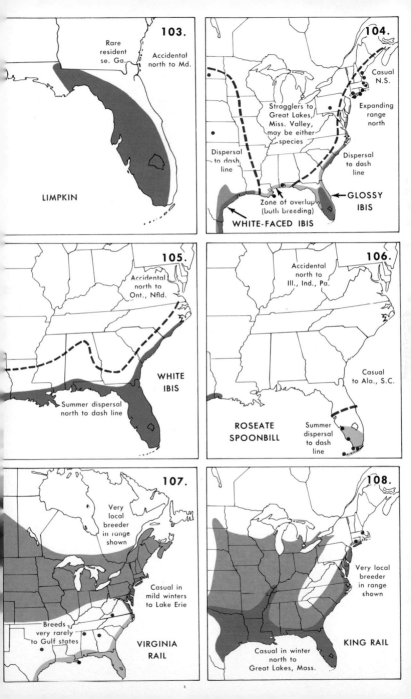

103.

Rare resident se. Ga.

Accidental north to Md.

LIMPKIN

104.

Casual N.S.

Expanding range north

Stragglers to Great Lakes, Miss. Valley, may be either species

Dispersal to dash line

Dispersal to dash line

Zone of overlap (both breeding)

←GLOSSY IBIS

WHITE-FACED IBIS

105.

Accidental north to Ont., Nfld.

WHITE IBIS

Summer dispersal north to dash line

106.

Accidental north to Ill., Ind., Pa.

Casual to Ala., S.C.

ROSEATE SPOONBILL

Summer dispersal to dash line

107.

Very local breeder in range shown

Casual in mild winters to Lake Erie

Breeds very rarely to Gulf states

VIRGINIA RAIL

108.

Very local breeder in range shown

Casual in winter north to Great Lakes, Mass.

KING RAIL

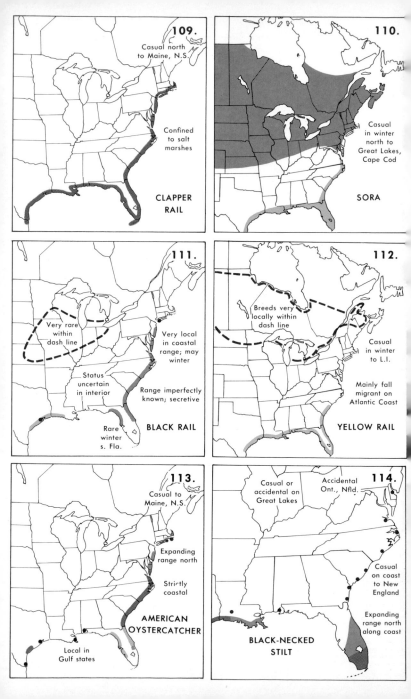

109.
Casual north to Maine, N.S.

Confined to salt marshes

CLAPPER RAIL

110.
Casual in winter north to Great Lakes, Cape Cod

SORA

111.
Very rare within dash line

Very local in coastal range; may winter

Status uncertain in interior

Range imperfectly known; secretive

Rare winter s. Fla.

BLACK RAIL

112.
Breeds very locally within dash line

Casual in winter to L.I.

Mainly fall migrant on Atlantic Coast

YELLOW RAIL

113.
Casual to Maine, N.S.

Expanding range north

Strictly coastal

Local in Gulf states

AMERICAN OYSTERCATCHER

114.
Casual or accidental on Great Lakes

Accidental Ont., Nfld.

Casual on coast to New England

Expanding range north along coast

BLACK-NECKED STILT

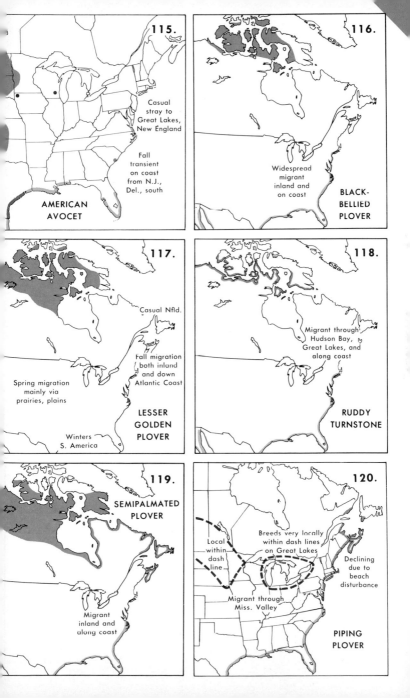

115.

Casual stray to Great Lakes, New England

Fall transient on coast from N.J., Del., south

AMERICAN AVOCET

116.

Widespread migrant inland and on coast

BLACK-BELLIED PLOVER

117.

Casual Nfld.

Fall migration both inland and down Atlantic Coast

Spring migration mainly via prairies, plains

Winters S. America

LESSER GOLDEN PLOVER

118.

Migrant through Hudson Bay, Great Lakes, and along coast

RUDDY TURNSTONE

119.

SEMIPALMATED PLOVER

Migrant inland and along coast

120.

Local within dash line

Breeds very locally within dash lines on Great Lakes

Declining due to beach disturbance

Migrant through Miss. Valley

PIPING PLOVER

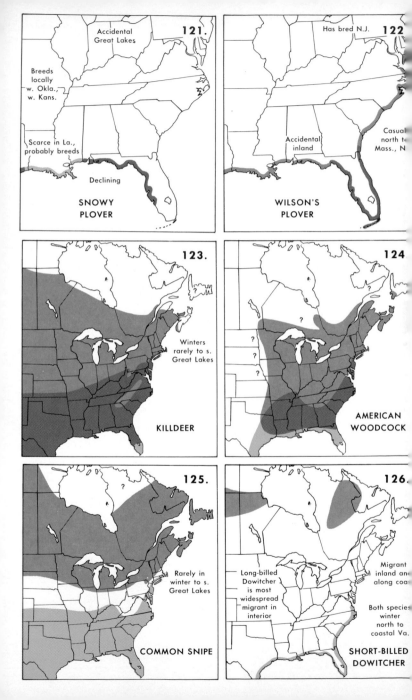

121. SNOWY PLOVER

Accidental Great Lakes

Breeds locally w. Okla., w. Kans.

Scarce in La., probably breeds

Declining

122. WILSON'S PLOVER

Has bred N.J.

Casual north to Mass., N

Accidental inland

123. KILLDEER

Winters rarely to s. Great Lakes

124. AMERICAN WOODCOCK

125. COMMON SNIPE

Rarely in winter to s. Great Lakes

126. SHORT-BILLED DOWITCHER

Long-billed Dowitcher is most widespread migrant in interior

Migrant inland and along coas

Both species winter north to coastal Va.

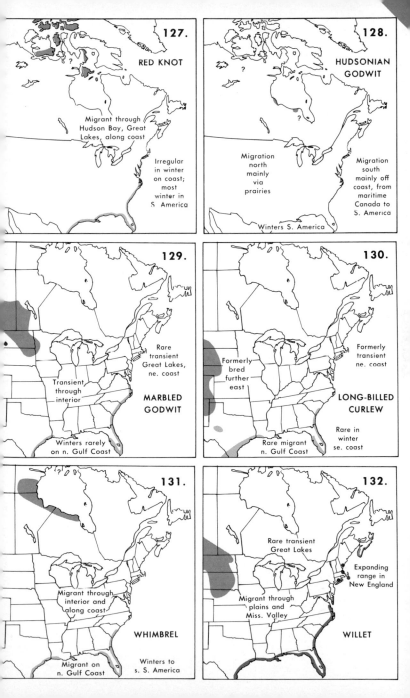

127. RED KNOT

Migrant through Hudson Bay, Great Lakes, along coast

Irregular in winter on coast; most winter in S. America

128. HUDSONIAN GODWIT

Migration north mainly via prairies

Migration south mainly off coast, from maritime Canada to S. America

Winters S. America

129. MARBLED GODWIT

Rare transient Great Lakes, ne. coast

Transient through interior

Winters rarely on n. Gulf Coast

130. LONG-BILLED CURLEW

Formerly transient ne. coast

Formerly bred further east

Rare in winter se. coast

Rare migrant n. Gulf Coast

131. WHIMBREL

Migrant through interior and along coast

Migrant on n. Gulf Coast

Winters to s. S. America

132. WILLET

Rare transient Great Lakes

Expanding range in New England

Migrant through plains and Miss. Valley

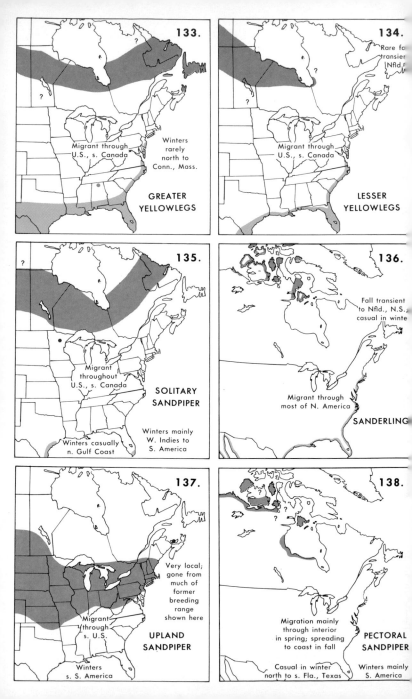

133.

Migrant through U.S., s. Canada

Winters rarely north to Conn., Mass.

GREATER YELLOWLEGS

134.

Rare fall transient Nfld.

Migrant through U.S., s. Canada

LESSER YELLOWLEGS

135.

Migrant throughout U.S., s. Canada

Winters casually n. Gulf Coast

Winters mainly W. Indies to S. America

SOLITARY SANDPIPER

136.

Fall transient to Nfld., N.S., casual in winter

Migrant through most of N. America

SANDERLING

137.

Very local; gone from much of former breeding range shown here

Migrant through s. U.S.

Winters s. S. America

UPLAND SANDPIPER

138.

Migration mainly through interior in spring; spreading to coast in fall

Casual in winter north to s. Fla., Texas

Winters mainly S. America

PECTORAL SANDPIPER

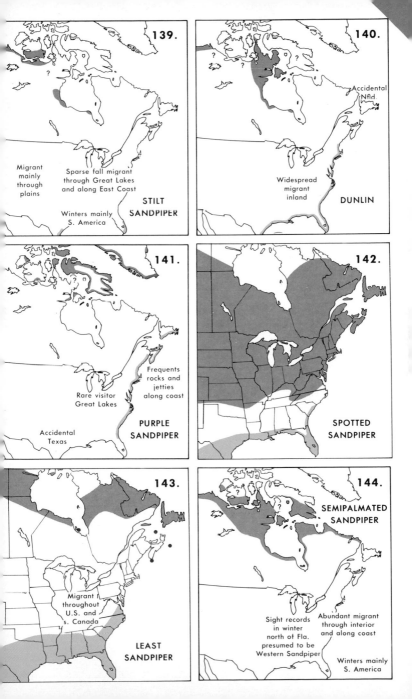

139.

Migrant mainly through plains

Sparse fall migrant through Great Lakes and along East Coast

Winters mainly S. America

STILT SANDPIPER

140.

Accidental Nfld

Widespread migrant inland

DUNLIN

141.

Frequents rocks and jetties along coast

Rare visitor Great Lakes

Accidental Texas

PURPLE SANDPIPER

142.

SPOTTED SANDPIPER

143.

Migrant throughout U.S. and s. Canada

LEAST SANDPIPER

144.

SEMIPALMATED SANDPIPER

Sight records in winter north of Fla. presumed to be Western Sandpiper

Abundant migrant through interior and along coast

Winters mainly S. America

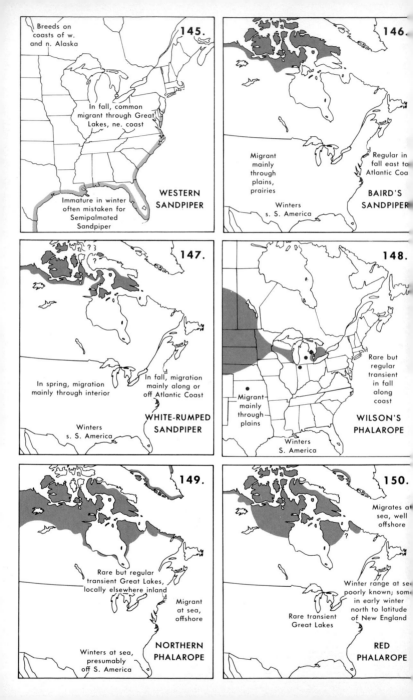

145. WESTERN SANDPIPER

Breeds on coasts of w. and n. Alaska

In fall, common migrant through Great Lakes, ne. coast

Immature in winter often mistaken for Semipalmated Sandpiper

146. BAIRD'S SANDPIPER

Migrant mainly through plains, prairies

Regular in fall east to Atlantic Coast

Winters s. S. America

147. WHITE-RUMPED SANDPIPER

In spring, migration mainly through interior

In fall, migration mainly along or off Atlantic Coast

Winters s. S. America

148. WILSON'S PHALAROPE

Migrant mainly through plains

Rare but regular transient in fall along coast

Winters S. America

149. NORTHERN PHALAROPE

Rare but regular transient Great Lakes, locally elsewhere inland

Migrant at sea, offshore

Winters at sea, presumably off S. America

150. RED PHALAROPE

Migrates at sea, well offshore

Winter range at sea poorly known; some in early winter north to latitude of New England

Rare transient Great Lakes

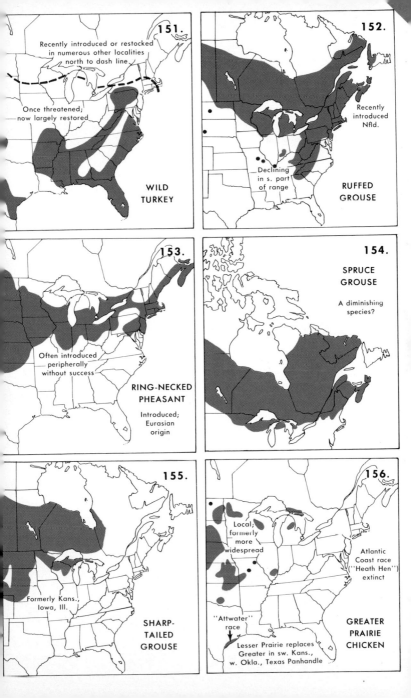

151. WILD TURKEY

Recently introduced or restocked in numerous other localities north to dash line

Once threatened; now largely restored

152. RUFFED GROUSE

Recently introduced Nfld.

Declining in s. part of range

153. RING-NECKED PHEASANT

Often introduced peripherally without success

Introduced; Eurasian origin

154. SPRUCE GROUSE

A diminishing species?

155. SHARP-TAILED GROUSE

Formerly Kans., Iowa, Ill.

156. GREATER PRAIRIE CHICKEN

Local; formerly more widespread

Atlantic Coast race ("Heath Hen") extinct

"Attwater" race

Lesser Prairie replaces Greater in sw. Kans., w. Okla., Texas Panhandle

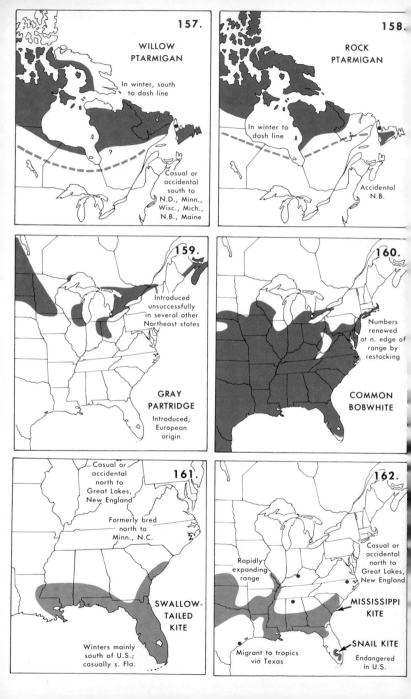

157.
WILLOW
PTARMIGAN

In winter, south
to dash line

?

Casual or
accidental
south to
N.D., Minn.,
Wisc., Mich.,
N.B., Maine

158.
ROCK
PTARMIGAN

In winter to
dash line

Accidental
N.B.

159.

Introduced
unsuccessfully
in several other
Northeast states

GRAY
PARTRIDGE

Introduced;
European
origin

160.

Numbers
renewed
at n. edge of
range by
restocking

COMMON
BOBWHITE

161.
Casual or
accidental
north to
Great Lakes,
New England

Formerly bred
north to
Minn., N.C.

SWALLOW-
TAILED
KITE

Winters mainly
south of U.S.;
casually s. Fla.

162.

Rapidly
expanding
range

Casual or
accidental
north to
Great Lakes,
New England

MISSISSIPPI
KITE

SNAIL KITE

Migrant to tropics
via Texas

Endangered
in U.S.

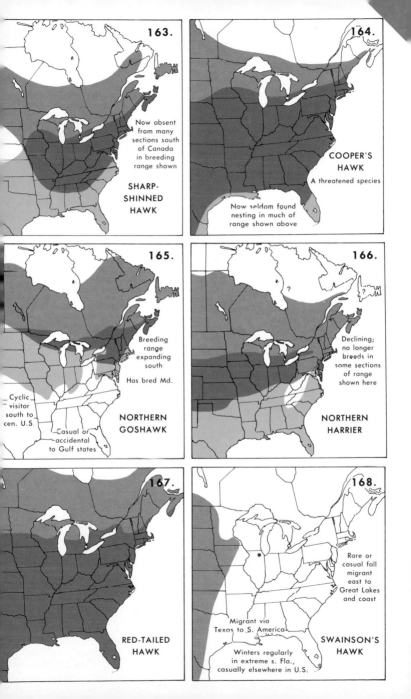

163.

Now absent from many sections south of Canada in breeding range shown

SHARP-SHINNED HAWK

164.

COOPER'S HAWK

A threatened species

Now seldom found nesting in much of range shown above

165.

Breeding range expanding south

Has bred Md.

Cyclic visitor south to cen. U.S

Casual or accidental to Gulf states

NORTHERN GOSHAWK

166.

Declining; no longer breeds in some sections of range shown here

NORTHERN HARRIER

167.

RED-TAILED HAWK

168.

Rare or casual fall migrant east to Great Lakes and coast

Migrant via Texas to S. America

Winters regularly in extreme s. Fla., casually elsewhere in U.S.

SWAINSON'S HAWK

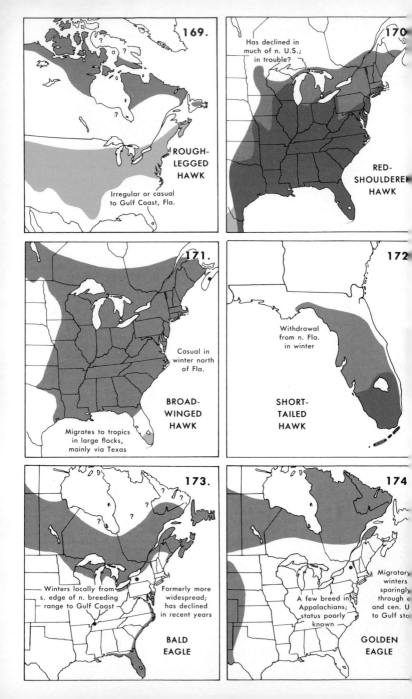

169.

ROUGH-
LEGGED
HAWK

Irregular or casual
to Gulf Coast, Fla.

170.

Has declined in
much of n. U.S.;
in trouble?

RED-
SHOULDERED
HAWK

171.

Casual in
winter north
of Fla.

BROAD-
WINGED
HAWK

Migrates to tropics
in large flocks,
mainly via Texas

172.

Withdrawal
from n. Fla.
in winter

SHORT-
TAILED
HAWK

173.

Winters locally from
s. edge of n. breeding
range to Gulf Coast

Formerly more
widespread;
has declined
in recent years

BALD
EAGLE

174.

Migratory;
winters
sparingly
through e.
and cen. U.
to Gulf sta

A few breed in
Appalachians;
status poorly
known

GOLDEN
EAGLE

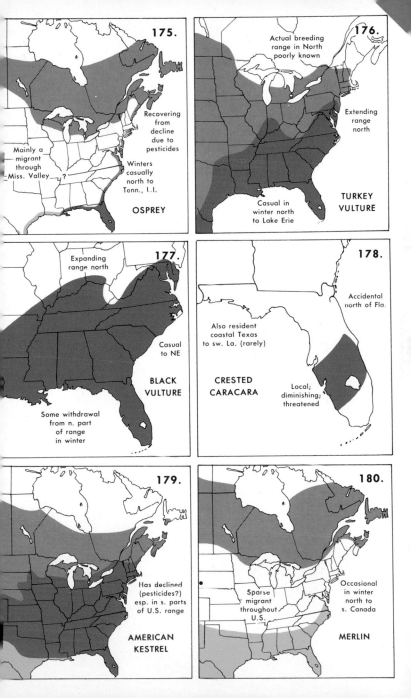

175. OSPREY

Recovering from decline due to pesticides

Mainly a migrant through Miss. Valley ?

Winters casually north to Tenn., L.I.

176. TURKEY VULTURE

Actual breeding range in North poorly known

Extending range north

Casual in winter north to Lake Erie

177. BLACK VULTURE

Expanding range north

Casual to NE

Some withdrawal from n. part of range in winter

178. CRESTED CARACARA

Accidental north of Fla.

Also resident coastal Texas to sw. La. (rarely)

Local; diminishing; threatened

179. AMERICAN KESTREL

Has declined (pesticides?) esp. in s. parts of U.S. range

180. MERLIN

Sparse migrant throughout U.S.

Occasional in winter north to s. Canada

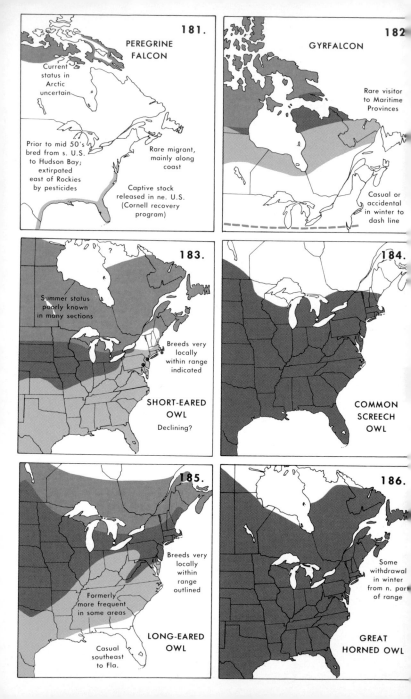

181.
PEREGRINE FALCON

Current status in Arctic uncertain

Prior to mid 50's bred from s. U.S. to Hudson Bay; extirpated east of Rockies by pesticides

Rare migrant, mainly along coast

Captive stock released in ne. U.S. (Cornell recovery program)

182
GYRFALCON

Rare visitor to Maritime Provinces

Casual or accidental in winter to dash line

183.
Summer status poorly known in many sections

Breeds very locally within range indicated

SHORT-EARED OWL

Declining?

184.
COMMON SCREECH OWL

185.
Breeds very locally within range outlined

Formerly more frequent in some areas

Casual southeast to Fla.

LONG-EARED OWL

186.
Some withdrawal in winter from n. part of range

GREAT HORNED OWL

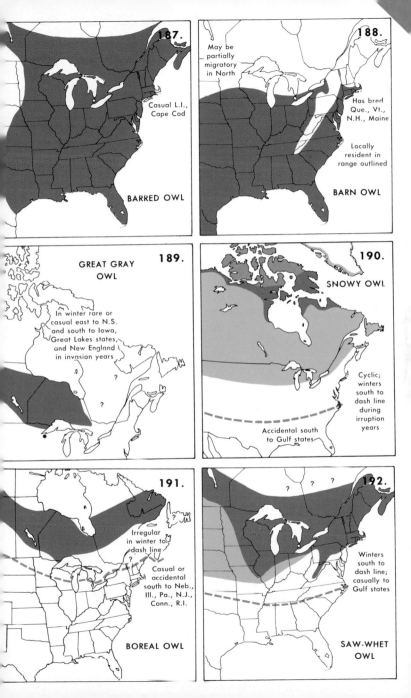

187. BARRED OWL

Casual L.I., Cape Cod

188. BARN OWL

May be partially migratory in North

Has bred Que., Vt., N.H., Maine

Locally resident in range outlined

189. GREAT GRAY OWL

In winter rare or casual east to N.S. and south to Iowa, Great Lakes states, and New England in invasion years

190. SNOWY OWL

Cyclic; winters south to dash line during irruption years

Accidental south to Gulf states

191. BOREAL OWL

Irregular in winter to dash line

Casual or accidental south to Neb., Ill., Pa., N.J., Conn., R.I.

192. SAW-WHET OWL

Winters south to dash line; casually to Gulf states

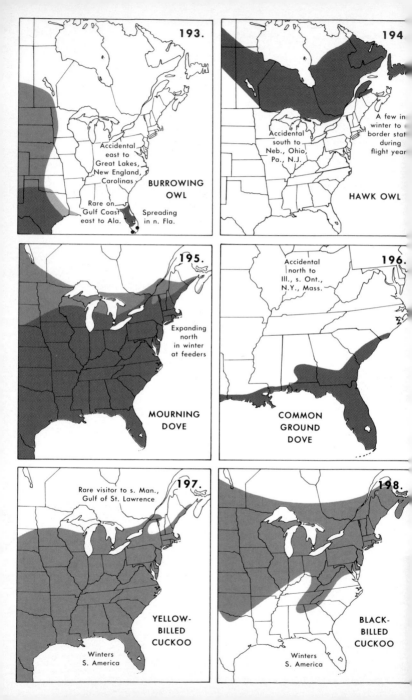

193.

Accidental east to Great Lakes, New England, Carolinas

BURROWING OWL

Rare on Gulf Coast east to Ala.   Spreading in n. Fla.

194

A few in winter to border stat during flight year

Accidental south to Neb., Ohio, Pa., N.J.

HAWK OWL

195.

Expanding north in winter at feeders

MOURNING DOVE

196.

Accidental north to Ill., s. Ont., N.Y., Mass.

COMMON GROUND DOVE

197.

Rare visitor to s. Man., Gulf of St. Lawrence

YELLOW-BILLED CUCKOO

Winters S. America

198.

BLACK-BILLED CUCKOO

Winters S. America

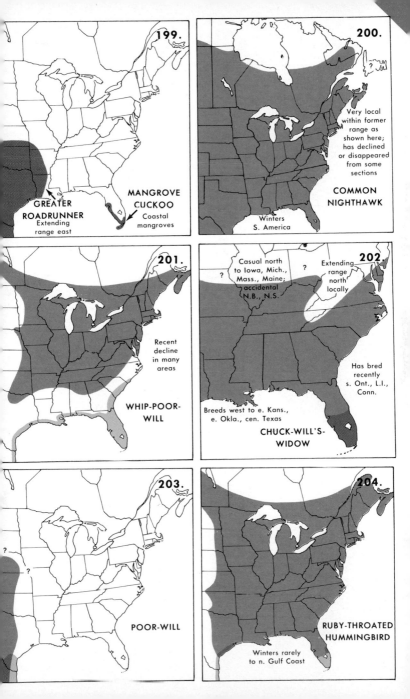

199. GREATER ROADRUNNER
Extending range east

MANGROVE CUCKOO
Coastal mangroves

200. COMMON NIGHTHAWK
Very local within former range as shown here; has declined or disappeared from some sections
Winters S. America
?

201. WHIP-POOR-WILL
Recent decline in many areas

202. CHUCK-WILL'S-WIDOW
Casual north to Iowa, Mich., Mass., Maine; accidental N.B., N.S.
Extending range north locally
Has bred recently s. Ont., L.I., Conn.
Breeds west to e. Kans., e. Okla., cen. Texas
?   ?

203. POOR-WILL
?
?

204. RUBY-THROATED HUMMINGBIRD
Winters rarely to n. Gulf Coast

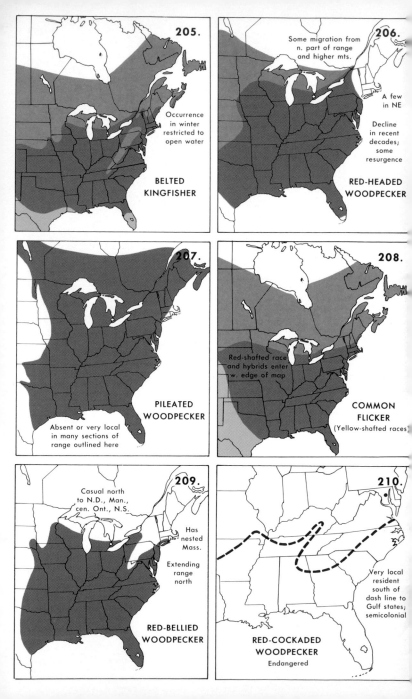

205.

Occurrence in winter restricted to open water

BELTED KINGFISHER

206.

Some migration from n. part of range and higher mts.

A few in NE

Decline in recent decades; some resurgence

RED-HEADED WOODPECKER

207.

PILEATED WOODPECKER

Absent or very local in many sections of range outlined here

208.

Red-shafted race and hybrids enter w. edge of map

COMMON FLICKER (Yellow-shafted races)

209.

Casual north to N.D., Man., cen. Ont., N.S.

Has nested Mass.

Extending range north

RED-BELLIED WOODPECKER

210.

Very local resident south of dash line to Gulf states; semicolonial

RED-COCKADED WOODPECKER

Endangered

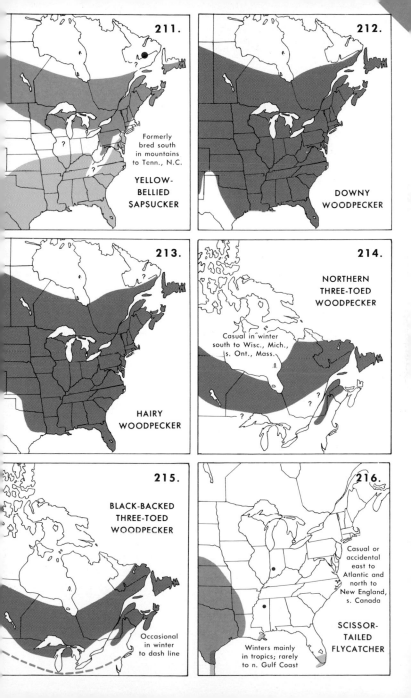

211.

Formerly
bred south
in mountains
to Tenn., N.C.

YELLOW-
BELLIED
SAPSUCKER

212.

DOWNY
WOODPECKER

213.

HAIRY
WOODPECKER

214.

NORTHERN
THREE-TOED
WOODPECKER

Casual in winter
south to Wisc., Mich.,
s. Ont., Mass.

215.

BLACK-BACKED
THREE-TOED
WOODPECKER

Occasional
in winter
to dash line

216.

Casual or
accidental
east to
Atlantic and
north to
New England,
s. Canada

SCISSOR-
TAILED
FLYCATCHER

Winters mainly
in tropics; rarely
to n. Gulf Coast

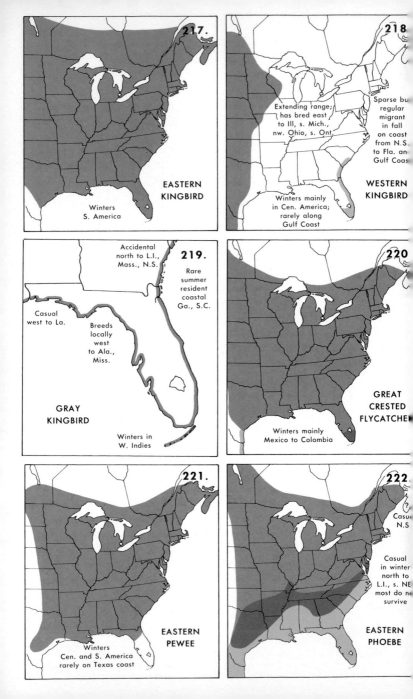

217. EASTERN KINGBIRD

Winters S. America

218 WESTERN KINGBIRD

Extending range; has bred east to Ill., s. Mich., nw. Ohio, s. Ont.

Sparse but regular migrant in fall on coast from N.S. to Fla. and Gulf Coast

Winters mainly in Cen. America; rarely along Gulf Coast

219. GRAY KINGBIRD

Accidental north to L.I., Mass., N.S.

Rare summer resident coastal Ga., S.C.

Casual west to La.

Breeds locally west to Ala., Miss.

Winters in W. Indies

220 GREAT CRESTED FLYCATCHER

Winters mainly Mexico to Colombia

221. EASTERN PEWEE

Winters Cen. and S. America rarely on Texas coast

222 EASTERN PHOEBE

Casual N.S.

Casual in winter north to L.I., s. NE most do not survive

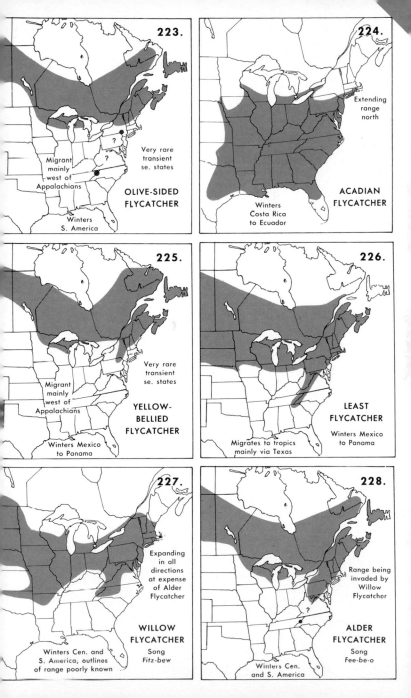

223.

Migrant mainly west of Appalachians

? ?

Very rare transient se. states

Winters S. America

OLIVE-SIDED FLYCATCHER

224.

Extending range north

ACADIAN FLYCATCHER

Winters Costa Rica to Ecuador

225.

Migrant mainly west of Appalachians

Very rare transient se. states

YELLOW-BELLIED FLYCATCHER

Winters Mexico to Panama

226.

LEAST FLYCATCHER

Winters Mexico to Panama

Migrates to tropics mainly via Texas

227.

Expanding in all directions at expense of Alder Flycatcher

WILLOW FLYCATCHER

Winters Cen. and S. America, outlines of range poorly known

Song Fitz-bew

228.

Range being invaded by Willow Flycatcher

ALDER FLYCATCHER

Song Fee-be-o

Winters Cen. and S. America

?

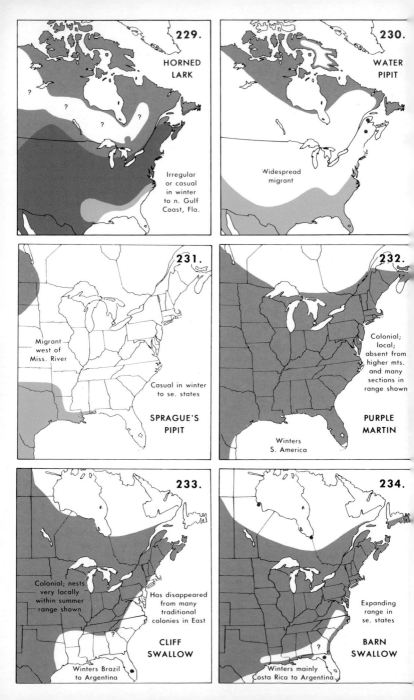

229.
HORNED LARK

Irregular or casual in winter to n. Gulf Coast, Fla.

230.
WATER PIPIT

Widespread migrant

231.
SPRAGUE'S PIPIT

Migrant west of Miss. River

Casual in winter to se. states

232.
PURPLE MARTIN

Colonial; local; absent from higher mts. and many sections in range shown

Winters S. America

233.
CLIFF SWALLOW

Colonial; nests very locally within summer range shown

Has disappeared from many traditional colonies in East

Winters Brazil to Argentina

234.
BARN SWALLOW

Expanding range in se. states

Winters mainly Costa Rica to Argentina

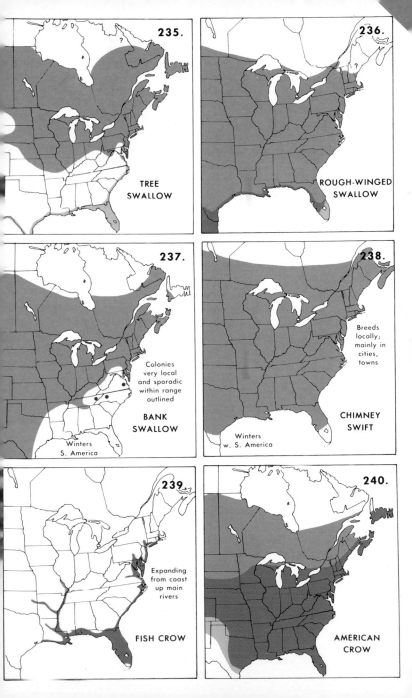

235.

TREE
SWALLOW

236.

ROUGH-WINGED
SWALLOW

237.

Colonies
very local
and sporadic
within range
outlined

BANK
SWALLOW

Winters
S. America

238.

Breeds
locally;
mainly in
cities,
towns

CHIMNEY
SWIFT

Winters
w. S. America

239.

Expanding
from coast
up main
rivers

FISH CROW

240.

AMERICAN
CROW

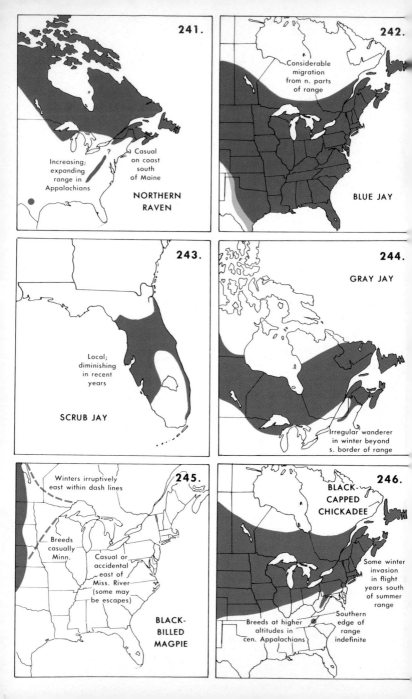

241.

Increasing; expanding range in Appalachians

Casual on coast south of Maine

NORTHERN RAVEN

242.

Considerable migration from n. parts of range

BLUE JAY

243.

Local; diminishing in recent years

SCRUB JAY

244.

GRAY JAY

Irregular wanderer in winter beyond s. border of range

245.

Winters irruptively east within dash lines

Breeds casually Minn.

Casual or accidental east of Miss. River (some may be escapes)

BLACK-BILLED MAGPIE

246.

BLACK-CAPPED CHICKADEE

Some winter invasion in flight years south of summer range

Breeds at higher altitudes in cen. Appalachians

Southern edge of range indefinite

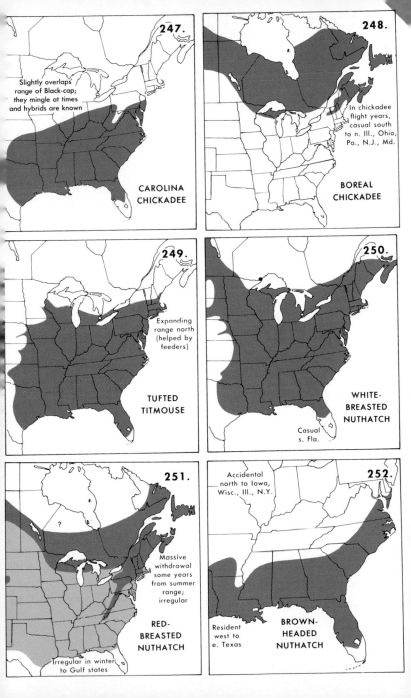

247.
Slightly overlaps range of Black-cap; they mingle at times and hybrids are known

CAROLINA CHICKADEE

248.
In chickadee flight years, casual south to n. Ill., Ohio, Pa., N.J., Md.

BOREAL CHICKADEE

249.
Expanding range north (helped by feeders)

TUFTED TITMOUSE

250.
WHITE-BREASTED NUTHATCH

Casual s. Fla.

251.
Massive withdrawal some years from summer range; irregular

RED-BREASTED NUTHATCH

Irregular in winter to Gulf states

252.
Accidental north to Iowa, Wisc., Ill., N.Y.

Resident west to e. Texas

BROWN-HEADED NUTHATCH

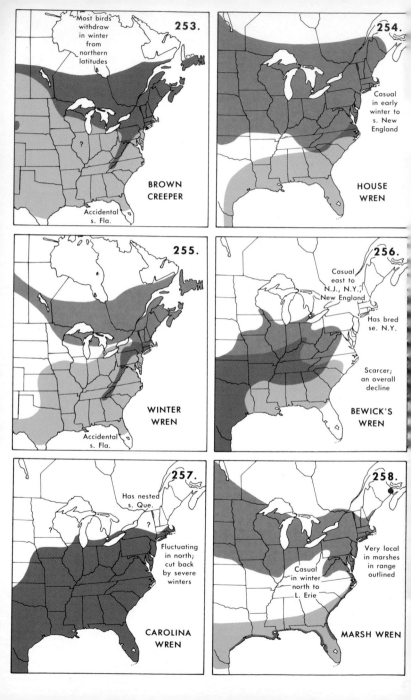

253. BROWN CREEPER

Most birds withdraw in winter from northern latitudes

Accidental s. Fla.

254. HOUSE WREN

Casual in early winter to s. New England

255. WINTER WREN

Accidental s. Fla.

256. BEWICK'S WREN

Casual east to N.J., N.Y., New England

Has bred se. N.Y.

Scarcer; an overall decline

257. CAROLINA WREN

Has nested s. Que.

Fluctuating in north; cut back by severe winters

258. MARSH WREN

Casual in winter north to L. Erie

Very local in marshes in range outlined

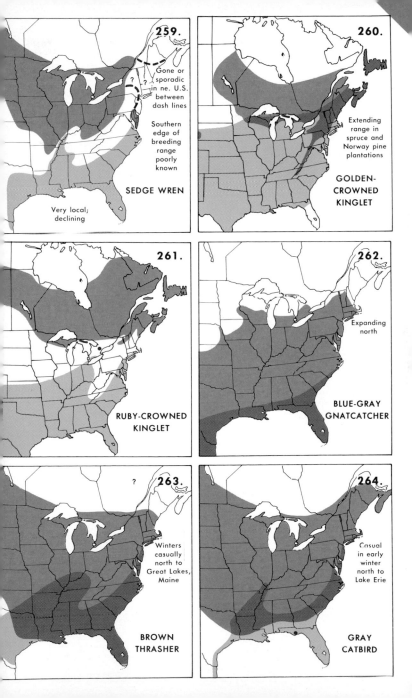

259.

Gone or
sporadic
in ne. U.S.
between
dash lines

Southern
edge of
breeding
range
poorly
known

SEDGE WREN

Very local;
declining

260.

Extending
range in
spruce and
Norway pine
plantations

GOLDEN-
CROWNED
KINGLET

261.

RUBY-CROWNED
KINGLET

262.

Expanding
north

BLUE-GRAY
GNATCATCHER

263.

Winters
casually
north to
Great Lakes,
Maine

BROWN
THRASHER

264.

Casual
in early
winter
north to
Lake Erie

GRAY
CATBIRD

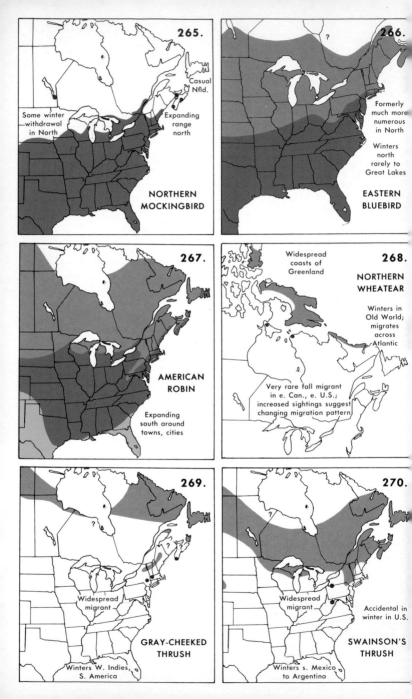

265.

Casual Nfld.

Some winter withdrawal in North

Expanding range north

NORTHERN MOCKINGBIRD

266.

?

Formerly much more numerous in North

Winters north rarely to Great Lakes

EASTERN BLUEBIRD

267.

AMERICAN ROBIN

Expanding south around towns, cities

268.

Widespread coasts of Greenland

NORTHERN WHEATEAR

Winters in Old World; migrates across Atlantic

Very rare fall migrant in e. Can., e. U.S.; increased sightings suggest changing migration pattern

269.

?

?

?

Widespread migrant

GRAY-CHEEKED THRUSH

Winters W. Indies, S. America

270.

?

Widespread migrant

Accidental in winter in U.S.

SWAINSON'S THRUSH

Winters s. Mexico to Argentina

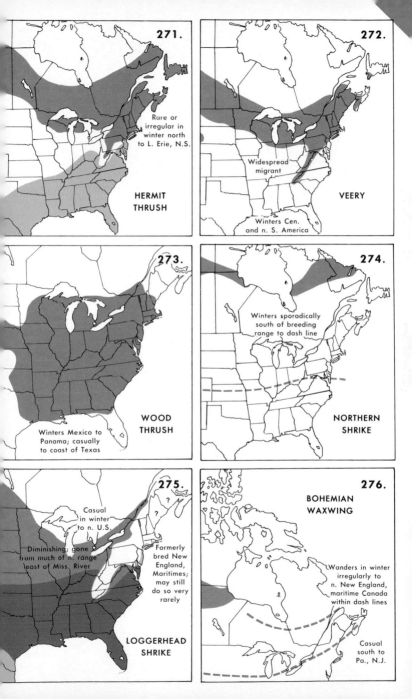

271.

Rare or irregular in winter north to L. Erie, N.S.

HERMIT THRUSH

272.

Widespread migrant

Winters Cen. and n. S. America

VEERY

273.

Winters Mexico to Panama; casually to coast of Texas

WOOD THRUSH

274.

Winters sporadically south of breeding range to dash line

NORTHERN SHRIKE

275.

Casual in winter to n. U.S.

Diminishing; gone from much of n. range east of Miss. River

Formerly bred New England, Maritimes; may still do so very rarely

LOGGERHEAD SHRIKE

276.

BOHEMIAN WAXWING

Wanders in winter irregularly to n. New England, maritime Canada within dash lines

Casual south to Pa., N.J.

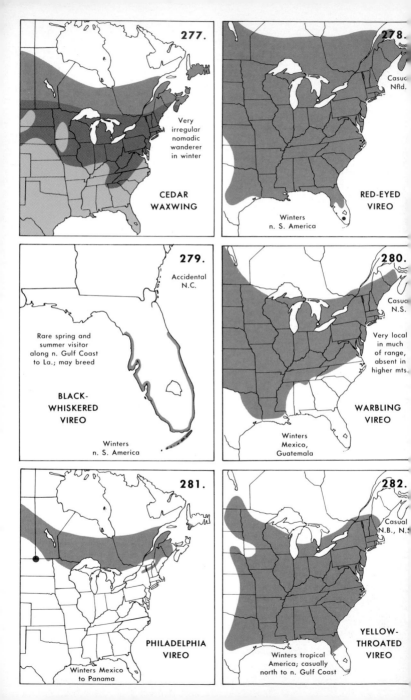

277.

Very irregular nomadic wanderer in winter

CEDAR WAXWING

278.

Casual Nfld.

Winters n. S. America

RED-EYED VIREO

279.

Accidental N.C.

Rare spring and summer visitor along n. Gulf Coast to La.; may breed

BLACK-WHISKERED VIREO

Winters n. S. America

280.

Casual N.S.

Very local in much of range, absent in higher mts.

WARBLING VIREO

Winters Mexico, Guatemala

281.

PHILADELPHIA VIREO

Winters Mexico to Panama

282.

Casual N.B., N.S.

YELLOW-THROATED VIREO

Winters tropical America; casually north to n. Gulf Coast

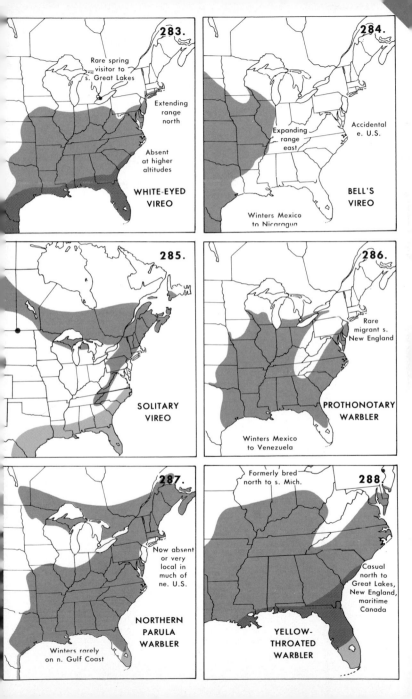

283. Rare spring visitor to s. Great Lakes

Extending range north

Absent at higher altitudes

WHITE-EYED VIREO

284. Expanding range east

Accidental e. U.S.

Winters Mexico to Nicaragua

BELL'S VIREO

285. SOLITARY VIREO

286. Rare migrant s. New England

Winters Mexico to Venezuela

PROTHONOTARY WARBLER

287. Now absent or very local in much of ne. U.S.

Winters rarely on n. Gulf Coast

NORTHERN PARULA WARBLER

288. Formerly bred north to s. Mich.

Casual north to Great Lakes, New England, maritime Canada

YELLOW-THROATED WARBLER

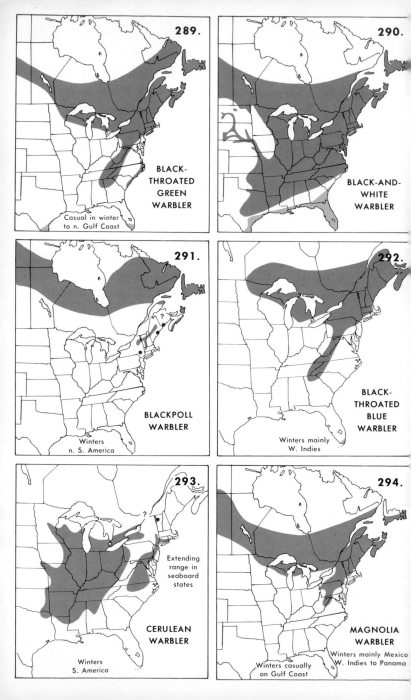

289. BLACK-THROATED GREEN WARBLER

Casual in winter to n. Gulf Coast

290. BLACK-AND-WHITE WARBLER

291. BLACKPOLL WARBLER

Winters n. S. America

292. BLACK-THROATED BLUE WARBLER

Winters mainly W. Indies

293. CERULEAN WARBLER

Extending range in seaboard states

Winters S. America

294. MAGNOLIA WARBLER

Winters mainly Mexico W. Indies to Panama

Winters casually on Gulf Coast

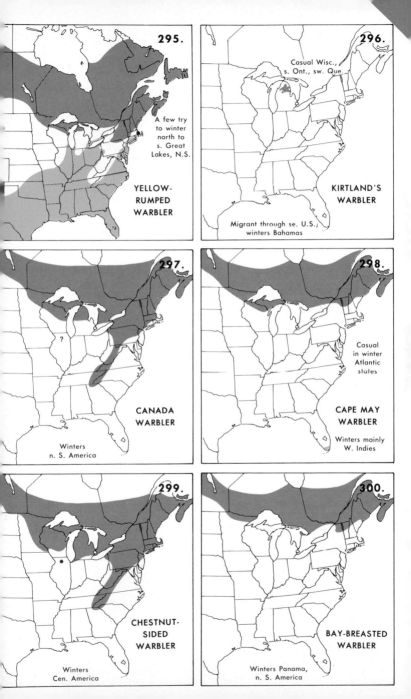

295.

A few try to winter north to s. Great Lakes, N.S.

YELLOW-RUMPED WARBLER

296.

Casual Wisc., s. Ont., sw. Que.

KIRTLAND'S WARBLER

Migrant through se. U.S.; winters Bahamas

297.

?

CANADA WARBLER

Winters n. S. America

298.

Casual in winter Atlantic states

CAPE MAY WARBLER

Winters mainly W. Indies

299.

CHESTNUT-SIDED WARBLER

Winters Cen. America

300.

BAY-BREASTED WARBLER

Winters Panama, n. S. America

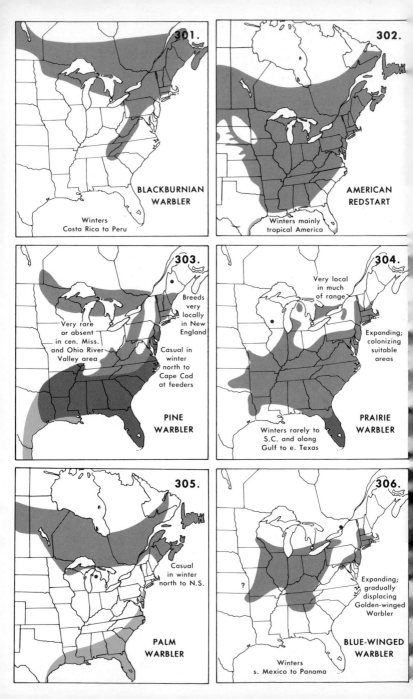

301.

BLACKBURNIAN
WARBLER

Winters
Costa Rica to Peru

302.

AMERICAN
REDSTART

Winters mainly
tropical America

303.

Very rare
or absent
in cen. Miss.
and Ohio River
Valley area

Breeds
very
locally
in New
England

Casual in
winter
north to
Cape Cod
at feeders

PINE
WARBLER

304.

Very local
in much
of range

Expanding;
colonizing
suitable
areas

Winters rarely to
S.C. and along
Gulf to e. Texas

PRAIRIE
WARBLER

305.

Casual
in winter
north to N.S.

PALM
WARBLER

306.

?

Expanding;
gradually
displacing
Golden-winged
Warbler

Winters
s. Mexico to Panama

BLUE-WINGED
WARBLER

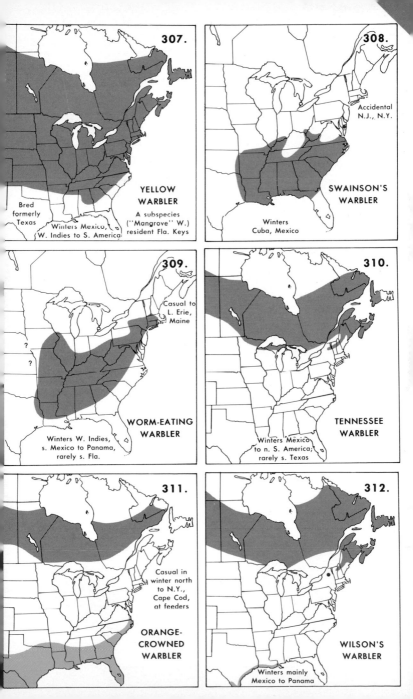

307.

YELLOW WARBLER

A subspecies ("Mangrove" W.) resident Fla. Keys

Bred formerly Texas

Winters Mexico, W. Indies to S. America

308.

SWAINSON'S WARBLER

Accidental N.J., N.Y.

Winters Cuba, Mexico

309.

WORM-EATING WARBLER

Casual to L. Erie, Maine

?
?

Winters W. Indies, s. Mexico to Panama, rarely s. Fla.

310.

TENNESSEE WARBLER

Winters Mexico to n. S. America; rarely s. Texas

311.

ORANGE-CROWNED WARBLER

Casual in winter north to N.Y., Cape Cod, at feeders

312.

WILSON'S WARBLER

Winters mainly Mexico to Panama

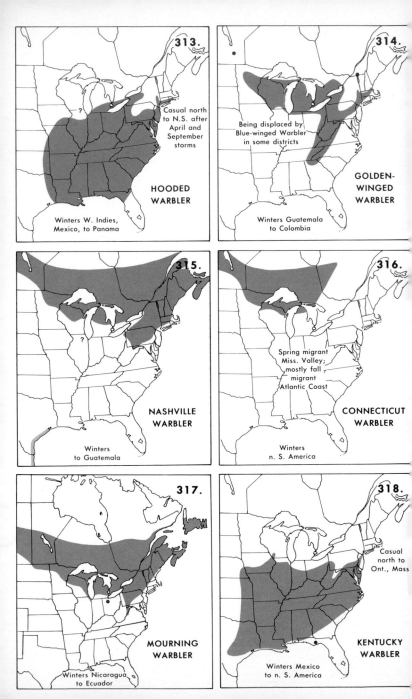

313.

? Casual north to N.S. after April and September storms

HOODED WARBLER

Winters W. Indies, Mexico, to Panama

314.

Being displaced by Blue-winged Warbler in some districts

GOLDEN-WINGED WARBLER

Winters Guatemala to Colombia

315.

?

NASHVILLE WARBLER

Winters to Guatemala

316.

Spring migrant Miss. Valley; mostly fall migrant Atlantic Coast

CONNECTICUT WARBLER

Winters n. S. America

317.

MOURNING WARBLER

Winters Nicaragua to Ecuador

318.

Casual north to Ont., Mass

KENTUCKY WARBLER

Winters Mexico to n. S. America

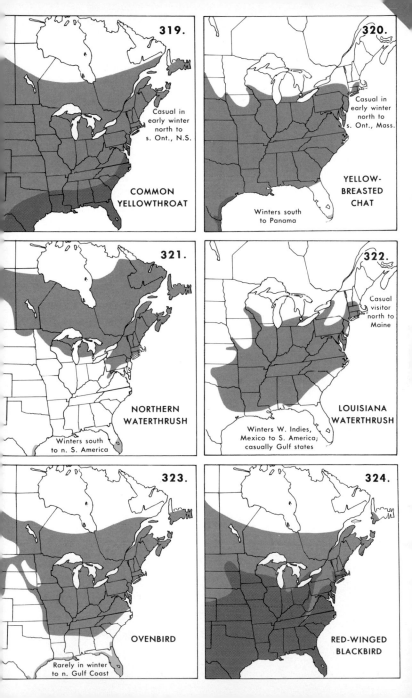

319.

Casual in early winter north to s. Ont., N.S.

COMMON YELLOWTHROAT

320.

Casual in early winter north to s. Ont., Mass.

YELLOW-BREASTED CHAT

Winters south to Panama

321.

NORTHERN WATERTHRUSH

Winters south to n. S. America

322.

Casual visitor north to Maine

LOUISIANA WATERTHRUSH

Winters W. Indies, Mexico to S. America; casually Gulf states

323.

OVENBIRD

Rarely in winter to n. Gulf Coast

324.

RED-WINGED BLACKBIRD

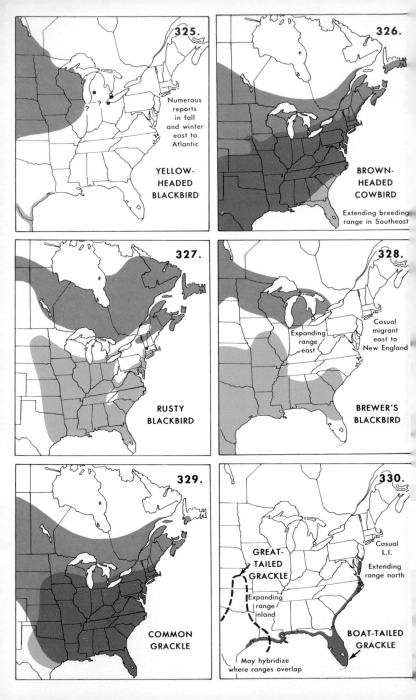

325.

Numerous reports in fall and winter east to Atlantic

YELLOW-HEADED BLACKBIRD

326.

BROWN-HEADED COWBIRD

Extending breeding range in Southeast

327.

RUSTY BLACKBIRD

328.

Expanding range east

Casual migrant east to New England

BREWER'S BLACKBIRD

329.

COMMON GRACKLE

330.

GREAT-TAILED GRACKLE

Expanding range inland

May hybridize where ranges overlap

Casual L.I.

Extending range north

BOAT-TAILED GRACKLE

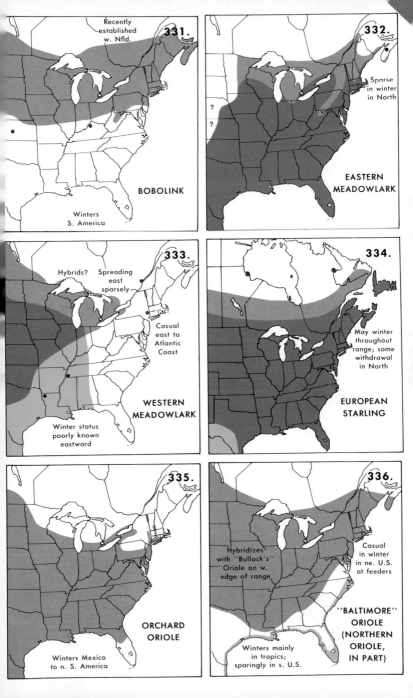

331.
Recently established w. Nfld.
BOBOLINK
Winters S. America

332.
Sparse in winter in North
EASTERN MEADOWLARK

333.
Hybrids? Spreading east sparsely
Casual east to Atlantic Coast
WESTERN MEADOWLARK
Winter status poorly known eastward

334.
May winter throughout range; some withdrawal in North
EUROPEAN STARLING

335.
ORCHARD ORIOLE
Winters Mexico to n. S. America

336.
Hybridizes with ''Bullock's'' Oriole on w. edge of range
Casual in winter in ne. U.S. at feeders
''BALTIMORE'' ORIOLE (NORTHERN ORIOLE, IN PART)
Winters mainly in tropics; sparingly in s. U.S.

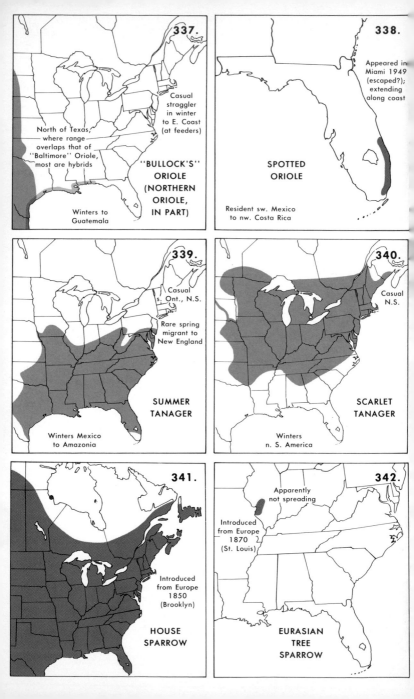

337. "BULLOCK'S" ORIOLE (NORTHERN ORIOLE, IN PART)

Casual straggler in winter to E. Coast (at feeders)

North of Texas, where range overlaps that of "Baltimore" Oriole, most are hybrids

Winters to Guatemala

338. SPOTTED ORIOLE

Appeared in Miami 1949 (escaped?); extending along coast

Resident sw. Mexico to nw. Costa Rica

339. SUMMER TANAGER

Casual s. Ont., N.S.

Rare spring migrant to New England

Winters Mexico to Amazonia

340. SCARLET TANAGER

Casual N.S.

Winters n. S. America

341. HOUSE SPARROW

Introduced from Europe 1850 (Brooklyn)

342. EURASIAN TREE SPARROW

Apparently not spreading

Introduced from Europe 1870 (St. Louis)

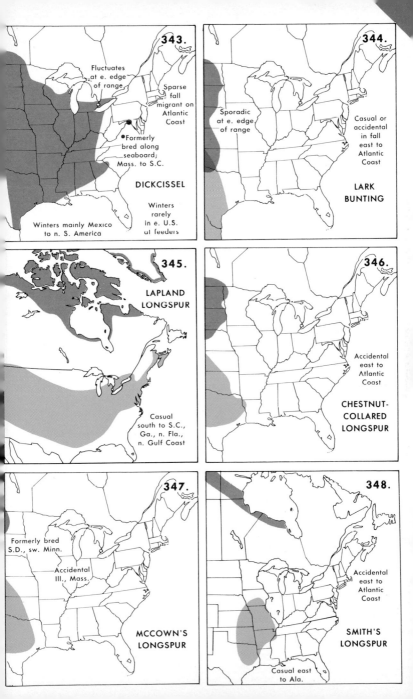

343.

DICKCISSEL

Fluctuates
at e. edge
of range

Sparse
fall
migrant on
Atlantic
Coast

●Formerly
bred along
seaboard;
Mass. to S.C.

Winters
rarely
in e. U.S.
at feeders

Winters mainly Mexico
to n. S. America

344.

LARK
BUNTING

Sporadic
at e. edge
of range

Casual or
accidental
in fall
east to
Atlantic
Coast

345.

LAPLAND
LONGSPUR

Casual
south to S.C.,
Ga., n. Fla.,
n. Gulf Coast

346.

CHESTNUT-
COLLARED
LONGSPUR

Accidental
east to
Atlantic
Coast

347.

McCOWN'S
LONGSPUR

Formerly bred
S.D., sw. Minn.

Accidental
Ill., Mass.

348.

SMITH'S
LONGSPUR

Accidental
east to
Atlantic
Coast

?

?

Casual east
to Ala.

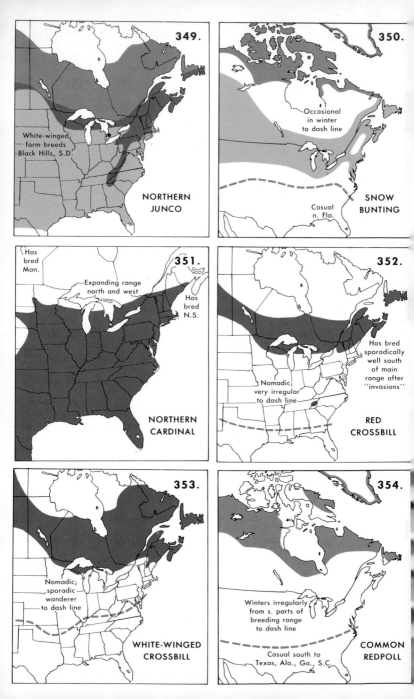

349.

White-winged
form breeds
Black Hills, S.D.

NORTHERN
JUNCO

350.

Occasional
in winter
to dash line

Casual
n. Fla.

SNOW
BUNTING

351.

Has bred
Man.

Expanding range
north and west

Has
bred
N.S.

NORTHERN
CARDINAL

352.

Has bred
sporadically
well south
of main
range after
"invasions"

Nomadic;
very irregular
to dash line

RED
CROSSBILL

353.

Nomadic;
sporadic
wanderer
to dash line

WHITE-WINGED
CROSSBILL

354.

Winters irregularly
from s. parts of
breeding range
to dash line

Casual south to
Texas, Ala., Ga., S.C.

COMMON
REDPOLL

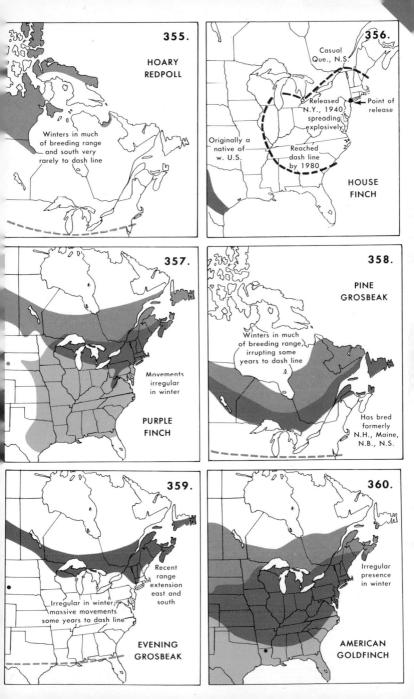

355.

HOARY REDPOLL

Winters in much of breeding range and south very rarely to dash line

356.

Casual Que., N.S.

Released N.Y., 1940, spreading explosively

Point of release

Originally a native of w. U.S.

Reached dash line by 1980

HOUSE FINCH

357.

Movements irregular in winter

PURPLE FINCH

358.

PINE GROSBEAK

Winters in much of breeding range, irrupting some years to dash line

Has bred formerly N.H., Maine, N.B., N.S.

359.

Recent range extension east and south

Irregular in winter; massive movements some years to dash line

EVENING GROSBEAK

360.

Irregular presence in winter

AMERICAN GOLDFINCH

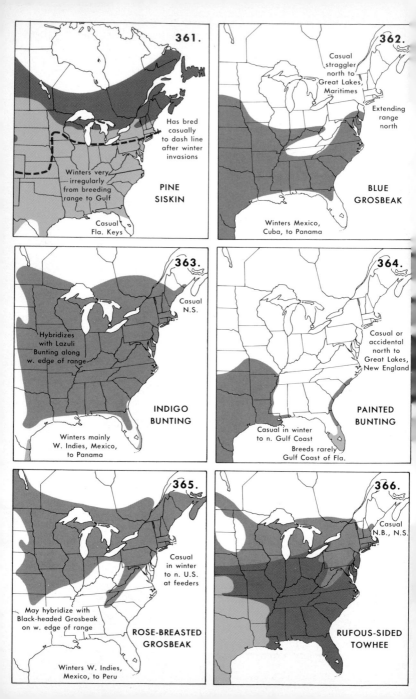

361. PINE SISKIN

Has bred casually to dash line after winter invasions

Winters very irregularly from breeding range to Gulf

Casual Fla. Keys

362. BLUE GROSBEAK

Casual straggler north to Great Lakes, Maritimes

Extending range north

Winters Mexico, Cuba, to Panama

363. INDIGO BUNTING

Casual N.S.

Hybridizes with Lazuli Bunting along w. edge of range

Winters mainly W. Indies, Mexico, to Panama

364. PAINTED BUNTING

Casual or accidental north to Great Lakes, New England

Casual in winter to n. Gulf Coast

Breeds rarely Gulf Coast of Fla.

365. ROSE-BREASTED GROSBEAK

Casual in winter to n. U.S. at feeders

May hybridize with Black-headed Grosbeak on w. edge of range

Winters W. Indies, Mexico, to Peru

366. RUFOUS-SIDED TOWHEE

Casual N.B., N.S.

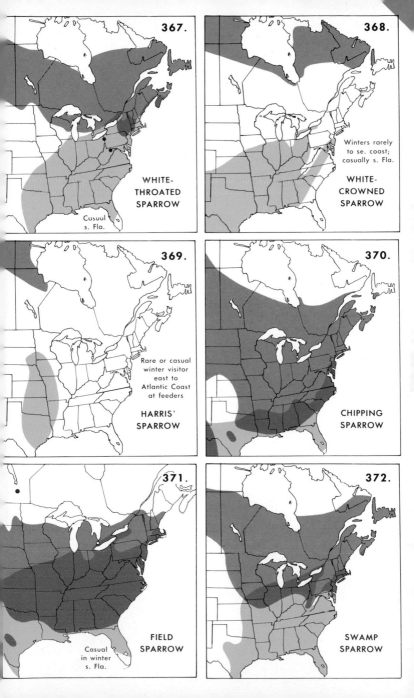

367. WHITE-THROATED SPARROW

Casual s. Fla.

368. WHITE-CROWNED SPARROW

Winters rarely to se. coast; casually s. Fla.

369. HARRIS' SPARROW

Rare or casual winter visitor east to Atlantic Coast at feeders

370. CHIPPING SPARROW

371. FIELD SPARROW

Casual in winter s. Fla.

372. SWAMP SPARROW

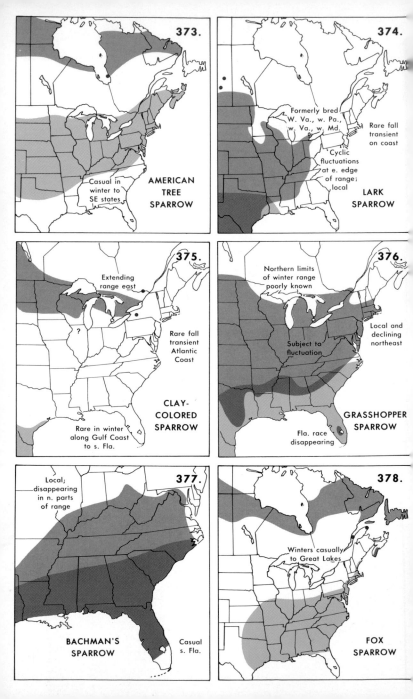

373.

Casual in winter to SE states

AMERICAN TREE SPARROW

374.

Formerly bred W. Va., w. Pa., w. Va., w. Md.

Rare fall transient on coast

Cyclic fluctuations at e. edge of range; local

LARK SPARROW

375.

Extending range east

?

Rare fall transient Atlantic Coast

Rare in winter along Gulf Coast to s. Fla.

CLAY-COLORED SPARROW

376.

Northern limits of winter range poorly known

Local and declining northeast

Subject to fluctuation

Fla. race disappearing

GRASSHOPPER SPARROW

377.

Local; disappearing in n. parts of range

Casual s. Fla.

BACHMAN'S SPARROW

378.

Winters casually to Great Lakes

FOX SPARROW

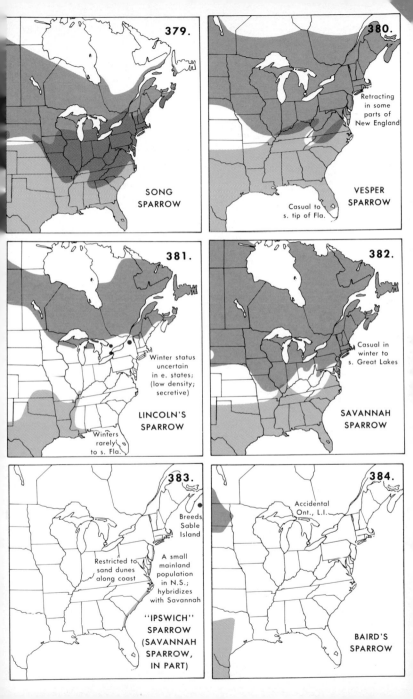

379. SONG SPARROW

380. VESPER SPARROW
Retracting in some parts of New England
Casual to s. tip of Fla.

381. LINCOLN'S SPARROW
Winter status uncertain in e. states; (low density; secretive)
Winters rarely to s. Fla.

382. SAVANNAH SPARROW
Casual in winter to s. Great Lakes

383. "IPSWICH" SPARROW (SAVANNAH SPARROW, IN PART)
Breeds Sable Island
Restricted to sand dunes along coast
A small mainland population in N.S.; hybridizes with Savannah

384. BAIRD'S SPARROW
Accidental Ont., L.I.

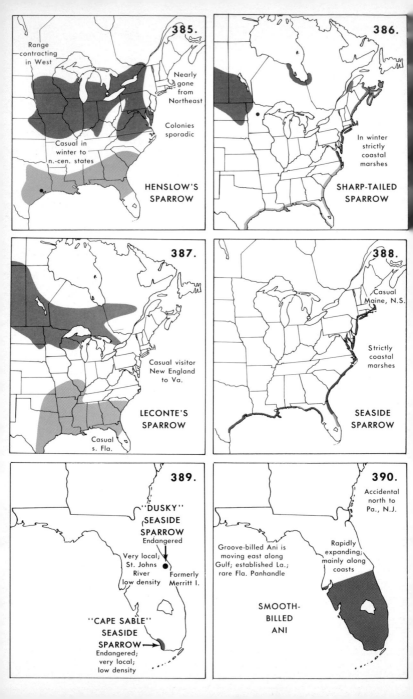

385.

Range contracting in West

Nearly gone from Northeast

Colonies sporadic

Casual in winter to n.-cen. states

HENSLOW'S SPARROW

386.

In winter strictly coastal marshes

SHARP-TAILED SPARROW

387.

Casual visitor New England to Va.

Casual s. Fla.

LECONTE'S SPARROW

388.

Casual Maine, N.S.

Strictly coastal marshes

SEASIDE SPARROW

389.

"DUSKY" SEASIDE SPARROW
Endangered

Very local; St. Johns River low density

Formerly Merritt I.

"CAPE SABLE" SEASIDE SPARROW
Endangered; very local; low density

390.

Accidental north to Pa., N.J.

Groove-billed Ani is moving east along Gulf; established La.; rare Fla. Panhandle

Rapidly expanding; mainly along coasts

SMOOTH-BILLED ANI

Index

All birds illustrated and described in this book are indexed. Those additional western accidentals that are mentioned on p. 304 but not described or illustrated are not indexed. The page number(s), with rare exception, refers to the text; it is understood that the illustration is on the right-hand facing page. Scientific names (in *italics*) are keyed to the pages on which the text appears, not the illustrations. The letter M before a number designates the appropriate range map; a gray corner facilitates quick thumbing to the map section in the rear of the book. The number of each map is in the upper right-hand corner.